Tourism in the Pacific:
Issues and Cases

Edited by

C. Michael Hall and Stephen J. Page

INTERNATIONAL
THOMSON
BUSINESS PRESS

INTERNATIONAL THOMSON BUSINESS PRESS
I(T)P An International Thomson Publishing Company

London ● Bonn ● Boston ● Johannesburg ● Madrid ● Melbourne ● Mexico ● City ● New ● York ● Paris
Singapore ● Tokyo ● Toronto ● Albany, NY ● Belmont, CA ● Cincinnati, OH ● Detroit, MI

Tourism in the Pacific
Copyright © 1996 C. Michael Hall and Stephen J. Page

First published by International Thomson Business Press

I(T)P   A division of International Thomson Publishing Inc.
The ITP logo is a trademark under licence

British Library Cataloguing-in-Publication Data
A catalogue record for this book is available from the British Library

First edition 1996

Typeset in Times by LaserScript, Mitcham, Surrey
Printed in the UK by Clays Ltd, St Ives plc, Bungay, Suffolk

ISBN 0–415–12500–6 (Pbk)

International Thomson Business Press   International Thomson Business Press
Berkshire House   20 Park Plaza
168–173 High Holborn   14th Floor
London WC1V 7AA   Boston MA 02116
UK   USA

Tourism in the Pacific

ook i
may be

TEL

SERIES IN TOURISM AND HOSPITALITY MANAGEMENT

Key Textbooks

Series Editors:
Roy C. Wood The Scottish Hotel School, University of Strathclyde, UK
Stephen J. Page Massey University, New Zealand

Series Consultant:
Professor C.L. Jenkins The Scottish Hotel School, University of Strathclyde, UK

Titles in this series:

Behavioural Studies in Hospitality Management
R. Carmouche and N. Kelly
ISBN 0 412 60850 2, 232 pages

Managing Human Resources in the European Tourism and Hospitality Industry
A strategic approach
T. Baum
ISBN 0 412 55630 8, 280 pages

Interpersonal Skills for Hospitality Management
M.A. Clark
ISBN 0 412 57330 X, 232 pages

Hospitality and Tourism Law
M. Popstie, N. Geddes, W. Stewart and J. Ross
ISBN 0 412 62080 4, 320 pages

Business Accounting for Hospitality and Tourism
H. Atkinson, S. Berry and R. Jarvis
ISBN 0 412 48080 8, 452 pages

Economics for Hospitality Management
P. Cullen
ISBN 0 412 60540 6, 224 pages

Doing Your Dissertation
A guide for students in tourism, leisure and hospitality management
M. Foley
ISBN 0 412 60840 5, 200 pages

Marketing Tourism, Hospitality and Leisure in Europe
Susan Horner and John Swarbrooke,
ISBN 0 412 62170 3, 728 pages

Managing Wine and Wine Sales
J.B. Fattorini
ISBN 0 412 72190 2, 200 pages

Books in the series are available on free inspection for lecturers considering the texts for course adoption. Details of these, and any other International Thomson Business Press titles are available by writing to the publishers (Berkshire House, 163–173 High Holborn, London WC1V 7AA) or by telephoning the Promotions Department on 0171–697 1423.

This work is dedicated to the memory of
Steve Britton
in recognition of the major contribution he made to the
understanding of tourism in the Pacific, and to
The Wandering Islands

Contents

List of Tables   ix
List of Figures   xi
List of Plates   xiii
Contributors   xv
Acknowledgements   xvii
Series Editors' Preface   xix
Foreword   x

1 Introduction: The context of tourism development in the
   South Pacific   1
   C. Michael Hall and Stephen J. Page

Part I: Issues in Pacific tourism

2 Tourism in the Pacific: Historical factors   19
   Norman Douglas and Ngaire Douglas
3 Economic impact of tourism in the Pacific   36
   Stephen Craig-Smith
4 Social and cultural impact of tourism in the Pacific   49
   Ngaire Douglas and Norman Douglas
5 Environmental impact of tourism in the Pacific   65
   C. Michael Hall
6 Political effects of tourism in the Pacific   81
   C. Michael Hall
7 Planning issues in Pacific tourism   91
   Michael Fagence
8 Tourism marketing and computer reservation systems in the
   Pacific   109
   Simon Milne
9 Health and tourism in the Pacific   130
   Brenda Rudkin and C. Michael Hall

10 Seeking quality in Pacific tourism   146
    Chris Ryan

Part II: Destination cases

11 Australia's and New Zealand's role in Pacific tourism: Aid,
    trade and travel   161
    C. Michael Hall and Stephen J. Page
12 Hawai'i   190
    Luciano Minerbi
13 Fiji   205
    Nii-k Plange
14 The Cook Islands   219
    Philip Buck and C. Michael Hall
15 Vanuatu   235
    Charles de Burlo
16 Papua New Guinea   256
    Ngaire Douglas
17 The Pacific Islands: Markets, development and
    planning issues   273
    Stephen J. Page and Glenda Lawton
18 Conclusion   304
    C. Michael Hall and Stephen J. Page

    Author Index   313
    Place Index   320
    Subject Index   323

List of Tables

1.1 Visitor arrivals in the Pacific, 1983–94   4
1.2 Characteristics of Pacific territories   6
1.3 Economic growth (GDP) in select Pacific countries, 1989–93   8
3.1 Tourism within selected Pacific economies   43
4.1 Comparison of population and visitor figures for Pacific Island countries, 1993   52
5.1 Environmental and ecological impacts of tourism on the Pacific Islands   70
6.1 Tourism and political instability   85
8.1 Corporate impacts associated with inclusion on computer reservation systems   115
8.2 CRS inclusion of microstate accommodation operations   117
8.3 Pacific destinations and airlines suggested by Montreal travel agents   117
9.1 Travel associated illness reported at the Infectious Disease Unit, Auckland Hospital   132
10.1 Characteristics of services   147
10.2 Definitions of quality and related concepts   148
10.3 Sections A and B of the Qualmark rating scheme   154
11.1 Aid from OECD Development Assistance Committee Donors to the Pacific Islands, 1973–91   165
11.2 Short-term visitors arriving in Australia from Oceania   167
11.3 Short-term departures of Australian residents by region, 1992–93   168
11.4 Australian residents departing for short-term stay in Oceania, 1985–93   168
11.5 Australian overseas aid as a percentage of total aid flows for Pacific Island countries   170
11.6 Australian Overseas Development Cooperation, 1989/90 to 1993/4   171
11.7 Australian Overseas Development Cooperation for Tourism, 1989/90 to 1993/4   172
11.8 Australian Overseas Development Cooperation for Transport and Navigation, 1989/90 to 1993/4   173

11.9 New Zealand's Official Development Assistance Programme,
       1994–5, bilateral assistance   179
11.10 New Zealand government aid to Pacific Island tourism-related
       projects, 1981–95   180
12.1 Visitor arrivals in Hawai'i, 1987–94   194
12.2 Visitor accommodation in Hawai'i by type and geographical area,
       Spring 1992   195
12.3 Visitor expenditure in Hawai'i by direction of travel, country of
       residence and islands, 1990 and 1991   195
12.4 Estimated direct visitor-related expenditure in Hawai'i, 1988–91 196
12.5 Economic activity generated by visitor-related expenditure in
       Hawai'i, by industry, 1991   197
13.1 Visitor arrivals in Fiji by major market, 1987–92   214
14.1 Cook Islands tourist arrivals   222
14.2 Visitor arrivals to the Cook Islands: total visitors by market,
       1983–94   224
14.3 Approved room stock, 1990–95   229
15.1 Visitor arrivals to Vanuatu, 1982–94   244
16.1 Economic profile of Papua New Guinea, 1993   259
16.2 Tourist arrivals in Papua New Guinea by purpose of visit, 1990–93 263
16.3 Short-term visitor arrivals in Papua New Guinea by major markets,
       1985–93   264
16.4 Milestones in tourism developed in Papua New Guinea since 1965   264
16.5 Comparative tourism indices for Papua New Guinea and other
       Pacific destinations, 1993   268
17.1 Visitor arrivals in Guam by origin, 1990–94   276

List of Figures

1.1	The Pacific: location map	2
12.1	Hawai'i: location map	192
13.1	Fiji: location map	206
15.1	Vanuatu: location map	236
16.1	Papua New Guinea: location map	257
16.2	Visitor arrivals to Papua New Guinea, 1986–91	265
17.1	Air New Zealand route network in the South Pacific and international connections	277
17.2	Visitor arrivals in Yap, 1989–94	283
17.3	Seasonality in visitor arrivals in New Caledonia, 1994–95	287
17.4	Forecasts of visitor arrivals for the Solomon Islands, 1991–2000	290
17.5	New Caledonia: location map	292

List of Plates

1.1 The quintessential tourist image of the South Pacific as an unspoilt tourist paradise. Outrigger canoe on an isolated beach in Vanuatu (Michael Hall)   5

2.1 Paradise encapsulated on a postcard of the 1920s from Hawai'i (Norman Douglas)   21

2.2 A popular magazine of the 1920s helped promote the myth of paradise (*Paradise of the Pacific*, Hawai'i State Archives)   22

2.3 Pineapples from Paradise: the industry, which was economically superior to tourism in Hawai'i in the early twentieth century, eventually yielded to it (Hawai'i State Archives)   23

2.4 The myth exported: surfing legend Duke Kahanamoku appears in Australia (State Library of New South Wales)   24

2.5 Paradise in overdrive: Pacific Islands tourism literature of the 1990s. (from top: CTC cruise brochure, Air Vanuatu in-flight magazine, Vanuatu holiday brochure, Air Niugini in-flight magazine, Solomon Airlines calendar, Cook Islands holiday brochure) (Norman Douglas)   33

4.1 Two major agents of cultural change 'video and tourism' combine in a village in the Papua New Guinea Highlands (Norman Douglas) 50

4.2 Ritual object as hotel decoration: a ceremonial slit gong from Ambrym Island, Vanuatu, adorns the new entrance to Le Meridien Hotel in Port Vila (Norman Douglas)   59

4.3 A cartoon from the defunct newspaper, *Fiji Sun* illustrates the dilemmas of European influence for the now Christianised islanders 61

5.1 Coastal tourism development at Waikiki, Hawai'i (Michael Hall)   71

5.2 Water access is a critical element in tourism development in Port Vila, Vanuatu (Michael Hall)   71

5.3 Tourism traffic along Rainbow Beach in Queensland, Australia is starting to place pressure on the environment (Michael Hall)   72

12.1 Sunbathing on Waikiki Beach, one of the classic tourist images of Hawai'i (Michael Hall)   191

12.2 Back from the beach at Waikiki. Tourism development has turned
      Waikiki into an urban environment little different from that which
      many of the tourists have escaped (Michael Hall)   191
15.1 Markets at Port Vila provide an opportunity for tourists to purchase
      local produce (Michael Hall)   239
15.2 The interplay of local and foreign commercial interests is seen
      in the availability of secondary tourist activities in Port Vila
      (Michael Hall)   240
16.1 A village on PNG's flood prone Sepik River. Tourist vessels
      cruise the river regularly (Norman Douglas)   261
16.2 Ambua Lodge, a resort in the Southern Highlands region
      of PNG (Norman Douglas)   267
16.3 A Huli Wigman of the Southern Highlands demonstrates his
      technique for tourists (Norman Douglas)   268
17.1 Noumea city   286
17.2 Le Surf Novotel Hotel, Noumea illustrates resort hotel
      development in New Caledonia, reproduced by courtesy of
      Destination New Caledonia, Auckland   288
17.3 Kou Bungy Resort, Isle of Pines, illustrates small-scale beach
      hotel development in New Caledonia   288

Contributors

Charles de Burlo, Department of Anthropology, University of Vermont, Vermont, USA

Philip Buck, Tourism Consultant, Kings Road, Nashua, New South Wales, Australia

Stephen Craig-Smith, Faculty of Business Studies, Gatton College, University of Queensland

Ngaire Douglas, Centre for Tourism, Southern Cross University, Lismore, New South Wales, Australia

Norman Douglas, Pacific Profiles, PO Box 229, Alstonville, New South Wales, Australia

Michael Fagence, Department of Geographical Sciences and Planning, University of Queensland, St Lucia, Queensland, Australia

C. Michael Hall, Tourism and Services Management, Victoria University of Wellington, New Zealand

Glenda Lawton, Department of Management Systems, Massey University–Albany, New Zealand

Simon Milne, Department of Geography, McGill University, Montreal, Quebec, Canada

Luciano Minerbi, Department of Urban and Regional Planning, University of Hawai'i at Manoa, Honolulu, Hawai'i, USA

Stephen J. Page, Department of Management Systems, Massey University–Albany, Auckland, New Zealand

Nii-k Plange, Department of Sociology, University of the South Pacific, Fiji

Brenda Rudkin, Department of Management Systems, Massey University–Albany, Auckland, New Zealand

Chris Ryan, Centre for Tourism and Visitor Management, Nottingham Trent University (formerly Massey University, Palmerston North, New Zealand)

Acknowledgements

The editors would like to take this opportunity to express their thanks to Mr Jim McCrae, Managing Director, Air New Zealand Ltd, Auckland, New Zealand for the very generous sponsorship provided in terms of a travel grant to assist the editors in fieldwork and travel to complete the book. The Public Relations Office at Air New Zealand, including David Beatson and Cameron Hill also provided help and assistance at different stages of the book. In addition, Olly Hardenburg in Strategic Planning, Air New Zealand Ltd, Auckland also provided invaluable assistance in data collection for the statistical sources used in Part II of the book. The help from Meegan Sarah at the New Zealand Tourism Board in Auckland with data sources is also gratefully acknowledged. The following organisations also kindly supplied data: Bureau of Tourism Research (Australia); Guam Visitors Bureau; Northern Marianas Visitor Bureau; Yap Commerce and Industries Division; Destination New Caledonia; Tahiti Tourist Board; Tonga Visitor Bureau; and the Ministry of Foreign Affairs in Wellington as well as access to their library. The provision of a Massey University Research Fund Grant in 1994–95 to Stephen Page also provided the vital support for additional fieldwork and assistance with a number of chapters.

The ongoing help and advice from Professor Paul Spoonley and Professor Ian Watson, Massey University–Albany, New Zealand have also provided a much needed source of encouragement and advice in relation to the research of Stephen Page. In the Department of Management Systems, Massey University–Albany the following people also deserve a special mention for their help and support during the preparation of the book: Mary Miller, Ruth Robison, Barbara Rom and Cecilia Williams for administrative assistance and for keeping a watchful eye on the hardworking fax machine. The research advice provided by Brenda Rudkin in relation to the Solomon Islands and data sources for other destinations is also gratefully acknowledged.

Support at the University of Canberra came from a number of sources. Infrastructural support was given by the Centre for Tourism and Leisure Policy Research while administrative assistance was provided by Stuart Christopherson, Michaela Saint and Sue Wright. The research assistance of Chris Hamon, Nicolle Lavelle, Vanessa O'Sullivan, and Kirsten Short is also gratefully acknowledged. Tracey Batchelor, Jeff Buckley, Dick Butler, Neil and Tim Finn, Julie Hodges, John Jenkins, Virginia Jones, Geoff Kearsley, Nikki Keirven, Simon McArthur, Sara McLachan, Declan MacManus, Peter Murphy, David Press, Evi Prin, Kirsten Short, Mark Snarski, Brian and Delyse Springett, Ingrid van Aalst and Chris Daly, and Chris Wilson provided welcome support during research conducted for the present book.

The editors would like to acknowledge the following for permission to reproduce material: Air New Zealand Ltd for permission to reproduce the front cover of the book and Figure 17.1 and Plate 1.1 from their 1995 Annual Report; Julie Cassin at Destination New Caledonia for permission to reproduce Plates 17.1, 17.2 and 17.3; and Douglas Lockhart for the use of Figure 1.1.

Chapter 9, 'Health and Tourism in the Pacific', by C. Michael Hall and Brenda Rudkin is a revised version of the health and special interest tourism chapter which appeared in *Health and the International Tourist*, edited by Stephen Clift and Stephen J. Page and published by Routledge in 1996. Chapter 17, 'Tourism in the Pacific Islands: Markets, Development and Planning Issues', by Stephen J. Page and Glenda Lawton is a substantially revised and updated version of the Pacific Islands report by Stephen J. Page which appeared in the *EIU International Tourism Reports*, January 1996.

At Routledge and International Thomson Publishing, Francesca Weaver provided her usual wonderful support, patience and encouragement that the editors have now come to expect from her overseeing their publishing projects and Caroline Law for her prompt attention to queries and detail. Finally, we would like to acknowledge Status Quo, Pebbles and Marina who provided such a memorable ending to the preparation of this manuscript.

Series Editors' Preface

The International Thompson Business Series in Tourism and Hospitality Management is dedicated to the publication of high quality textbooks and other volumes that will be of benefit to those engaged in tourism, hotel and hospitality education, especially at degree and postgraduate level. The series has two principal strands: core textbooks on key areas of the curriculum; and the *Topics in Tourism and Hospitality* series which includes highly focused and shorter texts on particular themes and issues. All the authors in the series are experts in their own fields, actively engaged in teaching, research and consultancy in tourism and hospitality. Each book comprises an authoritative blend of subject-relevant theoretical considerations and practical applications. Furthermore, a unique quality of the series is that it is student-oriented, offering accessible texts that take account of the realities of administration, management and operations in tourism and hospitality contexts, being constructively critical without losing sight of the overall goal of providing clear accounts of essential concepts, issues and techniques.

The series is committed to quality, accessibility, relevance and originality in its approach. Quality is ensured as a result of a vigorous refereeing process, unusual in the publication of textbooks. Accessibility is achieved through the use of innovative textual design techniques, and the use of discussion points, case studies and exercises within books, all geared to encouraging a comprehensive understanding of the material contained therein. Relevance and originality together result from the experience of authors as key authorities in their fields.

The tourism and hospitality industries are diverse and dynamic industries and it is the intention of the editors to reflect this diversity and dynamism by publishing quality texts that enhance topical subjects without losing sight of enduring themes. The Series Editors and Advisor are grateful to Steven Reed of International Thompson Business Press for his commitment, expertise and support of this philosophy.

Stephen J. Page
Massey University – Albany
Auckland, New Zealand

Roy C. Wood
The Scottish Hotel School
University of Strathclyde

Foreword

Tourism is one of the mainstays of the Pacific economy and has had dramatic impacts on the nations and island states of the Pacific. There is immense variation in the type of tourism in the Pacific, ranging from the developed destinations of Hawai'i, Australia and New Zealand through to the Pacific Island microstates of Kiribati and Niue. Despite the growing importance of tourism in the region and its significance in providing alternative models of tourism development, ranging from mass tourism in Guam and the Northern Marianas and Hawai'i to ecotourism in the Solomon Islands, a substantial gap exists in the recent tourism literature on tourism in the region.

During the 1970s and 1980s, a number of influential studies were published (e.g. Farrell 1977; Finney and Watson 1975; Pearce 1980; Rajotte 1982; Kissling 1984; Britton and Clarke 1987) as well as a number of overviews of tourism in specific destinations (e.g. Farrell 1982; Milne 1987; Hall 1995); while Hall (1994) highlighted the broader Asia-Pacific context of tourism. Such studies observe that the Pacific is a tourism marketplace which is increasingly developing interconnections between the various tourism generating regions of the world. However, there has been no attempt to provide a wide-ranging synthesis of the progress in research to date and of the current range of developments and issues affecting the Pacific Islands in the 1990s. It was this major gap in both the academic and tourism industry literature that prompted the editors to consider the idea of a wide-ranging review of the Pacific tourism business in 1994. The book recognises the relative inaccessibility of much of the existing literature on tourism in the Pacific at a time when there is a growing interest in the Pacific Rim as the fastest growing region of tourism activity. Although the Pacific Islands may not necessarily equate with such high growth rates, students of tourism cannot fail to have an interest in the developments, issues and debates associated with tourism in a region often characterised as a South Pacific Paradise.

As editors, the real challenge has been to commission a range of international researchers who have had a very close involvement in the Pacific Islands as observers, consultants and advisers on key challenges facing the region. It is the research and experience of the authors contained in this book that can offer detailed insights which have a meaning and application to the Pacific Islands. The chapters of the book go beyond mere description of tourist destinations to provide a critical analysis of the dynamics of tourism development. In doing so, it is hoped that this book will make a contribution not only to debates over tourism in the Pacific but to tourism in its global context. All too often researchers make assumptions that existing Western models of development, planning and business are appropriate to other contexts, such as the Pacific. When some of the authors in this book challenge such assumptions in relation to island microstates they are asking fundamental questions about the contextualisation, dynamics and complexities of contemporary tourism development.

The book is intended as a textbook for undergraduate and postgraduate students as well as industry practitioners who may want to use this as a source of easy reference to examine tourism in different Pacific Island contexts. By adopting a systematic approach to the factors and issues which have shaped the tourism patterns and processes within the region, the book provides a sound basis, in Part I, of the major issues and impacts affecting the region. This is followed in Part II by a range of detailed island cases which illustrate the range of issues in a local and regional context, as well as the interaction of different processes and factors affecting the development, planning, management and sustainability of tourism. Although Part II is not intended to be comprehensive for a region as diverse as the Pacific, it does deal with the three principal groupings of Micronesia, Melanesia and Polynesia, together with a range of small and larger island destinations.

As editors, one of our immediate concerns was to delimit the concept of the Pacific region by identifying what areas are within and outside of the Pacific region. For the purpose of this book, while the Pacific Ocean is intended as the containing context, the tourist destinations covered are bounded by Tahiti in the east Pacific, New Zealand and Australia in the South Pacific and Papua New Guinea in the west Pacific. The Northern Marianas and Hawai'i are the northern-most destinations covered. The major destinations are thus dealt with here for the first time, since all previous texts have only partially focused on the key destinations to the detriment of the smaller ones. It is in this context that this book offers a number of fresh insights and contributions to the growing literature on tourism.

C. Michael Hall
O'Connor, Canberra

Stephen J. Page
Albany

December 1995

REFERENCES

Britton, S. and Clarke, W.C. (eds) (1987) *Ambiguous Alternative: Tourism in Small, Developing Countries*, Suva: University of the South Pacific.

Farrell, B.H. (ed.) (1977) *The Social and Economic Impact of Tourism on Pacific Communities*, Santa Cruz: Center for South Pacific Studies, University of California, Santa Cruz.

—— (1982) *Hawaii, the Legend that Sells*, Honolulu: University of Hawai'i Press.

Finney, B.R. and Watson, K.W. (eds) (1975) *A New Kind of Sugar: Tourism in the Pacific*, Honolulu: East-West Centre.

Hall, C.M. (1994) *Introduction to Tourism in the Pacific: Development, Impacts, and Markets*, Melbourne: Longman Cheshire.

—— (1995) *Introduction to Tourism in Australia: Impacts, Planning and Development*, 2nd edn, Melbourne: Longman Australia.

Kissling, C.C. (ed.) (1984) *Transport and Communications for Pacific Microstates*, Suva: Institute of Pacific Studies, University of the South Pacific.

Milne, S. (1987) *The Economic Impact of Tourism in the Cook Islands*, Occasional Paper No. 21, Auckland: Department of Geography, University of Auckland.

Pearce, D.G. (ed.) (1980) *Tourism in the South Pacific: The Contribution of Research to Development and Planning*, Proceedings of UNESCO Tourism Workshop, Christchurch: Department of Geography, University of Canterbury.

Rajotte, F. (ed.) (1982) *The Impact of Tourism Development in the Pacific*, Peterborough: Environmental and Resource Studies Programme, Trent University.

Chapter 1

Introduction: The context of tourism development in the South Pacific

C. Michael Hall and Stephen J. Page

For many outsiders the term 'South Pacific' conjures up images of a region with eternally blue skies, palm trees swaying in tropical breezes, clear seas and islands surrounded by coral reefs and ocean breakers. It is the quintessential tourism image of 'sand, sea, sun and surf'. As with all images, there is a grain of truth in what the outsider imagines. However, the South Pacific is also an area beset with massive population, resource and environmental problems, and has an urgent need to find mechanisms which provides the peoples of the region with an improved quality of life (see Figure 1.1).

Into this dynamic situation steps tourism. In global terms tourism in the South Pacific is minute. The South Pacific Island region accounts for only approximately 0.15 per cent of the world's international tourism arrivals, with two-thirds of that figure being taken up by Fiji and Tahiti (Yacoumis 1990). However, in regional terms, tourism is a vital component of the economy and is a major employment provider for many of the countries of the reigon (Milne 1992; Hall 1994).

The problems that face the island nations of the South Pacific are typical of those which confront nearly all of the world's small island nations or island microstates (IMS). They lie at the margins of the global economy, are highly dependent on foreign aid and investment programmes, often have relatively little control over their natural resources, and have relatively little power to influence the economic and political direction of the region in which they are situated.

Pacific island economies generally share one feature in common: 'they are nett importers with minimal capacity to independently generate foreign exchange' (Department of Foreign Affairs and Trade 1994c: np). The Pacific islands have few natural resources which can be exploited and those that do exist, such as fish, minerals and timber, are rapidly dwindling due to the lack of economic alternatives and development options (Hall 1994). Furthermore, many of the economies of the Pacific island countries are based on one or two commodities that are subject to extreme price fluctuations. 'The outcome is that they generally have very few products to sell to sophisticated markets. There exists a small fragile private sector to pursue opportunities as they arise, but obtaining suitable, quality venture capital to finance sustainable globally

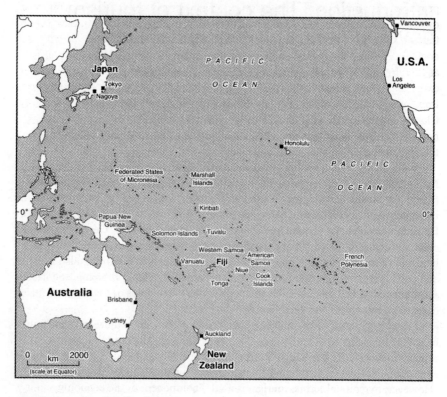

Figure 1.1: The Pacific: location map; reproduced courtesy of The Geographical
Association

competitive ventures is a chronic problem' (Department of Foreign Affairs and
Trade 1994c: np). It is therefore perhaps not surprising that given the need to
diversify their economic bases, rising social expectations and increasing
population pressures, great importance has been attached by Pacific island
governments to the development of service industries, such as tourism, as a
means of making an important contribution to economic growth and
employment (Dorrance 1986; Department of Foreign Affairs and Trade 1994c;
Hall 1994).

The predicament that faces the nations of the South Pacific has been well put
by Connell: 'For island states that have very few resources, virtually the only
resources where there may be some comparative advantage in favour of [island
microstates] are clean beaches, unpolluted seas and warm weather and water,
and at least vestiges of distinctive cultures' (1988: 62). However, while many
Pacific Islands appear to have competitive advantages in terms of natural tourism
resources, they generally lack the capital required to develop adequately tourism

products, transport and infrastructure. Therefore, foreign investment and ownership is virtually a necessity for the development of an international tourism industry in the region. It is for this reason that Lea (1980), in commenting on tourism development in Papua New Guinea, described tourism as 'the last resort'. Nevertheless, although governments and academics may have expressed reservations about the potential cultural, social and environmental impacts of tourism development (e.g. Farrell 1977; Dorrance 1986; Britton and Clarke 1987), tourism is an industry which, if only out of sheer economic necessity alone, many of the islands of the Pacific will have to embrace and learn to live with.

Pacific island tourism ranges from the developed destinations of Hawai'i and New Zealand to the Pacific island microstates of Vanuatu and the Cook Islands (Table 1.1). However, despite the significance of tourism in the South Pacific and its importance in providing alternative models of tourism development, ranging from mass tourism in Hawai'i to ecotourism in the Solomon Islands, there has existed a substantial gap in our understanding of tourism in the region. This book aims to help fill that gap by providing an overview of tourism development and the tourism marketplace in the Pacific. In addition to discussing the broad economic, social, planning and political frameworks within which tourism occurs, the book will examine the patterns and difficulties of development for particular countries and destinations. This first chapter provides an introduction to some of the major themes that need to be addressed in terms of examining the South Pacific as a region and is divided into four main sections. The first section examines the concept of the South Pacific as a region. The second discusses the role of trade in the economic integration of the South Pacific. The third identifies the emerging concerns for sustainable development which surround tourism and other economic activities in the region. The final section provides an outline of the book and emphasises some of the main themes and issues which emerge in any discussion of tourism in the South Pacific.

THE CONCEPT OF THE SOUTH PACIFIC

Despite the influence of tourist and romantic advertising on outsiders' images of the South Pacific as a distinct geographical region (see Plate 1.1), the delineation of the South Pacific as a readily identifiable geographic identity is fraught with difficulty. As Fuavao (1993: 22) observed,

> The South Pacific is unique, not because its geographical, biological, sociological characteristics are found nowhere else in the world, but because the combination of these characteristics in the region is special. The region is characterised by a high degree of ecosystem and species diversity, an extraordinary level of endemicity, a high degree of economic and cultural dependence on the natural environment, vulnerability to a wide range of natural disasters, a diversity of cultures and languages, and traditional

Table 1.1: Visitor arrivals in the Pacific, 1983–94 ('000)

	1983	1987	1990	1991	1992	1993	1994
American Samoa	17.7	17.3	30.3	22.2	15.9	15.3	17.9
Australia and New Zealand	1,452.4	2,629.2	3,190.9	3,333.4	3,658.9	4,153.2	41,684.2
Cook Islands	19.8	28.8	34.2	39.9	50.0	52.8	57.3
Fiji	191.6	189.9	278.9	259.3	278.5	287.4	318.8
Guam	345.0	484.0	769.8	728.7	863.0	784.0	1,086.7
Hawai'i	4,368.0	5,800.0	6,692.3	6,873.8	6,513.0	6,124.6	6,455.1
New Caledonia	90.3	62.2	85.2	83.5	80.8	82.9	88.2
Northern Marianas	128.0	194.7	435.4	429.7	505.2	545.8	596.0
Palau	–	–	32.8	32.7	36.1	40.4	40.5
Papua New Guinea	31.6	35.0	40.7	37.3	40.5	40.4	39.6
Solomon Islands	11.1	12.6	9.1	11.1	10.1	11.6	11.9
Tahiti	111.1	142.8	132.3	122.1	123.9	147.8	166.0
Tonga	15.8	21.2	20.9	20.5	23.0	25.5	28.4
Vanuatu	32.4	21.5	35.0	39.8	42.6	44.4	42.1
Western Samoa	36.7	41.1	48.0	34.9	38.6	47.0	50.7

Source: PATA; national data.

Plate 1.1: The quintessential tourist image as an unspoilt tourist paradise. Outrigger canoe on an isolated beach in Vanuatu (Michael Hall)

practices and customs which are central to the close and special relationship of Pacific people with their environment.

The 'South Pacific' is essentially a European invention. Unifying images of a South Pacific paradise are a cultural hangover from the imperial adventures of European powers in the eighteenth and nineteenth centuries. Given the enormous distances between the Pacific Islands, it was the European fleets that could best provide a notion of unity in such a vast physical and cultural space. Although the island colonising of the Polynesians in pre-European times did provide a limited degree of cultural unity for many of the Pacific Islands, it proved no match for the imposition of colonial control by Britain, Germany, France and the United States in the late nineteenth century.

The South Pacific nations are a political and economic legacy of the old colonial period. Colonial ties to the metropolitan areas of Australia, France, New Zealand and, to a lesser extent, the United States still dictate much development in the region. Australia and New Zealand in particular occupy a sphere of influence far in excess of what could normally be expected of such middle level powers on a global scale. Nevertheless, it is the constraints of colonial legacies and contemporary neo-colonial links which influence our perception of the South Pacific as a distinct geopolitical region (Britton 1987) (Tables 1.2 and 1.3).

Despite most of the Pacific Island nations gaining direct political independence from their colonial masters during the 1970s, most of the Pacific

Table 1.2: Characteristics of Pacific territories

	Status	Date of Independence/ Free Association	Former Colonial Power	Capital	Land Area (sq km)	Population
Australia	Independent State		United Kingdom	Canberra	7,682,300	17,600,000
American Samoa	Unincorporated US territory		United States	Pago Pago	197	50,923
Cook Islands	Self-governing in free association with New Zealand	1965	United Kingdom/ New Zealand	Avarua	240	17,400
Easter Island	Province of Chile	Annexed 1888	Chile	Hanga Roa	180	2,770
Federated States of Micronesia	Self-governing in free association with the US	1979	United States	Palikir	702	100,520
Fiji	Independent Republic	1970	United Kingdom	Suva	18,376	746,326
French Polynesia	Overseas territory of France	Annexed 1847	France	Papeete	3,521	201,400
Guam	Unincorporated US territory	Annexed 1898	Spain/United States	Agana	549	133,152
Hawai'i	State of the US	1959	United Kingdom/ United States	Honolulu	16,641	1,159,600
Irian Jaya	Indonesian province	1950	Netherlands	Jayapura	410,660	1,734,000
Kiribati	Independent republic	1979	United States	Tatawa	726	72,298
Marshall Islands	Self-governing republic in free association with the US	1979	United States	Majuro	720	49,969
Nauru	Independent republic	1968	United Kingdom	Yaren	21.2	9,919
New Caledonia	Overseas territory of France	Annexed 1853	France	Noumea	19,103	173,300

	Status	Year	Administering country	Capital	Area	Population
New Zealand	Independent state		United Kingdom	Wellington	270,500	3,434,900
Niue	Self-governing in free association with New Zealand	1974	United Kingdom/New Zealand	Alofi	258	2,532
Norfolk Island	Australian Territory	Annexed 1788	United Kingdom	Kingston	34.5	1,912
Northern Mariana Islands	Commonwealth of the US	1976	United States	Saipan	475	43,345
Palau (Belau)	Self-governing republic in free association with the US	1981	United States	Koror	500	16,386
Papua New Guinea	Independent State	1975	Germany/ Great Britain/Australia	Port Moresby	461,690	3,963,000
Pitcairn Island	Dependency of Britain	(1)	United Kingdom	Adamstown	4.5	65
Solomon Islands	Independent State	1978	United Kingdom	Honiara	29,785	35,055
Tokelau	Dependency of New Zealand	(2)	United Kingdom/ New Zealand		12.1	1,577
Tonga	Independent mcnarchy	1970	United Kingdom	Nuku'alofa	696,71	94,649
Tuvalu	Independent state	1978	United Kingdom	Funafuti	25.9	9,045
Vanuatu	Independent republic	1980	France/United Kingdom	Port Vila	12,189	150,864
Wallis and Futuna	Overseas territory of France	1961	France	Mata Utu	124	13,900
Western Samoa	Independent state	1962	United Kingdom	Apia	2,934	159,004

Notes: (1) In 1970, Pitcairn and its dependencies were transferred to the control of the British High Commission in New Zealand who is also the Governor of Pitcairn.

Notes: (2) In 1877, the British High Commission for the Western Pacific was given jurisdiction of the Islands. In 1948, the Islands were included in the territorial boundaries of New Zealand.

Source: Modified from the Pacific Islands Yearbook.

Table 1.3: Economic growth (GDP) in select Pacific countries 1989–93

Economy	1989	1990	1991	1992	1993
Fiji	12.0	4.8	0.7	2.8	4.5
Papua New Guinea	−1.4	−3.0	9.5	8.6	10.6
Samoa	1.3	−4.5	−1.5	−5.0	1.9
Solomon Islands	4.9	2.3	3.2	8.2	4.8
Tonga	1.6	−2.0	5.3	1.9	2.5
Vanuatu	4.5	5.2	4.1	0.0	1.9

Source: Economic and Social Commission for Asia and the Pacific 1994.

countries are still economically tied to the former colonial powers in terms not only of trade, but also of foreign aid and development assistance programmes. Although many of the countries are nominally independent, they remain dependent on political and economic linkages with Australia, New Zealand and France. However, in the contemporary global economy, the former colonial linkages of the South Pacific are being transformed into trade and economic linkages which are making the countries of the region more economically, politically and culturally interdependent and are therefore contributing to the development of an indigenous South Pacific economic and political identity.

As one of the economic mainstays of the South Pacific, tourism is playing an enormous part in the development of regional linkages. Substantial investment from Australia and New Zealand exists in tourism and aviation, while these countries are also major sources of tourists to the region. Furthermore, the creation of tourism organisations such as the Tourism Council of the South Pacific also contributes to consideration of regional economic and political development.

An understanding of linkage and interdependence is crucial to how we perceive tourism in the South Pacific. Too often, studies of tourism in specific destinations or countries have tended to examine those areas in isolation from the broader economic and political processes of which tourism is a part. In short, they have therefore failed to provide the overall *context* within which tourism development occurs. Therefore, the next section discusses the regional trade context, while the following section briefly examines concerns surrounding the need for sustainable development within the South Pacific.

REGIONAL TRADE ISSUES

The Pacific era has dawned. Today the region in and around the Pacific Basin – the largest of the world's oceans – holds most of the human and natural resources and is the most dynamic and prosperous area of the world (Kim 1987: 165).

The post-Second World War period has seen the emergence of the Pacific as a major geopolitical and economic force in world affairs. Economic growth in the Pacific Rim, and in Northeast Asia and ASEAN in particular, has been the most dynamic in the world over the past 40 years. It is also, therefore, not surprising that the Asia-Pacific region represents the world's fastest growing tourist region (Hall 1994). However, while the Pacific Rim is now a major element in economic and political thinking, the 'Pacific era' has not come to include the South Pacific.

Economic regionalism is the order of the day in East Asia and the Pacific Rim. The signing of the North American Free Trade Agreement (NAFTA) between Canada, Mexico and the United States; the Closer Economic Relationship (CER) agreement between Australia and New Zealand; and the establishment of the Association of South East Asian Nations (ASEAN) Free Trade Area (AFTA), all highlight the moves towards free trade and economic interdependency. However, of most significance is the establishment of an Asia–Pacific Economic Cooperation Forum (APEC), which has been championed by Australian Prime Minister Paul Keating. This combines the longer-standing economic powers of the region (Australia, Canada, Japan, New Zealand and the United States) with the newly industrialised economies of East Asia. With a goal of free trade in the Pacific, APEC has the capacity to provide the major impetus for economic and political development in the region well into the next century (Hall 1994).

Although the Pacific Islands have been largely bypassed by the development of Asia Pacific economic cooperation, substantial development opportunities may potentially be derived from involvement in the new economic regionalism which is impacting upon the Pacific. Mak and Naya (1992) note two reasons why the Pacific Islands have been generally omitted in discussion of Asia–Pacific cooperation. First, the size of the Pacific islands is small in terms of population and economic strength, representing less than 0.5 per cent of the total GDP and population of the Asia–Pacific region. Second, the island nations are spread over a wide area and are, they argue 'not recognized as a cohesive entity' (1992: 42). Nevertheless, Mak and Naya argue that the Pacific island nations have the capacity to be involved in APEC through their occupation of an important strategic position in the middle of the Pacific, while they also hold some potentially significant economic resources. Most notably in this regard, they highlight the 'significant flow of tourists from the APEC nations to the Pacific islands, as well as impressive and growing volumes of foreign investments in tourism and other economic activities' (1992: 42–3). In order to achieve involvement in APEC, Mak and Naya (1992) argue that it is essential that the Pacific island nations need to take a more regional approach to economic development. While a regional approach to Pacific economic development has received a substantial degree of support (Hall 1994), such regional agreements have been fraught with difficulties.

The South Pacific Regional Trade and Economic Cooperation Agreement (SPARTECA) is a unilateral trade and economic cooperation agreement between Australia and New Zealand, and the Forum Island Countries (Cook Islands, the

Federated States of Micronesia, Fiji, Kiribati, Marshall Islands, Nauru, Niue, Papua New Guinea, the Solomon Islands, Tonga, Tuvalu, Vanuatu and Western Samoa) which came into force on 1 January 1981 (Robertson 1986; Department of Foreign Affairs and Trade 1994a). In the case of PNG, SPARTECA superseded the Papua New Guinea Trade and Commercial Relations Agreement, which was a preferential, non-reciprocal arrangement between Australia and PNG which had been in place since 1 February 1977.

SPARTECA is intended to provide for freer trade in the South Pacific by granting duty-free access to the Australian and New Zealand markets, expanding and diversifying trade, stimulating investment, and providing for cooperation in marketing and other forms of commercial activity. However, in the early to mid-1980s, SPARTECA 'had very little impact on output, export and employment because the Australian and New Zealand markets are relatively unattractive and the South Pacific countries are not competitive in labour intensive products' (Robertson 1986: 23). Nevertheless, revisions to the agreement in 1987 and the general lowering of tariffs in Australia and New Zealand, has led to more positive outcomes for South Pacific nations from SPARTECA (Department of Foreign Affairs and Trade 1994b).

A dimension to SPARTECA of interest to tourism is the manner in which the trade agreement provides for the promotion of investment in the Forum Island Countries and cooperation in marketing and promotion, including funds for the Office of the South Pacific Trade Commissioner in Sydney and two International Trade Development Centres in Sydney and Melbourne (Department of Foreign Affairs and Trade 1994a). The South Pacific Trade Commissioner, in particular, has been aggressive in its promotion of tourism as an investment opportunity for Australian investors and as a growth industry in the South Pacific.

Trade agreements between the two dominant economic and political powers of the South Pacific – Australia and New Zealand – have also been of interest to the South Pacific island nations. In 1983 the Australia–New Zealand Closer Economic Relations/Trade Agreement (CER) came into force. The goal of CER is to establish a single trans-Tasman market within which tariff and other trade barriers are abolished, relevant business laws and administrative practices are harmonised and free trade encouraged in goods and services. Since 1983, New Zealand has become Australia's fourth largest market and Australia is New Zealand's most important trading partner, with trade between the two countries more than doubling since the agreement was signed (Hall 1994). Although initially only affecting goods, CER has now been extended to include services, such as aviation and tourism.

In 1985 Prime Minister Bob Hawke of Australia raised the possibility of extending CER to all Pacific Forum Countries. According to Robertson (1986: 23):

It was argued that such an arrangement would give security of investment for investors in the South Pacific because (following EC precedents), once it was established, it would be very difficult to dismantle. It was also argued that such an agreement would halt trends towards protectionism in some South Pacific economies because the reciprocity conditions would compel the reduction of existing trade barriers and prevent the erection of new ones.

Although the proposal was well intentioned in terms of attempting to provide a stable basis for economic development and investment in the region, it was fraught with difficulties. Island goods and services would potentially face increased competition from lower priced Australian and New Zealand goods and services which were products of businesses with larger economies of scale and more realistic exchange rates. However, the main problem was the difficulty in integrating economies which are markedly different in scale and level of development (Robertson 1986). Nevertheless, while CER has not yet been extended to Pacific Forum Countries, there is still an increasing level of regional economic integration. Australia and New Zealand have continued to develop trade and investment agreements with South Pacific governments, while the Pacific nations have also been extending links among one another. For example, the tripartite Melanesian Free Trade agreement between PNG, Solomon Islands and Vanuatu, came into effect in 1994 (Economist Intelligence Unit 1994).

An additional dimension to the region's economic structure is the increased level of investment from East Asian sources, particularly Japan, Taiwan and Malaysia. For example, a Taiwanese company, Olilian, announced a project in 1994 to boost the economy of Vanuatu's second largest city, Luganville, the project involves the construction of factories and medical, commercial, banking, and hotel facilities for an estimated 3,000 Taiwanese who are expected to settle in Luganville to take advantage of Vanuatu's tax-haven status. In addition, the Taiwanese are to fund a $US16 million upgrade of the international airport at Port Vila (Economist Intelligence Unit 1994).

Foreign investment from sources other than Australia and New Zealand has the capacity to reduce dependency on those countries and also diversify local economies. However, in light of APEC, it perhaps also illustrates the growing integration of the South Pacific within the Pacific Rim, and therefore highlights the potential for the development of new forms of economic regionalism and the role of tourism within such economic and political linkages.

SUSTAINABLE DEVELOPMENT

The essence of good resource management is to make economic growth sustainable – this principle applies equally to all countries regardless of their resource endowment.

(Gordon Bilney, Australian Minister responsible for the South Pacific Forum, 31 July 1994)

With the potential threat of disappearing under rising sea-levels should global warming continue, it is perhaps not surprising that the environment and sustainable development has emerged as a key issue for the South Pacific nations. Indeed, it should be noted that the governments of the South Pacific have attempted to adopt a regional approach to the implementation of the conventions on sustainable development which emerged from the 1992 Rio conference on environment and development (Fuavao 1993).

Tourism has increasingly been recognised as requiring the application of the principles of sustainable development. Sustainable tourism development requires the integration of economic, social and environmental considerations. By taking just one of these elements out of the sustainable equation, the prospects for sustainable tourism will be diminished. As Brookfield (1991: 42) commented, environmental sustainability not only refers to environmental regeneration and the maintenance of biodiversity but must also 'be measured by progress along a vector made up of attributes that include improvement in income and its distribution, in health, in education, freedoms, and access to resources'. Nevertheless, a number of problems surrounding the nature of tourism, require appropriate policy and planning responses if tourism is to be integrated into sustainable development frameworks. These are outlined by Butler (1990: 40):

- IGNORANCE of dimensions, nature, power of tourism;
- LACK OF ABILITY to determine level of sustainable development, i.e., capacity;
- LACK OF ABILITY to manage tourism and control the development;
- LACK OF APPRECIATION that tourism does cause impacts, is an industry, and can not easily be reversed;
- LACK OF APPRECIATION that tourism is dynamic, and causes change as well as responds to change;
- LACK OF AGREEMENT over levels of development, over control, over direction of tourism.

Undoubtedly, these issues regarding the nature of tourism will be highlighted as we examine the various destinations and countries in the chapters of this book. Nevertheless, it is worth noting that the position of tourism within the sustainable development of the Pacific Islands has been emphasised at recent Pacific island leaders' meetings.

The August 1994 Annual Summit of the South Pacific Forum, held in Brisbane, Australia, highlighted a number of issues with respect to the resources of the region. Sustainable development lay at the centre of Forum discussions; as the final communiqué stated,

> The Forum stressed the need to adopt a global perspective in regard to the development of economic policies, in particular ensuring the achievement of maximum sustainable economic returns on the region's resources, enhancing development of the private sector, responding to changing global conditions,

increasing the level of value-added production, and developing regional approaches to international trade.

(South Pacific Forum 1994: 3)

While attention has focused on logging and fisheries concerns, the Forum also recognised that tourism in the region was potentially unsustainable. From their retreat, the leaders released a statement noting that they had 'decided to take action in a number of areas', including airlines and tourism. They commented:

There was general agreement on the need to deal with airline losses. The leaders agreed to examine the options for a rationalisation of air services among Forum island countries, perhaps on a sub-regional basis. We agreed that given the problems of distance and size in the Pacific any reform of airline structures should take into account the need to ensure adequate services throughout the region. It would also need to look at factors such as the frequency and cost of operations, fares and safety . . . Tourism provides valuable employment opportunities. We recognised the excellent potential for tourism development in our region, provided its unique environmental features are preserved. In this regard, we noted the particular need to protect the region's fragile coastal zones.

(South Pacific Forum 1994: 11, 12)

The following chapters highlights the difficulties inherent in balancing tourism development with the conservation of the region's natural and cultural resources. While almost everyone agrees that sustainable tourism development is the most desirable outcome for tourism in the South Pacific, the political, economic and cultural pressures on tourism policy and development will make this outcome extremely difficult to achieve – a point that we will return to in the concluding chapter.

CONCLUSIONS

Tourism is undoubtedly a vital component in the economic development of the Pacific. However, our understanding of the role of tourism within the complex development process, including sociocultural, environmental and political impacts, is quite limited. While useful pieces of individual research have been conducted, a full account of the costs and benefits of tourism within the region has not been undertaken. Indeed, tourism is at times blamed for a range of ills which have more to do with former colonial linkages, the process of modernisation, and the intrinsic resource and economic characteristics of island microstates than the nature of tourism itself. Accordingly, it is appropriate that one of the recurring themes of the chapters in this book is that tourism development needs to be placed within its wider economic, environmental, sociocultural and political context if it is to be understood. Such an approach is important not only for understanding development processes but also for gaining a better appreciation of what governments should be seeking from tourism. As Richter (1989: 103) commented:

> In most countries, the industry's health is assumed to be the best indicator of a successful policy. This is not so. A tourism policy in a developing nation, particularly, should be judged by its net impact on the economic, social, and political life of the people. Since net economic benefits, as opposed to overall receipts, and social and political factors are seldom considered quantifiable, in many countries they are simply left out of the policy equation.

This chapter has helped place tourism development in the Pacific within the context of issues of island microstate development, the construction of the concept of the South Pacific, regional trade issues, and the goal of sustainable development. The series of chapters in Part I provide a much more thorough account of tourism in the Pacific in relation to a number of key dimensions of tourism development, and therefore provides a firm framework within which to highlight the nature and complexity of tourism in the region.

REFERENCES

Bilney, G. (1994) Address to the First Session of the 1994 South Pacific Forum, Sunday 31 July, mimeo.
Britton, S. (1987) 'New Zealand in the South Pacific: Towards a regional geography of colonial and capitalist relations', in P.G. Holland and W.B. Johnston (eds) *Southern Approaches: Geography in New Zealand*, Christchurch: New Zealand Geography Society, pp. 283–303.
Britton S. and Clarke, W.C. (eds) (1987) *Ambiguous Alternative: Tourism in Small Developing Countries*, Suva: University of the South Pacific.
Brookfield, H. (1991) 'Environmental sustainability with development: What prospects for a research agenda?', in O. Stokke (ed.) *Sustainable Development*, London: Frank Cass, pp. 42–66.
Butler, R.W. (1990) 'Alternative tourism: Pious hope or trojan horse', *Journal of Travel Research*, 28(3) 40–5.
Connell, J. (1988) *Sovereignty and Survival: Island Microstates in the Third World*, Research Monograph No. 3, Sydney: Department of Geography, University of Sydney.
Department of Foreign Affairs and Trade (1994a) *South Pacific Regional Trade and Economic Cooperation Agreement*, Canberra: Department of Foreign Affairs and Trade.
—— (1994b) *Australia's Trade Relations in the South Pacific*, Canberra: Department of Foreign Affairs and Trade.
—— (1994c) *Trade Patterns – South Pacific*, Canberra: Department of Foreign Affairs and Trade.
Dorrance, G.S. (1986) 'The desirability of tourism', *Pacific Economic Bulletin*, 1(2): 47–8.
Economic and Social Commission for Asia and the Pacific (1994) *Review of Tourism Development in the ESCAP Region*, ESCAP Tourism Review No. 15, New York: United Nations.
Economist Intelligence Unit (1994) *EIU Country Report*, 4th quarter, London: Economist Intelligence Unit.

Farrell, B.H. (ed.) (1977) *The Social and Economic Impact of Tourism on Pacific Communities*, Santa Cruz: Center for South Pacific Studies, University of California.

Fauvao, V.A. (1993) 'South Pacific Regional Environmental Programme: implications of Agenda 21 for the Pacific', *Pacific Economic Bulletin*, 8(2): 22–31.

Hall, C.M. (1994) *Tourism in the Pacific Rim: Development, Impacts and Markets*, South Melbourne: Longman Australia.

Kim, R. (1987) 'Pacific basin cooperation: problems and prospects', in R. Kim and H. Conroy (eds) *New Tides in the Pacific: Pacific Basin Cooperation and the Big Four (Japan, PRC, USA, USSR)*, Westport: Greenwood Press, pp. 165–91.

Lea, D.A.M. (1980) 'Tourism in Papua New Guinea: The last resort', in J.M. Jennings and G.J.R. Linge (eds) *Of Time and Place*, Canberra: Australian National University Press, pp. 211–31.

Mak, J. and Naya, S. (1992) 'Economic cooperation: Asia Pacific and the Pacific islands', *Pacific Economic Bulletin*, 7(2): 39–44.

Milne, S. (1992) 'Tourism and development in South Pacific microstates', *Annals of Tourism Research*, 19(3): 191–212.

Richter, L. (1989) *The Politics of Tourism in Asia*, Honolulu: University of Hawai'i Press.

Robertson, M. (1986) 'A comparison of SPARTECA and PACTRA', *Pacific Economic Bulletin*, July: 21–23.

South Pacific Forum (1994) *Forum Communiqué*, Twenty-Fifth South Pacific Forum, Brisbane, Australia, 31 July–2 August.

Yacoumis, J. (1990) 'Tourism in the South Pacific: A significant development potential', *The Courier*, 122, July–August: 81–3.

Part I

Issues in Pacific tourism

Chapter 2

Tourism in the Pacific: historical factors

Norman Douglas and Ngaire Douglas

THE MYTH OF PARADISE

Popular Western conceptions of the Pacific are founded on myth (Smith 1960; Cohen 1982). It was in the South Pacific, on the island of Tahiti specifically, that the modern version of the myth of an earthly Paradise was born; created, not by islanders, who had their own quite different belief systems, but by weary navigators from half a world distant to give expression to peculiarly European fantasies. 'I thought', wrote Louis Antoine de Bougainville, encountering the other-worldly landscape of Tahiti on 6 April 1768, and being greeted by superbly featured men and young, naked women, 'I was transported into the garden of Eden' (cited in Smith 1960: 25). Bougainville was not the first European to see Tahiti, but he made up for this by providing a description of it that to this day influences tourism promoters and advertising copy writers. Paradise had been disclosed, and the term, or a variation of it, became in time the most overworked expression in the lexicon of travel, particularly Pacific travel.

But if the myth was born in Tahiti, it was appropriated quite early by Hawai'i, to which commercial interests were applying the term 'Paradise' by the 1850s. Hawai'i's climate, more salubrious than most other Pacific Islands, and its topography, more dramatic than many, gave it an early appeal to Europeans. Its geographical proximity to the USA made it a relatively easy target for American missionaries and merchants, both groups strongly in evidence, if rarely in agreement, by the middle of the nineteenth century (Daws 1974). Mark Twain's *Letters from Hawaii*, written in 1866, helped popularise the islands ('the loveliest fleet of isles that lies anchored in any ocean') for mainlanders from the USA (Day 1966: vi). By the end of that decade these were represented in Hawai'i not simply by people of religion and commerce, with their own particular missions to fill, but also by those searching for the recuperative qualities of its climate, or by the merely curious visitor, especially from the west coast.

By that time visitors were also arriving from elsewhere, en route to the USA. The English traveller and writer, Isabella Bird, arriving in the islands from Auckland in 1873, fell easy prey to the growing force of the myth. Receiving her first glimpse of Honolulu 'beyond the reef and beyond the blue', she was moved to describe it as 'Bright blossom of a summer sea! Fair Paradise of the Pacific!' (Bird 1974: 14). Bird noted that there was already an excursion which most visitors took; a ride to the Pali, the forbidding, wall-like precipice a short distance from Honolulu. Hawai'i's visitor attractions were early established.

To accommodate at least some of the growing number of arrivals, the (Royal) Hawaiian Hotel (not the later hotel of the same name in Waikiki) was built at a cost of $US120,000 in Honolulu in 1871–2 by the native government, already under the influence of, but not yet overcome by, Americans. It was 'the perfection of an hotel', wrote Isabella Bird, 'the great public resort of Honolulu', where, among other types, one might find 'health seekers from California . . . [and] tourists from the British Pacific Colonies . . .' (Bird 1974: 23). 'Here', according to one historian, 'was the first bid for the tourist trade' (Judd 1961: 113). That bid was followed only gradually by others. Although it had been the residence of Hawaiian royalty and its potential as a resort area had been recognised by resident Europeans as early as 1865 (Kuykendall and Day 1948), Waikiki's time had yet to come, as had tourism's. Both would be spurred later by the entrepreneurial efforts of certain individuals, particularly Alexander Hume Ford, who is generally credited with boosting Waikiki's appeal by reviving the almost moribund sport of surfing (Furnas 1947; Judd 1961).

In the last two decades of the nineteenth century, however, there were other distractions – political and economic: a weak monarchy, further destabilised by American influence and the growth in power of plantation owners, rapidly expanding their estates in sugar, a crop which, with pineapples, was to dominate Hawai'i's economy for the next several decades. Plantations and politics were closely related; the overthrow of the Hawaiian monarchy in 1893 has been often referred to as the 'sugar revolution'. As though to illustrate the point, however, that everything is ultimately a resource for tourism, both sugar and pineapple plantations became essential elements in the growing catalogue of the territory's visitor attractions, and later were enshrined pictorially on that most distinctively touristic of all garments – the Aloha shirt. Tourism continues to subsume other forms of economic enterprise: in recent years large plantations, notably on Lanai (the 'pineapple isle') have been turned into resort development.

By the early 1900s both Matson Lines and the Oceanic Steamship Company – the latter established some years earlier by sugar magnate Claus Spreckels but later absorbed by Matson – were operating passenger services between the Hawaiian Islands and the US west coast (Stindt 1982). The largest of the vessels could accommodate almost 500 passengers in two classes, numbers to test the capacity of the visitor facilities of Hawai'i. Nevertheless, there were only five hotels listed for the Honolulu area in a 1917 guide book, two of them in Waikiki (Judd 1961). One of these, the Moana, completed in March 1901, was described the day after its opening as a 'magnificent hostelry which was dedicated as a resting place for the tourists of the wide, wide world who visit the Paradise of the Pacific' (*Pacific Commercial Advertiser*, 12 March 1901), thereby further entrenching the myth and the hotel's own place within it. Characteristic of the social climate in the now US territory, the official guest list of this new facility with its proudly Polynesian name included not one native Hawaiian. In any event, by this time Hawaiians – whether full or part – were already a minority in their own lands, outnumbered by Japanese as early as 1900, and by both Japanese and Caucasians a decade later (Lind 1969). Except as symbols, Hawaiians played little part in the growth of tourism and less in the ongoing development of the myth that was inextricably interwoven with it.

The latter activity was at least partly the preserve of a, by now, large community of *kamaaina haole* (locally born residents of European background), aided and abetted by mainland entrepreneurs and publicists who had interests of one kind or another in selling Hawai'i. These included Matson Navigation Company, whose magazine *Aloha*, published throughout the 1920s, was widely circulated, and whose ever-expanding interests began to include hotels. The first and still the best-known of these, the Royal Hawaiian, was completed in 1927:

Plate 2.1: Paradise encapsulated on a postcard of the 1920s from Hawai'i (Norman Douglas)

*Plate 2.2:   A popular magazine of the 1920s helped promote the myth of paradise
(Paradise of the Pacific:* Hawai'i State Archives)

five years later Matson took over the Moana (Stindt 1982). One historian has
questioned whether tourism was of much importance in the inter-war (1918–41)
period, pointing out that in 1922 there were fewer than 10,000 visitors, and in
1941 only 32,000 (Judd 1961). But relative to the resident population for those
years – 255,912 and 399,544 respectively – these numbers are impressive
enough, and when compared with visitor arrivals in several other Island
destinations – even in the 1990s – they seem still more impressive.

In any case the numbers alone hardly tell the entire story. At least as
important during these years was the fashioning of the image which would
represent Hawai'i for those thousands of visitors who came and for the millions
more yet to come. During the inter-war period, the commercialisation of the
myth that had taken root in the nineteenth century was brought to its peak of
development. It is fair to say that in the contrived imagery of Paradise nothing
really new has appeared for several decades (see Plates 2.1 to 2.4). In tourism –
and most other enterprises relying on illustrated advertising – the grass skirt (a

Plate 2.3:   Pineapples from paradise: the industry, which was economically superior to tourism in Hawai'i in the early twentieth century, eventually yielded to it (Hawai'i State Archives)

garment without traditional precedent in these islands) or the colourful *muumuu* (a variation on the shapeless gown introduced by missionaries) became the standard attire for Hawaiian women, a surfboard or an outrigger canoe the standard accoutrement for Hawaiian men. A ukulele might act as a prop for either. Countless variations of these symbols decorated almost every pictorial device from posters to pineapple cans, and from sheet music covers to cruise ship menus (Brown 1982). The process of disseminating a packaged Paradise was assisted by the wide release of a remarkable number of films made in or about Hawai'i – 72 between 1910 and 1941 – which, even if apparently unrelated to the subject of tourism, still functioned as promotional material for the Islands (Douglas 1994). Even while helping to fabricate the myth, the 'real Hawaiians' (in this case the second or third generation *kamaaina haole*) began to complain as early as the 1930s about the increasing numbers of tourists that the myth attracted (Furnas 1947; Judd 1961). So powerful did this stereotypical imagery eventually become that in the 1990s it even infuses the work of many contemporary native Hawaiian artists, in their own representations of the 'real' Hawai'i.

Plate 2.4:   The myth exported: surfing legend Duke Kahanamoku appears in Australia (State Library of New South Wales)

FIJI AS THE 'CROSSROADS OF THE PACIFIC'

Fiji, whose position in the central South Pacific made it a competitor with Hawai'i for the title 'Crossroads of the Pacific', was also an early beneficiary of steamship travel. In the 1930s Matson would help to popularise the South Pacific Islands with its South Seas itineraries, but well before that the Canadian–Australian Royal Mail Steamship Line and New Zealand's Union Steamship Line were using Fiji's capital, Suva, as a port of call. The former's activity, beginning in 1893, gave rise to one of the earliest examples of a travel guide to the Islands, Fiji for Tourists, written by one of the outstanding colonial administrators of the period, Basil Thomson (Thomson nd c1905); the latter's activity brought about the need for a hotel of some style to accommodate passengers in transit. This was the Grand Pacific, which was completed in May 1914 on reclaimed land on the Suva waterfront, its design based on that of 'the first class accommodation in ships of the day', its lavatory facilities 'most lavish and as sanitary as modern science can make it' (Schutz 1978: 28). There were a few other hotels already, 'all with marginal pretensions to being tourist accommodation' (Scott 1970: 1), but the GPH, as it was almost instantly known, set some distance from the busier part of Suva, quickly became and remained for decades the preferred establishment.

By 1923 a Suva Tourist Bureau had appeared, having been thought necessary by its parent organisation, the White Settlement League (Scott 1968), whose name adequately explained its aims. In addition to other functions, the Bureau published a gazette, containing 'all particulars useful to tourists, whether here for a day . . . or . . . an extended period' (cited in Scott 1970: 2), which was also sent to travel agencies overseas. Within a few months the Bureau was seeking support from the colonial government, which appointed a committee to make recommendations 'with a view to popularising the Colony to tourists, [and] to provide facilities to tourists to visit places of interest . . .' (cited in Scott 1970: 2). The following year the government established the Fiji Publicity Board, empowered with controlling the Tourist Bureau's minimal funds and directing its policy (Scott 1970).

In the opinion of some European residents, these initiatives by government were barely adequate. 'I beg my fellow citizens', one wrote to the colony's newspaper, 'to wake up to the possibilities of the tourist business . . . No visitor to Fiji is disappointed . . . Fiji is without peer in the South Pacific' (*Fiji Times and Herald*, 1 March 1927, cited in Scott 1970: 3). If the call failed to catch the ear of the administration, it was heeded and echoed by others keen to promote Fiji's charms. 'This place', wrote the editor of a new journal, *Pacific Islands Monthly*, ' . . . is destined to be the popular winter resort of Australians and New Zealanders' (*Pacific Islands Monthly* 16 August 1930). By 1930 there was enough shipping activity to at least partly justify this optimism. Monthly services through Suva were provided by four vessels of the Union Steamship Company and three of the Matson Line. In addition, Messageries Maritimes' bi-monthly service between Panama and Noumea also called at Suva. In one month in 1930, Suva might play host to 11 steamer visits (*Pacific Islands Monthly*, 16 August 1930). The Matson vessels, Sierra, Sonoma and Ventura, sister ships with almost identical specifications, each carried 221 passengers. In 1932 all three were retired from the Pacific run and their places taken by two more determinedly "luxury" ships, Mariposa and Monterey, each capable of accommodating 715 passengers in two classes (Stindt 1982), their numbers contributing mightily to the picture of the free-spending American abroad. Far more than earlier cruises from Australia to the islands of Melanesia, Matson's activity may be regarded as the precursor of modern-day luxury cruising in the Pacific.

By the mid-1930s greater attempts were being made to encourage visitors and entertain them once they had arrived. The custom of greeting cruise ships with a brass band, which was already popular in Honolulu, seems to have been introduced around this time. Pamphlets advising passengers how best to spend their day in Suva were distributed. Advertisements celebrating Fiji's visitor attractions appeared in the Australian and New Zealand press (Scott 1970). Guide books described what the day visitor could expect to find. For those with more time to spare, trips by small steamer to Fiji's outer islands were recommended. 'The outside world', read one enthusiastic account, lapsing easily into the already hackneyed phrase, 'is comparatively unfamiliar with this paradise of the Pacific' (Robson 1932: 74–5). In addition to two small, locally owned vessels, the outer islands were serviced by small steamers of the Burns Philp fleet.

CRUISES TO MELANESIA

While Fiji's geographical position made it likely that several steamship companies would take an interest in it, the islands of the western Pacific were for decades mainly the preserve of one organisation. The trading partnership of (James) Burns and (Robert) Philp was formed in April 1883. Less than one year later Burns Philp & Company Limited advertised the first 'New Guinea Excursion Trip', a five-week cruise out of Thursday Island, embracing 'about 250 miles of the most picturesque portion of the coast of New Guinea' (*Sydney Morning Herald*, 16 February 1884, cited in Douglas 1994: 60), a venture which has been described as the 'official beginning of tourist cruises in the South Pacific with particular reference to Melanesia' (Douglas 1994: 60–1). Two years later the company published the first tourist guide to British New Guinea (later Papua) and by 1894 had added the Solomon Islands and the New Hebrides (later Vanuatu) to their cruise itineraries, having shortly before obtained trade concessions in both places. Clearly aware of the significance of tourism, even at this early stage, the company established its own publication – *Picturesque Travel* – and in 1914 set up the Burns Philp Tourist Department. This was the 'natural outcome of the steady expansion of the company's business' (Picturesque Travel, 1914: 49), though it was unlikely to completely dominate the business, which was primarily focused on merchandise and commodity trading. 'Personally conducted tours' to various places, including Lord Howe and Norfolk Island, began to be featured, the latter now also contending for the title 'Paradise of the Pacific' (*BP Magazine*, 1 March 1934: 77).

It was as 'natural' an outcome that the company's activities should lead it into hotel investment, as early as 1901, when a lease on the Port Moresby Hotel was taken, leading in 1914 to acquisition. This was followed some years later by the purchase of the Papua Hotel. BP now owned both the 'Top pub' and the 'Bottom pub' in the Papuan capital, although like their counterparts in the once German colony of New Guinea, these were more likely to have entertained resident expatriates than recreational visitors.

Despite occasionally sharing passenger traffic to Papua New Guinea with P&O and that to the New Hebrides with Messageries Maritimes, Burns Philp maintained a near monopoly on passenger services to Melanesia until the outbreak of the war in the Pacific. To a great extent, the company defined tourism to the region, helping to maintain the image of the islands as places of 'romance . . . the twin sister to mystery' and their occupants as simple, colourful children – 'The "boys" are men of all ages, and all women are "Mary"' (*BP Magazine*, 1 March 1934: 40–1) – albeit not far removed from savagery and cannibalism. This picture of Melanesia and its inhabitants continues almost unchanged in tourist literature of the mid-1990s (Douglas 1994).

After the Japanese bombing of Pearl Harbour, Hawai'i, on 7 December 1941, international pleasure travel within the Pacific was brought to a standstill. Transport, communication and accommodation facilities that had grown to service the requirements of visitors were suddenly pressed into the immediate needs of the military. Luxury cruisers and passenger steamers became troop carriers; hotels throughout the Pacific from Hawai'i to the New Hebrides were turned into command centres, hospitals or officer quarters. In December 1941 Matson Navigation's entire facilities – including their four cruise liners – and staff were declared by the US government to be on a war footing; the company's Royal Hawaiian Hotel became a rest and recreation centre for the US navy (Stindt 1982). Several ships of the Burns Philp fleet were taken over even earlier by the British government; the company's vessel the *Macdhui*, so popular with passengers cruising the islands in the 1930s, was sunk at Port Moresby in 1942 on its first voyage as a troop carrier (Buckley and Klugman 1983).

The effects of the war in the Pacific were paradoxical. Those parts of the region which experienced direct conflict underwent enormous culture shock and suffered massive social dislocation; those not directly involved experienced only slightly less. The relatively small numbers of visitors in the years before the war were suddenly replaced by hundreds of thousands of troops, many of them Americans, some black. Military towns – among them Luganville on Espiritu Santo and Honiara on Guadalcanal – were created where before there had been little more than villages, and sophisticated transport and communications infrastructure took over from rudimentary, barely existent pre-war facilities.

But there were opportunities to be seized and sometimes profits to be made. The presence of so many outsiders stimulated the demand for locally produced goods and services. Throughout the Pacific Islands, particularly in Melanesia, craft production soared as soldiers sought local souvenirs (de Burlo 1989; Douglas 1994), helping to further stimulate a long-established trade and give additional impetus to the concept of the free-spending American; and in Samoa a part-Polynesian teenager who supplied US troops with hamburgers gained enough knowledge and experience from the encounter to later establish the best-known tourist hotel in the South Seas – Aggie Grey's (Eustis 1979). According to several accounts, the wartime experience gained by islanders in dealing with troops was later transferred to their dealing with peace-time tourists, many of whose expectations were seen as similar (de Burlo 1989).

War's waste would become tourism's treasures when visitor traffic revived:

the more violent the conflict, the more 'attractions' it provided. The Arizona Memorial at Pearl Harbour is the outstanding example of war disaster turned to peace-time profit. Elsewhere, the detritus of sea and air battles which filled lagoons in Micronesia and Melanesia would be eagerly sought by a new type of visitor, the scuba diver; much of the land based wreckage being reclaimed by the jungle would be dragged out and put on display for less agile tourists (Douglas 1994). Before their own ranks became depleted, the survivors of the Pacific War – allies and enemies alike – would be encouraged in large numbers to revisit the sites that they had hitherto been so anxious to leave. Nostalgia has long been a potent factor in tourism. The incorporation of the war's legacy into Pacific travel not only rekindled interest in some destinations, it was largely responsible for creating interest in others.

Other sites for which war had been ultimately responsible also became an essential part of the visitor experience, especially in those countries lacking historical monuments or other tangible evidences of antiquity. The National Memorial Cemetery of the Pacific is regarded by the Hawai'i Visitors Bureau as the major visitor attraction of Hawai'i. But on a smaller scale, cemeteries or memorial parks celebrating war dead also figure strongly in the promotional literature and local tour itineraries of New Caledonia, Papua New Guinea, Guam and Saipan. More ironic echoes of the war have also been incorporated into the catalogue of visitor attractions. In Vanuatu, the Jon Frum movement, a 'cargo cult' which had first appeared before the Pacific conflict, grew vigorously during those years, and incorporated much of the war time paraphernalia – (imitation) rifles, service uniforms, formation marching, and flag raisings – that its members had been exposed to (Douglas 1986). Fifty years after the war, members of the group who are too young to have had any experience of it still go through procedures determined by their seniors, but the rituals have now become a tourist spectacle, and are more likely to be maintained because of this. The promises of cargo made by the mythical founder are now at least partly fulfilled by tourists.

Among the most significant legacies of the Second World War were the airfields. Usually hurriedly constructed, with little respect for the landscape or forest that had to make way for them, they were intended to receive aircraft much larger than most parts of the Pacific had previously experienced, whether troop carriers, bombers or cargo transports. For many of the Islands air transport was still a novelty in 1941; some had had no experience of it whatsoever. Fiji first became a stop on Pan American Airways trans-Pacific service just two months before the bombing of Pearl Harbour (Robson 1959), an event which rapidly ended the service. But in a remarkably short time after the start of war in the Pacific, a series of airfields from Bora Bora in the eastern Pacific to Port Moresby in the western had been built, most of them by the Americans, and many of them named after the leading officer in their particular location: Jackson's Field in PNG, Henderson Field in Solomon Islands, Bauer Field in Vanuatu are notable examples. They required little conversion to civilian use, and as international gateways they bear the names to this day (Douglas 1994).

AUSTRALIA AND NEW ZEALAND IN THE PACIFIC: TOURISM DESTINATIONS AND MARKETS

Immediately following the Second World War, international tourism to Australia and New Zealand was relatively minor; travellers from Europe to either were far more likely to be emigrants aiming at resettlement than to be coming for purely recreational purposes. Those from the USA, if Matson Line's experience is evidence, were often more attracted by the islands en route. In the 1960s government-assisted migrants represented a large part of the passenger load for ships from Europe to Australia and for Australia's flag carrier Qantas, providing substantial revenue for both (Gunn 1990). After assisted migration ceased there was often more people leaving the two countries than coming to them: New Zealanders to Australia and Australians and New Zealanders to Britain and Europe. Protectionist policies put in place by national airlines – particularly Qantas – by keeping fares high did little to encourage international tourists. Within Australia, distances, limitations of transport, lack of infrastructure and a general indifference, if not hostility, to visitors added to the obstacles faced. No less an obstacle was the expense of domestic travel and accommodation. As resorts in the Pacific Islands and Southeast Asia began to proliferate in the 1970s, Australian residents were often surprised and delighted to find that they could holiday in an exotic location cheaper than at home. Regional destinations such as Bali and Fiji developed an appeal for Australians then that they retain, still, even after domestic destinations have become more competitive.

Nevertheless, domestic tourism in both Australia and New Zealand was always far more important than in any of the other countries discussed in this chapter, and of great significance to the economies of both. In 1992 New Zealand's domestic tourism accounted for half of tourism revenues (*New Zealand Yearbook* 1992). In Australia that year the proportion was even higher: domestic tourism generated more than twice as much revenue as international tourism (Commonwealth Department of Tourism 1995). But the sizes of their populations, their levels of disposable income, their proximity to and their historical associations with the Pacific Islands also made Australia and New Zealand significant as markets for the region, even while their own appeal as destinations for long-haul travellers was increasing. In the mid-1970s New Zealanders established their own patch of Paradise by both pioneering and dominating tourism (at least until 1992) to their one-time dependency – the Cook Islands.

THE EMERGENCE OF NEW DESTINATIONS: THE EXAMPLES OF GUAM, TAHITI AND NEW CALEDONIA

Hawaii's reputation as playground, securely established before 1941, took little time to recover in the post-war years. The recovery was aided by generous federal spending on defence, the acquisition of US statehood in 1959 and the increased frequency of air services from the mainland. Within two decades of these developments, tourist units had increased from 6825 to 55,700 (Farrell 1982) and visitor numbers from less than half a million to 3,934,504 (State of Hawai'i Data Book 1992). Japanese accounted for 15 per cent of visitors in 1980 and 17 per cent of hotel ownership. These percentages would grow during the following decade.

Despite the pivotal significance of Tahiti to' the myth of Paradise in the Pacific, tourism there was not pursued with any great enthusiasm until well after the Pacific war. The myth had been revived in the early twentieth century in both films and literature, and the widely read output of American writers Charles Nordhoff and James Norman Hall, resident in Tahiti from 1920 (Briand 1966), helped to disseminate it effectively. A Syndicat d'Initiative was established in 1933, ostensibly to encourage tourism (Robson 1956), but one of the main sources of visitors to the Pacific, Matson Line, did not include Tahiti in its South Pacific cruise itineraries until 1940 (Stindt 1982).

With the post-war restoration of shipping services, visitor traffic improved, although for fifteen years political tensions in the territory tended to assume far greater significance than other matters. The turning point for tourism came in 1960 with the opening of a new international airport at Faaa, near Papeete, an event that coincided with the filming in French Polynesia of a second Hollywood version of *Mutiny on the Bounty* (Langdon 1974). The publicity associated with this event helped to bring about a renewed interest in Tahiti that, combined with vigorous promotional campaigns, has remained buoyant ever since. In the South Pacific Islands, French Polynesia is now second only to Fiji in visitor numbers.

French Polynesia's sister territory, New Caledonia, lacking the former's mythic associations and largely indifferent to tourists from any source as long as nickel mining remained economically dominant, entered the contest for the visitor dollar much later. Without the requirements of the Korean and, later, the Vietnam War to sustain them, world prices for nickel collapsed in the 1970s: they have never fully recovered. At the height of the nickel boom, tourist numbers were insignificant – 450 in 1954 (Lyons 1986). After the slump, tourism marketing campaigns, aggressive to the point of desperation, were mounted, especially in the territory's nearest source market – Australia. The result was dramatic. Lured by the promise of the 'Paris of the Pacific' on their doorstep and the reassuringly cheap packages, visitors from Australia alone increased from less than 5000 to more than 20,000 in five years (Lyons 1986). Cruise ships – most of them sailing out of Australia – added another 37,000 visitors annually. The signs were encouraging enough to boost hotel building in Noumea during the 1970s, and to inspire, in 1979, the arrival of Club Méditerranée, which took over an existing facility in its enthusiasm to establish a presence (Carter 1981). Australians turned out to be an unreliable market, unable to distinguish between French territorial tourism and French military aims in the Pacific. They responded to political strife in New Caledonia and the continuance of nuclear testing in French Polynesia by taking their holidays elsewhere. By the late 1980s they were running a poor second to Japan in visitor numbers. The Japanese are now regarded by New Caledonia tourism authorities as the preferred market, accounting for more than one-third of the total.

Guam and most of Micronesia remained under US military control for several years after the Pacific war. Previously Guam had been merely a stopover on Pan Am's service to Hong Kong, and no visitor business of any consequence had developed. When civilian administration resumed in 1950 the military presence continued to be the most important economic factor, remaining so in the early 1990s after the numbers of service personnel in Guam were boosted by the closing of US bases in the Philippines.

It was not until 1962 that the administration removed the restrictions on access to the territory, giving US citizens visa-free entry, and encouraged the setting up of the Guam Visitors Bureau, thereby hoping to diversify the island's limited economic base, a decision inspired in part by the rest and recreation requirements of American forces in Vietnam. What happened could hardly have been foreseen. In just over a decade, from 1964 to 1974, visitor arrivals grew from 300 to 234,000. That was the first surprise, but there was a second: the great majority of visitors were not Americans but Japanese. The astonishing influx of Japanese visitors began in 1967–8 when Pan Am commenced services to Japan, later discounting the airfare. Guam, less than half the distance from Tokyo than it is from Honolulu, became the nearest tropical playground of the newly affluent Japanese. By 1970, 81 per cent of visitors were from Japan and only 13 per cent from the USA (Robson 1972).

THE REVIVAL OF CRUISING AND THE PACKAGED PACIFIC

The post-war revival of ocean cruising in the Pacific reached a peak in the 1960s and early 1970s. Matson revived its trans-Pacific services to New Zealand and Australia in 1955 with a reborn *Mariposa* and *Monterey*. During the 1960s the demand for migrant passages from Europe to Australia began to decline (Plowman 1992) and long distance travel became more and more the domain of wide-bodied jet aircraft. Cruises out of Australia to the Pacific Islands began to proliferate. In some years P&O/Orient, which had merged in 1960, had no fewer than seven ships (*Arcadia, Himalaya, Orcades, Orsova, Oriana, Iberia, Canberra*) offering five-day to thirty-one-day holidays in 'Australia's fastest growing resort – a P&O cruise liner'. In 1968 the company – by now using simply the P&O name – advertised twenty-one Pacific cruises out of Sydney (P&O 1968).

The international oil crisis in the early 1970s and the growing popularity of jet-serviced, land-based package holidays in the Pacific Islands obliged P&O to rationalise its fleet; *Iberia, Orcades, Orsova, Himalaya* had all gone to the ship breakers by 1974. But with the crisis over by the end of the decade, cruising and air travel started to become interdependent rather than competitive, and an increasing number of 'fly/cruise' packages were being offered from the late 1970s, many featuring a new generation of cruise ships which, in the face of determined competition from exotic resort hotels, placed ever greater emphasis on the floating resort concept.

REGIONAL PROMOTION AND DEVELOPMENT PLANS

Partly to rationalise the erratic growth of tourism in the South Pacific Islands, and to maximise the economic benefits derived from it, two trends became evident from the 1950s: attempts at regional cooperation and the formulation of plans for tourism development. The first of these emerged as early as 1952 in Honolulu, with the initial meeting of the Pacific Interim Travel Association (PITA), a group representing twelve Pacific countries. The following year the group became PATA (the Pacific Area Travel Association), an acronym it has retained ever since (although the geographical scope now includes Asia). In cooperation with the US Department of Commerce, PATA engaged the firm Checchi and Company to produce a report which appeared in 1961 and bore the title the Future of Tourism in the Pacific and Far East, although many Pacific destinations were omitted (Douglas 1994).

One of the earliest country-specific tourism plans for the islands region appeared in the Solomon Islands in 1968 (Scott 1968). A second attempt at cooperation between otherwise rival destinations, was tentatively introduced in 1971, having been suggested in the Solomons plan. But it involved three Melanesian countries only, Papua New Guinea, Solomon Islands and Vanuatu – all of which had been ignored in the Checchi report – and survived only until 1974. Two years later the Pacific Islands Tourism Development Council met in Tonga, in the first of a number of meetings which, in 1984, resulted in the formation of the Tourism Council of the South Pacific (TCSP) (Douglas 1994), a body whose regional importance grew in subsequent years. Substantially funded by the European Community, the TCSP began to initiate training programmes and to produce development plans for its member countries, adding to the already vast number of plans produced by the United Nations Development Programme, the World Tourism Organization, PATA and private consultants. By the mid-1990s tourism development plans were being formulated even for countries with no tourism infrastructure whatsoever and very little likelihood of acquiring any. The production of such plans had begun to take on the quality of a self-perpetuating industry, whose products often bore only a marginal relationship to the needs of the countries they purported to serve (Douglas 1994).

In the Pacific tourism continues to grow, quite often independently of the contributions of planners. Its economic significance to many countries is now beyond question: in several parts of the region – Hawai'i, Fiji, Cook Islands, Vanuatu, Guam and Tahiti, for example – it has displaced many earlier established enterprises and become the major revenue earner. In the metropolitan countries – Australia and New Zealand – it is regularly referred to as the fastest growing sector of the economy. The myth of Paradise is by now a thoroughly shop-worn cliché, which invests every kind of promotion (see Plate 2.5). Virtually every travel brochure on the region contains similar images, no longer the exclusive preserve of Tahiti, which inspired them, or Hawai'i which mass produced them. By the 1970s, aided by jet travel, packaged vacations and the relentlessness of brochure and television advertising, the myth had been exported more widely than any other regional product and was being applied indiscriminately and often incongruously to every part of the Pacific. It even included Australia and New Zealand, and reached at least temporary heights of absurdity in such examples as Air Vanuatu's promotion for its services, which announced that 'Air Vanuatu is Paradise to Paradise' (see also Douglas and

Plate 2.5:   Paradise in overdrive: Pacific Islands tourism literature of the 1990s (from top: CTC cruise brochure, Air Vanuatu in-flight magazine, Vanuatu holiday brochure, Air Niugini in-flight magazine, Solomon Airlines calendar, Cook Islands holiday brochure) (Norman Douglas)

Douglas 1990). The myth had become so pervasive that its presence was evident even in the work of those who ought to be critical of it. Farrell in his introduction to *Hawaii, the Legend that Sells*, is lured to its use thus: 'Take a group of breathtakingly beautiful islands set in the blue Pacific as close to paradise as you wish . . .' (Farrell 1982: xiii). For a number of Pacific Island countries, however, including Kiribati, Tuvalu, Nauru and the Marshall Islands, it appears that Paradise might have passed them by. The benefits conferred by tourism and the myth sustaining it continue to remain elusive. Despite the profusion of development or marketing plans and the remarkable projections contained in them, it seems unlikely that their participation in the region's visitor industry will ever be more than peripheral.

REFERENCES

Air Vanuatu (1991) Advertisement, *Islands Business Pacific*, March, inside back cover.

Anon. (1901) 'Moana Hotel Opened Last Evening With Glitter And Good Cheer', *Pacific Commercial Advertiser*, 12, March: 2.

Anon. (1930) Picture caption, *Pacific Islands Monthly*, 16 August: 9.

Anon.(1976) 'The First 25: PATA: For 25 years, a synergistic impact on Pacific tourism', *Pacific Travel News*, April: 34–5.

Bird, I. (1974, 1st edn 1890) *The Hawaiian Archipelago: Six Months among the Palm Groves, Coral Reefs and Volcanoes of the Sandwich Islands*, Rutland: Charles E. Tuttle.

Blanding, D. (1930) *Hula Moons*, New York: Dodd, Mead & Co.

BP Magazine (1934) 1 March.

Briand, P. (1966) *In Search of Paradise: The Nordhoff-Hall Story*, Honolulu: Mutual Publishing Company.

Brown, D. (1982) *Hawaii Recalls: Selling Romance to America; Nostalgic Images of the Hawaiian Islands 1910–1950*, Honolulu: Editions Limited.

Buckley, K. and Klugman, K. (1983) *The Australian Presence in the Pacific: Burns Philp 1914–1946*, Sydney: George Allen & Unwin.

Carter, J. (ed.) (1981) *Pacific Islands Yearbook, Fourteenth Edition*, Sydney: Pacific Publications.

Cohen, E. (1982) *The Pacific Islands from Utopian Myth to Consumer Product: the Disenchantment of Paradise*, Aix-En-Provence: Centre des Hautes Etudes Touristiques.

Commonwealth Department of Tourism (1995) *Impact, March*, Canberra: Commonwealth Department of Tourism.

Daws, G. (1974) *Shoal of Time: A History of the Hawaiian Islands*, Honolulu: University of Hawai'i Press.

Day, A. G. (ed.) (1966) *Mark Twain's Letters from Hawaii*, London: Chatto and Windus.

de Burlo, C. (1989) 'Islanders, soldiers and tourists: The war and the shaping of tourism in Melanesia', in G. White and L. Lindstrom (eds) *The Pacific Theater: Island Representations of World War II*, Honolulu: University of Hawai'i Press, pp. 299–325.

Douglas, N. (1983) 'Tourism in Vanuatu: Low Economic Priority, high public relations profile', *Pacific Islands Monthly*, March: 61–4.

—— (1986) *Vanuatu: A Guide*, Sydney: Pacific Publications.

—— (1994) 'Electric shadows in the South Seas: The Pacific Islands in film', in D. Aoki (ed.) *Moving Images of the Pacific Islands; A Guide to Films and Video*, Honolulu: Center for Pacific Islands Studies, pp. 3–19.

Douglas, N.I. and Douglas, N.M. (1990) 'Vanuatu's revival as untouched paradise', *Pacific Islands Monthly*, March: 37–9.
—— (1989) *Pacific Islands Yearbook Sixteenth Edition*, Sydney: Angus & Robertson.
—— (1994) *Pacific Islands Yearbook Seventeenth Edition*, Suva: Fiji Times.
Douglas, N.M. (1994) 'They came for savages: A comparative history of tourism development in Papua New Guinea, Solomon Islands and Vanuatu 1884–1984', unpublished PhD thesis, University of Queensland.
Eustis, N. (1979) *Aggie Grey of Samoa*, Adelaide: Hobby Investments.
Farrell, B. (1982) *Hawaii, the Legend that Sells*, Honolulu: University of Hawai'i Press.
Furnas, J. (1947) *Anatomy of Paradise: Hawaii and the Islands of the South Seas*, New York: William Sloane Associates.
Gunn, J. (1990) *High Corridors: Qantas 1954–1970*, St Lucia: University of Queensland Press.
Judd, G. (1961) *Hawaii: An Informal History*, New York: Collier Books.
Kuykendall, R.S. and Day, A.G. (1948) *Hawaii: a History: From Polynesian Kingdom to American Commonwealth*, New York: Prentice-Hall.
Langdon, R. (1974) *Tahiti: Island of Love*, 4th edn, Sydney: Pacific Publications.
Lind, A. (1969) *Hawaii: The Last of the Magic Isles*, London: Oxford University Press.
Lyons, M. (1986) *The Totem and the Tricolour: A Short History of New Caledonia since 1774*, Kensington: New South Wales University Press.
New Zealand Department of Statistics (1992) *New Zealand Official 1992 Yearbook*, Wellington: Government Press.
P&O (1968) *P&O presents 21 great cruises in 1968*, cruise brochure.
Parr, T. (1975) 'Tourism in the Pacific', *Pacific Perspective*, 4: 61–73
Picturesque Travel (1914) Sydney: Burns Philp.
Plowman, P. (1992) *Emigrant Ships to Luxury Liners*, Kensington: New South Wales University Press.
Robson, R. (ed.) (1932) *Pacific Islands Yearbook*, 1st edn, Sydney: Pacific Publications.
—— (1956) *Pacific Islands Yearbook*, 7th edn, Sydney: Pacific Publication.
—— (1959) *Pacific Islands Yearbook*, 8th edn, Sydney: Pacific Publications.
—— (1972) *Pacific Islands Yearbook*, 11th edn, Sydney: Pacific Publications.
Schutz, A. (1978) *Suva: A History and Guide*, Sydney: Pacific Publications.
Scott, R. (1968) *Report on the Prospects for the Tourist Industry in the British Solomon Islands Protectorate*, Honiara: British Solomon Islands Protectorate.
—— (1970) The Development of Tourism in Fiji since 1923. Unpublished paper, Fiji Visitors Bureau, Suva.
Smith, B. (1960) *European Vision and the South Pacific 1768–1850: A Study in the History of Art and Ideas*, London: Oxford University Press.
State of Hawai'i Department of Business, Economic Development and Tourism (1992) *State of Hawaii Data Book 1992: A Statistical Abstract*, Honolulu: Department of Business, Economic Development and Tourism.
Steele, H. T. (1984) *The Hawaiian Shirt*, London: Thames and Hudson.
Stindt, F. (1982) *Matson's Century of Ships: Modesto*, private.
Thomson, B. (nd c1905) *Fiji for Tourists*, London: Canadian-Australian Royal Mail Steamship Line.

Chapter 3

Economic impact of tourism in the Pacific

Stephen Craig-Smith

The economic reality for most of the Pacific Island countries falls a long way short of their popular utopian image with the vast majority of island countries facing severe balance of payment problems, unemployment and heavy aid dependence. Their small land areas, minuscule populations, limited natural resources, vulnerability to the vicissitudes of climate and geographic isolation works against their economic well being. For many of these countries the major economic constraint is heavy, if not total, dependence on foreign aid. Further compounding their problem is the world political restructuring following the end of the Cold War. No longer is there the need for the world superpowers to buy political support across vast areas of the South Pacific. As aid is such an important life line to so many of the island economies, the new political world order is likely to bring even greater hardship to many island communities. It is, therefore, little wonder that many Pacific island countries are turning their interest towards tourism development spurred on by the apparent success of Hawai'i and to a lesser extent Fiji, Guam and Saipan (Kissling 1990). With rapid industrial growth on the South East Asian rim a vast untapped tourism market is developing on their door step and tourism development is seen with great promise. To what extent are the Pacific islands in economic difficulty and can tourism provide an economic salvation?

To answer these and other questions this chapter is divided into a number of sections each with a particular focus. The special problems of Small Island Nations (SINs) are analysed together with reference to salient socioeconomic characteristics. While some of these issues have already been addressed in previous chapters, emphasis here is solely on their effects and influences on economic development. The specific problems of primary and secondary production are analysed together with an examination of the private and public sectors of the tourism industry. The chapter concludes with a brief review of future economic possibilities for small island economies with special reference to tourism development.

PACIFIC ISLANDS: THEIR ECONOMIC LEGACY

In a pre-industrial economy when many of the islands were first populated there were sufficient resources to support local island communities. However, by the late twentieth century with mass communication, the desires and expectations of most South Sea Islands is well beyond the support capacity of their local resources. While the resource base of the islands varies considerably even the most generously endowed are limited when compared with most larger metropolitan countries.

One of the greatest economic handicaps to the South Pacific Nations is the size of their land area. With the exception of Papua New Guinea (see Chapter 16) none of the islands can be considered large. Of greater significance than mere size is the paucity of their natural resources. Even further compounding their difficulties is the isolated and scattered nature of their location across the South Pacific. Only Papua New Guinea enjoys the advantages of both size and close geographic proximity to Australia and south-east Asia. Fiji and Hawai'i enjoy the status of region communication hubs but for most of the islands there exists the tyranny of small size and great distance. In the extreme case of Kiribati the distance between the most easterly and most westerly island is greater than the distance across the continental United States! Problems of isolation, smallness and limited resources have been highlighted by many studies over the last 30 years. As early as the mid-1960s, research was emphasising the problem of smallness and geographical isolation and the associated locational disadvantage, a feature highlighted again in 1993 in Lockhart *et al.*'s (1993) analysis of small islands.

Fairbairn *et al.* (1991) has grouped the island nations into four categories on the basis of their resource endowment:

- Papua New Guinea, Fiji, the Solomon Islands, New Caledonia and Vanuatu. These islands are of volcanic origin, tend to be endowed with commercially exploitable minerals and have over 85 per cent of the region's population. Papua New Guinea is a major producer of copper and gold and has recently made a series of oil discoveries, nickel is extensively mined in New Caledonia. The high volcanic islands tend to have adequate rainfall, good volcanic soils, the ability to exploit hydro electric power and sufficient land to support viable agricultural production including cash crops for export such as sugar. These nations enjoy a greater level of economic self-sufficiency than their neighbours and enjoy significant scope for developments in agriculture, forestry and fisheries as well as tourism;
- smaller islands such as Western Samoa, Tonga and French Polynesia which have fewer resources than the first group. Here there is some potential for agriculture and a few commercially exploitable mineral deposits do exist, but tourism may be the only industry with buoyant future prospects;

- small, remote, resource poor islands such as Kiribati, Niue, Tokelau and some of the Cook Islands. These have very limited agricultural potential and lack the financial resources to exploit their Exclusive Economic Zones (EEZs). Even tourism potential is limited on some of these islands; and
- a forth group includes Palau, Guam, the Marshall Islands and American Samoa. These islands either enjoy a strategic military advantage or are the recipients of considerable overseas aid. Unfortunately, many of the countries with the poorest resource base are also the countries facing the greatest challenge when it comes to tourism exploitation and development.

The social fabric of many of the island countries militates against strong economic growth. A socioeconomic structure well suited to pre-industrial society and self-sufficiency is now hindering modern economic development. Central to all Pacific societies is land. Over the centuries land ownership evolved for the benefit of a self-sufficient sea-faring community. Land is held in common ownership facilitating fair access and use of the land but working against sale or disposal. This traditional land holding system was designed for subsistence agriculture not modern cash crop farming, over-population pressure, the needs of urban development or other modern infrastructure. Considerable difficulties have been encountered in modern times by developers wishing to construct roads, hotels and resorts on custom-held land.

The region's colonial experience has not been without its economic difficulties (Fagence 1992). While the Pacific island region was one of the last areas to undergo colonisation, over the last 200 years, practically every island has come under the influence of the great nineteenth-century colonial powers. Only Tonga escaped full colonisation, but by signing a Treaty of Friendship and Protection with the United Kingdom in 1900, it too was subjected to some regulation and control from an outside authority.

While colonisation gave rise to a certain measure of protection and security and facilitated imperial investment, Frank (1967, 1979) pointed out that most investment in colonial countries was designed for the benefit of the imperial power and not the indigenous population. Colonialism has given rise to excessive concentration of power and development to specific urban areas (usually the capital town), an emphasis on infrastructure development focused on export, and over-reliance on the production of a few staple products for export. As Nurkse (1967: 72) has pointed out 'the halcyon days of staple exports have long since ended and that this century has seen the terms of trade turning against them . . .'

A further post-colonial legacy giving rise to modern-day economic difficulties, was the interference in the land owning system. The local system was little understood by the Western colonial powers and efforts to codify land ownership within the framework of Western law has proved far from satisfactory.

It is clear that most of the island nations of the South Pacific are at an economic disadvantage at the world level. It is therefore little wonder that many of these countries are hoping that tourism will bring the desired economic benefits. However, before tourism development can be analysed it is desirable to take a brief look at their existing non-tourism related economic development.

THE NON-TOURIST ECONOMY

Many of the Pacific Island countries are heavily dependent on the export of a few staple crops; this puts them in a very weak economic position on the global market. A legacy of the colonial era has been an over-emphasis on the export of staple crops. The primary reason for colonisation in the first place was the need for assured supplies of staple commodities by the major metropolitan powers and their geostrategic significance. Infrastructure development was geared towards the export of staples and the influence of that infrastructure is still present. SINs cannot afford to abandon the staple related infrastructures; unfortunately staple enterprises were rarely designed with the needs of the host community in mind (see Chapter 12).

The export infrastructure encouraged the development of urban migration, the focus of economic activity on just one island in a group and a heavy urban concentration leads to urban related problems of crime, unemployment and homelessness. These problems are not the sole prerogative of post-colonial legacy, as will be discussed presently, but the colonial heritage is not without its problems.

An over-concentration on a few export staples tends to retard inter-island trade opportunities and import substitution. Food imports are often necessary and economic dualism is common whereby a modern economy is superimposed on a less advanced system. Over-dependence on a few commodities for export, an ill-suited infrastructure, the rectification of which is often beyond the financial resources of the government, and an over-dependence on food imports are weaknesses of many of the islands in the Pacific. These problems have a direct bearing on the value of tourism to many island communities. Tourism merely exacerbates the existing need for imports and leads to heavy economic leakage. Infrastructure focus on the main point of export merely encourages tourism to locate in areas already developed, often retarding potential tourism growth in areas and regions where new development is more urgently needed.

Whereas many larger countries can turn towards a manufacturing base this is no easy task for small island nations. A manufacturing base geared towards an export market can often obscure serious ongoing economic difficulties and can further develop an outward-looking infrastructure. Export manufacturing will tend to locate in areas with a ready access to the world economy and/or foreign markets which tend to be in the major urban areas. The necessary development of airports, harbour facilities and other export orientated infrastructure can deflect much needed government finance for such pressing domestic needs as health or education. Parry (1973: 215) pointed out that 'the global basis of decision making which results in the tendency inherent in direct investment from abroad, to shift decision-making power in parts of the private sector outside the country'. International multinational corporations may, in many cases, have the financial strength and global workforce which can exceed the resources and the population of the smaller island nations. The financial interest of the multinationals may well be in direct conflict with the national interests of a small country (McKcc 1977). Corporate decision making can pose potential threats to sovereignty through the ability to circumvent domestic economic policy.

For isolated small nations such as those in the Pacific it may be particularly difficult to attract foreign investment for the manufacturing sector. Where an island country does not have a good locational advantage it may be tempted to offer greater and greater concessions in order to attract investors (Ramsaran 1985). The greater the incentives the greater are the costs of promoting industrial expansion and the less the economic return. According to Levy (1987) a considerable amount of local economic development activity has a zero-sum game character. Foreign manufacturing firms rarely locate on small islands without the offer of unrestricted remission of profits, tax holidays for a decade or more, duty free imports on machinery or raw materials and training programmes for the workforce.

With the possible exception of Papua New Guinea and Fiji, the South Pacific countries are at a disadvantage in the manufacturing sector to the superior competitive position of the newly industrialising countries on the Pacific Rim. The lack of supporting services, the limited home markets, the distance from most major international markets and the high transport costs make manufacturing production an unlikely economic saviour for most Pacific island nations. Economists are well aware that in small nations the opportunity for efficient import substitutory industrialisation is exhausted very quickly and that there is limited possibility for establishing an industrial mix which is not heavily export orientated.

Herbst (1988) suggested that many of the Pacific Island countries are so small, so poor and so bereft of natural resources that they will not demonstrate any significant development for many decades. As has been illustrated above, development of primary and secondary activities would appear to be associated with many pitfalls. What is the future for developing a tertiary sector? In the Pacific, governments rather than the private sector play a significant role in the provision of services. Government provided services include the marketing of agricultural export products, research and development services for agriculture and fisheries, education, health services, communications and some transport services.

The public sector of SINs is often large in comparison with other non-primary sectors in island microstates. This is particularly true in countries which receive considerable amounts of foreign aid. In many island states the government is the major employer of cash income earners. Pacific social structure and the communal ownership of land and marine areas tends to encourage the expansion of the public sector. Budget receipts in many of the islands are heavily dependent on foreign aid which not only covers the capital expenditure but operating expenses as well. This aid is a means whereby foreign governments can provide income support to islanders (McKee and Tisdell 1990).

Income sharing within extended families may mean that government funded jobs can lead to the social welfare of many people but social ties and clan relationships play a significant role in the allocation of jobs in many small island communities. Small economies suffer from lack of critical mass in the administration of the public service and a full range of service is rarely provided. There is also limited scope for specialisation. Administrative costs are proportionally higher in small micro-states especially those scattered across far flung archipelagoes.

Connell (1988) points out that social ties are sometimes so powerful and pervasive that anonymity, impersonal role relationships and impartiality are difficult to maintain. This makes the public service politically biased and corruption is frequently inescapable. In very small communities opposition to a party line is difficult if not impossible.

The funding of jobs in the public sectors comes from taxes as well as foreign aid. Income tax accounts for around 50 per cent of receipts in Fiji and Papua New Guinea but is of lesser significance in other Pacific island countries. The source of most income tax is the wages of public employees. A narrow tax base is unreliable and this makes long-term government planning very difficult.

The significance of foreign aid can be gained from a brief glance at the percentage figures for a few key countries. External grants in the early 1990s accounted for around 20 per cent of total government income for Fiji, Papua New Guinea and Tonga, around 30 per cent for the Solomon Islands and Western Samoa, and around 40 per cent for Kiribati and Vanuatu (Fairburn et al. 1991). The uncertainty of foreign aid further renders long-term government planning very difficult.

The expenditure of central governments in the Pacific island countries, as a proportion of GDP, indicates how important government expenditure is to these economies. In the early 1990s, it was 30 per cent in Fiji and Papua New Guinea, 45 per cent in Tonga, 50 per cent in Western Samoa, 60 per cent in Vanuatu and over 85 per cent in Kiribati (Fairburn et al. 1991). Clearly, the public sector has expanded out of all proportion to the rest of the economy and is totally unsustainable without the continuing support of foreign aid.

The dominant influence of the public sector has further influenced over-concentration on a few major urban areas, usually the seat of government which is invariably the major export port as well. In archipelagic nations the trend towards urban concentration has been centralised on the island containing the nation's capital leading to out-migration and under-development of out-lying islands.

The economic future for many small Pacific nations is far from optimistic with problems of size, isolation, small domestic markets, over-concentration on the export of a few staple commodities, difficulties concerning the introduction of a viable manufacturing sector and an unsustainable public sector heavily dependent on overseas aid. Unequal economic development, over-concentration on the capital town/port, rapid urbanisation, rural migration, crime, unemployment and homelessness are all common problems. Faced with these difficulties many of the Pacific island are seriously interested in tourism development but will tourism development be any more successful than any other sectors of the economy?

THE ECONOMICS OF TOURISM IN THE SOUTH PACIFIC

Tourism is a rapidly expanding industry and there is no reason why the Pacific Islands should not capitalise on their tourism potential (Biddlecombe 1981; Yacoumis 1991). The extent to which tourism can overcome their economic difficulties, however, is a matter of some debate and the focus of the rest of this chapter.

Recent advances in transportation technology have enabled more and more people to holiday in remote and exotic locations. As competition increases in the tourism industry there is a tendency to seek out new destinations. Less developed countries (LDCs) are popular with tourism industry professionals because of low labour costs, cheap land and their exotic destination appeal to the industrial tourist generating countries.

As early as the mid-1980s, Dwyer (1986) commented on the fact that many National Development Plans in the South Pacific saw tourism as contributing to many economic goals such as increasing foreign exchange earnings, reducing the balance of payments deficit, the generation of employment, the establishment of supportive linkages with elements of the non-tourism sector and reducing the reliance on staple exports and at the same time enhancing local culture and preserving local traditions. Such thinking merely transferred popularly held Western economic viewpoints to the island situation without realising that what might work well in a major metropolitan country might not work well in a small island microstate. Quite clearly, if there has to be large-scale imports of food, building materials and other tourism related resources the island might not actually increase foreign exchange earnings and reduce balance of payments difficulties. Furthermore, the import of overseas management expertise can scarcely reduce the employment impact of the industry for all but the least skilled and least paid. As has been pointed out above, tourism development tends to concentrate nearest the best developed infrastructure – usually the chief export town – thereby curtailing tourism's potential to encourage economic development in the remoter regions. This is not to say, however, that tourism is of limited value in all cases.

Tourism can and already does plan a significant role in the economic development of a number of Pacific Island countries. When international tourists visit a destination they bring with them income. Money spent on accommodation, food and beverage, local transport, sightseeing tours and the purchase of gifts and souvenirs goes into the local economy as tourist receipts. In some island countries this income is significantly larger than income from commodity exports (Table 3.1). In Western Samoa tourism income exceeds commodity income by 2.5 times, in Tonga it exceeds commodity income by 11 times and in Fiji with a larger and more diversified economy tourism accounts for almost one-third of all export income. Tourism is already a significant economic factor in many of these local economies. The balance of payments, national income, government revenue and employment are all helped with the presence of a viable tourism industry.

The increased economic activity generated by direct and indirect tourism expenditure can lead to other developments within the destination economy but as a general rule, the smaller the country the smaller the economic multiplier (Bull 1991). For a country the size of Canada the economic multiplier approximates to 2.43, for Greece it is only around 1.3 and for the smaller Pacific islands the multiplier is well below 1.0. As early as the 1970s the World Bank (1972) was estimating that the import content of Pacific Island tourism was in excess of 50 per cent and in some extreme cases exceeded 90 per cent. Fletcher and Snee (1989) estimated the tourism multiplier to be 0.36 to 0.41 in Palau (Micronesia), 0.52 in the Solomon Islands (Melanesia) and 0.38 in Western Samoa (Polynesia). High import requirements and heavy reliance on imported management are causes of serious leakages. Fletcher and Snee (1989) estimated that in Palau more than 53 cents in the dollar leaked out of the economy during the first round of expenditure and over 83 cents in the dollar dispersed offshore by the time the tourist dollar had finished circulating in the economy.

Actual figures of tourism receipts for the region as a whole are notoriously unreliable (Craig-Smith and Fagence 1992). For the 14 Tourism Council of the South Pacific (TCSP) member countries tourism income has been estimated to be worth around $US500 million (Bjarnason 1991). The figure represents between 5 and 10 per cent of GDP and 8 per cent of total government income. As the 14 TCSP member countries receive only 35 per cent of the region's tourist arrivals (all these figures exclude Hawai'i which is a state of the USA and is a

Table 3.1: Tourism within selected Pacific economies

Country	Gross tourist receipts as a percentage of all exports (%)	Gross tourist receipts as a percentage of GDP (%)
Tonga	70	32
Fiji	35	22
Vanuatu	27	11
Western Somoa	25	4

Source: Fairbairn *et al.* 1991.

special case) it is probable that tourism income to the 21 countries of the South Pacific is somewhere in the region of $US1.5billion (Craig-Smith and Fagence 1992). This is roughly equal to the level of aid given to the region and represents a significant element of the region's total economy.

Earlier in this chapter it was pointed out that employment was a significant problem for many of the island nations. Even with many island nationals living in New Zealand, Australia, Canada and the United States there is a high level of unemployment and underemployment within the islands. Tourism can and does create jobs. The advantage of the tourism and hospitality industry is its ability to provide gainful employment to semi-skilled workers. Furthermore, it is an industry which is difficult to automate; part of the essential fabric of any tourism experience is personal service. In the South Pacific the tourism element is even more essential – one of its chief attractions is its people and culture. Its low skill requirements and flexible working hours (tourism even in the Pacific is a seven-days a week, 24-hours a day industry) provide employment opportunities to teenagers, older sections of the community (especially in areas such as cleaning) and the female sector of the population which rosters around household family duties. It is estimated for instance that around 1,600 of Western Samoa's 16,000 jobs are tourism related. In the eight Association of Central Pacific countries Bjarnason (1991) estimates that 35,000 full-time equivalent jobs are tourism related and for all 14 TCSP members figure us somewhere between 50,000 and 55,000. If these figures are correct, it is estimated that thirteen international tourists create one full-time equivalent job. On the thirteen to one ratio it can be estimated that the 2 million visitors to the region generate approximately 150,000 jobs or 12 per cent of the region's total.

It stands to reason that the levels of tourism employment are intimately associated with the level of tourism development at any one place. The unequal distribution of tourism development between the national means that the majority of the 150,000 tourism related jobs within the region are focused on the four major honey pots of Guam, Saipan, Fiji and French Polynesia. At the national level the greatest levels of tourism employment are found near the major tourism resorts – normally located adjacent to a major air gateway and in many island countries focused on the capital settlement. Far from spreading employment opportunities tourism can in fact encourage inter-island migration, for example Fiji and Tuvalu.

While tourism is a significant contributor to the islands of the Pacific, generating as much income as the islands currently receive in foreign aid ($US1.5 billion), and 12 per cent of all jobs in the region, tourism should not be seen as the answer to all economic ills. Tourism comes with a high price tag and has many attendant problems.

One of the issues outlined earlier was the problem of economic over-concentration on the capital city/export harbour and depopulation and underdevelopment of the remoter outer islands. Because tourism is based on natural and cultural attractions it is tempting to believe that it has the potential to reverse current trends and act as an economic generator in more remote locations. Past evidence, however, would tend to suggest that this rarely happens (McKee and Tisdell 1990).

Cruise ships can be a potential source of income and can provide tourists for relatively short periods of time, thereby reducing undesirable impacts. Unfortunately, even cruise ships tend to focus rather than disperse economic activity. Cruise ships require a port for docking and an urban infrastructure capable of providing shopping, entertainment and cultural facilities for the passengers. Most Pacific Island countries have very few suitable docking facilities so even cruise ship trade tends to focus on the main areas of urbanism, infrastructure development and tourism plant availability. The majority of visitors enter a country at a specific point of entry (gateway) such as an airport or harbour with full customs and quarantine services. These are inevitably located adjacent to major urban complexes – usually the capital city. Onward travel to outer more remote islands extends the time and cost of the journey. This tends to deter foreign visitors on a limited budget or with limited time.

Furthermore, most foreign tourists demand services and facilities usually confined to existing urban countries; western style shopping, international banking facilities, medical and health infrastructure and good communications (radio, TV and telephones). These likewise tend to be concentrated around existing urban centres. Imported goods for resort construction, everyday operation and food and beverage products tend to be more readily available and at a cheaper cost on the less remote islands. Backward linkages to tourist agents, airlines and shipping companies also work against tourism development in isolated areas. Manpower requirements especially for those requiring management or operation training also work towards central location development. Current visitor arrival statistics in most Pacific island countries are incapable of indicating inter-island movement in any one country but Pearce (1990) has carried out an analysis of inter-island visitation in both French Polynesia and Tonga. In French Polynesia, Tahiti, with its international airport and almost 60 per cent of all visitor accommodation, is the prime focus. Out of every 19 visitors, only 9 spend the smallest part of their visiting time in Tahiti, and almost 60 per cent of all visitors confine their visit entirely to the island of Tahiti. In Tonga over 80 per cent of all visitors restrict their stay to the island of Tongatupu, the island with the international airport and capital settlement (Pearce 1990). These factors suggest that tourism in the Pacific Islands is likely to maintain the urban or central area location bias in spite of tourism resources being spread across isolated areas, islands or regions.

Although tourism is not overly capital intensive, when compared with some manufacturing industries, it can demand resources well beyond the means of small Pacific island communities. Airports, communications, resort development and hotel construction, and other tourism infrastructure often requires a high level of outside investment. The higher the level of outside investment the greater the economic leakage and the less the economic advantage to the local community. While high levels of leakage are common when mass tourism facilities and infrastructure are provided, not all tourism development is export intensive. In Tonga, for instance, the Royal Sunset Resort, developed on a small offshore island situated near the capital, has reduced outside dependence and export leakage to a minimum. The entire resort is designed around traditional styles, was built in traditional materials and almost entirely with local labour. It is estimated that almost 80 per cent of construction costs remained within Tonga, and much of the operating cost is retained on the small island – the bulk of the resort labour has been obtained by training the local village people (Craig-Smith 1990).

Import leakages from foreign tourist expenditure can be substantial. Some items related to transport, including fuel, are 100 per cent imported. Hotel construction can lead to leakage in excess of 78–85 per cent in some of the smaller Pacific countries as a result of the necessity to import a high percentage of the building materials and technical capability. For some of the hotel equipment the leakages can be greater than 90 per cent. Food consumption can have leakages of 65–75 per cent and for beverages up to 50 per cent (McKee and Tisdale 1990). Availability, reliability, quality control and western tastes dictate high levels of imports even when many food commodities can be obtained locally.

In many SIN's, general managers, accountants, chefs, management personnel, and operators with a command of foreign languages have to be imported. The employment-generating effects of tourism in SIN's, therefore tends to be lower than in larger metropolitan countries. Varley (1978) has pointed out that the employment generating impact of tourism in Fiji was less than all primary and secondary industry and less than the average for other tertiary industry.

Finally, on the economic front tourism can be seen as an inhibitor of economic development in the non-tourism sector. Problems of inflation, pressure on land, the attraction of labour away from the non-tourism sector and the diversion of scarce capital can actually inhibit other developments. This is not to suggest that tourism is bad for island economies but it does suggest that a balanced and well-considered view must be taken when considering tourism as a vehicle for island economic development.

In conclusion, a number of points can be made concerning the economic issues of tourism development within the South Pacific nations.

- The small islands of the South Pacific along with all small islands of the world face serious economic problems in today's global economy. Their small size, limited national resources, scattered and isolated locations and small economic base render them at as disadvantage on the world economic stage.
- Their traditional socioeconomic fabric including such things as land rights and ownership together with their colonial legacy inhibit modern economic development.
- Small islands face severe problems of over dependence on a few stable commodities on a world market; difficulties of scale and isolation are

considerable when contemplating developing a major manufacturing sector of the economy.

- Heavy dependence on overseas economic aid has given rise to a large and non-self-sustaining public sector and at a time when the future of overseas aid is in question.
- Given these economic difficulties and disadvantages the majority of Pacific island states are looking at tourism as a possible answer to their economic salvation.
- Even with only a few major tourism players the industry already contributes a sum approximately equal to that of foreign aid to the regional economy and accounts for around 12 per cent of island employment.
- Guam, Saipan, Fiji and French Polynesia already enjoy a considerable economic income from their respective tourism industries and countries such as Western Samoa, the Cook Islands and Vanuatu are steadily developing a sound tourism base.
- The scope for specific niche marketing, the development of specific special interest tourism and the attraction for off-beat high spending visitors will ensure a continued trend towards tourism development and increased regional reliance on tourism income.

With careful planning strategies, suitable marketing and appropriate development the island of the Pacific can continue to enjoy the benefits of tourism within the region but tourism should never be considered a cure for all economic ills. Problems of inflation, leakage, over-dependence on outside resources of the non-tourism sector of the economy and problems of over-concentration in a few areas must all be addressed. Careful and comprehensive tourism integrated planning is an absolute necessity. This and other related planning issues are addressed in Chapter 7.

REFERENCES

Biddlecombe, C. (1981) *Pacific Tourism – Contrasts in Values and Expectations*, Suva: Lata Padfika Productions.

Bjarnason, J.-B. (1991) 'Tourism in the Pacific – its economic significance and interaction with the environment'. Unpublished paper presented at Regional seminar of sustainable tourism development, Suva.

Bull, A. (1991) *The Economics of Tourism*, Melbourne: Pitman.

Connell, J. (1988) *Sovereignty and Survival, Island Microstates in the Third World*, Research Monograph No. 3, Sydney: Department of Geography, University of Sydney.

Craig-Smith, S. (1990) 'Tourism in developing countries – some implications for resort development: The Tonga experience', in *Proceedings of Conference of International Association of Hotel Management Schools*, Melbourne: Footscray Institute of Technology.

Craig-Smith, S.J. and Fagence, M. (1992) *Sustainable Tourism Development in Pacific Island Countries*, New York: UN-ESCAP.

—— (1994) 'Factors affecting tourism development in Pacific Island Countries', in *Investment and Economic Co-operation in the Tourism Sector in Pacific*

Island Countries, ESCAP Tourism Review No. 13, New York: UN-ESCAP, pp. 237–54.

Dwyer, L. (1986) *Tourism*, Islands/Australia Working Paper No. 86/3, Canberra: Australian National Unversity, National Centre for Development Structures.

Fagence, M. (1992) 'The legacy of Europe in the Pacific region.' Paper to Tourism in Europe Conference, Centre for Travel and Tourism, Newcastle Polytechnic, Durham.

Fairbairn, T., Morrison, C., Baker, R. and Croves, S. (1991) *The Pacific Islands – Policies, Economics and International Relations*, Honolulu: East-West Center.

Fletcher, J. and Snee, H. (1989) 'Tourism in the South Pacific Islands', in C. Cooper (ed.) *Progress in Tourism, Recreation and Hospitality Research*, Vol. 1, London: Belhaven Press, pp. 114–24.

Frank, A.G. (1967) *Capitalism and Underdevelopment in Latin America*, New York: Monthly Review Press.

Frank, A.G. (1979) *Dependent Accumulation and Underdevelopment*, New York: Monthly Review Press, New York.

Herbst, J. (1988) 'Migration helps poorest of the poor', *The Wall Street Journal*, June 15.

Kissling, C. (ed.) (1990) *Destination South-Pacific – Perspectives on Island Tourism*, Aix-en Provence: Centre des Hautes Etudes Touristiques.

Levy, J.M. (1987) 'The limits of local economic development programs', in D.L. McKee and R.E. Bennett (eds) *Structural Change in an Urban Industrial Region*, New York: Praeger.

Lockhart, D., Drakakis-Smith, D. and Schembi, J. (eds) (1993) *The Development Process in Small Island States*, London: Routledge.

McKee, D.L. (1977) 'Facteurs extérieurs et infrastructure das pays en voie de développement', *Revue Tiers-Monde*, 18(70): 293–300.

McKee, D.L. and Tisdell, C. (1990) *Development Issues in Small Island Economies*, New York: Praeger.

Nurkse, R. (1967) *Problems of Capital Formation in Underdeveloped Countries and Patterns of Trade and Development*, New York: Oxford University Press.

Parry, T.G. (1973) 'The international firm and national economic policy', *The Economic Journal*, 84(332): 1201–21.

Pearce, D. (1990) 'Tourist travel patterns in the South Pacific: Analyses and implications', in C. Kissling (ed.) *Destination South Pacific – Perspectives on Island Tourism*, Les Cahiers du Tourisme Series B, No. 60, Centre des Hautes Etudes Touristuques, pp. 31–50.

Ramsaran, R.F. (1985) *US Investment in Latin America and the Caribbean*, London: Hodder & Stoughton.

Varley, R.C. (1978). *Tourism in Fiji. Some Economic and Social Problems*, Cardiff: University of Wales Press.

World Bank (1972) *Tourism – Sector Working Paper*, Washington, DC: World Bank.

Yacoumis, J. (1991) 'Tourism in the South Pacific: An overview.' Unpublished paper presented to Regional Conference on Tourism and National Development Planning in the South Pacific, Tourism Council of the South Pacific, Suva.

Chapter 4

Social and cultural impact of tourism in the South Pacific

Ngairie Douglas and Norman Douglas

INTRODUCTION

There is little consensus on the extent of social and cultural impacts of tourism on host communities. For some time the scales have been tipped in favour of negativity, particularly in academic studies which focus on the South Pacific (Farrell 1977, 1978, 1979; Bolabola 1981; Dwyer 1986, 1988; Baines 1987; Britton 1987; Crocombe 1987; de Burlo 1987, 1989; Helu-Thaman 1993). However, this could well change as more indigenous researchers gain access to the avenues which allow them to defend their rights to the commodities of the twentieth century compared to the currently fashionable academic stance of apology for the apparent imposition of anything 'foreign' upon indigenous communities. The notion of 'impact' itself may have perjorative connotations. Mansperger (1992) found that in some Pacific areas where the impacts of tourism are more positive than negative and therefore less detrimental, local communities do not recognise any impacts at all, thus presenting a discrepancy between what is perceived and what is real. What must also be further defined, according to Harrison (1992: 20), is the distinction between social *consequences* and social *problems*. The former, primarily the results of modernisation, can be 'described, demonstrated and, in principle, explained'. The latter are listed according to an individual's perception of *development*, resulting in a highly subjective appraisal. The assessment of social and cultural impacts is elusive because they are difficult, if not impossible, to quantify, to subtract costs from benefits, and draw conclusions. It is also difficult to separate social and economic costs and benefits since they are so interrelated (Crandall 1987).

Tourism does not occur within a vacuum. Its effects upon a community must be considered within a complex web of political, economic, environmental and historical factors, many of which have been powerful agents of change well before the introduction of tourism (see Plate 4.1). Christianity, colonialism, education, urbanisation and the increasing adoption of cash economies to replace more traditional agrarian subsistence economies have been affecting Pacific communities at various levels for some 200 years. Tourism in a form substantial enough to make significant impacts has only infiltrated Pacific communities, excluding

Hawai'i, in the past 40 years or so. Sofield (1990) also observed that many critics single out tourism as the most socially destructive force of the modernisation process, with little regard to other historical developments.

Butler's (1980) model of the cycle of development of a tourist area suggests that tourism goes through several stages before it reaches a critical level where, among other factors, guests outnumber hosts. This condition has the potential for considerable negative consequences, especially when there are major cultural and economic differences between the visitor and the visited. Others argue that the introduction of outside ideologies and foreign ways of life into societies that have been relatively closed or isolated can lead to changes in attitudes, values or behaviour which can result from merely observing tourists. The demonstration

Plate 4.1:   Two major agents of cultural change, video and tourism, combine in a village in the Papua New Guinea Highlands (Norman Douglas)

effect,[1] they claim, is inevitable and unavoidable (de Kadt 1979; Murphy 1985; Fletcher and Snee 1988). But these claims do not take into account the nature of the relationship which existed between the indigenous people and the resident expatriates prior to the introduction of 'mass' tourism. De Kadt (1979) also writes that small, relatively underdeveloped countries in terms of infrastructure and skills training are likely to experience more negative sociocultural effects as a result of tourism development than larger, more developed countries. However, de Kadt qualifies this statement by adding that if the rate of tourism growth is neither rapid nor massive, then the negative impacts are likely to be reduced. For many South Pacific countries tourism development on any significant level will never amount to much more than inflated rhetoric on the part of foreign consultants, entrepreneurs and some indigenous politicians (Table 4.1). Tiny Niue's host to guest ratio, for example, which looks overwhelming in the table, must be considered in context. The majority of arrivals are Niueans returning to visit friends and relatives or to check on their abandoned family land holdings. It is one of the few countries in the world which could hang a vacancy sign up referring to the state of the country rather than the availability of a hotel bed! It has many of the attributes Pacific tourism thrives on – tropical weather, swaying palms, warm waters, white sand, friendly people – but most Niueans prefer to live in New Zealand where they have right of residence and access to education and employment opportunities. Indeed, over 12,000 Niueans live there. Thus, in order to understand tourism's impacts on the sociocultural fabric of a Pacific community, it is important to examine the political, geographical, economic, social and historical environment of each community. Broad generalisations are usually suspect. Indeed, the figures in Table 4.1 need clarification. Visitor arrivals refers to all arrivals including returning residents and citizens, business people and the ever-increasing itinerant band of international consultants and experts who play regularly at venues throughout the less developed countries. National tourism offices have a vested interest in promoting the highest possible arrival figures in order to secure their own positions. If, however, the category of arrivals of people pursuing leisure and pleasure is separated (column 4), then a somewhat different picture emerges of the extent of tourism in a number of destinations.

The magnitude and significance of the impacts of tourism increase according to a number of identified variables:

- the nature and extent of social, economic and cultural differences between tourists and hosts;
- the ratio of visitors to residents;
- the distribution and visibility of tourist developments;
- the speed and intensity of development;
- the extent of foreign ownership and employment.

This chapter discusses each of these issues and concludes that, with a couple of exceptions, tourism itself has not been a greatly significant agent of change throughout the Pacific.

Table 4.1: Comparison of population and visitor figures for Pacific island countries, 1993

	Population	Total visitor arrivals	Holiday arrivals (%)
American Samoa	50,923	15,368	35
Cook Islands	17,400	52,868	85
Fed. States of Micronesia	100,520	29,000	60
Fiji	746,326	287,462	81
French Polynesia	201,400	147,847	85
Guam	133,152	784,018	85
Hawai'i	1,159,600	6,124,230	83
Kiribati	72,298	4,225	24
Marshall Islands	49,969	5,055	15
Nauru	9,919	*16,500	25
New Caledonia	173,300	80,754	73
Niue	2,532	3,441	39
Northern Marianas	43,345	536,263	85
Palau	16,386	40,497	80
Papua New Guinea	3,963,000	33,441	29
Solomon Islands	350,553	11,570	40
Tonga	94,649	25,513	54
Tuvalu	9,045	929	25
Vanuatu	150,864	44,562	71
Western Samoa	159,004	46,806	18

Note: *1994 estimate only

HOSTS AND GUESTS

In order to understand the nature and extent of differences between these two parties, it is necessary to know something about the basic nature of the people who live in the region. There are three ethnic categories: the Micronesians live predominantly in the area north of the equator. Physically they are relatively fair-skinned, straight-haired and of smaller stature than the Polynesians. Their relationship to the peoples of Asia is more obvious. Micronesian society is hierarchical and their contact with external forces has been long and varied, ranging from Spanish and Portuguese explorations and annexation of the sixteenth century to German, Japanese and American occupation throughout the nineteenth and twentieth centuries. Assimilation, integration and imposition have produced a confetti of Spanish architecture, Japanese and German languages and family names, American food and popular culture sprinkled over Micronesian tradition. The twentieth-century tourist, unless very well informed, would find it difficult to separate the cultural layers which make up modern Micronesia. For the Micronesians, the tourists who visit the area have essentially the same cultural differences as the various foreign hordes before them had. Americans and Japanese in the main dominate tourist numbers. Indisputably their economic, cultural and social differences are obvious to their hosts – but not new. The demonstration effect of tourism, therefore, may be minimal. Far more significant has been the effect of the half-century of US administration of, and involvement in, most of Micronesia. It is arguable that the misplaced generosity of the US funding of Micronesia, while many of the islands formed part of the Trust Territory of the Pacific, had a far greater economic and cultural impact than anything to do with tourism, which remains barely developed in most of these islands.

South of the equator lie the islands inhabited by Melanesians. In stark contrast to the people of the north, the Melanesians have very kinky hair and number among them some of the darkest skinned people on earth. Their societies are based on the merit principle where leadership is earned, not inherited. Over 80 per cent of them live in isolated rural settlements practising subsistence agriculture. Access to education and health systems is often poor. Unlike their Polynesian neighbours to the east, Melanesians rarely travel abroad to establish communities in countries like Australia, New Zealand, Canada and the United States. Those who move overseas are likely to be from the small group of educated elite who seek to further their opportunities or who are on government business.

The countries of Melanesia – Papua New Guinea, Solomon Islands, Vanuatu and New Caledonia – have had long and controversial colonial histories. Fiji, long regarded as part of Melanesia, is now considered by an increasing number of scholars to be geographically, culturally and historically peripheral to this region (Routledge 1985; Thomas 1989; Tuimaleali'ifano 1990). The effects of colonialism on Fiji, however, have been profound, and remain very obvious. Papua New Guinea had Australian administrators, Solomon Islands was a British protectorate, Vanuatu had a joint French/British condominium government, New Caledonia was, and firmly remains, a French territory. But Australians as traders, settlers, planters and missionaries were most prolific throughout the area and they continue to maintain this visible presence as the largest tourist segment. Douglas (1994) argues that the demonstration effect of tourism alone in Melanesia has been slight because colonialists and tourists exhibited the same degree of social, economic and cultural difference from their hosts. Papua New Guinea, the Melanesian country with one of the least developed tourism industries in relation to its size and the variety of its resources (see Chapter 16), exhibits by far the greatest number of social and cultural difficulties, but they are difficulties readily traceable to its indigenous political organisation and its colonial history and have very little connection specifically with tourism.

The third region is Polynesia, a vast area sweeping across half the Pacific Ocean from New Zealand in the south to Hawai'i in the north, from Tonga in the west to Easter Island in the east. Polynesian society is hierarchical and physically the people are taller, lighter skinned and have straighter hair than Melanesians. Their colonial histories are varied: British, French, German, New Zealand and American dominated administrative areas with Australians often present in the private sector. Polynesians have long been adventurers and great seafarers as their historical migrations indicate and they have continued this pattern in the twentieth century. There are large communities of Polynesians in Australia, Canada and the United States as well as mixed communities in other Polynesian states, for example in New Zealand and Hawai'i where they perceive greater access to opportunities. These people move frequently between their new communities and their traditional villages, bringing from the first to the second as many symbols of industrialised western culture as they can manage. Videos, films, education, trade, missionisation and other agents of the process of modernisation and transformation have had enormous impacts on Pacific communities and cultures. The attempt to separate tourism as an independent and more profound influence is not only exceedingly difficult, it is ultimately pointless.

RATIO OF VISITORS TO RESIDENTS

There are parts of the Pacific where tourist numbers exceed residents in staggering proportions and, in order to facilitate their stay, the demands of tourism have had a dramatic impact on communities. Hawai'i is perhaps the most obvious example of this. Over six million tourists arrive on the island of Oahu every year; the majority of whom stay in the enclave of Waikiki Beach. The requirements of new resorts and golf courses mean that land on the island is at a premium, and those still fortunate enough to have land are often seduced by the high prices offered by developers. Thus in Hawai'i a situation exists where most staple foods must be imported from, mainland USA, East Asia or South America because there is not enough land available for viable agriculture. Land is central to a Pacific Islander's sense of place. It shapes both identity and, in many communities, economic sustainability. Ownership of land is often communal and problems of social displacement and unrest have occurred where rights to land have been traded by a few rather than the community as a group. During the 1980s a prime location in the Cook Islands was offered by some leading figures in the community as a site for a Sheraton hotel. So incensed were other members of the community by the deal that they reportedly arranged a *tapu* (forbidden access) to be put on the site. In subsequent months several accidents occurred on the site which were attributed to the power of the *tapu*. Work has consequently halted and the resort sits in an incomplete state. Non-believers point to the appalling economic planning and political débâcles which have dogged the project from the beginning as the reasons for this hiatus but many Cook Islanders have their own cultural interpretation of events based firmly on the consequences of alienation from their land.

THE DISTRIBUTION AND VIABILITY OF TOURIST DEVELOPMENTS

Throughout the Pacific tourism development is confined to two identifiable areas, the designated 'capital' island and small, isolated, often unpopulated islands. Tourism developments tend to be concentrated because of several factors.

- accessibility and transport possibilities from international airports;
- accessibility of supporting infrastructure such as wholesalers, banking systems, and communication;
- accessibility to potential workforce;
- the support network of other tourist developments.

The capital islands of Viti Levu in Fiji, Rarotonga in the Cook Islands, Tongatapu in Tonga, Upolu in Western Samoa, Efate in Vanuatu and Oahu in Hawai'i, for example, conform to this pattern. This means, however, that in many places, the majority of the indigenous population actually have little or no direct contact with tourists because they do not live in proximity to the tourist enclave. Apart from Guam, Niue and Nauru, the first with a very large tourism industry, the latter two with virtually non-existent tourism development, Pacific states consist of many islands scattered widely over large sea areas and the majority of the populations live on the many farflung islands rather than in the urban areas. Although this situation in some places is falling victim to the twentieth-century's internationally experienced rural-urban drift, for the most part the demographic balance between the two sectors remains in favour of the former, even in such a country as Fiji which has experienced a greater degree of modernisation than many others.

The other preferred location of a tourist facility is on an isolated island where it stands alone, significantly removed from the host culture except in areas deemed appropriate by management. The nearest village, whether it be on the same island or within a short canoe ride, is the source of employees, entertainers and even the site of controlled village visits which themselves may become part of the visitor's experience. These locations can be so insular and self-contained that tourists may be unaware that they have actually visited a particular Pacific country, but rather identify their holiday destination by the name of the resort. Fiji is especially notable for the number of its small, exclusive island resorts, the guests at which are unlikely to see any other part of the country, except for the airport. Thus, in either scenario, the distribution and visibility of tourist development is selective. This situation is further reinforced by poor internal transport and resort design which seeks to provide for the total holiday experience, thereby discouraging too much independent movement.

THE SPEED AND INTENSITY OF DEVELOPMENT

Tourism development throughout the Pacific has generally proceeded on a 'Pacific time' calendar. The tourist area cycle proposed by Butler (1980) can be applied comfortably to most Pacific nations. A number of countries such as Papua New Guinea, Solomon Islands, Tonga, Western Samoa and American Samoa, are unlikely to progress beyond the initial stages of the development phase within the foreseeable future. Nauru, Niue, Kiribati and Tuvalu are unlikely to even reach it, remaining locked into the first exploration level. Others like Fiji, the Cook Islands, French Polynesia, New Caledonia, Vanuatu, the Federated States of Micronesia and Hawai'i may already be in the zone of critical capacity and even now deliberating on how to determine movement into the next level. The exception to an orderly procedure through the life cycle is Guam which, following the inauguration of direct flights from Tokyo in 1967, experienced intense and rapid development, and for a market culturally quite different to that of the foreign presence which had been dominant up to that time. However, the Americanisation of Guam (still a US territory) has far more to do with the long-term presence of the US military and other areas of US federal expenditure, than with the island's experience of international tourism. In 1993 US federal spending in Guam amounted to $US952 million, of which $US748 million was spent on the military presence. In comparison an estimated $US200 million annually is generated by tourism (Guam Visitors Bureau 1993). One-third of Guam's total land area is given over to military use (Douglas and Douglas 1994). Compared to this, the tourist enclave of Tumon Bay appears small indeed. Even in Hawai'i, which hosts 6.2 million tourists annually, Farrell (1982) states that the use of land for tourism purposes was initially slow compared to other forms of economic development; thus the degree of impacts have been far more gradual, although to the first time visitor to Waikiki it may appear otherwise.

THE EXTENT OF FOREIGN OWNERSHIP AND EMPLOYMENT

This is the major area of concern in discussing the social and cultural impact of tourism in the Pacific. In countries where tourism is the leading economic sector, foreign ownership, high leakage and expatriate domination of management levels are at high levels. Hawai'i, Guam, Fiji, the Cook Islands and Vanuatu exemplify this. Britton (1987) and Nash (1989) propose that tourism is a form of neo-colonialism, its spatial and economic organisation designed to accommodate foreign as opposed to indigenous interests. In this situation indigenous people have little control over the direction of development or the type of tourism to be fostered. Their participation is primarily as employees in the lower ranks where they are at the mercy of seasonal variations, international tourism fashions and transnational business practices. Samy (1975) adds that employment is based on racial and ethnic criteria. His study in Fiji found that Fijians employed in public areas of a large resort were constantly being told how to behave like the friendly smiling natives promoted in the advertising material while Indians were mainly employed in the back-of-house areas and saw little opportunity to move into the public arena.

Bolabola (1981) goes even further and suggests that there is an association between malnutrition and tourism caused by workers abandoning their more traditional subsistence agricultural pursuits, in preference for employment in resorts. They then turn to processed, purchased foods which are dearer and less suitable as staple dietary items. However, tourism alone cannot be blamed for changing food preferences. In Pacific communities which have little or no association with tourism, the ability to purchase a sack of rice rather than investing the labour required to cultivate a staple root crop is considered a visible sign of wealth, modernisation and status. This behaviour, and the nutritional problems associated with it, has long been evident in Nauru – an island barely affected by tourism, although with a high per capita income – and is increasingly evident in Western Samoa and Tonga, where it is a consequence of income from overseas remittances rather than tourism. The proposed 1996 establishment of a McDonalds restaurant in Apia, Western Samoa, has far less to do with catering for the needs of European tourists than it does with an accurate assessment of local preferences, many of which have been formed by Samoan travel to the USA and New Zealand. The driving force behind the new outlet is a Samoan, who is also a wealthy business person and a member of parliament.

The appearance of a Tonganised 'Paddy's Market' near the Nuku'alofa waterfront in recent years, reflects the increasing influence on the town's residents of those Tongans who journey frequently outside the country and return to sell their cheaply acquired clothing, electronic goods and other household items, thus contributing in a far more direct manner to changes in social and cultural behaviour than any tourist is capable of doing. Similarly, the T-shirt worn by a Solomon Islander or Papua New Guinean, bearing a commercial or obscene message, is as likely to have come from an indigenously owned used clothing store as from a foreign visitor. Pacific Islanders themselves as agents of cultural change have been around at least since the first indentured labourer returned to his island from the cane fields of Queensland. He would regale his village with stories of his exploits in towns like Cairns, and display the contents of the box he had brought with him; axes, knives, tobacco and other commodities, thus encouraging fellow visitors to sign on for a similar experience when the next labour recruiting vessel appeared.

In countries where tourism is a low priority – Papua New Guinea, the Solomon Islands, the Samoas and Tonga for example – indigenous and local European ownership and control are high, leakage is not excessive and economic benefits are more likely to stay within the community. It can be argued that the historical government attitudes towards tourism in these countries which range along a spectrum from hostility, ambivalence and indifference to unequivocal enthusiasm (but little financial and infrastructural support) have actually cushioned their cultures from tourism impacts of any magnitude. It is also destinations of this sort which have inadvertently become the focus of the changing dimensions of tourism in the 1990s. Ecotourism, currently the most desirable product package, has the cornerstones of tradition, culture, environment and quality of experience, all resources which these places have in abundance. Having discussed the factors which are identified as important in determining the level of social and cultural impacts of tourism on host communities in small developing countries and explained the degree to which these occur in various South Pacific nations, it is necessary to look at areas where specific changes can be identified.

TRADITIONAL ARTEFACT OR AIRPORT ART?

Pacific Islanders have been trading their sacred objects and secular goods and chattels (now defined as artefacts) since Europeans sailed over the horizon (and long before that with each other). A traveller/photographer of the late nineteenth century reported being informed by Melanesians that curio prices went up whenever there was a ship in the area, and collectors under the auspices of museums, art galleries and national geographical societies carried off vast quantities until governments finally began to acknowledge the loss of many national treasures and set up laws prohibiting export without special licence (Douglas 1994). Last century Victorian moral codes called for the removal of the exposed genitals of many of the carvings, a prolific artistic feature throughout the Pacific. For the first part of this century moral guardians were calling for the practice to be continued so that the sensitivities of the twentieth-century female tourists were not offended (Douglas 1994). Curiously, however, and presumably as a concession to tourist expectations regarding 'primitive' cultures, genitalia have now been restored – even exaggerated – by some island artisans.

By the 1970s a debate on whether tourism was destroying the authenticity of Pacific artefacts had reached academic circles. One side argued that the effects of tourism were ambiguous, change was inevitable, culture was dynamic and besides artefact production provided access to a cash income in otherwise deprived areas (May 1975; Graburn 1976; de Kadt 1979). The counter-argument was that tourist demand for cheap, portable, suitcase-sized souvenirs debased both the culture and the craft and resulted in 'airport art' (Mackenzie 1977). Whether determined by tradition or popular demand, the commoditisation of artefacts has enabled indigenous people to retain autonomy. The demand for souvenirs in the tourist enclaves ensures that people in remote locations can produce saleable commodities. They determine what they will make, when, how, where and at what price with little or no contact with tourists. Another outlet for production is in the designer trend to decorate resorts, restaurants and tourism offices with local craft. This can range from small pieces adapted to key rings to huge ceremonial carvings which grace gardens and lobbies (see Plate 4.2). Men, women and children are engaged in production in areas which are traditionally determined; men carve, women weave and make tapa cloth, children collect raw

Plate 4.2:   Ritual object as hotel decoration: a ceremonial slit gong from Ambrym
Island, Vanuatu, adorns the new entrance to Le Meridien Hotel in Port
Vila (Norman Douglas)

materials. In Papua New Guinea's Sepik River villages, the artefacts from which
have long excited collectors, the visitor may find seemingly 'authentic' replicas
of traditional and ritual objects alongside wooden representations – no less
painstakingly crafted – of the nation's flag or coat of arms. Is this the
bastardisation of traditional forms or merely the astute recognition of newly
significant symbols?

The argument assumes a similar stance when discussing cultural
performances and behaviours. Does performance on demand debase the
meaning of a dance or ritual, or does demand, and the resulting income,
stimulate renewed vigour and interest among younger people in particular who
may otherwise not retain the tradition? This issue is often obscured by the
'human zoo' concept. Tourists are encouraged by marketing techniques to
expect interaction with 'traditional' and 'tribal' peoples in many small
developing countries. Indeed, terms like 'stone age, savages and primitives,
smiling natives, child-like' appear frequently in promotional literature. They
express disappointment if the 'natives' they encounter wear watches with their
war paint or T shirts with their tattoos. This problem has been dealt with in the
Pacific in two ways. The first is the creation of theme parks like the Polynesian
Cultural Centre in Laie, Hawai'i and the Pacific Harbour Cultural Centre at
Deuba, Fiji. Here the visitor can experience a 'packaged paradise' depicting the

noble savage at work and play – the difficulty in distinguishing between the two activities is part of the appeal – and have no concerns about safety, sanitation or sickness (Douglas and Douglas 1991). The performer has paid employment in regions where there are few, if any, other economic opportunities, and the incentive to develop traditional skills which may or may not be required in his/ her daily twentieth-century lifestyle. Both hosts and guests understand the position of the display in terms of Cohen's (1979) authenticity matrix.

The second is the arrangement whereby tourists are taken to specific, real villages at a time suitable to the inhabitants who must put aside their daily routines in order to accommodate the agreement they have made with the tour operator. This is more prevalent in Melanesia because, unlike their Polynesian neighbours who are far more extrovert in their behaviour, Melanesians are more inward looking. This difference is particularly reflected in the dancing styles of both groups. For some tourists this experience is more satisfying but for the majority of tourists to the South Pacific the convenience of cultural commoditisation is experience enough. As a footnote to the issue of commoditising indigenous cultures, however, it is worth pointing out that early brochure advertising to certain Pacific countries, particularly New Caledonia and Vanuatu, often omitted mention of indigenous peoples completely, since it was felt that their cultures offered little interest. Instead, the prevailing European culture – French in both of these cases – was emphasised as the major attraction.

STANDARD OF LIVING

Many small Pacific states have few exploitable resources and rely heavily on foreign aid (see Chapter 11) and remittances from the nationals who work overseas to subsidise their economies. Health and education facilities, the two fundamental rights of any people, must necessarily be sustained in part by payments from the population. Clothing, housing and food all require participation in a cash economy. Therefore, the opportunity to obtain paid employment in a tourist facility which may well be the only commercial venture within miles is considered highly desirable, seasonality, low pay and menial work notwithstanding. Throughout the Pacific there are enormous discrepancies between the built environment of the hotels and resorts and those of the majority of staff, as there are between the income levels of host and guest: the price a visitor pays for a meal may be the equivalent of a week's wage for the waiter. But it would seem that too often the tourism industry is the focus of studies which seek evidence of inequality and suppression. The same imbalances exist in most commercial developments throughout the region. The garment factories owned by expatriate companies, the value added ventures scattered throughout the islands and supported by bilateral trade agreements, the car dealerships, the logging companies, the burgeoning breweries all offer similar terms and conditions. But in times when workforces are increasing rapidly at the same time as opportunities are decreasing, then employment in any industry is desirable.

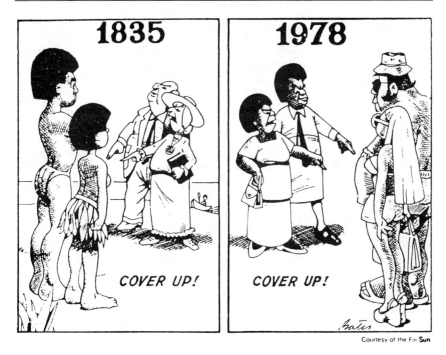

Courtesy of the Fiji **Sun**

Plate 4.3:   A cartoon from the defunct newspaper, *Fiji Sun* illustrates the dilemmas of European influence for the now Christianised islanders.

Tourism is undeniably an agent of social and cultural change but in a region where there are so many other factors to consider it is impossible to isolate it as a single influence. A number of historical and economic processes, including western religion, colonialism, education, indigenous travel, television, video, and the entire insidious process of modernisation must all be considered, not simply as backgrounds to tourism, but as a relentless continuum of change, of which tourism is merely the most recent and perhaps most visible part (see Plate 4.3). It must also be realised that, in many of these processes, indigenous people have not been simply passive victims but have been willing participants. The image of the hapless islander being forced to accept every western introduction from Victorian Christianity to video cassettes has long been far too simplistic, although it continues to be invoked by researchers with little knowledge of the region's history. Islanders themselves have often displayed a different point of view. In 1976 Peter Kenilorea, a future Prime Minister of Solomon Islands, wrote that 'outside forces could not be held responsible for every aspect of cultural change' (Kenilorea 1976). Islanders, he argued, had assisted the process by allowing the changes to take place. If anything was to blame it was the 'intrinsic and innate face of human acquisitiveness'.

ENDNOTE

1 The 'demonstration effect' refers to the tendency for a person to imitate the behaviour, language, dress or other cultural attributes of another and to assimilate it as their own. It is usually applied to behaviour modification in developing countries where it is associated with the demand for imported goods.

REFERENCES

Baines, G.B.K. (1987) 'Manipulation of islands and men: Sand-cay tourism in the South Pacific', in S. Britton and W.C. Clarke (eds) *Ambiguous Alternatives: Tourism in Small Developing Countries*, Suva: Institute of Pacific Studies: 16–24.
Bolabola, C. (1981) 'Does tourism cause malnutrition: They seem to be connected', *Pacific Perspective*, 10(1): 72–7.
Britton, S. (1987) 'Tourism in small developing countries: Development issues and research needs', in S. Britton and W.C. Clarke (eds) *Ambiguous Alternatives: Tourism in Small Developing Countries*, Suva: Institute of Pacific Studies, pp. 167–87.
—— (1987) 'Tourism in Pacific islands states: Constraints and opportunities', in S. Britton and W.C. Clarke (eds) *Ambiguous Alternatives: Tourism in Small Developing Countries*, Suva: Institute of Pacific Studies, pp. 113–39.
Butler, R.W. (1980) 'The concept of a tourist area cycle of evolution: Implications for management of resources', *Canadian Geographer*, 24(1): 5–12.
Cohen, E. (1979) 'Rethinking the sociology of tourism', *Annals of Tourism Research*. 6(1): 215–37.
Crandall, L. (1987) 'The social impact of tourism on developing regions and its measurement', in J.R. Brent Ritchie and C.R. Goeldner (eds) *Travel, Tourism and Hospitality Research: A Handbook for Managers and Researchers*, 1st edn, Toronto: John Wiley, pp. 373–83.
Crocombe, R. (1987) *The South Pacific: An Introduction*, Auckland: Longman Paul.
de Burlo, C. (1987) 'Neglected social factors in tourism project design: The case of Vanuatu', *Tourism Recreation Research*, 12(2): 25–30.
—— (1989) 'Land alienation, land tenure and tourism in Vanuatu, a Melanesian island nation', *GeoJournal*, 19(3): 317–21.
de Kadt, E. (1979) *Tourism – Passport to Development?*, New York: Oxford University Press.
Douglas, N. (1994) 'They came for savages: A comparative history of tourism development in Papua New Guinea, Solomon Islands and Vanuatu, 1884–1984.' Unpublished PhD thesis, University of Queensland, Brisbane.
Douglas, N. and Douglas N. (1991) 'Where the tiki are wired for sound and poi glow in the dark: A day at the Polynesian Cultural Centre', *Islands Business Pacific*, 17(12): 60–4.
—— (eds) (1994) *Pacific Islands Yearbook*, 17th edn, Suva: Fiji Times.
Dwyer, L. (1986) 'Tourism in the South Pacific', in R.V. Cole and T.G. Parry (eds) *Selected Issues in Pacific Islands Development*, Canberra: Australian National University Press, pp. 226–61.
—— (1988) 'Import content of tourist hotel food and beverage purchases in the South Pacific', *Pacific Economic Bulletin*, 3(2): 37–67.
Farrell, B. (ed.) (1977) *The Social and Economic Impacts of Tourism on Pacific Communities*, Santa Cruz: University of California, Santa Cruz.
—— (1978) *The Golden Hordes and the Pacific People*, Centre for South Pacific Studies Data Paper, Santa Cruz: University of California, Santa Cruz.

—— (1979) 'Tourism's human conflicts: Cases from the Pacific', *Annals of Tourism Research*, April/June: 122–36.

—— (1982) *Hawai'i the Legend that Sells*, Honolulu: University of Hawai'i Press.

Finney, B.R. and Watson, K.A. (eds) (1975) *A New Kind of Sugar*, Honolulu: University of Hawai'i Press.

Fletcher, J. and Snee, H. (1988) 'Tourism in the South Pacific islands', in C.P. Cooper (ed.) *Progress in Tourism, Recreation and Hospitality Management*, London and New York: John Wiley, pp. 114–24.

Graburn, N.H.H. (1976) *Ethnic and Tourist Arts: Cultural Expression From the Fourth World*, Berkeley: University of California, Berkeley.

Guam Department of Commerce (1994) *1993 Guam Annual Economic Review*, Agana, Guam Department of Commerce.

Guam Visitors Bureau (nd c1993) *Manual for Agents*, Agana: Guam Visitors Bureau.

Harrison, D. (1992) 'Tourism to less developed countries: The social consequences', in D. Harrison (ed.) *Tourism and the Less Developed Countries*, London, Belhaven Press, pp. 19–34.

Helu-Thaman, K. (1993) 'Beyond hula, hotels and handicrafts: A Pacific Islander's perspective of tourism development', *The Contemporary Pacific*, 5(1): 103–12.

Huffman, K. (1987) *Socio-cultural Consideration in Tourism Development: the Case of Vanuatu*, a tourism foundation course sponsored by the Tourism Council of the South Pacific and the World Tourism Organization, 27 October–6 November, Nuku'alofa: Tourism Council of the South Pacific and the World Tourism Organization.

Kenilorea, P. (1976) 'Cultural values verses the acquisitiveness of man', *Pacific Perspective*, 5(2): 3–8.

Lefevre, T. (1975) 'Making do with the leftovers from Pacific tourism', in S. Tupouniua (ed.) *The Pacific Way – Social Issues in National Development*, Suva: Institute for Pacific Studies, pp. 215–21.

Mackenzie, M. (1977) 'The deviant art of tourism: Airport art', in B.H. Farrell (ed.) *The Social and Economic Impact of Tourism on Pacific Communities*, Santa Cruz: University of California, Santa Cruz, pp. 83–4.

Mansperger, M.C. (1992) 'Yap: A case of benevolent tourism', *Practising Anthropology*, 14(2): 10–13.

May, R. (1975) 'Tourism and the artefact industry in Papua New Guinea', in Finney. B.R. and Watson, K.A. (eds) *A New Kind of Sugar: Tourism in the Pacific*, Honolulu: University of Hawai'i Press.

Murphy, P. (1985) *Tourism: A Community Approach*, New York: Methuen.

Nash, D. (1989) 'Tourism as a form of imperialism', in V.L. Smith (ed.) *Hosts and Guests: The Anthropology of Tourism*, 2nd edn, Philadelphia: University of Pennsylvannia, pp. 38–52.

Rajotte, F. and Crocombe, R. (1980) *Tourism as Pacific Islanders See it*, Suva: Institute of Pacific Studies.

Ranck, S. (1987) 'An attempt at autonomous development: The case of the Tufi guest houses, Papua New Guinea', in S. Britton and W.C. Clarke (eds) *Ambiguous Alternatives: Tourism in Small Developing Countries*, Suva: Institute of Pacific Studies, pp. 154–67.

Routledge, D. (1985) *Matanitu: The Struggle for Power in Early Fiji*, Suva: University of the South Pacific.

Samy, J. (1975) 'Crumbs from the table? The workers' share of tourism', in B.R. Finney and K.A. Watson (eds) *A New Kind of Sugar*, Honolulu: University of Hawai'i Press, pp. 111–21.

Sofield, T.H.B. (1990) 'The impact of tourism development on traditional socio-cultural values in the South Pacific: Conflict, coexistence and symbiosis', in M.L. Miller and J.

Auyong (eds) *Proceedings of the 1990 Congress on Coastal and Marine Tourism*, Newport: National Coastal Resources Research and Development Institute, pp. 49–66.

Thomas, N. (1989) 'The force of ethnology: origins and significance of the Melanesian/ Polynesian division', *Current Anthropology*, 30(1): 27–34.

Tuimaleali'ifano, M. (1990) *Samoans in Fiji: Migration, Identity and Communication*, Suva: University of the South Pacific.

Chapter 5

Environmental impact of tourism in the Pacific

C. Michael Hall

INTRODUCTION

The natural environment is a focal point for the selling of the South Pacific to tourists. As has already been noted in earlier chapters (see Chapters 2 and 4), images of a pristine environment – sun, sand, sea and palm trees – have been at the forefront of Western images of the South Pacific. The European Community funded Tourism Council of the South Pacific (TCSP) undertook a series of visitor surveys in member countries which indicated that 50–80 per cent of all tourists to the region regarded the natural environment as one of the principal attractions of the host country (Kudu 1992). As Connell (1988: 62) observed, 'For island states that have very few resources, virtually the only resources where there may be some comparative advantage in favour of [island microstates] are clean beaches, unpolluted seas and warm weather and water, and at least vestiges of distinctive cultures'. It is perhaps for this reason that fears of tourism's impacts on the natural environment have often been at the forefront over debates surrounding tourism development in the region (Finney and Watson 1977; Farrell 1982; Hay 1992; Minerbi 1992).

Unfortunately, tourism's impacts on the natural environment have likely been exaggerated in the same way that tourism has often been blamed for many of the cultural and social ills of the South Pacific (see Chapter 4). This is because the impacts of tourism have often failed to have been distinguished from other forms of development impact or even such factors as overpopulation, poor agricultural practice or poor resource management. This is not to say that tourism has not affected the Pacific environment. However, what is often at issue are aesthetic or cumulative impacts rather than effects that can be isolated solely as relating to tourism development. Indeed, to focus on tourism as a form of negative impact on the natural environment is to miss the far greater environmental problems which face the South Pacific: global warming, depletion of fisheries and forest resources and the need to maintain biodiversity, and overpopulation (Hall and Batterham 1991).

Although tourism is undoubtedly an important issue for the Pacific island nations, for several of them their very existence is threatened by the prospect of sea-level rise as a result of global climate change. Tonga, Kiribati and several island chains in the Federated States of Micronesia are extremely vulnerable to sea-level increase. The prospects of such environmental change has raised the spectre of dramatic population movements in the region. Partially as a result of the potential of global warming, countries such as Australia have embarked on environmental and climate monitoring projects as part of their aid and assistance programmes to Pacific Island states (Australian International Development Assistance Bureau 1994).

Concerns have also been expressed by governments and conservation organisations at the exploitation of the natural resources of the Pacific islands, particularly their fish stocks and forests, and the loss of biodiversity (Fuavao 1993). During the 1970s and 1980s, Japanese, Taiwanese and American fishing fleets over-exploited fish stocks, and tuna in particular, leading to a fisheries management crisis with major economic ramifications for the resource-poor island microstates. Although the decline in fish stocks has been arrested in recent years thanks to the implementation of international fisheries management regimes, the stocks still remain low with doubts remaining about the longer-term economic viability of some species (Hall and Batterham 1991).

Tropical log exports have been banned all over the world, leaving today just two major sources in the Pacific: Papua New Guinea, which is 70 per cent covered by rainforest, and the Solomon Islands. According to the World Bank, logging in the Solomons is being conducted at three times the rate of sustainability (Callick 1993). As Keith-Reid (1993: 38) noted:

> Foreign logging companies are intensifying the raváging of Solomon Islands rainforest at a rate that will destroy the last commercial stands of natural forest by the end of the 1990s . . . Three to four years ago critics alarmed by the devastation of the forest said all commercial stands would be wiped out within 15 years. Since then the average volume of exports has doubled . . . This is nearly three times the rate that an Australian aid inventory of the forests now being completed indicates is the sustainable rate.

Given their sociocultural, as well as ecological significance, substantial concerns have been expressed about the loss of forest cover. As Community Aid Abroad (1990: 3) observed, 'Destruction of the forest from logging or other causes means reduced access to sources of food, building materials and fuel and loss of ancestral and burial sites. Women in particular have to walk further each day to find fuel and water'. The removal of the tree cover leaves the soil more susceptible to erosion, landslides and loss of productivity. The increased sediment load in the run-off from deforested sites leads to increased silting of the waterways, thereby polluting sources of fresh water and impacting on coastal and marine ecology.

The general impact of resource practices is not divorced from tourism development (Hall 1994a). Indeed, tourism is seen by many as providing an economic and sustainable alternative to present unsustainable patterns of resource development, particularly with respect to logging (e.g. Lees 1991, 1992; Sofield 1992; Valentine 1992a; Young 1992). Ecotourism is being promoted by the TCSP to ensure the establishment of protected areas on communal land through the 'potential of considerable economic benefits to the landowners'. Nevertheless, 'the TCSP is cognizant about the problems of convincing communal landowners that their land often serves better unexploited than exploited, in particular as the latter often provide the landowners with immediate and visible economic benefits' (Kudu 1992: 158). This somewhat problematic relationship between tourism and the environment serves as the underlying theme for this chapter.

The chapter is divided into two main sections. The first section discusses the environmental impacts of tourism in the region, while the second examines the way in which tourism may potentially contribute to conservation through nature-based or 'eco'-tourism. However, the chapter concludes by observing that it is possible to identify ecotourism as a new form of ecological imperialism which imposes Western conservation ideas on the region and argues that the notion of 'environment' needs to be placed within a broader sociocultural context.

THE IMPACTS OF TOURISM

That tourism can have harmful impacts on the physical environment of island microstates has now become well recognised within the tourism literature (e.g. Beekhuis 1981; Mathieson and Wall 1982; Archer 1985; Murphy 1985). However, that tourism automatically has a negative effect has now become something of a truism in much of the contemporary travel literature. Undoubtedly, unplanned and poorly managed tourism development can damage the natural environment, but the overall understanding of the interaction between tourism and the environment is quite poor, with debates over the impacts of tourism development often dealing in generalities rather than the outcomes of scientific research on tourist impacts in a specific environment or on a specific species.

Within the context of the South Pacific there has been no systematic study of the environmental impacts of tourism over the region as a whole. Data and information is highly fragmented (Milne 1990). Base-line data, that is information regarding the condition of the natural environment prior to tourism development, is invariably lacking (Carpenter and Maragos 1989). Even in Australia, one of the most economically developed nations of the region, information about the environmental impacts of tourism is relatively poor and, where it does exist, it tends to be available for areas, such as national parks or reserves, which are under government control, rather than for private lands (Buckley and Pannell 1990; Hall 1995a). In addition, development-specific reports, such as environmental impact statements on resort or tourism developments which are required by law in many Western countries, are often not required in the countries of the South Pacific because environmental planning legislation is still being developed (Tourism Council of the South Pacific 1988; Fuavao 1993).

The lack of information on the environmental impacts of tourism in the South Pacific has arisen for several reasons. First, substantial business and political concern over environmental conditions has only emerged in recent years. Second, many of the governments of the region have had far greater priorities, for example economic development, health, welfare and education, for their limited financial resources than environmental monitoring or conservation. Third, and as a partial consequence of the above two factors, the resources and scientific expertise was not generally available to undertake the vast amount of research required.

In recent years, however, greater concern has been expressed over the condition of the Pacific environment. This has not been due to tourism alone. Nevertheless, the increasing economic significance of tourism and the perceived desire of many consumers to experience the pristine Pacific of the tourist image will likely contribute to an increase in research on the environmental impacts of tourism.

Minerbi (1992), as part of a paper for the Greenpeace Pacific Campaign, recorded a number of environmental and ecological impacts associated with tourism development on the Pacific Islands (Table 5.1). The range of tourism-related impacts is similar to that for many other environments (Edington and Edington 1986; Hall 1995a). However, in the case of Pacific, tourism impacts may be more problematic due to the tendency for tourism development and tourists to concentrate on or near the ecologically and geomorphologically dynamic coastal environment (see Plates 5.1, 5.2 and 5.3). Indeed, with a few notable exceptions, for example the highlands of Papua New Guinea, the small size of many of the Pacific Islands means that tourism activities *have* to be located within the coastal zone. Because of the highly dynamic nature of the coastal environment and the significance of mangroves and the limited coral sand supply for island beaches in particular, any development which interferes with the natural system may have severe consequences for the long-term stability of the environment. The impact of poorly developed tourism projects on the sand cays (coral sand islands) of the Pacific, for example, has been well documented:

- near-shore vegetation clearing exposes the island to sea storm erosion and decreases plant material decomposition on the beach, thereby reducing nutrient availability for flora and fauna;
- manoeuvring by bulldozer (instead of hand clearing) results in scarring and soil disturbance and makes sand deposit loose and vulnerable to erosion (e.g. Treasure Island in Fiji);
- excessive tapping of the fresh groundwater induces salt water intrusion which then impairs vegetation growth and human water use and renders the cay susceptible to storm damage and further erosion;
- sewage outfall in shallow water and reef flats may led to an excessive build-up of nutrients thereby leading to algal growth which may eventually kill coral (e.g. Green Island in Australia in the 1980s);

- seawalls built to trap sand in the short-term impair the natural seasonal distribution of sand resulting, in the long run, in a net beach loss and in a reduction of the island land mass;
- boat channels blasted in the reef act as a sand trap; in time they fill with sand which is no longer circulating around the island; in turn this sand is replaced by other sand eroded from the vegetated edges, changing the size and shape of the island and in time threatening the island's integrity (Baines 1987).

Another component of the coastal environment which can be substantially affected by tourism is the clearing and dredging of mangroves and estuaries for marinas and resorts. Mangroves and estuarine environments are extremely significant nursery areas for a variety of fish species. The loss of natural habitat due to dredging or infilling may therefore have dramatic impact on fish catches. In addition, there may be substantial impacts on the whole of the estuarine food chain with a subsequent loss of ecological diversity. A further consequence of mangrove loss is reduced protection against erosion of the shoreline thereby increasing vulnerability to storm surge. Removal of mangroves will not only impact on the immediate area of clearance, but will also affect other coastal areas through the transport of greater amounts of marine sediment (Clarke 1991). Tourism development has been responsible for mangrove clearance in several countries of the South Pacific, including Hawai'i, Vanuatu, and Fiji. In the case of the Denarau Island resort development in Fiji, 130 hectares of mangrove forest was dredged to construct an 18-hole golf course and create an artificial marina (Minerbi 1992; Hall 1994b).

One of the most obvious ways in which tourism-related development has impacted on the coastal environment is the effect of tourism and tourist activities on coral reefs. 'Coral reefs are very vulnerable, and adverse human activities may result in a lower capacity to regenerate, or the death of entire coral colonies' (Tourism Council of the South Pacific 1988: 12). Tourists can directly impact on coral reefs in a number of ways. Skin divers and snorklers can damage coral by hitting it with their fins. In order to restrict such damage, Vanuatu has been actively educating divers on the importance of maintaining correct buoyancy. In other parts of the Pacific, such as Australia's Great Barrier Reef, reef walking by tourists at low tide has resulted in substantial damage to sections of the reef within easy shore access.

The major indirect aspect of tourism's impacts on coral reefs is the environmental effects of urban and resort development, land clearing, and pollution. Pollutants can come from both land, for example resorts, and marine sources, such as tourist boats. Land-based pollution is often in the form of excessive nutrients from sewage and fertilisers. While both of these types of pollution may come from non-tourism sources it should be noted that septic tanks or inadequate sewage systems at resorts, or fertiliser run-off from golf courses may substantially impact on reef systems (Kuji 1991). Excessive nutrients promote algal growth at the expense of coral, leading to the smothering

Table 5.1: Environmental and ecological impacts of tourism on the Pacific Islands

Environmental degradation and pollution
- Degradation and pollution of the environment due to golf courses
- Pollution by littering

Destruction of habitats and damage to ecosystems
- Poorly managed tourism may result in destruction of high quality natural environments
- Unmanaged human interference of specific species of fauna and flora
- Dynamite blasting and overfishing

Loss of coastal and marine resources
- Interference with inland and coastal natural processes
  - excessive groundwater extraction by large resorts induces salt-water intrusion and deterioration of water quality and recharge of the aquifer
- Coastal ecosystem damage and destruction through tourism development
- Terrestrial run-off and dredging on coastal areas
  - damage to coral reef and marine resources caused by the construction of tourist infrastructure such as runways, marinas, harbours, parking areas and roads, and use of coral limestone in hotels and resort developments
- Destruction by tourist activities
  - destruction of coral reefs, lagoons, mangroves, saltwater marshes, and wetlands due to excessive visitation and/or unmanaged exploitation of those resources
  - disturbance to near shore aquatic life due to thrill crafts and boat tours
- Introduced exotic species
  - increased sea and air inter-island traffic creates the danger of accidental importation of exotic species, which can be very destructive to indigenous flora and fauna
  - tourism enterprises alter the integrity of the environment and encroach on local lifestyles with imported exotic species for safari hunting
- Damage to sand-cay ecosystems
- Damage to mangrove ecosystems
- Damage to coastal rainforest ecosystems
- Loss of sandy beaches and shoreline erosion
  - loss of sandy beaches due to onshore development and construction of seawalls

Coastal pollution
- Waste water discharge and sewage pollution
- Coastal water pollution and siltation due to near shore resort construction and run-off from resort areas results in the destruction of natural habitat, coral and feeding grounds for fish
- Marine and harbour pollution
  - coastal oil pollution due to motorised vehicles and ships

Surface water and ground water diversion
- Diversion of streams and water sources from local use to resort use, with resulting decline in water availability for domestic and other productive uses and farming, particularly taro cultivation

Source: After Minerbi 1992; also Milne 1990; Hay 1992; Weiler 1992.

Plate 5.1:   Coastal tourism development at Waikiki, Hawai'i (Michael Hall)

Plate 5.2:   Water access is a critical element in tourism development in Port Vila, Vanuatu (Michael Hall)

Plate 5.3: Tourism traffic along Rainbow Beach in Queensland, Australia is starting to place pressure on the environment (Michael Hall)

of coral and its eventual death. Similarly, sedimentation leads to silting and water cloudiness which cuts off sunlight to the coral reef also killing it. In the case of the Cape Tribulation Road constructed near Daintree in northern Queensland by the state government in the mid-1980s in an effort to develop tourism (Hall 1992), sedimentation on adjacent coral reefs increased more than sixfold in comparison with undisturbed catchments in the same area (Fisk and Harriot 1989; Partain and Hopley 1990; Hopley *et al.* 1993).

In concluding his examination of the impacts of tourism development on the Pacific Islands, Minerbi (1992: 69) was scathing in his criticism of the environmental impacts of tourism:

Resorts and golf courses increase environmental degradation and pollution. Littering has taken place on beaches and scenic lookouts and parks. Marine sanctuaries have been run over and exploited by too many tourists. Resorts have interfered with the hydrological cycle by changing groundwater patterns, altering stream life, and engaging in excessive groundwater extraction. Coastal reefs, lagoons, anchialine ponds, wastewater marshes, mangroves, have been destroyed by resort construction and by excessive visitations and activities with the consequent loss of marine life and destruction of ecosystems. Beach walking, snorkeling, recreational fishing, boat tours and anchoring have damaged coral reefs and grasses and have disturbed near shore aquatic life . . .

Tourism has presented itself as a clean and not polluting industry but its claims have not come true . . .

Despite the litany of damage noted by Minerbi, it must be emphasised that the environmental impacts of tourism are certainly less than other industries on the Pacific Islands such as agriculture, fishing, forestry, and mining. Furthermore, many of Minerbi's sources for his review were derived from newspapers and research conducted on similar island environments in other parts of the world, such as the Caribbean. This is not to deny that tourism has had substantial impacts on the South Pacific, rather it is to emphasise that specific regional research on environmental impacts is sparse (Milne 1990). Given this situation, it may well be the case that tourism is receiving the blame for various forms of environmental degradation for which it is only partially responsible. Other forms of 'indigenous' impact, such as overpopulation, inappropriate urban development, and land clearance may be far more significant but are perhaps not so easy to blame as an industry as visible as tourism, particularly when businesses will often be owned by foreigners. Correctly managed therefore, tourism may well be more ecologically sustainable than many other industries in the South Pacific.

Biodiversity, sustainable development and tourism

Island ecosystems, such as those of the Pacific, are substantially different from those of continental areas. They are characterised by limitations of space, restricted habitats, lower species numbers compared to continental areas of similar ecological diversity, and a high degree of species endemism. The islands' biota is a culmination of a long history of geographical isolation, species dispersal, climatic factors, and community interaction. The specialisation of island biota means that they are highly vulnerable to external disturbance and environmental change, particularly human-induced impacts. The extinction of species is particularly common on islands when new competitors or physical conditions are introduced. Nevertheless, while the conservation of biodiversity as a component of sustainable development is clearly a major concern (Fuavao 1993), the nature of biodiversity has not been understood by many commentators on the relationship between tourism and the physical environment (e.g. Hay 1992).

Biodiversity (also referred to as biological or biotic diversity) is the diversity of living things. There are three related levels of biodiversity: genetic, species and ecosystem. When one is seeking to conserve diversity it is necessary therefore to be aware of the interaction that exists between all levels and the means by which they are measured. For example, clearing a rainforest for a walking track, access road or a resort development may well *increase* the number of species in a given area, because the forest clearing has created a new ecological niche with a different set of light and micro-climatic conditions. Therefore, if one was measuring diversity at a species level the clearing may well be perceived as positive. However, at an ecosystem level, clearance may result in fragmentation of the forest with a consequent loss of ecological integrity and an increased likelihood of plant and animal extinctions (Diamond 1975; Harris 1984). This example highlights the complexity of biological conservation – a complexity which needs to be reflected in the debate over the relationship between tourism and the environment.

Clearly, tourism needs to be placed within the context of the wider push for biological conservation within the South Pacific and the series of sustainable development measures proposed under Agenda 21, the United Nations Conference on Environment and Development (UNCED), including the development of national environmental strategies for the Pacific island nations (Fuavao 1993). This will require an understanding of the institutional components which are necessary for comprehensive and sustainable conservation of the Pacific environment:

- knowledge of local biological diversity;
- social recognition and valuation of local biological diversity;
- resilience of local patterns of tenure;
- range of viable categories of protected areas;
- systems of ecological impact assessment;
- conservation interest groups;
- comprehensive land use planning;
- site planning and the spatial decision making at appropriate scales;
- extent of ongoing monitoring;
- level of adaptibility of land use planning and subsequent implementation;
- extent of management and regulation of adjacent land uses; and
- mechanisms for channeling benefits of conservation back into local communities.

(Ingram 1994)

In addition, it will require a better understanding of the way in which the tourism-environment relationship is integrated into the economic and cultural aspects of development, a point that will be addressed in the next section.

ECOTOURISM

Ecotourism has become a major feature in the promotion of the Pacific to tourists and the development of tourism product (Economic and Social Commission for Asia and the Pacific 1994). Although the environment has long been a feature of tourist images of the Pacific, ecotourism represents a new phase in the commodification of the environment in that it now provides a justification for the establishment of conservation reserves and their consequent packaging for the tourist dollar. As Helu-Thaman (1992, p. 26) argued:

Ecotourism is fast becoming the modern marketing manager's source of inspiration for the new sale. It's got a lot going for it: it gives great pictures; it offers pretty much what people want when they wish to escape from pressured polluted urban living, and it offers a sort of moral expiation of guilt for our contribution to the degradation of our own planet.

The term 'ecotourism' as it is commonly used in the Pacific, refers to two different dimensions of tourism which, although interrelated, pose distinct management, policy, planning and development problems:

- Ecotourism as 'green' or 'nature-based' tourism which is essentially a form of *special interest* tourism and refers to a specific market segment and the products generated for that segment, e.g. 'wilderness' tours in Fiji;
- Ecotourism as *any* form of tourism development which is regarded as environmentally friendly.

(Hall 1994a)

In both of its common usages, ecotourism is widely promoted as a positive dimension of tourism which integrates economic development and income generation with environmental preservation (Sofield 1992; Young 1992). However, substantial criticism has emerged with a concept of ecotourism that leaves out the sociocultural dimensions of development (Cater and Bowman 1994). For example, Helu-Thaman (1992: 26) expressed concerns at a business culture in much of ecotourism 'which places the concern with profitability before that of conservation' and argued for the adoption of the concept of 'ecocultural tourism':

tourism development based on the culture of the host community and not on the culture of the tourists or developers or aid donors. This is particularly relevant given the fact that for the land-based semi-subsistence societies of the Pacific islands, people and their cultures are inextricably part of their ecosystems. A people's CULTURE . . . logically the most appropriate basis and the framework for development, not a mere variable within it.

(Helu-Thaman 1992: 27)

As Brookfield (1991: 42) has argued, environmental sustainability not only refers to environmental regeneration and the maintenance of biodiversity but must also 'be measured by progress along a vector made up of attributes that include improvement in income and its distribution, in health, in education, freedoms, and access to resources'. More often than not ecotourism has come to be regarded as tourist visitation to national parks and reserves (Hay 1992; Valentine 1992a, 1992b; Weiler 1992; Hall 1994a). However, such a notion of ecotourism not only provides an extremely limited approach to ideas of environment, ecology, and the maintenance of biodiversity, but it also indicates the inherent bias of much ecotourism and conservation thinking toward Western ideas of environmental conservation which tend to separate humankind from nature (Hall and McArthur 1996).

In most western societies in which conservation land is set aside, natural heritage values predominate and evidence of recent human settlement is often removed or not interpreted for visitors. Nevertheless, the split of heritage into natural and cultural components is somewhat artificial, as the values which are associated with areas such as national parks, wilderness, and scientific reserves are cultural in nature. To retain an area as a national park is as much a cultural decision, and hence a cultural landscape, as it is to use the land for grazing, plantation cropping, or swidden agriculture (Hall and McArthur 1996). Indeed, the legitimacy of the cultural practices of indigenous peoples in areas set aside as national parks and conservation reserves is slowly being recognised by some governments and conservation agencies (West and Brechin 1991; Birckhead *et al.* 1992).

For the indigenous peoples of the Pacific who retain their cultural traditions, humankind is not regarded as separate from the landscape but is part of an indivisible whole, that is the physical environment is an everyday lived experience (Weaver 1992; Hall 1996; Hall and McArthur 1996). For example, despite the efforts of the TCSP in establishing conservation legislation for tourism (e.g. TCSP 1988), 'existing legislation is usually unenforceable, particularly where it conflicts with the national culture' (Fuavao 1992: 153). Indeed, Fuavao goes on to note that the weight of environmental policy and the degree of on-site control that government agencies have is quite restricted and, in some cases, may actually expose landowners to exploitation. As Kudu (1992: 158) observes, ecotourism projects need 'to be managed by local landowners' so that they are 'not seen as an alien imposition'.

Similarly, in the case of New Zealand, the increase in European (*Pakeha*) concern for conservation of the natural heritage of New Zealand is seen by some Maori as prejudicially affecting them. For example, Maori groups at present own more than 50 per cent of native bushland in private hands, the reservation of which has been a central point of *Pakeha* conservation group concerns over the past 20 years. Nevertheless, as one Maori put it 'Pakehas are all conservationists when it comes to Maori land – the Pakeha attitude seems to be what's yours is ours, but what's mine is my own' (*The Dominion*, 18 October 1989).

Hall (1994a, 1995b) has described the contemporary push for ecotourism as a new form of 'ecological imperialism'. In his book *Ecological Imperialism: The Biological Expansion of Europe, 900–1900*, Crosby (1986) described the, sometimes forced, Europeanisation of the global environment through the spread of the plant and animal species most-desired by the European peoples. In the current age of supposed environmental awareness, many western conservationists are seeking ways to preserve biodiversity through a global system of conservation reserves. In the Pacific, ecotourism is being promoted as a means to achieve both environmental conservation and economic returns. However, in so doing, the indigenous cultural dimension of development is often either lost or ignored while conservation mechanisms are often being seen through western eyes. Therefore, the Pacific is perhaps facing a form of ecological imperialism in the region in which a new set of European cultural values are being impressed on indigenous cultures through ecotourism development.

CONCLUSION

This chapter has highlighted the somewhat problematic nature of the relationship between tourism and the environment in the Pacific. From an ecological perspective, tensions exist in our understanding of the relationship because a detailed knowledge of the impacts of tourism on the environment in the Pacific, and on specific ecosystems and species in particular, does not exist. Within the cultural dimension, tensions exist because conservation and perhaps the nature of negative environmental impacts is typically perceived from Western rather than indigenous cultural perspectives.

Sustainable tourism means conserving the productive basis of the physical environment by preserving the integrity of the biota and ecological processes and producing tourism commodities without degrading other values, including sociocultural and economic values. Having no form of tourism in the Pacific islands may well be the most advisable strategy in terms of the ecological integrity of the islands. However, it is also unrealistic.

In order to ensure that biodiversity is preserved, management agencies must, somewhat paradoxically, allow people to visit 'natural' areas so that policy makers can be persuaded to establish institutional arrangements, which may include the establishment of reserved areas, to assist in achieving conservation objectives. The desire of many westerners to engage in ecotourism activities is undoubtedly attractive to many of the island states of the Pacific. Ecotourism has the potential to provide an economic return to some locations and can also generate employment opportunities over a range of different tourism services, such as guided tours. Nevertheless, tourist numbers cannot be allowed to grow to the point where the environment is degraded and the tourist experience lessened. Furthermore, ecotourism must be placed within the local indigenous context. Without such restraints tourism may not only become a new form of ecological imperialism but may also, in the longer term, be counter-productive in the search for what should be primary objective of tourism development, the conservation and maintenance of biological and cultural diversity.

REFERENCES

Archer, E. (1985) 'Emerging environmental problems in a tourist zone: The case of Barbados', *Caribbean Geography*, 2: 45–55.

Australian International Development Assistance Bureau (1994) *Australian Overseas Development Cooperation 1989 to 1993/94: Official Expenditure by Country, Region and Sector*, Canberra: Australian International Development Assistance Bureau.

Baines, G.B.K. (1987) 'Manipulation of islands and men: Sand-cay tourism in the South Pacific', in S. Britton and W.C. Clarke (eds) *Ambiguous Alternative: Tourism in Small Developing Countries*, Suva: University of the South Pacific, pp. 16–24.

Beekhuis, J.V. (1981) 'Tourism in the Caribbean: Impacts on the economic, social and natural environments', *Ambio*, 10: 325–31.

Birckhead, J., De Lacy, T. and Smith, L. (eds) (1992) *Aboriginal Involvement in Parks and Protected Areas*, Canberra: Aboriginal Studies Press.

Brookfield, H. (1991) 'Environmental sustainability with development: What prospects for a research agenda?', in O. Stokke (ed.) *Sustainable Development*, London: Frank Cass, pp. 42–66.

Buckley, R. and Pannell, J. (1990) 'Environmental impacts of tourism and recreation in national parks and conservation reserves', *Journal of Tourism Studies*, 1(1): 24–32.

Callick, R. (1993) 'Fighting the rush to chop down the trees', *Island Business Pacific*, July: 35–8.

Carpenter, R.A. and Maragos, J.E. (eds) (1989) *How to Assess Environmental Impacts on Tropical Islands and Coastal Areas*, South Pacific Regional Environment Programme (SPREP) Training Manual, Honolulu: Environmental and Policy Institute, East-West Center.

Cater, E.A. and Bowman, G.A. (eds) (1994) *Ecotourism: A Sustainable Option?*, Chichester/London: John Wiley/Royal Geographical Society.

Clarke, W.C. (1991) 'Time and tourism: An ecological perspective', in M.L. Miller and J. Auyong (eds) *Proceedings of the 1990 Congress on Coastal and Marine Tourism*, Honolulu: National Coastal Research and Development Institute, pp. 387–93.

Community Aid Abroad (1990) 'Rainforests and the people of Solomon Islands', *CAA Review*, Summer: 3–6.

Connell, J. (1988) *Sovereignty and Survival: Island Microstates in the Third World*, Research Monograph No. 3, Sydney: Departrment of Geography, University of Sydney.

Crosby, A.W. (1986) *Ecological Imperialism: The Biological Expansion of Europe, 900–1900*, Cambridge: Cambridge University Press.

Diamond, J. (1975) 'The island dilemma: Lessons of modern biogeographic studies for the design of nature reserves', *Biological Conservation*, 7: 129–46.

Economic and Social Commission for Asia and the Pacific (1994) *Review of Tourism Development in the ESCAP Region*, ESCAP Tourism Review No. 15, New York: United Nations.

Edington, J.M. and Edington, M.A. (1986) *Ecology, Recreation and Tourism*, Cambridge: Cambridge University Press.

Farrell, B.H. (1982) *Hawaii: The Legend That Sells*, Honolulu: University of Hawai'i Press.

Finney, B.R. and Watson, K.A. (eds) (1977) *A New Kind of Sugar: Tourism in the Pacific*, Santa Cruz: Centre for South Pacific Studies, University of California, Santa Cruz.

Fisk, D.A. and Harriott, V.J. (1989) *The Effects of Increased Sedimentation on the Recruitment and Population Dynamics of Juvenile Corals at Cape Tribulation, North Queensland*, Great Barrier Reef Marine Park Authority Technical Memorandum 20, Townsville: Great Barrier Reef Marine Park Authority.

Fuavao, V.A. (1992) 'Operating within natural policy and legal environments', in J.E. Hay (ed.) *Ecotourism Business in the Pacific: Promoting a Sustainable Experience, Conference Proceedings*, Auckland: Environmental Science, University of Auckland, pp. 151–3.

—— (1993) 'South Pacific Regional Environmental Programme: implications of Agenda 21 for the Pacific', *Pacific Economic Bulletin*, 8(2): 22–31.

Hall, C.M. (1992) *Wasteland to World Heritage: Preserving Australia's Wilderness*, Carlton: Melbourne University Press.

—— (1994a) 'Ecotourism in Australia, New Zealand and the South Pacific: Appropriate tourism or a new form of ecological imperialism?', in E.A. Cater and G.A. Bowman (eds) *Ecotourism: A Sustainable Option?*, Chichester/London: John Wiley/Royal Geographical Society, pp. 137–58.

—— (1994b) *Tourism in the Pacific Rim: Development, Impacts and Markets*, South Melbourne: Longman Australia.

—— (1995a) *Introduction to Tourism in Australia: Impacts, Planning and Development*, 2nd edn, South Melbourne: Longman Australia.

—— (1995b) 'Ecotourism or ecological imperialism?', *Geographical: The Royal Geographical Society Magazine*, 67(2): 19.

—— (1996) 'Tourism and the Maori of Aotearoa (New Zealand)', in R. Butler and T. Hinch (eds) *Tourism and Native Peoples*, Chichester: John Wiley.

Hall, C.M. and Batterham, I. (1991) 'Trouble in paradise: A special report on the state of the South Pacific environment', *Alternatives: Perspectives on Science, Technology and the Environment*, 18(1): 14–15.

Hall, C.M. and McArthur, S. (1996) 'The human dimension of heritage management: Different values, different interests . . . different issues', in C.M. Hall and S. McArthur (eds) *Heritage Management in Australia and New Zealand: The Human Dimension*, Melbourne: Oxford University Press.

Harris, L.D. (1984) *The Fragmented Forest: Island Biogeographic Theory and the Preservation of Biotic Diversity*, Chicago: University of Chicago Press.

Hay, J.E. (ed.) (1992) *Ecotourism Business in the Pacific: Promoting a Sustainable Experience, Conference Proceedings*, Environmental Science Occasional Publication No. 8, Auckland: Environmental Science, University of Auckland.

Helu-Thaman, K. (1992) 'Ecocultural tourism: A personal view for maintaining cultural integrity in ecotourism development', in J.E. Hay (ed.) *Ecotourism Business in the Pacific: Promoting a Sustainable Experience, Conference Proceedings*, Auckland: Environmental Science, University of Auckland, pp. 24–9.

Hopley, D., van Woesik, R., Hoyal, D.C.J.D., Rasmussen, C.E. and Steven, A.D.L. (1993) *Sedimentation Resulting From Road Development, Cape Tribulation area*, Great Barrier Reef Marine Park Authority Technical Memorandum 24, Townsville: Great Barrier Reef Marine Park Authority.

Ingram, G.B. 1994, 'Institutional obstacles to conservation: Fergusson Island, Papua New Guinea', *Pacific Affairs*, 67(1): 26–45.

Keith-Reid, R. (1993) 'The rapid rape of the forests of the Solomons', *Island Business Pacific*, July: 38.

Kudu, D. (1992) 'The role and activities of the Tourism Council of the South Pacific, particularly in relation to ecotourism development', in J.E. Hay (ed.) *Ecotourism Business in the Pacific: Promoting a Sustainable Experience, Conference Proceedings*, Auckland: Environmental Science, University of Auckland, pp. 154–60.

Kuji, T. (1991) 'The political economy of golf', *AMPO, Japan-Asia Quarterly Review*, 22(4): 47–54.

Lees, A. (1991) *A Representative Protected Forests System for the Solomon Islands*, report to the Australian National Parks and Wildlife Service, Maruia Society, Nelson.

—— (1992) 'Ecotourism – restraining the big promise', in J.E. Hay (ed.) *Ecotourism Business in the Pacific: Promoting a Sustainable Experience, Conference Proceedings*, Auckland: Environmental Science, University of Auckland, pp. 61–4.

Mathieson, A. and Wall, G. (1982) *Tourism: Economic, Physical and Social Impacts*, London: Longman.

Milne, S. (1990) 'The impact of tourism development in small Pacific Island states', *New Zealand Journal of Geography*, 89: 16–21.

Minerbi, L. (1992) *Impacts of Tourism Development in Pacific Islands*, San Francisco: Greenpeace Pacific Campaign.

Murphy, P.E. (1985) *Tourism: A Community Approach*, New York: Methuen.

Partain, B.R. and Hopley, D. (1990) *Sedimentation Resulting From Road Development, Cape Tribulation Area*, Great Barrier Reef Marine Park Authority Technical Memorandum 21, Townsville: Great Barrier Reef Marine Park Authority.

Sofield, T. (1992) 'The Guadalcanal track ecotourism project in the Solomon Islands', in J.E. Hay (ed.) *Ecotourism Business in the Pacific: Promoting a Sustainable Experience,*

Conference Proceedings, Auckland: Environmental Science, University of Auckland, pp. 89–100.

Tourism Council of the South Pacific (1988) *Nature Legislation and Nature Conservation as a Part of Tourism Development in the Island Pacific: A Report Covering Cook Islands, Fiji, Kiribati, Niue, Papua New Guinea, Solomon Islands, Tonga, Tuvulu, Vanuatu and Western Samoa*, Suva: Tourism Council of the South Pacific.

Valentine, P.S. (1992a) 'Ecotourism and nature conservation: A definition with some recent developments in Micronesia', in B. Weiler (ed.) *Ecotourism Incorporating The Global Classroom, 1991 International Conference Papers*, Canberra: Bureau of Tourism Research, pp. 4–9.

—— (1992b) 'Nature-based tourism', in B. Weiler and C.M. Hall (eds) *Special Interest Tourism*, London: Belhaven Press, pp. 105–27.

Weaver, S. (1992) 'Eco-fix that needs fixing', *Pacific Islands Monthly*, January: 54.

Weiler, B. (ed.) (1992) *Ecotourism Incorporating The Global Classroom, 1991 International Conference Papers*, Canberra: Bureau of Tourism Research.

West, P.C. and Brechin, S.R. (eds) (1991) *Resident Peoples and National Parks*, Tucson: University of Arizona Press.

Young, M. (1992) 'Ecotourism – profitable conservation', in J.E. Hay (ed.) *Ecotourism Business in the Pacific: Promoting a Sustainable Experience, Conference Proceedings*, Auckland: Environmental Science, University of Auckland, pp. 55–60.

Chapter 6

Political effects of tourism in the Pacific

C. Michael Hall

INTRODUCTION

The political nature of international tourism has received only scant attention in the tourism research literature (Matthews 1978; Richter 1989; Hall 1994a; Hall and Jenkins 1995). However, an appreciation of the political context of tourism is critical to an understanding of the complex nature of tourism development. Issues of political stability and political relations within and between states are extremely important in determining the image of destinations in tourist generating regions and, of course, the real and perceived safety of tourists (Hall and O'Sullivan 1995).

Politics is an essential element in understanding tourist relationships in the South Pacific. While the romantic image of the South Seas colours many tourist perceptions of the South Pacific as a destination, it is important to recognise that there are complex sociopolitical structures and issues behind this facade which must be understood if a more complete picture of tourism in the region is to be established. Patterns and processes of tourism development will be related to government policies and regulations, power relationships between interests in the development process, and competing sets of ideologies and values. 'Tourism is ... very much part of the competition for and consumption of scarce resources, the seeking of which *must* surely lead one to the essential elements of the politics of tourism: *Politics is about power, who gets what, where, how and why*' (Hall 1994a: 195).

This chapter discusses the relationship between tourism and politics in the South Pacific in terms of tourism and dependency, relations between states, perceptions of political stability, and community opposition to tourism development. Clearly, this account of the political dimensions of tourism in the South Pacific is not exhaustive. However, it is intended that it will assist the reader in identifying some of the key issues which arise in the analysis of the politics of tourism in the South Pacific.

TOURISM AND DEPENDENCY IN THE PACIFIC

The fundamental characteristics of the Pacific island economies have been primarily determined by their colonial history. Tourism has therefore been seen 'to have been grafted on to a once colonial economy in a way that has perpetuated deep-seated structural anomalies and inequalities' (Britton 1983: v). Because of this, tourism in the Pacific Islands may illustrate some of the conditions of dependency.

Dependency can be conceptualised as an historical process which alters the internal functioning of economic, political and social subsystems within a developing country. This conditioning causes the simultaneous disintegration of an indigenous economy and its reorientation to serve the needs of exogenous markets, such as international tourists. 'As a product, and an extension, of metropolitan capital, the international tourist industry acts to extend [structural dependency] in those island tourist destinations where it operates' (Britton 1983: 2). This internal transformation determines the specific roles and articulation of various modes of production within a developing country, and thereby creates specialised commodity export enclaves, such as tourism or primary agricultural production (e.g. sugar) and structural inequality between social groups (Britton 1982; Hall 1994a, b).

The notion of dependency has been influential to the understanding of the tourism development process in developing countries and island microstates, particularly those with a colonial legacy (Connell 1988; Nash 1989). For example, Crick (1989: 322) argued that the manner in which the tourism industry is planned and shaped with respect to the attraction of international tourists, 'will recreate the fabric of the colonial situation'. Indeed, Crick (1989: 322) went on to argue that tourism was a form of 'leisure imperialism' and represented 'the hedonistic face of neocolonialism'.

The clear concern in most studies of dependency is that the locus of control over the development process shifts from the people that are most affected by development, the host community, to the tourism generating regions (Hall 1994a: 123). As Erisman (1983: 339) observed 'beyond economics lies the deeper and generally unarticulated fear that the industry's impact is even more pervasive and insidious, that it will somehow shape and affect in adverse ways the entire fabric of . . . society'. According to Connell (1988: 64), 'The inevitability of foreign ownership, the uneven development that has followed tourist development, but above all the cultural conflict argued to inevitably ensue, initially discouraged Pacific states from orienting development strategies towards tourism'. However, limited economic growth with the island economies, improvements in transport technology, and greater development interest from overseas tourism companies have resulted in tourism now being central to development in the Pacific. Moreover, for most of the island economies of the South Pacific 'virtually the only resources where there may be some comparative advantage . . . are clean beaches, unpolluted seas and warm weather and water, and at least vestiges of distinctive cultures' (Connell 1988: 62). Somewhat paradoxically, this last point may lead to substantial cultural impacts because of its potential attractiveness to culture seeking tourists. For example, in the case of

Fiji, the World Bank (1987: 14) noted that 'the local culture has not been tailored and projected so as to attract tourist attention as has been done in Hawaii and Bali'.

Although tourism does have a significant colonial history in the Pacific Islands (see Chapter 2), the vast majority of tourism development has occurred in the post-colonial period. In their efforts to broaden their economic base and generate employment, Pacific countries, such as Fiji and Vanuatu, encouraged overseas investment in the tourism sector. Britton (1983: 23) observed that tourism was a mechanism for alleviating Fiji's dependence on sugar and would also 'diversify [the] economic base, increase foreign exchange, and reduce the country's exposure to the vagaries of the international sugar market'. With only a minute domestic tourism market and small amounts of local capital, tourism development *must* require the involvement of foreign capital in order to gain access to the overseas markets and to develop tourism infrastructure. For example, the region's main tourism marketing, planning and promotion body, the Tourism Council of the South Pacific, is primarily funded by the European Union as part of its overseas aid package, while Australia and New Zealand have contributed to the development of transport infrastructure as part of their aid contributions (see Chapter 17). Therefore, tourism in much of the Pacific has little option but to build upon the economic and political legacies of the colonial period.

In the case of Fiji, for example, Britton (1983: 201) observed that international tourism operated 'in two contradictorary directions. It helps to alleviate problems derived from Fiji's colonial legacy. But tourism is itself a product of this colonial structure and acts to exacerbate many essential features of this original condition'. In contrast, 'without the involvement of foreign and commercial interests, Tonga has not evolved the essential ties with metropolitan markets and their tourism companies. It would seem that Tonga's tourist industry has paradoxically suffered because the country was not exploited as a fully-fledged colony' (Britton 1987: 131).

In the case of the Pacific Islands, tourism has, by its very nature, maintained some of the economic and political effects of colonial rule. Tourism contributes to dependency on foreign capital, primarily from Australia and New Zealand, but increasingly from Japan (Hall 1994b). As Britton (1983: 6–7), recognised over a decade ago with respect to tourism development in the Pacific: 'Immobile tourism plant in the periphery relies on foreign corporations to supply tourists. The flow of tourists is achieved by gaining the cooperation of foreign interests or by national bargaining power over factors affecting the profitability of these foreign investments.' In this situation, political concerns over power, interests and values must be of major importance for our understanding of tourism in South Pacific.

POLITICAL STABILITY AND DESTINATION IMAGE

A favourable image is an essential requirement of any tourist destination. The problem with any kind of civil unrest is that unfavourable images are beamed across the world, so that even those who are not afraid of terrorism will be discouraged from taking a holiday there. It is not so much that the area is dangerous; more that it does not look attractive.

(Buckley and Klemm 1993: 193–4)

Perceptions of political stability and safety are a prerequisite for tourist visitation (Brackenbury 1995). Violence, political protest, social unrest, civil war, terrorist actions, perceived violations of human rights, or even the mere threat of these activities, can all serve to cause tourists to alter their travel behaviour (Lea and Small 1988, Hall and O'Sullivan 1995). Although the South Pacific has been relatively safe in terms of terrorist attacks against tourists or civil war, there have been a number of events which have contributed to perceptions of political instability in the region and, hence, have contributed to a decline in the tourist attractiveness of the Pacific Islands in major tourist generating regions. Since the early 1980s coup attempts have been staged in Fiji and Vanuatu, civil wars of independence have been waged in New Caledonia and Papua New Guinea (PNG) (Bougainville), criminal attacks against tourists and European expatriates have occurred in PNG, and direct attacks and protests against tourist developments have occurred in Fiji and the Solomon Islands. Examples of the different types of political instability and their significance in the South Pacific are illustrated in Table 6.1.

Given the potential for political unrest and instability in the region, tourism managers and planners need to become far more sophisticated in their approach to crisis management and be more aware of the political dimensions of tourism development. At present, 'when problems arise, the only response the industry knows is to market more vigorously, regardless of the likelihood of success' (Richter and Waugh 1986: 232). For example, in response to the 14 May 1987 military coup in Fiji, the Fijian tourism industry, aided by the devaluation of the Fiji dollar, slashed holiday prices. By August 1987 there was an increase in Australian and New Zealand arrivals of 9.6 per cent, and by September these markets were up 40 per cent. Then on September 28 a second coup occurred leading to a further 30 per cent drop in arrivals. The Fijian response to the second coup was to launch a promotional campaign with the theme 'I wonder whether Fiji is still a paradise?' with the emphasis 'that all is normal and "ordinary Australians" are featured to reassure potential visitors that the destination is safe' (Lea and Small 1988: 8). However, despite the best efforts of marketers the instability of Fijian politics continued to have an impact on tourist arrivals, with the 1986 visitor arrival total not being reached again until 1990 (Fiji Visitors' Bureau 1992). Indeed, given their substitutability for the Fijian tourism product, both Bali and north Queensland benefited from the coups.

Table 6.1:   Tourism and political instability

Dimension	Examples
International relations and wars	Although modern tourism in the South Pacific has not been directly affected by war, there is some evidence to suggest that international disputes such as the 1991 Gulf War crisis did affect international travel to the South Pacific because of fears of terrorist activity. International relations can also affect tourist visitation. The announcement in June 1995 by the French Government that it would resume underground nuclear testing at Mururoa Atoll was perceived as being potentially damaging to tourism in Tahiti and Tonga.
Civil wars	Kanak separatism in New Caledonia in the mid-1980s led to perceptions of the islands as being unsafe for tourists. The Australian government issued warnings to its nationals advising against non-essential travel. The troubles in New Caledonia affected tourist visitation in neighbouring countries, such as Vanuatu, because tourists in generating regions, such as Australia, could not easily distinguish between the various nations of the South Pacific.
Coups	Following the May 1987 coup in Fiji, Japanese visitation was halved during June, and dropped further during July and August. Tourist arrivals from Australia, New Zealand and the United States was cut by almost 75 per cent. From the 85,000 visitors in April, arrivals fell to 5000 in June. The Australian and New Zealand governments advised their nationals not to travel to Fiji and the occupancy rate in Fiji dropped to approximately 10 per cent.
Terrorism	Tourism in the South Pacific has not been directly affected by terrorism in the same way as Europe or the Middle East. Direct attacks on tourists have been extremely rare. However, the hijacking of an Air New Zealand jet at Nadi airport during the 1987 coups did dramatically affect New Zealand confidence in Fiji as a destination.
Riots/political protests/social unrest	Political and social unrest has had a substantial impact on tourism in the South Pacific. Social unrest in Papua New Guinea, particularly through the activities of 'rascal' gangs, has affected the perceived safety of PNG as a tourist destination in Australia and New Zealand. Tourism developments may also be directly targeted by protestors if members of the local community are opposed to the development of a tourist resort. Protests and occupations of tourist resorts by locals has occurred in Fiji and the Solomon Islands.
Strikes	Following the 1989 Australian domestic air pilots dispute, the Australian Tourism Industry Association estimated 457,000 people cancelled their holiday plans altogether and a further 556,000 had to change their holiday plans due to the dispute. While being a domestic dispute, the strike also affected feeder services for international travel operations.

Source: Hall 1994a, b; Hall and O'Sullivan 1995.

According to Lea and Small (1988: 9), 'Several destinations used the Fijian coups to highlight the appeal and safety of their own resorts: "Golden beaches, coconut palms and *no* coups!", was the message used to attract visitors to Magnetic Island [Queensland] in October 1987; and "War in the Solomons ended in 1945. Why risk Fiji?".' Cut-price fares and accommodation were only a short-term solution to the problems posed by the coups, longer-term solutions required a complete reassessment of the way in which consumers perceived Fiji as a tourist destination (Burns 1995).

Role of the media

One of the major points to appreciate in understanding the relationship between political instability and its affect on tourism, is the role of the media. While government policy is important in regulating tourist flows and also influencing tourist visitation through the articulation of national government policies towards current or potential tourist destination regions, it is the media which will have the greatest influence on the creation of destination images in tourist generating regions (Hall and O'Sullivan 1995).

Books, magazines and newspapers have always had a substantial influence on images of destination areas. However, the telecommunications revolution of the late twentieth century has created a visual immediacy to image creation unmatched in human history. Thanks to satellites and cable links, events in destinations in countries and regions far away from the tourist generating regions can now be seen as they happen. The media acts as an image filter between the tourist destination and generating regions. Sometimes the filter will emphasise particular issues or events; at other times events may be ignored. Either way the media will be a major force in creating images of safety and political stability in the destination region. Indeed, it is the very potential for media coverage that provides some political groups with the rationale for attacks on tourists (Hall and O'Sullivan 1995), although fortunately this situation does not seem to have occurred in the South Pacific.

The media select particular representations and interpretations of places and events amid a plethora of potential representations in terms of time, content, and images. Therefore, it is the portrayal of political instability rather than political instability itself which becomes uppermost as a factor in tourist destination choice behaviour. For example, political instability can affect regional tourism as well as the particular destination in which the violence or unrest actually occurs. As Lea and Small (1988: 9) commented in relation to the effects of political violence on tourism in the region, 'the main lesson for South Pacific destinations is that trouble in one country means trouble for the region'. In 1985 the South Pacific nation of Vanuatu suffered as a result of the political unrest in neighbouring New Caledonia (Hall 1994b). In 1986 arrivals from Australia, the major source of international tourists, were the lowest for nine years. 'Unfortunately, as very little image building had been done there was confusion in many tourism source countries over whether Vanuatu was or was not a part of New Caledonia and Vanuatu's tourism industry suffered accordingly' (National Tourism Office of Vanuatu 1990: 3).

A more recent case of the affect of the media on tourist attitudes in tourism generating countries was the effect of the French Government's announcement in June 1995, that it would resume nuclear weapons testing at Mururoa Atoll in French Polynesia. The announcement not only led to strained political relations between the French Government and other South Pacific nations, but also led to fears that the weapons testing would affect tourist arrivals in terms of both perceived safety and a protest against the French actions. The tests were regarded as potentially affecting not only French Polynesia, and Tahiti in particular, but also other South Pacific nations in Visit South Pacific Year (see Chapter 17).

An official of the Tonga Visitors Bureau, Semisi Taumoepeau, argued that the French nuclear tests would threaten the Tongan economy which is heavily reliant on tourism, and the promotion of images of white sands, clear lagoons and palm trees. Tonga lies approximately 6000 kilometres west of Mururoa Atoll. However, as noted above, tourist decisions are often motivated by perceptions rather than by the reality of a situation. According to Taumoepeau:

> People have this mental picture of the South Pacific where they think Tonga is only a few yards away from Mururoa Atoll . . . It [the drop in tourism] could be as high as 30 per cent because most of our visitors are from America. Most Americans are not very good at geography and think that Tonga and Western Samoa are right next door to Mururoa Atoll.
>
> (Le Grand 1995: 15)

Tourism as an object of protest

Political protest is not only targeted at such activities as French nuclear testing. Tourism may also be the direct object of social and political opposition. In many destination areas around the world, local attitudes and opinions regarding tourism development are often ignored by government and tourism developers in their search for profit, foreign exchange and other perceived benefits of tourism. However, if local people are excluded from planning and decision-making processes and from their lands and resources, then their way of life will undoubtedly change, possibly resulting in resentment and negative social and environmental impacts. For example, following a change of ownership at the Anuha Island Resort in the Solomon Islands and a consequent series of actions which angered the customary landholders, 'The angered islanders dug holes in the airstrip, sent painted warriors to force guests off the islands, and closed down the resort in spite of a court ruling against them' (Minerbi 1992: 19).

Of all New Caledonia's industries, tourism was 'the most dramatically affected, and [was] almost destroyed, by political unrest' in 1984 (Connell 1987:

148). However, Melanesian opposition to tourism and its association with the French colonists had taken the form of direct action prior to the troubles of 1984. Land issues had led to the closure of several hotels owned by outside interests in rural areas in the early 1980s. According to Connell (1987: 147), 'on the Isle of Pines local Melanesians have been just as opposed to French "tourist merchants" as they were to Americans or Japanese, on the grounds that they all merely offered false promises of new riches but only alienated their land':

> How did we gain from tourism? . . . Where is the money that we were promised? Strangers have pocketed the millions that tourists have brought to our islands. And, as if that weren't enough, they have tried to impose Club Med on us. We would be invaded and submerged without the least real benefit.
>
> (Kohler 1984: 98 in Connell 1987: 147)

Protest against non-indigenous ownership has also occurred in Fiji. An Australian-owned resort in Fiji was forced to close temporarily in April 1995 after Fijian protesters occupied a 15-hectares island they wanted to reclaim for their village. Protestors burned tyres on the beach and asked the owner of the Paradise Island Resort on Bekana Island to leave following a breakdown in negotiations between the local villagers and the owner over the sale of the resort lease. The protestors' actions forced the cancellation of all bookings at the resort. The protesters' leader, Ratu Nacanieli Nava, claimed that the resort owner had breached the terms of the resort's 99-year lease, which is administered by the Native Land Trust Board, through inadequate lease payments and had not observed a requirement that Namoli villagers be given priority of employment at the resort.

The events in Fiji and the Solomon Islands highlight the extent to which tourism development in the Pacific needs to be able to understand the sociopolitical environment if it is to be successful. Across the Pacific, indigenous islanders are increasingly asserting their rights over their traditional resources. Native Hawaiians have protested about golf course and hotel development and their effect on agriculture, fisheries, and environmental quality (Hall 1994b). As Minerbi (1992: 9) observed, 'many resort communities imposed on local communities have run into oppositions at zoning and at shoreline management permit hearings, run into delays of years and have been stalled by law suits in the courts'. For example, a native Hawaiian group, the Hui Alanui o Makena, filed six lawsuits against a Japanese resort developer, Seibu Hawai'i, because they had cut public access to the coast at a section of a traditional trail which had been built around the island of Maui in the sixteenth century. After three years a settlement was reached which bound the corporation and its successors to keep the trail open and restore, at its own expense, public access. 'In addition Seibu contributed half a million dollars for a community based corporation to perpetuate Hawaiian culture and dedicated 3 acres of land for a living cultural centre' (Minerbi 1992: 52).

Undoubtedly, the political context of tourism development is regarded as being significant. However, probably one of the greatest challenges to tourism development will be the ability to translate Western models and frameworks of tourism planning into a South Pacific cultural and political context which has been traditionally dominated by the rule of 'big men', and more recently by Western educated elites (Sofield 1990). Indeed, it is possible that, over time, we will see the development of a distinctive South Pacific tourism planning framework which specifically incorporates indigenous political structures (see particularly Chapters 4, 7 and 15).

CONCLUSIONS

Politics is an important dimension of tourism development in the South Pacific. This chapter has concentrated on two main elements of tourism politics in the region, dependency and political instability. The nature of the current pattern of dependency in the South Pacific is a legacy of the region's colonial past. Nevertheless, the pattern of economic dependency has mixed economic and political blessings for the tourism dependent nations of the South Pacific. It may possibly be a blessing in the sense of providing a ready-made link to tourist generating regions and also the foreign capital needed to attract tourists from those regions. However, patterns of dependency may be extremely hard to break out of, particularly given the costs in developing tourism infrastructure and aviation connections for overseas markets.

Political stability has been highlighted as an extremely significant component of tourism in the region. Although the duration of political instability may be shortlived, the longer-term implications for tourism can last for many years, affecting the confidence not only of tourists, but also of potential investors in the tourism industry. Given the increasing potential for destination substitution in the highly competitive global tourism marketplace, many destination regions need to pay greater heed to the potential impact of political instability on the image of the destination. In the case of the Pacific Islands this may necessitate not only the development of crisis management strategies, but also greater attempts to market the region for its unique properties rather than compete with other sun, sand and surf destinations on cost alone.

REFERENCES

Brackenbury, M. (1995) *Managing the Perceptions and Realities of Physical Safety and Security in Tourism Destinations*, PATA Occasional Papers Series No. 13, San Francisco: Pacific Asia Travel Association.
Britton, S.G. (1982) 'The political economy of tourism in the Third World', *Annals of Tourism Research*, 9(3): 331–58.
—— (1983) *Tourism and Underdevelopment in Fiji*, Development Studies Centre Monograph No. 31, Canberra: Australian National University.
—— (1987) 'Tourism in Pacific island states, constraints and opportunities', in S. Britton

and W.C. Clarke (eds) *Ambiguous Alternative: Tourism in Small Developing Countries*, Suva: University of the South Pacific: 113–39.

Buckley, P.J. and Klemm, M. (1993) 'The decline of tourism in Northern Ireland', *Tourism Management*, June: 185–94.

Burns, P. (1995) 'Sustaining tourism under political adversity: The case of Fiji', in M.V. Conlin and T. Baum (eds) *Island Tourism: Management Principles and Practice*, Chichester: John Wiley, pp. 259–72.

Connell, J. (1987) *New Caledonia or Kanaky? The Political History of a French Colony*, Pacific Research Monograph No. 16, Canberra: National Centre for Development Studies, Australian National University.

Connell, J. (1988) *Sovereignty and Survival: Island Microstates in the Third World*, Research Monograph No. 3, Sydney: Department of Geography, University of Sydney.

Crick, M. (1989) 'Representations of international tourism in the social sciences: Sun, sex, sights, savings, and servility', *Annual Review of Anthropology*, 18: 307–44.

Erisman, H.M. (1983) 'Tourism and cultural dependency in the West Indies', *Annals of Tourism Research*, 10: 337–61.

Fiji Visitors' Bureau (1992) *A Statistical Report on Visitor Arrivals into Fiji, Calendar Year 1991*, Suva: Fiji Visitors Bureau.

Hall, C.M. (1994a) *Tourism and Politics: Policy, Power and Place*. Chichester: John Wiley.

—— (1994b) *Tourism in the Pacific: Development, Impacts and Markets*. South Melbourne: Longman Cheshire.

—— (1995) *Introduction to Tourism in Australia: Impacts, Planning and Development*, 2nd edn, Melbourne: Longman Cheshire.

Hall, C.M. and Jenkins, J. (1995) *Tourism and Public Policy*, London: Routledge.

Hall, C.M. and O'Sullivan, V. (1995) 'Tourism, political stability and violence', in A. Pizam (ed.) *Tourism and Violence*, Chichester: John Wiley, pp. 105–22.

Le Grand, C. (1995) 'Tonga fears explosions will damage tourist trade', *The Weekend Australian*, 17–18 June: 15.

Lea, J. and Small, J. (1988) 'Cyclones, riots and coups: Tourist industry responses in the South Pacific'. Paper presented at Frontiers in Australian Tourism Conference, Australian National University, Canberra, Australia, July.

Matthews, H.G. (1978) *International Tourism: A Social and Political Analysis*, Cambridge: Schenkman.

Minerbi, L. (1992) *Impacts of Tourism Development in Pacific Islands*, San Francisco: Greenpeace Pacific Campaign.

Nash, D. (1989) 'Tourism as a form of imperialism', in V. Smith (ed.) *Hosts and Guests: The Anthropology of Tourism*, 2nd edn, Philadelphia: University of Pennsylvania Press, pp. 37–52.

National Tourism Office of Vanuatu (1990) *A History of Tourism in Vanuatu: A Platform for Future Success*. Port Vila: National Tourism Office of Vanuatu.

Richter, L.K. (1989) *The Politics of Tourism in Asia*. Honolulu: University of Hawaii Press.

Richter, L.K. and Waugh, W.L., Jr. (1986) 'Terrorism and tourism as logical companions', *Tourism Management*, December: 230–8.

Sofield, T. (1990) 'The impact of tourism development on traditional sociocultural values in the South Pacific: Conflict, coexistence, and symbiosis', in M. Miller and J. Auyong (eds) *Proceedings of the 1990 Congress on Coastal and Marine Tourism*, Honolulu: National Coastal Research and Development Institute, pp. 49–66.

World Bank (1987) *Fiji. A Transition to Manufacturing*, Washington, DC: International Bank for Reconstruction and Development.

Chapter 7

Planning issues in Pacific tourism

Michael Fagence

INTRODUCTION

The frame of reference for this chapter has been the various development issues which are evident in the Pacific region as a consequence of the commitment to the application to tourism of the general principles of 'planning'. Almost inevitably, the interpretation placed upon the term 'tourism planning' has been broad, covering a number of different hierarchical levels, types and scales of tourism activity, and extending into the special areas of economic/social/cultural/environmental/land use and other related aspects of the general activity of 'planning'. In this respect 'tourism planning' is scarcely more than 'a specialised type of development planning' (Inskeep 1988: 360) in which the principal thrust is to achieve orderly development, to avoid or mitigate potentially undesirable consequences of tourism activity, and to achieve the systematic integration of tourism with all other aspects of the governance of a locality, region or nation (Gunn 1977; Mill and Morrison 1985; ESCAP forthcoming a). This broad scope is in evidence in the main sections of the chapter which consider some of the principal challenges to be faced in the region, and the means which are being drawn up to meet them.

In his advocacy of systematic tourism planning, Travis (1985) has articulated a hierarchical model of coherence in which planning at the local, regional and national levels is integrated through sets of objectives, concepts and operational procedures. A similar advocacy in systematic planning is evident in Gunn (1993), Inskeep (1989; 1991), Baud-Bovy and Lawson (1977) and others. Despite Moorehead's (1966) prognosis of internationalism in planning and practice being the inevitable outcome of the waves of ubiquitous international experts working in the Pacific region, there is little evidence of consistency in approach to tourism planning among the 21 island nations in the Pacific region. Even in the few cases in which national tourism strategies are in evidence there is little conspicuous hierarchical coherence in economic, environmental and especially spatial terms. There are cases of marketing strategies, and the 'set' of Tourism Council of the South Pacific (TCSP) studies of Solomon Islands (1990), Western Samoa (1992) and Tuvalu (1992) and the recently completed World

Tourism Organization/United Nations Development Program (WTO/UNDP) funded national strategy for Vanuatu (1995) may be exceptions to this generalisation. Apart from TCSP studies, most 'plans' have focused on marketing, human resource development, and economic strategy. This chapter seeks to address the often overlooked component of spatial planning.

Recent examinations of the status of tourism planning and development in the Pacific Island countries (such as Bjarnason for TCSP 1991; Sofield for Australian International Development Assistance Bureau (AIDAB) 1991; Craig-Smith and Fagence for Economic and Social Commission for Asia and the Pacific (ESCAP) 1992; and Muqbil for ESCAP 1995) have revealed the diversity of approaches and commitment to tourism planning. Across the region, the individuality and personality of 'the Pacific Way' is clearly in evidence in the diversity of scope, emphasis, content, focus and implementability. For some island countries there is no specific tourism plan; rather, tourism is incorporated (not necessarily integrated) as one sector in a general national economic strategy (Bjarnason 1991; Craig-Smith and Fagence 1994b). Kissling and Pearce (1990: 1) observed in their assessment of 'Destination South Pacific' that, while many island leaders acknowledge the potential significance of tourism activity, they 'are [not] prepared to accord promotion of tourism sufficiently high priority to ensure that it competes on even terms with other segments of local economies'. One serious debilitating consequence of this reduced profile accorded to tourism is that it may fail to attract funding for infrastructure or technical assistance from agencies such as the Asian Development Bank (Hanton 1995). This lack of commitment to a general tourism strategy is surprising when it is becoming evident that some island governments are considering developing a specialised ecotourism strategy (Fagence 1995). At a recent ESCAP-TCSP Workshop in Port Vila (June 1995) it was evident that many island governments remain sceptical about the benefits to be achieved from a commitment to a national tourism strategy; it seems the economic, environmental and social consequences are not considered to be conclusively positive.

Although there is an increasing awareness of the need for the systematic planning of tourism, and there is increasing evidence of commitment in many internationally funded studies, workshops, programmes, plans and reports, it is becoming apparent that there is little consistency in approach across the Pacific region, not least because the approach adopted and the process pursued is dependent on the professional idiosyncrasies of the consultants. This lack of consistency may be due to the variations in the briefs to which the consultants work. Some consistency may be derived from the experience of the TCSP studies, the recent innovative approach adopted for Vanuatu, the guidelines produced by ESCAP (1990, and forthcoming a), and the content and focus of the Pacific Island Development Program (PIDP) studies (1990). Without reasonable consistency in approach, process and method, any thought of mounting a region-wide strategy will be frustrated (Craig-Smith and Fagence, 1992). One of the elements often overlooked in the strategy formulation is that of spatial planning.

As tourism activities take place in space and are space-demanding it should be inevitable that the spatial (or geographical) element of the plan would receive due consideration. This is the focus of this chapter.

Before addressing the possible parameters of spatial planning for tourism in the special context of the Pacific Islands it is appropriate to consider some of the principal challenges that have to be faced. It will be the spatial component of these challenges which will be considered.

PRINCIPAL CHALLENGES

The principal challenges which may be encountered in the preparation of a distinctive tourism plan in the context of the Pacific Island countries have been discussed in various sources (such as Cole and Parry 1986; Brookfield and Ward 1988; Fairbairn *et al.* 1991; Hall 1994). The particular challenges in spatial planning have received less specific attention (see Craig-Smith and Fagence 1992; Fagence and Craig-Smith 1993). From the various commentaries readily accessible there is some concurrence that the principal challenges to be faced include the following:

- identity and image
- accessibility and location
- foreign investment
- colonial legacy and independence
- resource base (for tourism)
- infrastructure system capacity
- land tenure systems.

Identity and image

In a commentary on the political economy of tourism in developing countries, Britton (1982: 331) expected these countries to become 'enmeshed in a global system over which [they] have little control'. One aspect of this globalisation is a generalisation of identity in that travellers from the major metropolitan source markets of North America and Europe have an expectation that the Pacific region has a common culture based on tropical settings of the sun, sand, surf, coral reefs and palm trees. In some of the volcanic islands this extends to rainforests, waterfalls, mountainous scenery and volcanoes. To this exotic physical image could be added the mystery of the Polynesian, Melanesian and Micronesian cultures. This romantic and exotic image has been referred to as the 'tourist paradise' (Hall 1994) and 'the stuff of which many tourist dreams are made' (EIU 1989: 71). In recent years, some island countries have added to their spectrum of attractions adventure tours, diving, exploring relics of early indigenous occupancy and of the Second World War, and the specialist naturalist activities of ornithology and lepidoptery.

The image of affordable exotica is secure. However, a number of major problems are present. First, the marketing campaigns of 'the South Pacific Village', as waged by TCSP, tend to generalise the image, masking the subtle differences between independent countries. This means that the popularised exotic image becomes closely identified with the four 'honey pots' of Guam, Hawai'i, Saipan and Tahiti, while the 'lesser lights' have their distinctiveness dissolved into the generalised image. This is a marketing and promotion matter. Of more concern to the focus of planning adopted in this chapter is a series of physical circumstances. It may be that the sustainability of this exotic image is put at risk by high concentrations of tourists, especially where degradation of the environment occurs through poor behaviours in sensitive areas and through problems of waste disposal. The opening up of new niche markets may put at risk the sustainability of quality of heritage relics and sites and natural fauna and flora habitats. An ongoing challenge to planning, especially if the focus of the attractiveness of a destination changes, is to determine, monitor and then manage carrying capacity so that the separate identity of island countries and their distinctive images are preserved (Fagence 1995).

Location and accessibility

In other chapters reference has been made to the significance of the geographical location of the island countries in the Pacific basin and the problems of access, especially the difficulties of movement within the region. Some of the mystique of the tourism destination is derived from the relative remoteness and small scale of the Pacific Islands (Page 1996). Despite these attractions, as by-products of image and identity, many commentators (such as Farrell 1985; Kissling 1990; ANZ McCaughan 1993) have referenced the problems of air communication within the region, pointing out particularly the low volumes of traffic, the dispersed nature of the destinations, and especially the changes to airline policy which are made in boardrooms outside the region. Location and size of the island countries are immutable. However, levels of accessibility and route connections are amenable to planned action. Faktaufon (1995) has commented on the inextricable link of tourism and air transport in the region. In his view, regional airlines should pursue aggressive commercial policies to fit airline routes, capacities and schedules to the needs of tourism destinations, rather than pursue policies which are driven by social (returning resident) policies. This is a critical mass issue (Craig-Smith and Fagence 1994b). To bring into harmonious balance air routes, capacities, schedules, and airport infrastructure with tourism infrastructure requires the development of compatible policies. The planning challenges are:

• to accept the 'hub and spoke' principles of air traffic in the region and to develop a regional tourism strategy which recognises and supports it;
• to create critical mass nodes of tourism infrastructure (accommodation,

attractions, services) which can be adequately serviced by the preferred air routes;

- to integrate air route and airport planning with tourism planning;
- to pre-plan new tourism development which can easily improve the viability of the dominant air routes.

As the 1994 South Pacific Forum resolved, air routes in the Pacific region need to be complementary and cooperative rather than competitive. Too many airline failures and international carrier withdrawals from the region will seriously limit accessibility to and within the region, thereby disrupting balance between servicing capacity and tourism destination attraction.

Foreign investment and aid

The relevance of these matters to tourism planning has been discussed generally in Fagence and Craig-Smith (1994), and particularly in so far as they have an impact on the life-cycle of tourism development and the creation of tourism critical mass (Craig-Smith and Fagence 1994a). It is recognised that where domestic resources are inadequate to finance tourism development, foreign investment and aid would be needed as the catalyst for tourism activity and development. In planning terms, there is advantage to be gained in that investment and aid is directed at activity which could 'harmonise with local circumstances to achieve critical mass, to integrate enclaves of development, to optimise infrastructure services and networks, and to create a balanced structure of tourism activity' (Fagence and Craig-Smith 1994: 859). Any tendency to generalise forms of tourism development across the region at the whim of entrepreneurial agencies and investors would need to be monitored carefully, not least to protect the individuality of each island country. A particular concern of tourism planning is the need to achieve compatibility of capacities of transport, accommodation and services, and attractions – the critical mass – within capacity thresholds that do not bring about the deterioration of the quality of the natural environment and indigenous culture which has been the initial generator of visitor interest.

There are three major problems for planning. The first is that tourism activity becomes so successful that it comes to dominate economic strategy making with little regard for establishing upper limits. This may be so where foreign investment seeks to capitalise on attractive and successful destinations with typical model 'islander' design. The second is that aid for infrastructure development may not be able to keep pace with free enterprise development, unless the national governments give tourism a high profile in the national strategy in funding negotiations with agencies such as the Asian Development Bank (Hanton 1995). Third is that national incentive programmes need to be devised so as not to frustrate the achievement of appropriate projects (TCSP 1992).

The colonial legacy and independence

The remnants of the colonial legacies across the region provide other challenges and opportunities for tourism. Moorehead's (1966) prognosis that the waves of European and other exogenous influences would accelerate and then extend a process of internationalisation in heritage content and institutional process is clearly manifest across the region. The colonial legacy is evident in the built environment, in isolated settings and in distinct precincts in some of the major towns. These remnants are providing significant attractions to the new forms of special interest tourism. Of relatively more recent origin are the relics of the Second World War activity in the region, providing a focus of interest to particular visitor groups and a magnet for some diving destinations. There is the emotional linkage of some European countries with certain Pacific islands, and this is manifest in the visitor profiles (Fagence 1992), this link also exists in the sources of economic assistance through aid and technical advice (Fairbairn 1991). Heritage resources provide both an opportunity and challenge to tourism planning, especially in the creation of the tourism master plans which include site or precinct development levels of details.

Another aspect of the colonial legacy is the perpetuation or adaptation of the institutional processes and styles. Evidence of former British and French colonial administration styles are pervasive, despite widespread national independence. In some cases the former colonial systems and the recent independent systems have not fused too well. For tourism planning, the increasing emphasis on nationalism has provided an additional tourism-relevant opportunity with the requirement that sacred sites and places of significance to the indigenous communities are incorporated in the spatial strategy. They should also be included in any new thrusts of special interest tourism and become focal points in strategies which increase indigenous participation in tourism activity and development. It may well be that this is the level at which the individuality of each island country can be expressed best in the tourism strategy. Fiji, Western Samoa, Tonga and the Solomon Islands in particular are raising the profile of indigenous culture in their tourism strategies.

Resource base for tourism

It is the exotic base which provides the fundamental attraction for tourism in the Pacific Islands. The principal tasks for tourism planning include pursuing strategies to achieve the sustainability of those resources and to 'package ' them so that they contribute to the 'South Seas' image which is expected by tourists. This is so far both natural and cultural resources. Various typologies of tourism resources have been developed (e.g. Gunn 1993), but the range in most Pacific island countries is often restricted (except in the four 'honey pots' – Guam, Saipan, Fiji and Hawai'i) and is focused particularly on the features which contribute to the general image of the region. As the range of experiences being sought by tourists is expanding, particularly moving into new areas of adventure tourism and what is referred to as 'secondary tourism' (King 1992), there is an increasing need of vigilance in tourism planning.

The potential for a number of conflicts increases as the volume of tourist traffic and its penetration into environmentally and culturally sensitive areas increases. Environmental, cultural and social sensitivity is of growing concern, particularly in those circumstances where the behaviour of tourists is not respectful of the resources. The potential destruction of the very resources which provide the attractiveness rationale has become a matter of increasing concern, progressing beyond the focus of particular cases to the general cautions in recent international conferences in Rio de Janerio (1992) and Barbados (1994). In particular, the Barbados Global Conference on *Sustainable Development of Small Island Developing States* drew attention to the likelihood that without the appropriate planning and management tourism could lead to the degradation of the environment, especially in coastal zones and unspoilt island areas, and to the disruption of indigenous culture and economic sectors such as indigenous subsistence agriculture. It has yet to be recognised that the mere availability of the requisite resources may not be sufficient to sustain a viable tourism industry. The basic requirement is for the resources to be incorporated into comprehensive land use and economic activity plans after careful assessment of tourism needs and the consequential impacts. As the international meetings recorded, it is comprehensive and integrated planning that is the key (ECSAP forthcoming a).

Infrastructure

The infrastructure issues in the Pacific region are those common to most developing countries: the adequacy of a support infrastructure of 'hardware' (such as roads, utility services, buildings, terminals) and 'software' (such as commercial services, security and safety, health, education and human resources and institutional processes). There are differences in performance in infrastructure support across the region, due in part to the attentiveness and efficiency of pre-independence administration, and in part to the commitment of any administration to infrastructure development. The geography of most island countries, composed as they are of many islands and island groups, is a serious impediment to cohesive infrastructure planning. This is aggravated by the differences in population levels and economic potential.

It has been asserted that the calibre of the infrastructure systems is of 'paramount importance' to successful tourism (McIntosh and Goeldner 1992), and a determinant of critical mass (Craig-Smith and Fagence 1994b) in the potential life-cycle development of a resort area. For tourism destinations to be continuously successful, the infrastructure services of water supply, sewerage disposal, power supply, electronic communications, drainage, road systems and networks, airports and harbours need to be at a level of proficiency at least commensurate with the standards expected by potential tourists in their respective metropolitan centres. It is not only physical availability of the system, but the quality of that system which is important as a planning issue. The novelty of inferior, inadequate and inconsistent systems has little duration for the international tourist who will approach the chosen exotic destination with an expectation that the standards of their 'ecological bubble' will be present. Some countries have recognised the need to ensure the provision of infrastructure services before the development of the facilities of attractions and accommodation can be entertained; for example, one of Fiji's distinct advantages in the region is its commitment to infrastructure development to support its tourism industry. The challenge for planning is to integrate the infrastructure with tourism development, to use infrastructure as the catalyst to attract other forms of development, and to promote tourism-related infrastructure in the profile of the national development strategy to achieve a broad scope of economic and social improvement.

Land tenure systems

One of the most difficult problems encountered by tourism investors and entrepreneurs in the Pacific Islands is the system of customary land ownership. It is a multi-faceted sociocultural, political and economic issue (Crocombe 1986; Acquaye 1987). In many island countries there are complicated land ownership traditions in which land is owned communally rather than by individuals, and in which land is held in trust to be used to sustain a community group (or tribe) rather than a commodity to be traded. This is a circumstance which may act as a constraint on the free-form creation of a conventional form of land use strategy for tourism. Development can take place in the three cases: on publicly owned land (often a legacy of colonial administration), on the small allotments of privately owned land (also, in part, a legacy of colonial periods), or by negotiation on communally owned land through a lease. Often, the most extensive and attractive tracts for tourism development purposes are communally owned, and there are recorded cases where appropriate forms of development have been impeded because the customary owners are not convinced that their land should be used for tourism.

For the purposes of tourism planning and development the issue of land tenure continues to be vexatious, not least in the difficulty of negotiation between potential developers and either the land owners directly or through native land trust boards. These negotiations pose one more potential delay in the decision-making process. Land is held to be such a precious commodity by indigenous people that there can be little certainty that any tourism land use strategy can be implemented fully. This is particularly true if a whole community decides to opt out of any form of development; if the demands made upon the developer threatened the viability of the project; or, worst still, if after a developer has commenced some members of the community decide to renege on the deal and embark in a process of destruction. The Pacific region is littered with examples of abandoned projects. The ideal situation occurs where the developer is able to conclude negotiations with the communal land owners such that the land owners benefit through employment opportunities and realistic returns from the developer's profits. Fiji has some examples of successful ventures of this kind. One further aspect of this matter is worthy of comment. There is an increasing realisation by national governments that niche markets of special interest tourism may be best serviced if the accommodation, tour operation and interpretation facilities are operated by indigenous groups in their own communal territory.

The issue of land tenure in Pacific island countries is contentious, and is a matter raised regularly at international meetings in the region. Certainly, this appears to be one of the most intractable problems and challenges faced in tourism planning not least because it engenders uncertainty about the successful achievement of the objectives and the spatial configurations of any formal tourism plan or strategy.

FACING THE CHALLENGES

Various institutional mechanisms have been tried by the Pacific island countries acting independently or in one or other forms of regional cooperation to meet the challenges described in the previous section. In addition, international organisations have participated in different degrees to provide technical advice and assistance, forums for discussion, and in some cases direct funding to Pacific island countries. Some island countries have forged ahead with their comprehensive tourism strategy, most often funded (and in some cases undertaken) by agencies such as TCSP, WTO, ESCAP, UNDP and others. This section reviews the various mechanisms which have been devised and put in place.

As Jenkins and Henry have observed (1982: 519), 'in developing countries, limitations inherent in the private sector require government to take an operational role in the tourism industry'. The entrepreneurial role, not always appreciated and welcomed by the industry, is in addition to the conventional role of the government pursued 'in the public interest' and at the levels of policy making and decision making about particular forms of tourism development. There is not a common pattern across the region as is evident in the descriptions of patterns of organisations and their responsibilities provided, for example by Arase (1988), Elak (1991), Harris (1991), Woods (1991) and Yahuda (1988). Studies of some of the Pacific island countries by PIDP (1990) drew attention to the difficulties of tourism planning and organisation across the region (with reference to particular case studies), and the matter was highlighted in the report to ESCAP by Craig-Smith and Fagence (1992).

In this section reference will be made to:

• the various commitments to tourism strategies in some Pacific island countries;

- the impact of international agencies and assistance programmes;
- regional cooperation.

Commitment to national strategies

As noted in the previous section, tourism planning in the Pacific region has not achieved consistency and coherence. In some cases this is due to Pacific island governments neglecting to give official recognition to the potential advantages of tourism development *per se* and a failure to recognise the advantages of coordination, cooperation and coherence both within any island country and across the region. Some of the issues examined previously may not be capable of solution on a country-by-country basis. Two comments made at a regional seminar in Suva in 1991 highlighted the need for integrated tourism planning at two levels – national, regional/international:

> in many ways the future of tourism in the individual countries of the Pacific is bound up with the future of tourism in others . . . given the common interest, it must be greatly to our advantage to present a common front to the world.
> (Kamikamica 1991: 11)

> [tourism] requires an integrated institutional and planning framework.
> (Yacoumis 1991: 7)

There has been a tendency for most island countries to pursue strong marketing initiatives and strategies, a commitment which has been supported by TCSP with its general 'South Pacific Village' promotional strategy and its more recent 'Visit South Pacific Year' programme. While promotion has been pursued with some vigour, less evident has been the conspicuous success of tourism planning practice (Craig-Smith and Fagence 1994b). There is a wave of enthusiasm for the production of national tourism strategies, although the production process often seems to take much longer than expected. Even for those countries with adopted strategy, there is often more commitment in rhetoric than in substance. A few examples of the diversity of circumstances may explain the region-wide dilemma.

Island nations, such as Tonga and Fiji, have conspicuous and separate tourism policies within the structures of their national development strategies (in some cases supported by special statutory provisions, such as the Tonga Tourism Act, 1976). Others, such as Kiribati and the Marshall Islands, have incorporated tourism as integral elements in broadly based economic development plans. In the case of Kiribati two ministries have responsibility for tourism matters with coordination being effected through the Tourism Advisory Committee. For the Federated States of Micronesia (FSM) national tourism development policies have been merged into the current National Development Plan (NDP). Another 'model' of tourism policy-making operates in the Commonwealth of the Northern Mariana Islands (CMNI) where the principal administrative body is the

Mariana Visitors Bureau (MVB). This agency is untypical of visitors bureaux in general in that the functions assigned to it include research, promotion, regulation, supervision of tourism enterprises, development of tourism facilities, tourism manpower development and the formulation of the comprehensive tourism development plan. These examples do little more than provide evidence of the diversity prevalent in the region. They also are indicative of the difficulty in determining which agency or ministry is 'really' responsible for directing tourism policy and planning. This confusion is exacerbated by what may be described as political and professional 'turf battles' in which agencies of even strong-minded individuals (politicians or bureaucrats) strive to preserve their operational 'territory'. Thus, in the very creation of an institutional framework the previously considered problems become enmeshed in another set of problems.

The passage of time is beginning to provide opportunities for some of the institutional problems to be overcome. For example, Bjarnason (1991) reported that the national development plan of Tuvalu (1987–91) failed to mention tourism; however, in the following year TCSP produced a tourism strategy for Tuvalu. In contrast, Fiji, PNG and Tonga have long-standing commitments to tourism development as part of their respective national economic development strategies. Until the early 1990s, the national development plan for Kiribati omitted specific reference to tourism in its principal set of objectives, policies and strategies. A similar case existed in the Solomon Islands until the production of the TCSP plan (1992), although it is interesting to note that the Western Provinces of Solomon's listed tourism as a matter of policy significance in its separate strategy. Western Samoa has accorded tourism its own set of tourism-specific objectives. Some of these matters are being re-addressed (see the destination case studies later in this book), especially with the new scope of plans as evidenced by the recently released national tourism development for Vanuatu (McVey 1995).

Even so, the differential level of commitment to and performance in tourism planning, especially in the revelation of the principles and objectives to be adopted, is evident in the lack of coherence and consistency in the structure and content of those plans which exist. The 'plans' prepared for some island nations in the 1970s were essentially marketing strategies. By the late 1980s there was an increasing realisation that tourism plans should incorporate responses to the concerns of environmental and social impact, matters of land tenure and ownership, and the challenge that 'even within a tourist region only certain areas are absolutely necessary for tourist development' (Baud-Bovy and Lawson 1977: 181). In their studies of ten Pacific island nations PIDP (1990) proposed a basic structure for national tourism plans. However, the reality of the situation in the different case studies forced departures from the 'model' framework, reflecting what were considered to be the crucial issues. For example, in the Kiribati exercise there was a strong focus on social and economic safeguards, and for the Solomon Islands an emphasis was on rendering tourism development more

appropriate to indigenous circumstances: the creation of appropriate planning and implementation processes was considered important for the Cook Islands and the FSM. The outcomes of the PIDP studies have been uneven, with some initiatives being carried forward into the preparation of a tourism policy and plan (as in the case of Solomon Islands), others being incorporated into nationally generated strategies of various types (as in the case of the Cook Islands), and still others awaiting serious attention and commitment.

A degree of consistency is apparent in the plans prepared by TCSP to a standardised framework (Bjarnason 1991) which is capable of manipulation to suit the circumstances of each special case. The plans prepared according to this framework so far have been for the Solomon Islands (1990), Western Samoa (1992) and Tuvalu (1992). There is another 'set' to be undertaken under current funding of TCSP through the Pacific Regional Tourism Development Program (PRTDP). If there is consistency between these two sets a 'model' framework could become established, which might provide the basis for regional coordination across the Pacific. There is a tendency for the plans for tourism development in the region to appear largely restrained; in terms of spatial or physical strategy there are recommendations for (or expectations of) conspicuous concentrations of tourism development near international airports, in enclaves at the coast or in major towns, or in isolated sites in areas of spectacular natural attractions. Such concentrations reflect the adoption of industry pragmatism rather than efficient strategic tourism planning (Gunn 1977). It is the evidence of the domination of pragmatism over strategic planning which has prompted some regional NGOs (such as TCSP, ESCAP, SPREP) to promote workshops and conferences in the region. At these the need to pursue ecologically and culturally sustainable tourism development have received priority consideration (see, for example, ESCAP forthcoming b, and the strategy reference documents of SPREP and TCSP). Another tool in this domain has become the recommended guidelines (ESCAP 1990, forthcoming a).

Pacific Regional Tourism Development Programme

The former colonial associations with countries in the region are perpetuated, if disguised, through various forms of aid and technical assistance. In a general case, European countries and the US are involved in various schemes of bilateral and multi-cultural aid and technical assistance for countries in the African, Asian, Caribbean and Pacific regions. These linkages sometimes continue previous colonial associations, even following independence; other linkages are developed out of strategic mutual advantage (see Chapter 11). The European Union has created for itself an influential role in providing assistance of various kinds to developing countries, with the most significant output being through the development cooperation policy of the Lomé Convention. Through the Lomé Convention of rolling five-year programmes, the Union provides grants and 'soft loans' (through European Development Fund (EDF)), and the European

Investment Bank (EIB) provides loans for programmes of national or regional development, including tourism. Tourism was scarcely noted in the first two of the Lomé Conventions (1975–80, 1981–6); however, by the Third Convention, tourism was incorporated as a conspicuous component of cooperative assistance programmes (Lee 1987a). In order to receive European Union funding or assistance any applicant country is required to reveal its recent performance in tourism activity (such as tourism exchange earnings, employment, contributions to economic prosperity and diversification, its integration with other economic sectors, the maintenance of indigenous crafts and skills, and marketing). In addition, reflecting the worldwide conservationist ethic, dependent countries are required to respond to questions concerning proposals to identify and maintain tourism assets of the cultural and natural heritage, and to contribute to ecologically sustainable development.

An important force in the region, the work programme of which is facilitated in part by financial assistance from EU under the PRTDP, is the Tourism Council of the South Pacific (TCSP). Initially established in 1983 as an informal association of national tourism organisations in the region of the South Pacific, the TCSP was promoted as a suitable vehicle for coordinating tourism policy. The first programme (PRTDP) of technical and development assistance was supported under the Lomé II Convention and included the establishment of the TCSP Secretariat (Suva, Fiji). Member countries (American Samoa, Cook Islands, Fiji, Kiribati, Niue, PNG, Solomon Islands, French Polynesia, Tonga, Tuvalu, Vanuatu, Western Samoa and FSM) contribute to some of the funding needs of TCSP. However, the bulk of the financial support is through the PRTDP (from EU), with other aid donors such as Australia and New Zealand. (Note that of the TCSP member countries only eight are Pacific ACP countries recognised by the Lomé Convention for the purpose of aid and technical assistance: Fiji, Kiribati, PNG, Solomon Islands, Tonga, Tuvalu, Vanuatu, Western Samoa.) The 'power of the purse' provides the EU with considerable influence on the programmes which are supportable through PRTDP (Lee 1987a, b), and the emphasis which is appropriate, such as conservation, guidelines for environmental protection, measures to protect indigenous cultures and lifestyles, a distinctive marketing strategy, and cost-efficient research and data collection. The emphasis in the current phase of funding (which extends to the end of 1997) has been on marketing and promotion, not least because the EU considers that regional funding should focus on those matters which benefit the region as a whole, and that product development is essentially a matter for national programmes of assistance (Tuinabua 1995). Recent indications are that EU funding is unlikely to continue in 1998 (Islands Business Pacific 1995). If this is so, new partnership and funding arrangements will become necessary, forcing new interpretations of regional cooperation.

Regional cooperation

One of the particular challenges being faced in the region is that of securing region-wide cooperation in tourism policy development. Evidence from regional seminars suggests there is increasing recognition that cooperative action is needed to conserve natural resources, to increase the sustainability level of local customs and traditions, to maintain international attention, to create the circumstances for viable inter-country air transport, and to achieve necessary infrastructure funding. However, segmented national interests intrude, perhaps derived from a suspicion that participants in cooperative tourism may not benefit equally (PIDP 1990).

Expert group meetings, forums, and workshops have been held in the Pacific region under the auspices and direction of UN-ECSAP, SPREP, TCSP, WTO, UNDP – singly and in various combinations – to probe the potential for regional cooperation in, for example, investment and economic cooperation (Tokyo 1993), promotion of sustainable tourism development (Suva 1991), integrated tourism planning (Port Villa 1995), human resource development and training (Bangkok 1993), and environmental management (Bali 1993). In the sensitive matter of aviation in the region, efforts have been made at political, administrative and operator levels to achieve cooperation between island countries in the provision of services (Kissling 1990), while the Association of South Pacific Airlines (ASPA) has promoted the integration of tourism and aviation policy across the region (Faktaufon 1995). There is evidence of an increasing commitment within the region to cooperation and the pursuit of common practices, especially in respect of information and data collection and sharing, technical assistance, facilitation procedures, human resource development and training and inter-agency operations. The challenge of cooperation is being faced, but the suitability of agency structures and political commitment may frustrate the good intentions (Fagence forthcoming). Policy and planning cooperation and coordination may become the important issue of the 1990s as the region attempts to at least maintain share of international tourism traffic, and as it attempts to meet the challenges of economic and ecological sustainability (Craig-Smith and Fagence 1992).

TOURISM PLANNING – THE PARADIGM DILEMMA

The performance of tourism planning in the Pacific region is disparate (Fletcher and Snee 1989; Craig-Smith and Fagence 1994a). The reasons for this include the evident preference for planning to be conducted in a manner described by Lea (1988: 78) as according to the 'western notions of running an efficient industry', but with distortions which embrace the equally evident preferences for pragmatism, opportunism and stereotype solutions. In addition, as this chapter has shown, there are peculiar circumstances which impede the development of a consistent approach across the region – even if such consistency was to be considered desirable. A further set of impediments to an even quality of performance in tourism planning is the plethora of overlapping agencies and interests which become confused in the maelstrom of nationalistic parochialism (EIU 1989). The concept of harmony which is reflected in the marketing strategy of TCSP – the 'South Pacific Village' – and which is embodied in the notion of the 'Pacific Way' is not evident in tourism planning.

There is a further complication in respect of tourism planning in the region. This has been discussed in Fagence and Craig-Smith (1993) in the examination of the challenges the circumstances in the Pacific region pose to orthodox planning theory, especially in the use of spatial models. The basic argument is that the current orthodox is composed of a set of conventional stereotypical solutions which have pragmatic appeal but which have some incapacity to reflect the special circumstances of the region. It is the peculiarity of the geographical circumstances of each island microstate which demands special treatment on a case-by-case basis (Craig-Smith and Fagence 1992: para. 153). Although the PIDP summary report (1990) recommended the adoption of planning orthodoxy, it acknowledged that each island country should emphasise its uniqueness and its niche opportunities. As Gunn (1988: 281) has claimed, 'stereotyping is an easy trap for tourism planners', and a trap which may impede the optimal realisation of tourism potential. Recent attempts by island countries to create ecotourism strategies out of sequence with the formulation of a comprehensive tourism strategy provide evidence of the tendency towards opportunism (Fagence 1995). It has been claimed that the general conduct of tourism planning is fashioned by the interaction of compelling and at times competing forces. The differential interaction of these forces, and their composition at any one time created the prevailing paradigm of orthodoxy. As can be expected from evolutionary processes, paradigm change occurs as the outcome of challenge to conventional theory and practice in which the current prospectus is found to be inadequate to meet the needs of different geographical, environmental, sociocultural, political and economic circumstances (Kuhn 1970). To be universally appropriate, even a current orthodox paradigm should be composed of a set of principles rather than a set of stereotype solutions. In the geographical context of the Pacific region there is evidence that the 'tried and trusted' tourism planning strategies and solutions used in other geographical circumstances (such as the developed nations of Europe and North America) are being introduced into the region of Pacific micro states with little conspicuous translation or modification to fit local circumstances (Fagence 1992).

The potential for the mismatch of paradigms in the context of the Pacific region has been presented in Fagence and Craig-Smith (1994), and the general points of orthodoxy have been argued in Fagence (1990, 1991, 1995). In particular, and in the context of pursuing strategies of sustainable tourism, it is necessary for tourism planning in the region to respond intelligently to the issues canvassed in this chapter and throughout this book. The region has special attributes, and it is variegated rather than general in its attribute types and distributions. It is in need of tourism planning approaches which do more than repair 'the shallow simplicity of past approaches' and which are, instead, based on 'innovation and creativity' (Gunn 1988: 278). Gunn and others have been critical of the adoption of tourism planning orthodoxy (even if those precise terms have not been used), especially when it has been derived by convenience of administration, by the routine application of policies and development standards, by the mere evidence of project success elsewhere, by the fear of failure with innovation, and by the failure to accurately determine the planning issue or problem or opportunity.

As in so-many cases, Gunn's remarks are apposite: 'the strength of tourism lies in how well the spatial assets of an area are planned and developed' (1988: 273). In the case of the Pacific island microstates the challenge to spatial and conceptual orthodoxy is crucial. If the region is to maximise its tourism potential it needs its special paradigm, a Pacific orthodoxy which will enable it to develop its idiosyncrasies rather than facilitate the re-deployment of an orthodoxy developed in other parts if the world where the particular circumstances of this region do not exist. The tendency towards pragmatism, opportunism and the adoption of stereotypical solutions is well-entrenched; but, there is more than a smidgen of concern that 'spatial orthodoxy may not service the South Pacific well' (Fagence and Craig-Smith 1993: 147).

REFERENCES

Acquaye, E. (1987) *Land Tenure and Rural Productivity in the Pacific Islands*, Suva: University of the South Pacific.

ANZ McCaughan (1993) *Aviation Industry Research Report: Vol. 1, Tourism in the Asia/Pacific Region*, Melbourne: ANZ McCaughan.

Arase, D. (1988) 'Pacific economic co-operation: Problems and prospects', *The Pacific Review*, 1(2): 128–44.

Baud-Bovy, M. and Lawson, F. (1977) *Tourism and Recreational Development*, London: Architectural Press.

Bjarnason, J. (1991) 'Tourism and national development planning.' Unpublished paper to TCSP Regional Conference on Tourism and National Development Planning in the South Pacific, Suva, November.

Britton, S. (1982) 'Political economy of tourism in the Third World', *Annals of Tourism Research*, 9(3): 331–58.

Brookfield, M. and Ward, R. (1988) *New Directions in the South Pacific*, Canberra: Academy of Social Sciences.

Cole, R. and Parry, T. (1986) *Selected Issues in Pacific Island Development*, Canberra: National Centre for Development Studies, Australian National University.

Craig-Smith, S. and Fagence, M. (1992) *Sustainable Tourism Development in Pacific Island Nations*, Lawes, Department of Business Studies, Gatton College, University of Queensland.

—— (1994a) 'A critique of tourism planning in the Pacific', in C. Cooper and A. Lockwood (eds) *Progress in Tourism, Recreation and Hospitality Management, Vol. 6* Chichister: John Wiley, pp. 92–110.

—— (1994b) 'Factors affecting tourism development in Pacific island nations', *ESCAP Tourism Review*, 13: 237–54.

Crocombe, R. (1986) *Land Tenure in the Pacific*, rev. edn, Suva: University of the South Pacific.

Economist Intelligence Unit (1989) 'The Pacific Islands', *EIU International Tourism Reports*, 4: 70–99.

Elak, A. (1991) 'The challenge of Asian-Pacific economic cooperation', *The Pacific Review*, 4(4): 322–32.

ESCAP (1990) *Guidelines for the Production of a Standard Tourism Paper*, New York: United Nations.

—— (1993) *Sustainable Tourism Development in Pacific Island Countries*, New York: United Nations.

—— (forthcoming a) *Guidelines on Integrated Planning and Tourism in Pacific Island Countries*, New York: United Nations.

—— (forthcoming b) *Guidelines on Environmentally Sound Development of Coastal Tourism*, New York: United Nations.

Fagence, M. (1990) 'Geographically referenced planning strategies', *Journal of Environmental Management*, 3(1): 1–18.

—— (1991) 'Geographic referencing of public policies in tourism', *Revue de Tourisme*, 3(3): 8–19.

—— (1992) 'The legacy of Europe in the Pacific region', *Proceedings, Tourism in Europe Conference*, Durham: Centre for Tourism Studies, F1–11.

—— (1995) 'Ecotourism and Pacific Island Nations: Towards a realistic interpretation of feasibility', *Cahiers du Tourisme*, Series C, No. 189.

—— (forthcoming) 'Regional cooperation in tourism in the Asia-Pacific region', *Annals of Tourism Research*.

Fagence, M. and Craig-Smith, S. (1993) 'Challenge to orthodoxy', in *Building a Research Base in Tourism*, Canberra: Bureau of Tourism Research, pp. 141–9.

—— (1994) 'Foreign investment and technical cooperation needs in the Pacific region', *Annals of Tourism Research*, 21(4): 858–60.

Fairbairn, T. (ed.) (1991) *The Pacific Islands: Politics, Economics and International Relations*, Honolulu: East-West Centre, University of Hawaii.

Faktaufon, G. (1995) 'Aviation issues for expansion of tourism in Pacific island countries.' Unpublished paper to ECSAP workshop, Port Vila, Vanuatu, June.

Farrell, B. (1985) 'South Pacific tourism in the mid-1980s', *Tourism Management*, 6(1): 55–60.

Fletcher, J. and Snee, H. (1989) 'Tourism in the South Pacific Islands', in C. Cooper (ed.) *Progress in Tourism, Recreation and Hospitality Management*, Vol. 1, London: Belhaven, pp. 114–24.

Gunn, C. (1977) 'Industry pragmatism v. tourism planning', *Leisure Sciences*, 1(1): 85–94.

—— (1988) *Tourism Planning*, 2nd edn, Philadelphia: Taylor and Francis.

—— (1993) *Tourism Planning*, 3rd edn, Philadelphia: Taylor and Francis.

Hall, C.M. (1994) *Tourism in the Pacific Rim: Impacts, Planning and Markets*, Melbourne: Longman Cheshire.

Hanton, P. (1995) 'ADB's economic and technical cooperation in tourism development.' Unpublished paper to ESCAP workshop, Port Vila, Vanuatu, June.

Harris, S. (1991) 'Varieties of Pacific economic co-operation', *The Pacific Review*, 4(4): 301–11.

Inskeep, E. (1989) 'Tourism planning', *American Planning Association Journal*, 54(3): 360–72.

—— (1991) *Tourism Planning*, New York: Van Nostrand Reinhold.

Islands Business Pacific (1995) 'The Tourism Council of the South Pacific must carry on', *Islands Business Pacific*, 21(9) September: 11.

Jenkins, C. and Henry, B. (1982) 'Government involvement in tourism in developing countries', *Annals of Tourism Research*, 9(4): 499–521.

Kamikamica, J. (1991) Opening address to TCSP Regional Conference on Tourism and National Development Planning in the South Pacific, Suva, Fiji, November 1991.

King, B. (1992) 'Cultural tourism and its potential for Fiji', *Journal of Pacific Studies*, 16: 74–89.

Kissling, C. (1990) 'Management issues in Pacific island aviation and tourism', in C. Kissling and D. Pearce (eds), *Destination South Pacific*, Cahiers de Tourisme, Series B No. 60, pp. 13–30.

Kissling, C. and Pearce, D. (eds) (1990) *Destination South Pacific*, Cahiers de Tourisme, Series B, No. 60.

Kuhn, T. (1970) *The Structure of Scientific Revolutions*, 2nd edn, Chicago: University of Chicago Press.

Lea, J. (1988) *Tourism and Development in the Third World*, London: Routledge.

Lee, G. (1987a) 'Tourism as a factor in development co-operation', *Tourism Management*, 8(1): 2–19.

—— (1987b) 'Future of national and regional tourism in developing countries', *Tourism Management*, 8(2): 86–8.

McIntosh, R. and Goeldner, C. (1992) *Tourism: Principles, Practices, Philosophies*, 5th edn, New York: Wiley.

McVey, M. (1995) 'Vanuatu Tourism Development Master Plan.' Unpublished paper to ESCAP Workshop, Port Vila, Vanuatu, June.

Mill, R. and Morrison, A. (1985) *The Tourism System*, Englewood Cliffs: Prentice-Hall.

Moorehead, A. (1966) *The Fatal Impact*, London: Hamish Hamilton.

Muqbil, I. (1995) 'Study on regional co-operation in the tourism sector in the Asian and Pacific region.' Unpublished paper to ESCAP Expert Group Meeting, New Delhi, April.

Page, S.J. (1996) 'Pacific Islands', *EIU International Tourism Reports*, pp. 67–102.

Pacific Islands Development Programme (1990) *Pacific Islands Tourism Case Studies: Regional Sumary*, Honolulu: East-West Centre, University of Hawaii.

Sofield, T. (1991) *Tourism for Development in the South Pacific Region*, 2 vols, Townsville: James Cook University of North Queensland.

Tourist Council of the South Pacific (TCSP) (1992) *Tourism Investment Guide*, Suva: Tourism Council of the South Pacific.

Travis, A. (1985) *Collected Papers on Leisure and Tourism*. Occasional Paper No. 12, Birmingham: Centre for Urban and Regional Studies, University of Birmingham.

Tuinabua, L. (1995) 'South Pacific tourism: An overview.' Unpublished paper presented to ESCAP Workshop on Integrated Tourism Planning in Pacific Island Countries, Port Vila, Vanuatu, 5–9 June, 1995.

Woods, L. (1991) 'Non-governmental organizations and Pacific cooperation: back to the future?', *The Pacific Review*, 4(4): 312–21.

Yacoumis, J. (1991) 'Tourism in the South Pacific – an overview.' Unpublished paper to Tourism Council of the South Pacific Regional Conference on Tourism and National Development Planning in the South Pacific, Suva, Fiji.

Yahuda, M. (1988) 'The "Pacific community"; not yet', *The Pacific Review*, 1(2): 119–27.

Chapter 8

Tourism marketing and computer reservation systems in the Pacific

Simon Milne

INTRODUCTION

In recent years social scientists have begun to pay increasing attention to the links that exist between the tourism industry and rapidly evolving information technologies (IT). While some commentators have focused primarily on the intra-firm impact of IT in certain sectors (Haywood 1990; Pohlmann 1994) others have provided a more far-reaching analysis pointing to the central role that IT is playing in transforming the travel distribution network (Collier 1989; Bennett and Radburn 1991; Mowlana and Smith 1992) and in creating a new industry-wide 'best practice' (Poon 1988a, 1989). Indeed, one of the leading researchers on the links between tourism and information technology, argues that information technology:

> facilitates the production of new, flexible and high-quality travel and tourism services that are cost competitive with mass, standardized and rigidly packaged options . . . IT helps to engineer the transformation of travel and tourism from its mass, standardized and rigidly packaged nature into a more flexible, individual-oriented, sustainable and diagonally integrated industry.
>
> (Poon 1993: 13)

Of all the IT developments that have captured the imagination of tourism researchers, computer reservation systems (CRS) have gained the most attention (Collier 1989; Tremblay 1990; Truitt *et al.* 1991; Go 1992). These powerful travel distribution technologies are seen to offer significant opportunities for the travel industry to improve customer service, efficiency and flexibility and seem certain to exert an increasingly important influence over future travel patterns and industry performance (Poon 1993). At the same time, several authors are cautious about the concentration of control over vital information flows associated with the rise of CRS which may be a cause for concern for smaller, independent, tourist operations and destinations that are relatively under-represented on these systems (Bennett and Radburn 1991; Milne and Grekin 1992; Milne and Nowosielski 1995).

This chapter examines the impact of CRS and other emerging travel distribution technologies (e.g. the Internet) are having on the ability of small Pacific island tourism destinations and the activities of Pacific island tourism businesses to market themselves as destinations and products. The chapter commences with a review of the literature on the travel distribution system and its influence on tourism development in Pacific island microstates. The role of information technologies, especially computer reservation systems, in influencing the ability of small Pacific island states to reach key overseas markets and achieve higher levels of local ownership within their tourism industries are reviewed followed by a discussion of research conducted by the McGill Tourism Research Group (MTRG) in both the South Pacific and Canadian contexts. Following a brief overview of the ability of more traditional marketing tools such as brochures to meet the marketing needs of Pacific island microstates, the ability of the internet, and particularly the worldwide web (WWW), is examined as a basis to offer new prospects for the marketing of niche tourism products in the region. The implications for Pacific microstates to improve their ability to develop and use this emerging and extremely powerful travel distribution technology is discussed, followed by the implications for local ownership and control.

TRAVEL DISTRIBUTION AND PACIFIC ISLAND TOURISM

The microstates of the South Pacific represent some of the smallest and most isolated players in the global economic system. Their distance from major markets, and limited domestic capital have forced them to rely heavily on a travel distribution system controlled by external corporations. Because of their key position between the traveller and the tourist destination, airlines, travel agents and tour operators are perhaps the most vital links in the travel distribution chain (Tourism Canada 1994). Of these sectors it is air transport that has gathered most attention from Pacific tourism researchers.

Britton and Kissling (1984) stress the fact that Pacific microstates rely heavily on overseas owned airlines to bring visitors to their shores and have little control over the routing and scheduling decisions of these companies (see also Kissling 1980; King 1984; Taylor and Kissling 1984; Airline Business, 1992). Most of the nations are dependent on a small number of foreign carriers with only a handful boasting their own small international/regional airlines. The fickle nature of international routing has hurt several tourist industries. For example, Air New Zealand's decision to cut back services to the Cook Islands in the early 1980s led to a significant reduction in tourist flows, while a pilot's strike at Air Nauru in mid-1988 cut the only commercial air service between the Niue and New Zealand (Britton and Kissling 1984; Milne, 1992).

Despite the fact that international air transportation has evolved considerably since the mid-1980s concerns about the uncertainty of transportation links between the region and its markets still hold true. While continued deregulation of the international airline industry may have opened up new markets and provided the customer with cheaper prices on some routes, ownership concentration has also grown – with small and mid-sized carriers giving way to international mega-carriers. Deregulation also means that less profitable routes (both domestic and international) are under pressure to cease or are subject to dramatic fare increases (Bryant 1995).

Attempts to form regional airlines to escape the dependence on larger carriers have been fraught with difficulties. Air Pacific was initially established by Qantas and Air New Zealand to create a regional feeder network for the major airlines (Britton and Kissling 1984). While the airline was supposed to increase microstates' access to the international airline network, disagreements over routes and frequencies of service have led Tonga, Western Samoa and other islands to establish their own national airlines. The re-establishment of a truly regional airline has been suggested and studied by the Association of South Pacific Airlines, but it is doubtful whether such a goal is practically feasible. Instead, the emerging trend in the South Pacific, as elsewhere, is towards inter-airline cooperation characterised by bilateral agreements and sub-regional partnerships (Interavia Air Letter 1994; Vandyk 1995). Although a few of the smaller South Pacific carriers have made some strides towards profitability, the future remains uncertain (Airline Business 1992) and several airlines such as Air Vanuatu and Air Pacific (now essentially a flag carrier for Fiji) have had little choice but to link themselves with larger carriers through code sharing agreements or joint marketing initiatives.

Tour operators and wholesalers consolidate various travel products into packages which are then offered to the consumer. By purchasing individual products in large quantities and arranging them into packages, these operators bring a variety of multifaceted products to travel agents or to customers directly (Holloway 1990). The structure of a tour package will influence destination development with the common assumption being that most package tours are associated with a high degree of sociocultural disruption and a low degree of economic benefit (Macnaught 1982; Grekin and Milne 1994). Tour operators are accused of siphoning off high proportions of tourist expenditure, creating enclave developments, and of directing visitor's expenditures to businesses offering the best commissions (Britton 1981). In South Pacific island destinations it is argued that wholesalers rely extensively on foreign owned air carriers and hotels, resulting in a drain of profits from the microstates. With transportation and accommodation usually accounting for over 80 per cent of a tour operator's expenses (Tourism Canada 1994), the loss of income by tourist destinations can be sizable (Britton 1982; Pearce 1989).

By marketing and selling the products and services of tour operators and airlines, travel agents can play a key role in influencing a traveller's choice of destination. Research in Canada has shown that 50 per cent of vacationers seek the advice of travel agents in making their choice of airline and that 66 per cent of those seeking tour packages are strongly influenced by travel agent recommendations. Similar figures exist for customers making inquiries on car rentals or hotel accommodation (Tourism Canada 1994). The ability of travel agents to act as information brokers is limited by an agent's knowledge of a region (Wilkinson 1991; Milne and Grekin 1992). Travellers unsure of a destination can be at the mercy of travel agents' suggestions. Thus, without an effective link through travel agencies, less well-known destinations in the South Pacific are likely to have difficulty attracting potential visitors.

Drawing heavily on dependency theory, Britton (1981, 1982) focuses on the influence that this three-way grouping of metropolitan based corporations exerts over the nature of tourism development in small Pacific island nations. Microstates are seen to be enmeshed in a global tourism system over which they have little or no influence. The advertising strategies of wholesalers and airlines shape tourist expectations, leading visitors to seek the types of experiences and facilities associated with mass tourism. Island governments are forced, in turn, to use multinational companies to provide the necessary capital to finance large-scale international style hotels and provide trained staff. The ability of these larger operations to offer higher commissions to overseas tour operators also enables them to gain control over various sectors of microstate tourist industries. Small-scale, locally owned enterprises are either relegated to activities which lie beyond the immediate interests of larger companies, or find roles as subcontractors. The final outcome is a form of tourism that primarily satisfies the commercial interests of overseas concerns and only partially meets local development needs (Britton 1987; Milne, forthcoming). While the dependency approach can be criticised for downplaying the role that local or 'bottom-up' factors can play in determining the outcomes of Pacific Island tourism Britton's work remains an important contribution to our understanding of the tourism development process in the region (Milne, forthcoming).

Computer reservation systems

The literature on tourism development in the South Pacific region has largely ignored a key feature of the evolving travel distribution system – the increasing dominance of airline CRS (sometimes called global distribution systems). A CRS is a central database connected to a network of terminals (usually housed in travel agencies) from which bookings and reservations are made. The global distribution system, or airline CRS, caters to airline schedule and rate management but has grown to include schedules and rates for a range of other tourism products. During the late 1960s, CRS were developed as reservation and accounting systems for internal use by airlines and hotels. Reduced costs and improvements to computer networking encouraged the extension of the systems and they evolved to provide reservation and distribution links between travel service providers (airlines, hotels, tours and car rentals) and the consumer, with travel agents usually acting as the intermediaries (Ellig 1991; Crayston 1992; Leaming 1993). According to a 1992 survey conducted by Travel Weekly (1992), US travel agents used CRS to book 92 per cent of domestic airline flights, 80 per cent of international flights, 68 per cent of car rentals, 53 per cent of hotel nights, 51 per cent of rail travel, 10 per cent of tours and 6 per cent of cruises (see also Tremblay 1990). Over 95 per cent of North American travel agencies are linked into one or more reservation systems. SABRE, the largest CRS (operated by American Airlines) handles over 500,000 reservations a day and has over 45 million prices in its data bank representing 650 airlines, 21,000 hotels, 52 rental car companies and 8 railroads. The system has over 100,000 terminals in more than 25,000 agencies spread throughout 64 countries (Carper 1993). As Collier (1989: 87) notes 'This is not an airline booking system, or a marketing system but a huge travel distribution network'. The continued deregulation of the airline industry, increasing strategic alliance activity between major operators, and improvements in the sophistication of both hardware and software are leading to the development of 'mega-CRSs' – with control of vital travel information being concentrated in an ever smaller number of hands (Scocozza 1989; Poon 1993).

There have been relatively few attempts by tourism researchers to ascertain the implications of these developments for small, tourism-orientated, island economies. Much of the existing knowledge has been based on the research by Poon (1988b, 1993). Poon takes a relatively positive perspective on the various impacts associated with the tourism industry's evolving use of CRS technology. Poon argues that the wide range of tourism products available on a CRS allows firms to move into new, interrelated activities, generating synergies, systems gains and economies of scale. As a result it often becomes more profitable to produce clusters of interrelated services instead of single, unrelated items. Poon (1989) maintains that new technologies and diagonal integration are making it possible to produce flexible and segmented vacations that are cost-competitive with 'traditional' mass, standardised holidays.

While Poon is well aware of some of the negative implications associated with the development of CRS the potential costs are generally felt to be outweighed by the benefits associated with their growth. Thus Poon argues that the greater array of tourist products available through CRS will facilitate the access of niche products to the travel consumer – either as stand-alone entities or as components of more flexible package structures. In simple terms this enhanced 'product depth' may translate into greater opportunities for small locally controlled businesses to gain access to a consumer seeking more flexible travel products (see also Bennett and Radburn 1991). The link between CRS and local ownership of the industry is vital because, as Poon (1993: 331) notes, true long-term sustainability is predicated upon the development of an indigenous entrepreneurial class. While Poon acknowledges that small industry players and peripheral destinations may lose market share by not having the skills or resources to participate in these systems, it is acknowledged that small firm networking and public sector intervention can overcome these hurdles (1993).

Although research on the links between CRS and the broader structure of the tourism industry in small island states is thought-provoking and has opened up important new dimensions in tourism research it tends to over-emphasise the positive elements ascribed to the technology and downplays what is, in fact, a rather harsh reality for small independent operators. The costs of joining CRS and the skilled labour required to operate them may place them out of the hands of smaller, locally owned concerns. Typically, CRS subscription will involve a 'join-up' fee and charge per booking made. The latter may be a percentage of the cost of the product sold – 10 per cent is a common figure – or a fixed flat rate which is highly unlikely to be less than $US10 per booking (see Carper 1993; Gill and Milne 1995).

It could also be argued that Poon and others have had a tendency to over-emphasize the 'flexibility' of these systems. It is indeed possible to display a range of different products and create new synergies through CRS, but a number of important rigidities remain. It is no coincidence, for example, that tour operators and their relatively complex products are the least well-represented components of the travel industry on CRS (Travel Weekly 1992; Collier 1989). Those tours that are represented tend to be highly packaged and relatively standardized in nature such as cruises and 'all-inclusive' hotel stays (Bennett and Radburn 1991). The rigidities of CRS display protocol also make it difficult for niche tour and travel operations to market themselves effectively. Several studies have also shown that travel agents are highly likely to draw information from the first page of CRS information that appears on their terminal screen (Leaming 1993). It is clearly in the interest of the CRS owner to present their own airline/ business information (or that of their partners) on the opening page. Despite attempts to regulate this type of bias larger operations controlling a system are still able to prioritise their own products (Ellig 1991; Leaming 1993).

The high cost of CRS membership, the relatively rigid structure of the information that can be displayed, and potential display bias, may tend to lead to the exclusion of many smaller South Pacific operations from these powerful distribution systems while larger, often foreign owned, concerns are likely to reap the competitive rewards associated with access to these networks. Recent research conducted in Canada by Pohlmann (1994) and Gill and Milne (1995) has shown that accommodation and attraction operations reap a number of rewards from CRS access (Table 8.1). The most important benefits lie in gaining a competitive edge – primarily through achieving a greater corporate profile in the marketplace. The impact on revenues is considered to be far more minimal – a consequence of the various membership fees and commissions charged. This latter point reinforces the important role that economies of scale play in the decision to enter a CRS. Companies also appear to have seen little increased fee setting flexibility or networking opportunities stemming from CRS membership (Table 8.1). This leads one to question the assumption that CRS automatically enables the creation of 'deeper', more flexible, tourism products. Another important factor to bear in mind is that if a destination is characterised by only a handful of multinational operations, its presence on global distribution systems is likely to be relatively limited – putting it at a disadvantage *vis-à-vis* larger, more internationally, established destinations.

Table 8.1: Corporate impacts associated with inclusion on CRS*

Area of impact	Impact
Competitiveness	Good
Bookings	Good
Marked exposure	Good
Revenues	Acceptable
Rate flexibility	No impact
Alliance formation	No impact

Note: *Data drawn from 1994/5 surveys of 85 accommodation and attraction operations in Toronto and Montreal.

Source: Gill and Milne, 1995.

CRS AND MICROSTATE MARKETING – RESEARCH FINDINGS

The following discussion of CRS inclusion is based on 1988 tourism industry surveys conducted for the United Nation's Development Program in five South Pacific islands (see Milne 1992). While this work is dated and focused primarily on economic linkage issues the fact that the survey instrument and interviews analysed corporate cost structures in detail allows an analysis of the number of tourism operations paying for links to some form of CRS. Due to the small scale of the countries' tourism industries and the interest of the participants it was possible to obtain excellent survey coverage. In Niue and Kiribati all relevant businesses participated in the survey while in Tonga, Papua New Guinea and Vanuatu the majority of tourist facilities were surveyed. In this paper we focus on the key accommodation sector.

CRS related biases in travel flows were analysed through a 'shadow shopping' survey of Montreal travel agents conducted by MTRG researchers between May and July, 1995. Eighty agents (randomly chosen from the Montreal Yellow Pages) were asked a 'general' question:

I would like travel to New Zealand, and as part of the trip I would like to visit an island in the South Pacific. I am looking for an island that is less developed, off the beaten track, *not* like Hawai'i. Can you suggest an island?

The stopover option was chosen because of the long-haul nature of the Montreal market for South Pacific travel. While no accurate statistics exist it was assumed that the majority of Montrealers travelling to the region are taking a multi-destination holiday – often involving Australia, New Zealand and one or more Pacific islands. This assumption was reinforced when experimenting with a non-stopover general question for a short period – several agents refused to take the enquiry seriously. In addition to flight information, the agents were asked to provide information on hotels, activities, and general background information on the island(s) suggested. Twenty additional travel agencies were visited in person to determine whether responses would differ with a face-to-face approach. These agents were asked the same 'general' question. The methodology used is consistent with other travel agency 'shadow shopping' exercises that have been conducted in recent years (Wilkinson 1991; Milne and Grekin 1992).

A second component of the survey sought to determine what specific information was available on three destinations – Vanuatu, Tonga and the Cook Islands. An additional 75 agents (25 per destination) were asked a more refined question:

> I would like to take a vacation in the South Pacific for three weeks. Some friends of mine recommended an island called _____. Could you provide me with some additional information.

The agents were then asked to provide as much information as possible about the island. This included background information on hotels, activities, local weather, suggestions for visits to adjacent islands, as well as the basic information on flights.

As Table 8.2 shows the vital accommodation sector, large overseas chain-owned hotels were very well represented on both hotel and airline reservation systems. Large independent operations, some of which were under management contract to chains, were also relatively well represented – with a tendency to be part of either a voluntary hotel reservation consortia or hotel chain CRS. The former are central reservation systems which cater to predominantly independent accommodation properties. Without exception small and medium-sized operations were excluded from CRS, with most citing costs and skills as being the major barrier to entry. This clearly places smaller operators at a competitive disadvantage in the marketplace. Small and medium-sized operators in the tour sector were also under-represented compared to their larger counterparts (Milne and Nowosielski 1995).

While these results are now becoming dated it is interesting to note that they are consistent with more recent studies of differential CRS inclusion conducted by MTRG researchers. For example, Pohlmann (1994) in her study of the Montreal hotel industry found that 90 per cent of small and 62 per cent of medium-sized independent hotels were not listed on a CRS. By contrast, hotels either affiliated to, or part of, chains had 100 per cent representation. Gill and Milne (1995) found similar variations in CRS adoption among Toronto hotels.

The results of the travel agent survey also support earlier statements regarding the impacts of CRS on the distribution of tourist flows; with certain South Pacific destinations clearly being favoured over others. Fiji and French Polynesia dominated initial suggestions while further research saw an increasing profile for the Cook Islands. Other island destinations such as Vanuatu or Tonga, were rarely mentioned (Table 8.3). Further details provided by agents were generally limited to information on flights, with the three major airlines flying to the South Pacific from Canada (Canadian, Qantas, Air New Zealand) dominating. Air Pacific was only mentioned twice by agents, who advised a return side trip from Auckland to an island destination.

Table 8.2: CRS inclusion of microstate accommodation operations[1]

Type of accommodation	Included on CRS (%)[2]
Small/medium independent	0
Large independent[3]	35
Chain affiliate	75
Large/medium chain member	95

Notes: [1] Data drawn from 1988 UNDP/WTO study of the economic impact of tourism in Niue, Tonga, Papua New Guinea, Kiribati and Vanuatu. Total number of accommodation operations surveyed = 62.
[2] Represents percentage of firms in each category that are included on some form of CRS/GDS.
[3] Large independent accommodation operations usually include an element of overseas ownership.

Source: Milne and Nowosielski, 1995.

Table 8.3: Pacific destinations and airlines suggested by Montreal travel agents (n = 80)

Destination	Initial suggestion	Suggested after research
Fiji	19	25
French Polynesia (Papeete, Tahiti)	12	15
Cook Islands	7	15
New Caledonia	4	1
Hawai'i	4	7
Tonga	3	9
Vanuatu	1	1
Western Samoa	1	5
Other*	7	11
No suggestion	21	–

Airline	Number of times suggested
Air Fiji (Air Pacific)	2
Canadian Airlines	16
Qantas	17
Air New Zealand	25

Note: * Includes Australia, New Zealand, Tuvalu, Marquesas, Sumatra, Nauru, Niue, Papua New Guinea.

Source: Milne and Nowosielski, 1995.

Half of the agents suggested a stopover en route to New Zealand, generally in Nadi, Papeete or Honolulu, consistent with the hub and spoke network observed by Page and Lawton in Chapter 17. This is cheaper than making a routing to New Zealand and then travelling out again to the islands on a round trip excursion. Five agents looked up fare information to New Zealand and suggested that the caller buy a South Pacific island vacation package in New Zealand. These agents stated (incorrectly) that this would be a less expensive option and that the caller would have a greater variety of destinations to choose from. It is clear that if an airline does not make a stopover at a smaller island en route, those destinations tend to be neglected by the travel agents. Most of the major carriers flying from North America to Australia or New Zealand make scheduled stops at either Hawai'i, Fiji or Tahiti. When the agent looks up flight information on the CRS one of these destinations is sure to appear as part of a traveller's potential flight itinerary.

From the standpoint of the smaller islands, this is unfortunate, since travellers that would willingly visit more *remote* nations are being channelled to the *mainstream* South Pacific destinations. In spite of the CRS and airline imposed bias, smaller islands could tap into this 'stopover' market with relative ease. Air New Zealand, the most commonly suggested carrier, has cooperative marketing agreements with Air Vanuatu, Air Pacific, Solomon Airlines and Air Calédonie, all of which provide service to destinations that can be included as stopovers en route to New Zealand for little additional cost. Generally, the least expensive tickets are only valid for a month and allow no stopovers en route. For only an additional $100–200, however, the traveller may stay three months and is allowed one stopover. Additional stopovers on these three-month fares are allowed for only $150 per destination. Stopovers can be made at numerous South Pacific destinations: Air New Zealand offers Fiji, Tahiti, Tonga, Western Samoa, and the Cook Islands. Qantas and Canadian Airlines' stopovers options are limited to Los Angeles, Papeete, Hawai'i and Fiji respectively (see Chapter 17). Although 25 agents mentioned Air New Zealand as a carrier, only nine suggested the possibility of such multiple stopovers.

Hotel information was provided by only four agents from the 'general' grouping. These agents only gave a price range and suggested making arrangements once at the destination. From the information provided it seems likely that these hotel prices were obtained from brochures in the travel agency. Ten agencies either mailed brochures or prepared packages for the researcher to pick up, stating that this was the best way to get information on the destinations.

Several responses revealed that agents have only limited awareness of the South Pacific region beyond what is available on their CRS terminals. One agent did not think any South Pacific packages were available from Canada. Another agent began by mistakenly stating that New Zealand was a destination in Australia and a further seven suggested Hawaii in spite of being asked for a destination 'not like Hawai'i'. One of these agents mentioned that only the main island of Hawai'i was developed and that outlying islands were pretty much untouched. Rarotonga, the main island of the Cooks group, was introduced by one travel agent as being a beautiful destination in Tahiti.

The travel agents survey revealed findings similar to those of the telephone survey. The agents visited tended to limit their research to looking for flight details, but often gave additional information in the form of numerous brochures on Australia, New Zealand and the South Pacific. Early into the 'specific' question section of the research it was noted that almost all of the responses for each destination were identical. In fact, a single wholesaler dominates the South Pacific travel market in Montreal. In the case of Tonga and the Cook Islands, the wholesaler was sending the agents a photocopy of a few pages from an Air New Zealand package brochure and the information was then passed on to the caller. These pages had brief descriptions of the islands and a listing of 3–5 hotels available as part of a package deal. Questions related to Vanuatu were met with a similar response, although it was not possible to determine the source of the information. In the few cases where agents did not call a wholesaler, responses were limited to providing flight information only (this is often all that is available on the CRS). It is clear from the responses to the 'specific' questions that Montreal travel agents knew little or nothing about destinations such as the Cook Islands, Tonga or Vanuatu.

Because of the relative lack of information available on the CRS, brochures were often resorted to by agents in their search for information. As a supplement to the 'shadow shopping' exercise a content analysis of the brochures was provided by agents to assess the type of information that a traveller wishing to wander off the beaten track would require. Twenty-three different brochures were collected describing South Pacific packages, with Fiji and Tahiti appearing in every one. The Cook Islands was listed in only five brochures while Tonga is only briefly mentioned once. Air New Zealand dominates, with Qantas only appearing in four pamphlets. The smaller South Pacific airlines receive little or no mention in the brochures with Air Pacific the only regional carrier listed, and even then it is only mentioned as a partner to Qantas. At the same time niche, or small-scale, tour operators tend to be excluded. The Fiji and Tahiti material presents resort holidays aimed at the *sun, sea and sand* market. All involve staying at larger hotels or resorts. If smaller hotels are listed they are, in every case, deluxe 'boutique' operations. If one considers only those brochures listing Tonga or the Cook Islands, a similar pattern holds true – wholesalers limit themselves to a very small number of large, usually foreign owned, resort hotels.

Brochure suggestions for activities are generally limited to water sports, sunbathing and shopping with niche products (emphasising culture, nature and wildlife) being excluded. One wholesaler's brochure includes the following description of the Cook Islands: 'There is very little to do except soak up the sun, surf and sand' while another company, calling itself 'Cultural Tours' offers a three-day stopover in Rarotonga to 'bask in the sunshine . . . hire a jeep . . . or discover exotic flowers'. Nowhere is there mention of any interaction with Cook Island Maori culture, nor is there any detailed description of the Cook Islands themselves. Faced with such limited information, it is not surprising that agents were unable to turn to brochures to provide them with information on alternative tourism products in the region.

The CRS and brochure review revealed that tourists who contact Montreal travel agents for information on niche orientated microstate tourism products in the South Pacific are highly likely to be pushed towards more established destinations such as Fiji, and larger, often foreign owned, accommodation operations. Perhaps most importantly the inaccuracy of much of the information provided can create problems for tourists arriving in the region, with any dissatisfaction that results potentially leading to negative feedback being passed on to friends and relatives. This has clear implications for the quality of tourism experience provided to visitors, as emphasised in Chapter 10, where gap analysis highlights the difference between the visitors expectations and the tourism industry's delivery of a product and service.

Small islands do have some potential strategies to assist them in overcoming these CRS entry barriers (Poon 1993). The use of networking and strategic alliances will become increasingly important competitive tools for firms of all sizes. Smaller or independent companies can overcome disadvantages associated with limited size by forming networks – which allow for the pooling of marketing resources, or enable joint access to essential technologies (Poon 1993). There are already several examples of small adventure-orientated operators setting up alliances in North America and elsewhere in order to gain access to elusive consumers (Del Rosso 1991a, b), while small accommodation complexes have a long tradition of pooling resources to maximise market profiles (see Pohlmann 1994; Gill and Milne 1995). While research on similar themes in the South Pacific is non-existent there are already examples in destinations such as the Cook Islands and Vanuatu, of locally owned or small-scale accommodation operations joining forces to improve marketplace and lobbying profiles. It should be noted, of course, that networks of any sort rely on patterns of trust and reciprocity: for this reason it is not always an easy task to establish or maintain such groupings.

The regions' suppliers could also benefit from the establishment of Destination Information Systems (DIS) or databases – electronic information technology accessed via videotext, CD-Rom, and personal computers. The DIS can provide pre-trip information about a destination's accommodation, transportation, tours, and attractions to the travelling public either directly through home computers, or through travel agents or national/regional tourist offices. There is also potential for connecting the DIS with CRSs which would link the respective suppliers to travel agents around the world (Sheldon 1993). Such systems can be developed on a national or regional basis; examples of the latter exist in the Scottish Highlands and the Tyrolean region of Austria (Vlitos-Rowe 1992). In market regions 'characterised by small independent businesses and individualistic holidays', centralisation of information can increase visibility as well as ease of reservation (Vlitos-Rowe 1992: 102). Indeed government and aid donor assistance (see Chapter 11) in the establishment and running of such networks may be one of the most effective ways to foster small enterprise development in the South Pacific tourism industry. Yet such systems are expensive to establish, rely on trust and reciprocity among participants and must also pay fees to allow them to 'switch' into CRS. It seems unlikely that they can provide a cost-effective answer to microstate marketing needs.

THE INTERNET

One of the greatest prospects for the marketing of niche operators and products in the South Pacific lie in the emergence of the Internet as a powerful tool for global information transfer.[1] The Internet is composed of thousands of computer networks which utilise a universal protocol enabling them to communicate with each other (Hoffman 1993; Davies 1995). The concept of the Internet was developed by the US Defense Department in the 1960s. The idea was to develop a computer network which had no central control and could therefore be protected from strategically placed enemy attacks. Just as there is no central authority which oversees the internet there is no organisation which collects fees to maintain the network. Each provider pays for its own component. Thus each university pays for its own campus network and then decides how to connect to the Internet through a regional network, which in turn pays a national provider for its access. Telephone companies provide most of the long-distance interconnections, with companies in each country running parts of the system. The ultimate authority for Internet development rests with the Internet Society (ISOC), a voluntary organisation whose purpose is to promote global information exchange through Internet technology. It appoints committees which have responsibility for the technical management and direction of the system.

For some time the Internet was restricted to the US, its allies and related military bases. Political shifts and reductions in the costs of telecommunications have enabled the expansion of the system into eastern European and developing nations (Kroll 1992). By 1994, 159 countries had Internet access and it is estimated that some 40 million people worldwide have access to the system. The US continues to account for the bulk of users (76 per cent) with Canadians being the next major national grouping (9 per cent) (Yahoo 1995; TIC/MIDS 1995). User numbers are now growing rapidly in European, Asian and Latin American nations as local networks and Internet service companies expand in number. While the majority of Internet users work at large corporations (42 per cent at companies with over 1000 employees) (O'Reilly and Associates 1995) access is also becoming a household affair with a range of companies offering easy access to homes with a personal computer and a modem.

The mean age of the average Internet user is 35 and they are 2.5 times as likely to have a university degree than the general population – earning 50 per cent more than the average income in their respective countries (TIC/MIDS 1995). It is interesting to note that this is the same type of 'high-end' socioeconomic profile ascribed to the types of eco/alternative travellers that are most likely to demand niche Pacific island products (see Eagles 1992 for a review of ecotourist traits).

As a marketing and advertising medium the Internet has the potential to radically change the way tourism firms and destinations do business with their potential clients by offering an efficient and extremely flexible means of contacting customers, providing product information, direct selling, and providing technical assistance. The different components of the Internet which are of most use to tourism businesses include:

- discussion groups which provide online correspondence between parties interested in a particular topic. Advertisers can post listings in related groups, or set up their own group;
- file transfer and software distribution (FTP). Allowing users to download files and software for detailed evaluation;
- electronic mail (email). This provides instant communications for customer inquiries, feedback, and technical support;
- information distribution (gopher, and the worldwide web – WWW). These allow users to view, save and print detailed product information.

(Davies 1995; Kimel 1995)

The worldwide web is a distributed, hypermedia-based Internet information browser and offers the greatest marketing potential for small tourism operations. It presents users with a user-friendly point and click interface to a wide variety of types of information (text, graphics, sound and movies) and Internet services. It is possible to use the web to access FTP archives, databases and even gopher servers. The WWW is the fastest growing component of the Internet, with an estimated expansion rate of 10–15 per cent per month (Kimel 1995). The reason for such rapid growth is the easy to use 'windows' type platform it employs and the growth of popular web browsers such as Netscape's Navigator and Microsoft's Internet Explorer (see Gleick 1995).

The WWW allows tourism destinations and businesses to present information to the world. Customers can visit a company or destination's online 'colour brochure' which is stored in 'pages' or files which can be viewed in both text and pictures. When a customer sees something that interests them on a destination index or home page they can click on highlighted links, allowing them to access a greater depth of information. Potential customers can view as little or as much as they want, and business owners can update prices or product profiles at any time. The technology also brings the advantage of knowing how many people have looked at your web site, where they come from, and what aspects of the product seem to be of most interest.

To make use of the web, a destination and/or the companies that comprise its tourist product place their web pages on a host computer's storage bank. The only telephone charge is the cost of a call to the Internet service provider. Messages are then relayed to other larger host computers via leased, high speed telephone lines and satellite systems. The telephone costs are normally included in a flat monthly Internet service provider fee. Potential customers find their way to a web site by using one of several search engines (such as *Yahoo*, *Lycos* and *Web Crawler*) that rely on the customer entering key words (e.g. *Tourism, South Pacific, Samoa*). A web page designer registers the destination's pages with these indexes. It is also possible to email press releases to services which track what is new on the Internet, and make people aware of a company's web site by means of Internet mailing lists and news groups (Davies 1995).

Clearly, the Internet adds tremendous marketing power to both small and large tourism businesses. It is interesting to note that CRS operators have not been slow to see the power of the Internet. Airlines and hotel chains are hoping to cash in by providing easy to use reservation systems over the Internet, with Holiday Inn recently becoming the first major hotel chain to offer such a service. American Airlines' *Easy-Sabre*, already available through Compuserve, will soon be available via the worldwide web and other CRS are sure to follow. Estimates suggest that up to 10 per cent of travel arrangements in the United States are now made through such networks with this figure expected to rise rapidly (Tourism Canada 1994). More importantly the WWW may actually begin to eat into the dominance of CRS as travel distribution networks. Web sites offer the possibility to break out of some of the rigidities associated with CRS while the increased use of home computers and the growing accessibility of Internet may play a role in the demise of traditional non-specialised travel agencies (Pohlmann 1994).

To complement this CRS research, a search of the Internet for the same three destinations (Tonga, Vanuatu and the Cook Islands) was undertaken. Western Samoa was also added because it was the only microstate in the region at the time to have an active tourism orientated web site. Using a variety of WWW search mechanisms including *web crawler*, *yahoo* and *virtual tourist*, the information found on the Internet can be broken down into four categories:

General information

The information is usually limited to basic geographical, political and economic data and resembles that found in encyclopedias. Information on all four case study nations was available, although it would be of very limited use to potential tourists seeking details on travel and accommodation.

Private, special interest sites

These are sites established by private individuals with a highly focused interest. The Tonga search identified a site located in Berlin, Germany. Apparently, the designer had visited Tonga and wanted to promote the islands over the Internet. The site includes numerous photos, descriptions of the archipelago, and limited travel information. Vanuatu is promoted through a similar site, located at Clark

University in Massachussetts. Here, Internet 'surfers' can view photos of various parts of the islands, listen to an excerpt from a local radio broadcast, and see an excellent bibliography of books and travel guides about Vanuatu.

Commercial sites

The search for information on the microstates also highlighted several travel agencies, wholesalers and airlines operating in the South Pacific. To date, the use of the Internet for commercial purposes has been frowned upon, but this is changing as large and small businesses discover its wide-reaching advertising potential. One travel agency, based in Australia, sells various packages to the South Pacific destinations included in this study and its web pages include airfares, numerous hotel listings as well as descriptions of activities, climate and limited information on various island cultures. The web pages gave more information about the islands than could be found by our survey of Montreal travel agents. The company maintaining the web site operates as a full service travel agency in Australia and is only using the Internet as an extension of their regular services. A representative of the agency claimed to receive 10 to 20 enquiries per day in response to the Internet advertisements: about 10 per cent of these are converted into sales. Numerous airlines are also jumping into the Internet fray. Of the South Pacific carriers, only Qantas and Ansett Australian Airlines had operating web pages at the time of the search but others are likely to follow. Several wholesalers were also advertising on the Internet, though all of those dealing with the South Pacific were advertising packages to established destinations such as Fiji, Tahiti and Hawai'i.

Government sponsored travel information

Western Samoa was the only nation studied with a WWW home page. Here one can find background information on the islands, how to get there, hotel listings and information on tour operators. There is also a listing of upcoming events. These sorts of sites may offer the best hope for niche tourist products. The Western Samoa site lists more than a dozen local tour operators, most of whom offer small-scale eco-tours or cultural visits, and an extensive listing of accommodation operations – many of them small scale in nature. These are exactly the types of operations that find it difficult to access CRS.[2]

The potential of the Internet to assist smaller destinations seeking to develop tourism industries characterised by higher levels of local ownership is clearly enormous. With the popularity of the Internet constantly growing, destinations seeking to develop niche markets can promote themselves at a relatively low cost to an expanding, high income/well-educated market. Smaller operators can bypass the traditional tourist distribution network and access customers directly.

From this research it is evident that several key factors determine the relative success of an web site (Davies 1995; Kimel 1995) including:

- *Immediate gratification.* There are literally millions of pages to chose from and unless a page grabs the consumer's attention they will simply move on;
- *Choice.* Images usually take a long time to download, thus users should be given the option of seeing an image using thumbnail sketches or hypertext. The easiest way to lose a potential user is to make them wait 30 seconds for an image they do not actually want;
- *Related links.* Good links are a valuable asset to any web page as users want to know where to find more information on related topics;
- *Being up-to-date.* Regularly updated sites will tend to encourage return visits;
- *Ease of use.* A site should lead users through the information and provide clear choices;
- *Sites which support all forms of Internet browsers,* including text based browsers.

One must, however, be wary of over-hyping the current potential of the WWW to act as an effective marketing tool for Pacific microstates as several problems remain to be solved. Telecommunication services on many islands are of poor quality and computer literacy and hardware availability is limited. The onus will clearly be on governments, aid donors and prospective Internet service providers to solve these problems. It is interesting to note that Western Samoa's home page was created on that island's behalf by a company based in San Francisco – showing that infrastructural problems on the islands can be circumvented.

Companies and destinations gain access to potential customers through an Internet service provider, with fees usually ranging from $US25–35 for initial set-up and approximately $US35 per month for user fees. Costs will be higher in areas such as the South Pacific where telecommunications links are more expensive but these can be expected to fall – especially with the growth in wireless, satellite-based communication (Cairncross 1995; Davies pers. comm.). The cost of a professional web site designer to help in the preparation of web pages will vary from $US1,000 to $US10,000 depending on the complexity of the material. It is also important to note that credit card payments cannot yet be made securely over the Internet because VISA, Mastercard and Microsoft have yet to provide a standard encryption technology. As a result companies must still rely on customers to telephone, fax or mail an order. There is also the important concern that when a standardised charging approach is developed, a company such as Microsoft may charge a fee for every commercial transaction that is conducted (Gleick 1995). Despite these provisos it is clear that the Internet provides small companies and peripheral nations with the potential to gain access to an international clientele that has largely evaded them in the past and at a price far below the costs of joining a CRS or attempting to use other mainstream advertising media.

CONCLUSION

As the island microstates of the South Pacific prepare to enter the twenty-first century they face the major challenge of how to fine tune tourism product development and marketing strategies to meet the changing needs of the traveller, while at the same time creating a more sustainable industry – with increased levels of local ownership being an essential element in the sustainability equation.

Initial concerns regarding the ability of CRS to enable Pacific microstates to meet these challenges have been confirmed by the research findings. The growing power of CRS, together with increased ownership concentration, appears likely to lead to the further strengthening of large enterprises, especially multinational chains. Mid-sized or smaller independent firms will suffer from a distinct competitive disadvantage, as will destinations that are relatively underrepresented on these systems. Biases in travel flows will not only disadvantage small operators and destinations in the marketplace but will also tend to facilitate against the achievement of higher levels of local ownership and, by default, the creation of more sustainable forms of tourism development. Milne and Nowosielski (1995) outline a range of implications for sustainable tourism development that stem from CRS-biased tourism flows:

- Several studies (e.g. Milne 1987) have shown that large-scale foreign concerns exhibit higher economic leakages than their smaller, locally owned counterparts. If tourist flows are directed to large operations we may well see a commensurate increase in economic leakages. Larger operations also tend to be relatively less intensive in their use of labour resources.
- While larger operations have been shown to generate proportionately more government revenue than their smaller counterparts it must also be remembered that they often require extensive infrastructure and may also be the recipient of government incentives and loans designed to attract initial investment.
- A lack of local participation in the industry may also have undesirable cultural and environmental consequences. The concentration of travel distribution, with high levels of expatriate ownership and management, may tend to alienate the local population (Macnaught 1982; Wilkinson 1989). This will also, in the longer term, have significant social and environmental impacts as local owners may be more likely to exhibit improved stewardship of natural resources, and may also exhibit greater sensitivity toward conflicting land use issues.

While one is wary of slipping into a technologically deterministic stance the findings presented here will hopefully encourage researchers to broaden the array of factors that they deal with in trying to ascertain the very real marketing problems facing niche forms of tourism in the South Pacific. There is clearly a great deal more research to be conducted on the ways in which evolving travel distribution technologies can influence the success of government strategies to increase the marketability and sustainability of their tourism industries.

ENDNOTES

1 Tourism researchers have been slow to integrate the Internet into their analyses of the links between tourism and information technology. Indeed Poon (1993), in what is probably the most thorough overview of the tourism–IT interface, fails to address the Internet at all.
2 The Western Samoan site can be viewed at: *http://www.intergroup.com/interweb/ samoa*

ACKNOWLEDGEMENTS

I gratefully acknowledge the assistance provided by the Montreal travel agents included in the 'shadow shopping' survey. The staff of ICAO's head offices in Montreal also provided invaluable guidance on the airline sector. Leszek Nowosielski and Kara Gill of the McGill Tourism Research Group provided much needed research assistance. I am also grateful for the helpful insights provided by Mr Bradley Davies, Director of New Business Development, Commercial Internet Services, Toronto. The research was funded by Quebec's FCAR (Team Grant #290–37).

REFERENCES

Airline Business (1992) 'Oceans apart', *Airline Business*, March: 60–3.
Bennett, M. and Radburn, M. (1991) 'Information technology in tourism: The impact on the industry and supply of holidays', in M.T. Sinclair and M.J. Stabler (eds) *The Tourism Industry: An International Analysis*, Oxford: CAB International, pp. 45–65.
Britton, S.G. (1981) *Tourism, Dependency and Development: A Mode of Analysis*, Australian National University Occasional Publication No. 23, Canberra: Australian National University.
—— (1982) 'The political economy of tourism in the Third World', *Annals of Tourism Research*, 9(3): 331–58.
—— (1987) 'Tourism in Pacific Island states: Constraints and opportunities', in S. Britton and W. Clarke (eds) *Ambiguous Alternatives: Tourism in Small Developing Countries*, Suva: Institute of Pacific Studies, University of the South Pacific, pp. 113–39.
Britton, S.G. and Kissling, C.C. (1984) 'Aviation and development constraints in South Pacific microstates', in C.C. Kissling (ed.) *Transport and Communication in Pacific Microstates: Issues in Organization and Management*, Suva: Institute of Pacific Studies, University of the South Pacific, pp. 79–96.
Bryant, A. (1995) 'On a wing and a prayer: deregulation decoded', *New York Times*, November 5: Sect. E, 5.
Cairncross, F. (1995) 'The death of distance, a survey of telecommunications', *The Economist*, September 30.
Carper, J. (1993) 'A brief look at today's reservation systems', *Hotels*, September: 68–70.
Collier, D. (1989) 'Expansion and development of CRS', *Tourism Management*, 10(2): 86–8.

Crayston, J. (1992) 'Worldwide code of conduct adopted for CRS operations', *ICAO Journal*, 47(3): 7–8.

Davies, B. (1995) 'Introduction to the Internet', mimeo, Commercial Internet Services, Toronto. *cis@ftn.net*

Del Rosso, L. (1991a) 'Adventure operators hope to gain visibility through association', *Travel Weekly*, 50(12): 22.

Del Rosso, L. (1991b) 'Adventure firms combine operations', *Travel Weekly*, 50(46): 14.

Eagles, P.F. (1992) 'Motivations of Canadian ecotourists', *Journal of Travel Research*, 31(2): 3–7.

Ellig, J. (1991) 'Computer reservation systems, creative destruction, and consumer welfare: Some unsettled issues', *Transportation Law Journal*, 19(2): 287–307.

Gill, K. and Milne, S. (1995) 'Differential CRS adoption and corporate competitiveness: Some examples from Montreal and Toronto.' Paper presented at the Annual Meeting of the Canadian Association of Geographers, Montreal, May 30–June 3.

Gleick, J. (1995) 'Making microsoft safe for capitalism', *New York Times Magazine*, November 5: 57–64.

Go, F.M. (1992) 'The role of computer reservation systems in the hospitality industry', *Tourism Management*, 13(1): 22–6.

Grekin, J. and Milne, S. (1994) *Understanding the Impacts of Tourism Development in the Baffin Region, NWT: The Role of Tour Operators*, McGill Tourism Research Group Industry Report No. 6, Montreal: McGill Tourism Research Group.

Haywood, K.M. (1990) 'A strategic approach to managing technology', *Cornell Hotel and Restaurant Administration Quarterly*, May: 39–45.

Hoffman, E. (1993) 'What is the Internet', Network Working Group, University of Illinois and Merit Network, Inc., *ftp://nic.merit.edu/documents/fyi/fyi_04.txt*

Holloway, J.C. (1990) *The Business of Tourism*, 3rd edn, London: Pitman.

Interavia Air Letter (1994) 'Royal Tongan strikes Air Pacific partnership', *Interavia Air Letter* 2.

Kimel, S. (1995) 'Questions small businesses ask about the Internet' mimeo, Commercial Internet Services, Toronto, *cis@ftn.net*

King, J.M. (1984) 'The air traffic market and tourism: Some thoughts on the South Pacific', in C. C. Kissling (ed.) *Transport and Communication in Pacific Microstates: Issues in Organization and Management*, Suva: Institute of Pacific Studies, University of the South Pacific, pp. 113–24.

Kissling, C.C. (1980) *International Civil Aviation in the South Pacific: A Perspective*, Development Studies Centre Occasional Paper No. 19, Canberra: Australian National University.

Kroll, E. (1992) 'The whole Internet user's guide and catalog', O'Reilly & Associates, Inc., *http://www.ora.com*

Leaming, M. (1993) 'Enlightened regulation of computerized reservation systems requires a conscious balance between consumer protection and profitable airline marketing', *Transportation Law Journal*, 21(2): 469–517.

Macnaught, T.J. (1982) 'Mass tourism and the dilemmas of modernization in Pacific Island communities', *Annals of Tourism Research*, 9(3): 359–81.

Milne, S. (1987) 'Differential multipliers', *Annals of Tourism Research*, 14(4): 499–515.

—— (1992) 'Tourism and development in South Pacific island microstates', *Annals of Tourism Research*, 19(2): 191–212.

—— (1995) 'Beyond the vicious cycle?: tourism, dependency and South Pacific microstates', in D.G. Lockhart and D. Drakakis-Smith (eds) *Island Tourism*, London: Mansell.

Milne, S. and Grekin, J. (1992) 'Travel agents as information brokers: The case of the Baffin Region, Northwest Territories', *The Operational Geographer*, 10(3): 11–15.

Milne, S. and Nowosielski, L. (1995) 'Travel distribution technologies and sustainable tourism development: the case of South Pacific Microstates.' Paper presented to the Regional IGU workshop on Sustainable Tourism Development in the South Pacific, Canberra 1–4 September.

Mowlana, H. and Smith, G. (1992) 'Trends in telecommunications and the tourism industry: Coalition, regionalism and international welfare systems', in F. Go and D. Frechtling (eds) *World Travel and Tourism Review*, Vol. 2, Oxford: CAB International, pp. 163–7.

O'Reilly and Associates (1995) 'Internet survey: Preliminary results', O'Reilly and Associates, Inc., *http://www.ora.com/survey*

Pearce, D. (1989) *Tourist Development*, 2nd edn, London: Longman.

Pohlmann, C. (1994) 'The restructuring of Montreal's tourism industry: A sectoral analysis.' MA Thesis, Department of Geography, McGill University, Montreal.

Poon, A. (1988a) 'Tourism and information technologies – ideal bedfellows?', *Annals of Tourism Research*, 15(4): 531–49.

—— (1988b) 'Innovation and the future of Caribbean tourism', *Tourism Management*, 9(3): 213–20.

—— (1989) 'Competitive strategies for a "new tourism"', in C.P. Cooper (ed.) *Progress in Tourism, Recreation and Hospitality Management*, Vol. 1, London: Belhaven Press, pp. 91–102.

—— (1993) *Tourism, Technology and Competitive Strategies*, Oxford: CAB International.

Scocozza, M. (1989) 'Deregulation – a recipe for prosperity', *IATA Review*, 1: 8–11.

Sheldon, P. J. (1993) 'Destination information systems', *Annals of Tourism Research*, 20: 633–49.

Taylor, M.J. and Kissling, C.C. (1984) 'National sovereignty and corporate dependence in South Pacific aviation', in C.C. Kissling (ed.) *Transport and Communication in Pacific Microstates: Issues in Organization and Management*, Suva: Institute of Pacific Studies, University of the South Pacific, 97–112.

TIC/MIDS, (1995) 'Internet demographic survey', Austin, Texas: TIC/MIDS *http://www.tic.com/mids*.

Tourism Canada (1994) *Product Distribution in the Tourism Industry: A Profile of Tour Operators and Travel Agencies in Canada*, Ottawa: Supply and Services Canada.

Travel Weekly (1992) 'Travel agent survey – special issue', *Travel Weekly*, 51 (65).

Tremblay, S. (1990) 'Les systemes informatises de reservations dans l'industrie touristique', *Teoros*, 9(3): 14–21.

Truitt, L.J., Teye, V.B. and Farris, M.T. (1991) 'The role of computer reservation systems: international implications for the travel industry', *Tourism Management*, March: 21–36.

Vandyk, A. (1995) 'Think small in South Pacific', *Air Transport World*, 32: 22.

Vlitos-Rowe, I. (1992) 'Destination databases and management systems', *EIU Travel and Tourism Analyst*, 5: 84–108.

Wilkinson, P. (1989) 'Strategies for tourism in Island microstates', *Annals of Tourism Research*, 16(2): 153–77.

—— (1991) 'Travel agents as information brokers: the cases of Anguilla and Dominic', *The Operational Geographer*, 9(3): 37–41.

Yahoo (1995) Yahoo Internet Survey Results, *http://www.yahoo.com/survey/results.html*.

Chapter 9

Health and tourism in the Pacific

Brenda Rudkin and C. Michael Hall

INTRODUCTION

> Tropical travel carries risks. Before . . . travel we need to organise
> vaccinations in a timely manner, advise on protection from insect biting
> and on water and food-borne disease, and be aware of chronic illness which
> may complicate travel arrangements. On return we need to know that we are
> dealing with a traveller.
>
> (Ellis-Pegler 1992: 111)

The romantic image of the South Pacific has long fascinated the international
traveller (see Chapter 2). As travellers increasingly seek to experience 'unspoilt'
'natural' areas and indigenous Pacific cultures they invariably venture off the
conventional tourist track. However, expectations by travellers that remoteness
provides isolated indigenous peoples an idyllic lifestyle without the pressures of
polluted urban living and an abundance of locally produced or gathered foods is
far from reality. Many of these Pacific communities live in areas with inadequate
housing, unreliable fresh water, and poor sanitation, conditions that can lead to
severe illness for locals and visitors alike. Furthermore, medical personnel,
health facilities and supplies may be absent or inadequate at the local level.
Indeed, most Pacific island economies face rapidly rising populations and
deteriorating balance deficits thereby straining health and infrastructure budgets.

This chapter was prompted by the authors' research into sustainable tourism
development in the South Pacific and by their own health experiences as a
consequence of such research. Undoubtedly, tourism is seen as a critical element
of economic development in the South Pacific. The microstates of the region
have few, if any, other development alternatives (see Chapter 1). However, health
requirements of both travellers and local people have generally not been
considered in the tourism development process (Clift and Page 1996), and
particularly in the Pacific (Minerbi 1992; Economic and Social Commission for
Asia and the Pacific 1994). For example, despite substantial media publicity of
the deaths of Australian and New Zealand holidaymakers from tropical diseases
(e.g. Australian Associated Press 1991; Howarth 1992) and associated reports of
tropical diseases in return travellers (e.g. New Zealand Herald 1993a), many

tourists are not specifically warned by tour operators or travel agents of the potential health dangers of travelling in the South Pacific, even though relevant health literature is available (e.g. Wilson and Baker 1992; Department of Health 1993). According to the World Health Organisation (in PATA Advisory Council 1992), for every 100,000 people who travel overseas to tropical areas:

- 50,000 have health problems
- 30,000 get travellers diarrhoea
- 3000–4000 will contract malaria
- 8 will die
- 2 will contract typhoid
- 0.1 will contract cholera.

Furthermore, when travellers require medical treatment when they are visiting destination areas in some parts of the South Pacific, they may be placing a strain on already scarce medical resources. Therefore, the authors argue that it is essential that the health dimensions of travel in the region be considered, particularly in the development of special interest travel opportunities, such as nature-based and adventure tourism.

One of the difficulties in researching the relationship between tourism and health in the South Pacific is that specific data on travel-related illness is generally unavailable in Australia and New Zealand and even less so in Pacific Island microstates (Ellis-Pegler 1992). Therefore, the authors have drawn data from a wide range of sources, including interviews with staff of infectious disease units in Australia and New Zealand, other health professionals, and special interest travel operators, in order to ascertain the level of awareness of travel-related health issues in Pacific countries. The chapter is divided into two sections. First, a review of the main diseases affecting travellers in the region: malaria, cholera/diarrhoea, and dengue fever. Second, an examination of the potential health implications of special interest tourism development in the region. This section focuses on the health implications of the development of nature-based and cultural tourism which promotes contact with regions away from the main tourist centres. It is argued that such travellers are exposing themselves to malaria and other infectious diseases, such as dengue fever and typhoid, which are prevalent among some South Pacific communities. Similarly, warm clear waters laden with colourful coral and marine life and numerous sunken war wrecks are a divers paradise, but a lack of knowledge of the dangers that lurk in the waters could result in dire consequences for the unprepared, including pollution, coral cuts, food poisoning and decompression sickness (Nicholls 1992).

TRAVEL-RELATED ILLNESS IN AUSTRALIA AND NEW ZEALAND

Australia and New Zealand are two of the major tourist markets for the countries of the South Pacific. While both countries have comprehensive disease reporting mechanisms and produce regular bulletins on communicable diseases, sources of exposure to diseases are rarely reported, with disease information only being available at an aggregate level. Therefore, one of the great difficulties in evaluating the extent of travel-related diseases in Australia and New Zealand is the lack of a specific travel disease database. Furthermore, not all travel-related diseases are notifiable and, as in the case of one of the authors, one individual may have multiple cases thereby leading to double counting. In most cases it is up to the individual doctor to note the areas visited by a patient. In addition, problems in identifying disease sources arise when people have visited multiple destinations.

As far as can be ascertained, the only published systematic survey of travel associated disease in either Australia or New Zealand is a study of travel-related illness undertaken at the Infectious Disease Unit at the Auckland Hospital from July–December 1989 (Table 9.1). The survey reported on 140 telephone consultations, 18 outpatient assessments and 29 hospital admissions. Significantly in terms of the relative impact of travel-related illness, the 29 admissions constituted 20 per cent of the total admissions (127) during the survey period (Wallace *et al.* 1992). Malaria was the most common problem for which consultation was sought, with the next major diagnostic groups being diarrhoeal disease and dengue fever. Although a clear profile of travel-related illness in Australia and New Zealand is not available, evidence suggests that the pattern of disease reported in the Wallace *et al.* (1992) study is broadly representative of cases in the two countries (Ellis-Pegler 1992).

Malaria

Malaria is increasing as a problem disease for Australian and New Zealand travellers in the South Pacific (Cook 1992; Ellis-Pegler 1992; Wallace *et al.* 1992). Malarial cases in travellers is reported to have doubled in the past decade (Howarth 1992). Malaria is caused by *Plasmodium*, a single-cell parasite. There are four types which cause the disease in humans: *Plasmodium falciparum*

Table 9.1: Travel associated illness reported at the Infectious Diseases Unit, Auckland Hospital, July–December 1989

	Total	Diagnoses		Diarrhoea	Dengue	Other
		Malaria				
		Prophyclaxis	*Treatment*			
Telephone calls	141	46	29	20	3	43
Outpatient clinics	18	–	6	1	4	7
Hospital admissions	29	–	9	4	5	11
Total	188	46	44	25	12	61

Source: Wallace *et al.*, 1992: 315.

(commonly known as cerebral malaria), *P. vivax*, *P. ovale* and *P. malariae*. The parasite produces attacks of fever varying in severity and frequency with the most serious symptoms being caused by *P. falciparum*. Malarial parasites are injected into the human bloodstream by the bite of an infected *Anopheles* mosquito. The number of cases of malaria is rising worldwide. Malarial parasites now infect an estimated 489 million people every year, killing up to 2.8 million people, which is far more than AIDS, and causing up to 100 million cases of acute illness (Turley 1990).

The World Health Organisation (WHO) announced in 1955 that the disease would soon be eradicated (Newsweek 1993). However, such optimism was not to be met. The WHO approach to eradicating malaria was twofold. First, attempting to halt the passing-on of malaria by attacking infected mosquitoes with residual pesticides such as DDT. Second, to destroy malaria parasites in the human blood through treatment with anti-malarial drugs. Unfortunately, the success of the strategy was short-lived. The relative high cost of anti-malarial programmes for developing countries meant that such programmes were either stopped or severely curtailed when foreign aid was withdrawn. The wide and often indiscriminate use of chemical pesticides has meant that many malaria carriers have now developed high genetic resistance. In addition, the use of insecticides often had numerous unintended side effects on 'friendly' insects which reduced local support for spraying programmes. Malarial parasites have also developed resistance to anti-malarial drugs. For example, in the case of Thailand, the liberal use of of anti-malarial medications has led to increasing drug resistance in malarial strains. According to *Newsweek* (1993: 14):

> Chloroquine and Fansidar, still marginally effective in most parts of the world, are virtually useless against the falciparum parasite . . . Backup drugs such as mefloquine and halofantine are fast losing their effectiveness, and so is the old standby quinine. Experts say that without new therapies, Asia could face wholly untreatable strains of malaria by the end of the decade.

The expansion of transport and development infrastructure in developing countries has also hastened the spread of malarial-carrying mosquitoes and parasites. Furthermore, many developing countries have not been able to place enough investment into health, sanitation and education (Turley 1990). All of these problems are represented to varying degrees in special interest tourism destinations in the Asia-Pacific region (see World Health Organisation 1993b, 1993c).

Resistance to malarial medication in the South Pacific is an increasing problem in Papua New Guinea, the Solomon Islands, Vanuatu and several other South Pacific islands. For example, the Solomon Islands has one of the highest rates of malaria in the world, with the capital Honiara, on the island of Guadalcanal, having one of the largest number of cases reaching almost 800 per thousand population in 1991, down from a high of over 900 cases in 1990 (Honimae 1992). Given the role of tourism in the economic development of the

Solomons through such activities as scuba-diving and ecotourism projects, the high incidence of malaria should clearly be of concern to tourism operators and travellers themselves.

Precise figures about the proportion of *Plasmodium falciparum* infections that are resistant to chloroquine in the Pacific Islands are unavailable. It is known that a 'significant number of travellers to nations such as the Solomon Islands and Papua New Guinea develop malaria due to *Plasmodium falciparum* while taking chloroquine' (Auckland Hospital Infectious Diseases Unit, pers. comm., 30 September 1992). Although exact details are unknown, it appears that chloroquine resistant *Plasmodium falciparum* is quite prevalent and that its frequency approaches that of the worst affected parts of Africa and South East Asia.

Dengue fever

Like malaria, dengue fever is a mosquito borne viral disease transmitted by *Aedes aegypti* which is endemic throughout the tropics. Dengue belongs to the flavivirus group of viruses. In recent years epidemics of dengue fever have occurred in Fiji, French Polynesia, Vanuatu, New Caledonia and other Pacific islands. As a result of an increase of dengue in south-east Asia and the Pacific Islands and increased travel to this region from Australia and New Zealand it is expected that the disease will present itself more frequently in Australian and New Zealand tourists returning from tropical areas (Mills 1991).

The prevention of dengue fever in tourists at present depends on prevention of transmission as there are no vaccines available to prevent the disease. The behaviour of the dengue vector is substantially different from that of the Anopheline mosquito responsible for malaria. '*Aedes aegypti* prefers to feed on humans during the daytime and most frequently is found in or near human habitations. Personal mosquito avoidance measures are the most important means of reducing the risk of acquiring dengue infection' (Mills 1991).

Dengue fever is also endemic to the tropics of northern Queensland. The vector of the dengue virus, *Aedes aegypti*, is known to occur only in Queensland. Outbreaks of dengue fever occurring in Townsville and Cairns in 1992, both major tourism centres, indicate the potential of the disease to spread in tropical Queensland (Sinclair 1992). Although the outbreak of dengue fever did receive some publicity in the national media, as far as can be ascertained travellers to the region did not receive formal warning of the outbreak by tour operators. However, the threat of dengue fever was regarded as so serious by the city of Rockhampton on the central Queensland coast that they placed four flocks of chickens, known as 'sentinel hens', on the outskirts of the city in order to check for the arrival of dengue carrying mosquitoes (New Zealand Herald 1993b).

Cholera and diarrhoea

Cholera is a disease endemic in many less developed nations. Cholera is essentially a disease of poverty, poor health, housing and malnutrition, and often accompanies natural disasters such as floods and earthquakes. The seventh world pandemic that started in Indonesia in 1961 reached South America in 1991 after traversing Asia and Africa. The arrival of the pandemic heralded the first significant occurrence of cholera and subsequent mortality for a century in South America (Godlee 1991).

The World Health Organisation (1993a) currently advises that cholera vaccination is not a legal requirement for international travel and travel does not need to be restricted on account of cholera. According to the *New Zealand Medical Journal* (1991: 274) 'Cholera vaccination has no part to play in the control of epidemics and the current inactivated vaccines give protection for three months in half the inoculated. The main problem concerns the traveller who is at low risk.' Nevertheless, travellers to Asia from New Zealand are being warned of a new strain of cholera (*Vibrio cholarae* (serotype 0139)) which is sweeping through Asia. The New Zealand Ministry of Health's adviser on public medicine Dr Arvind Patel has stated that the cholera vaccine, already of relatively limited use against the usual strains of cholera, was probably of no use against the new strain. The new strain of *Vibrio cholarae* was regarded as five times as lethal as the common strain, killing 5 per cent of those infected. Dr Patel explicitly noted the danger of the new strain for tourists and commented that although food prepared in top quality hotels was unlikely to be a problem, food and drink from other sources was likely to be suspect (Townsend 1993). In October 1993 the New Zealand Ministry of Health started to issue official warnings to travellers regarding the dangers presented by the new strain.

Similar to the effects of cholera but far more prevalent are diarrhoeal diseases (Barer 1989). By far the most common cause of travellers' diarrhoea is the enterotoxigenic *E coli* that may affect between 20–50 per cent of tropical travellers (New Zealand Medical Journal 1991). Therefore, advice about food and oral rehydration are probably more important than vaccination for many travellers. While knowledge of 'Delhi belly' or other such euphemisms, seems good among the backpacking fraternity and is often noted in guide books, such as *Lonely Planet*, awareness of tropical diarrhoea does not seem to be as prevalent among more up-scale travel groups in the South Pacific. This may be partly because of improved food hygiene by tour operators. However, it may also be a result of an unwillingness of some operators to disclose such perils of travelling or perhaps even a lack of field experience.

Other diseases

One of the major health issues of the late twentieth century is concern over the spread of AIDS (acquired immune deficiency syndrome). AIDS is not a single disease, but a complex of symptoms caused by a virus – HIV (human immunodeficiency virus) – which damage the human immune system and leave the infected person open to a wide array of opportunistic infections. HIV is acquired almost entirely through sexual intercourse and intravenous drug use. HIV and AIDS (which, strictly speaking, refers to the final, fatal stage of HIV infection) have become a significant tourism issue for four major reasons. First, travel has been a major factor in the spread of HIV (Lange and Dax 1987; Chinn 1988; De Schryver and Meheus 1989; Shannon and Pyle 1989; Australian Doctor 1995). Second, specific forms of tourism, particularly sex tourism, may put travellers and their sexual partners in a high risk category of contracting HIV (Hall 1994c, 1995; Australian Doctor 1995). Third, fears about the spread of AIDS have led some countries to consider bans on travellers who are HIV positive (Lewis 1989; Panos Institute 1989). Fourth, those destinations which are perceived as being HIV high risk areas may have considerable damage done to their image in the tourism marketplace (Asia Travel Trade 1990; Hall 1994b).

HIV infection is not a serious problem in the South Pacific (excluding Australia and New Zealand) in comparison with the developing nations of Africa or Asia (Karel and Robey 1988; Lewis 1989). However, the growing rate of travel between the Pacific Islands and countries with significant HIV populations, increases in the incidence of sexually transmitted diseases (STDs), and the possibility visits by HIV positive individuals who then engage in inappropriate sexual or drug using behaviour at the destination, means that the relationship between the spread of HIV and tourism is coming under increased scrutiny.

Given the enormous costs of screening travellers for HIV, let alone the immense ethical and human rights questions such a response would provide, a number of countries in the region have embarked on educational campaigns with respect to HIV and other diseases associated with travellers (Australian Doctor 1995). As Lewis (1989: 18) commented:

> The HIV pandemic raises the same questions in the Pacific as it does elsewhere across the globe. The region's major sources of tourists are Japan, North America, Australia and New Zealand, and the United Kingdom and Western Europe. The fifth source of travelers are from within the region. Included in these source regions are those with the highest rates of HIV endemicity, e.g., the United States. Most potential visitors from these source locations, however, remain uninfected, and . . . HIV screening of visitors is unlikely to stop the pandemic. Most cases of HIV infection in the region involve returning residents . . . and the key and sole way to reduce the impact of this disease is through HIV prevention education. Culturally sensitive education must be directed at the general population, high-risk groups, the travel industry, and arriving tourists.

In the Pacific islands the incidence of sexually transmitted diseases have greatly increased over the past two decades thereby indicating that the potential for the spread of HIV is substantial (Wilcox 1980a, 1980b; Lombange 1984; Gyaneshwar *et al.* 1987; Mulley 1995). However, development of a comprehensive HIV and STD education programme for the region is difficult because contemporary patterns of sexual behaviour are only poorly understood, with 'the values and mores that govern sexual behavior [being] a complex mix of traditional, Christian, and modern values' (Lewis 1989: 20).

Education has been a key component of Australia's national HIV/AIDS strategy which has been highly regarded throughout the South Pacific as a model HIV/AIDS campaign (Commonwealth Department of Health, Housing, Local Government and Community Services [DHHCS] 1993). The major goals of the National Strategy are to eliminate transmission of HIV and to minimise the personal and social impact of HIV/AIDS. Since 1991 the DHHCS has been operating an education campaign aimed at Australians travelling overseas, domestic travellers, and tourists visiting Australia, as a primary target group in the national HIV/AIDS strategy (National Evaluation Steering Committee 1992). The campaign arose because of 'the discovery of HIV infection amongst travellers returning to Australia . . . travellers need targeting to reinforce the risks of unprotected sex and needle use, as well as risks of infection through other means such as unsecured blood supplies or high levels of infection amongst sex workers in some countries' (DHHCS 1993: 28).

The campaign has utilised a series of widely distributed brochures and posters, a video, the inclusion of HIV information on airline tickets, and advertising in airport toilets (DHHCS 1992). The national campaign is not primarily targeted at those travellers who are normally categorised as sex tourists, that is those who participate in formally organised sex tours to southeast Asia, but instead the campaign is aimed towards the recreational traveller (Hall 1995). Traveller education campaigns are clearly an essential element in reducing the spread of HIV/AIDS and other STDs (Lewis 1989). However, concerns have arisen in some quarters that governments 'must not be seen to be condoning sex tourism in its educative approach to safe sex practices of tourists' (McMenamin 1993: 20). Such concerns illustrate the political tightrope that governments and health authorities have to walk when embarking on travel health education campaigns. Too far one way and the campaigns are criticised for not being effective, too far the other and they are open to criticisms of encouraging promiscuity.

The political dimensions of travel health do not just apply to sexual diseases. Growth in the number of typhoid and tuberculosis (TB) cases in New Zealand has been related to increased travel from the South Pacific Islands. Typhoid is a bacterial infection of the intestines caused by contaminated food and water. Often patients who have recovered become carriers. One of the prime sources of the disease in New Zealand has been dead fish brought in from Western Samoa and other Pacific countries as gifts by visitors or returning residents. However, while the New Zealand Ministry of Health has been approached to educate travellers over the potential problem with fish, little action has been taken.

According to Dr Lester Calder, Central Auckland's Medical Officer of Health, this is because the Ministry 'seem worried about it being a political thing' (Tiffany 1995: 51). Similarly, while TB among Pacific Islanders in Auckland is 30 times that of Europeans, the New Zealand government does not appear to be willing to impose a more rigorous health screening process on immigrants or on travellers from Niue, Tokelau and the Cook Islands, who are New Zealand citizens and are therefore able to travel to and from the Pacific islands without health checks.

HEALTH AND SPECIAL INTEREST TRAVEL

Special interest travel, particularly nature-based and cultural tourism, is becoming an increasingly important element of travel marketing and promotion of the Pacific Island states (Hay 1992; Hall 1994a, 1994b). Although traditional recreational tourism is important in destinations such as Fiji, Hawai'i, Tahiti and the Cook Islands, special interest travel, such as dive holidays, cultural tours, and ecotourism activities, are increasingly being promoted throughout the region. For example, marine tourism is being promoted by Fiji, Vanuatu, and the Solomon Islands; while 'ecotourism', often tied into the creation of new national parks, is being promoted heavily throughout the region (Hall 1994a).

The spatial distribution of special interest travel activities is substantially different from that of recreational tourism. Whereas recreational tourism tends to be resort centred and focused on 'sun, sand, sea, and surf', special interest travel activities tend to be dispersed and occur in areas away from mass tourism. Indeed, one of the primary motivational factors of special interest tourists is regarded to be the desire for novelty and authenticity in the tourist experience (Hall and Weiler 1992). Therefore, contact with areas and peoples that are not exposed to mass tourists is probably fundamental to the success of any special interest travel operation. However, the very factor which may make an area attractive to special interest tourists, that of relative isolation, also has potential health implications for host and guest alike. First, sick tourists may place significant demands on local health services (if they are available), and the availability of services should be taken into account in the promotion of destinations. Second, the local population may be at risk of diseases transmitted by tourists. Third, tourists may be at risk from exposure to local diseases with the returning tourist potentially introducing diseases into his or her country of origin (Alleyne 1990a; Shaw 1993). However, it should be acknowledged that diseases do not distinguish between special interest travellers and recreational tourists; given the presence of diseases throughout the region, all travellers would appear to be at risk.

By their very nature special interest travellers are seeking to get off the conventional tourism routes and away from mass tourist resorts. In doing so they are also potentially exposing themselves to a range of diseases that for hygiene, sanitation, health education, and environmental reasons are not found in many of the resort areas of the region. As the above discussion indicates, tropical diseases that were previously thought to be under control are becoming increasingly virulent and threatening to travellers. Nevertheless, many travel operators and national and regional tourism bodies are often failing to acknowledge such health threats perhaps because of a fear of scaring potential visitors away or because of the damage it could do to a country's or region's image.

An example of the manner in which decision-making processes ignore the health dimensions of special interest tourism can be provided from an ecotourism development in the Solomon Islands. In October 1988 a proposal for a rainforest wilderness trail traversing Guadalcanal 'under the control of an indigenous company of customary landowners' (Sofield 1992: 96), originated from within the Prime Minister's Office. It was proposed that the walk would start at Aola on the north coast of Guadalcanal and end at Lauvi Lagoon on the southern Weather Coast. However, the coastal area of the Weather Coast has only poor quality agricultural land and is beset by health problems, such as malaria, and by natural disasters including cyclones, flooding and earthquakes. Health facilities and the general level of sanitation, hygiene, and water quality is grossly inadequate for local people let alone tourists. Malaria is a major problem on the Weather Coast and has been described by the Director of Health Services of Guadalcanal Province (Guadalcanal Province 1991) as 'crippling attempts at developing a tourist industry and it would appear to be getting worse not better. In short, it is a major social, economic and health disaster in this small developing country'.

Despite such health warnings, and widespread local concerns surrounding the Lauvi Lagoon tourism resort project, the Tourism Council of the South Pacific (TCSP) (1991) produced a report highlighting the potential of the area for ecotourism development. Indeed, the *Solomon Islands Tourism Development Plan, 1991–2000*, (TCSP 1990) stated that the Lauvi Lagoon

> has potential for development of a small scale nature-oriented attraction with associated visitor accommodation and other services. There appears to be scope for developing and managing the crocodile populations for tourist viewing, this being the major attraction. Other attractions which should be developed are trails in the surrounding forest, and trips to the outlying reef. It may also be possible to integrate custom and traditional villages with tourism depending on the wishes of the people.
>
> (TCSP 1990: 359)

Unfortunately, the lagoon area and the Weather Coast in general provides the breeding ground for mosquitoes and a number of intestinal diseases at least in part because of poor water quality and sanitation, as well as a number of other diseases including leprosy and tuberculosis (Guadalcanal Province 1991). Following substantial local opposition, the ecotourism development proposal was dropped with Ezekiel Alebua, a government minister, concluding that given the opposition to the resort project it may be appropriate to divert TCSP funding into the Lees Lake area in the highlands of Guadalcanal which had substantially less health problems, primarily malaria, than the lagoon (Hall and Rudkin 1993), although it should be noted that malaria does still exist in the region (Bennett 1987).

In January 1993 cyclone Nina devastated many of the villages along the Weather Coast. In the village nearest the lagoon not a single house was left standing. The airstrip was covered with logs and other debris. It took several days of clearing by the local people before flights could resume. Nevertheless, despite health, social, environmental and broader development concerns, proposals for ecotourism development in the region were still being pursued (Hall and Rudkin 1993), with no provision for the access of water supply, sanitation for the locals or any economic benefits generated through the development to improve the inadequate health or educational facilities of the area.

The Weather Coast of Guadalcanal is not an isolated example of inadequate consideration of health matters. The health dimension is being all but forgotten within the tourism development process (Hay 1992; Hall 1994a), both in terms of the local people and in the potential impacts of travellers on the already scarce health resources of many countries in the region. The ignorance of health issues is not isolated to tourism developers as many operators and travel agents are also either ignorant or naive about the health dangers that exist for those travellers who intend to venture outside of the main tourist resorts (Ellis-Pegler 1992).

Another area of special interest tourism in the Asia-Pacific region in which the health risks have not received the attention they deserve is that of diving. Countries such as the Solomon Islands, Fiji, and Vanuatu have invested heavily in the promotion of their underwater attractions at remote locations. As with other forms of special interest tourism it is the isolation of many dive sites which represents a potential health threat. Decompression sickness is probably the most well-known hazard for divers, particularly if it is exacerbated by flying home from a diving holiday (Edmonds *et al.* 1992). For example, the carrying of portable personal decompression chambers is now compulsory for Australian commercial dive operators, although such measures are not enforced in the Pacific Islands. However, in reality the greatest marine health threat arises from contact with stinging fish and shells and ciguatera fish poisoning.

The South Pacific region abounds with hazardous fish and shells, while media attention is often focused on the danger of shark attack, in reality far more danger from contact with poisonous animals including stonefish (*Synanceia trachynis, S. verrucosa*), stingrays, jellyfish, fire coral, butterfly cod (*Pterois volitans*), cone shells (*Conus sp.*), sea snakes and the blue-ringed octopus (*Hapalochlaena maculosa*) (Wilson and Gillett 1971; Edmonds 1978; Colfelt 1985). Cone shells, for example, have been responsible for many serious stings and a number of fatalities as divers collect shells as souvenirs. Several of the cones are highly dangerous as their venom is a powerful neurotoxin and can only be safely collected with tongs and should be placed in a thick collecting bag or pail, particularly as their harpoon can penetrate heavy clothing.

Ciguatera fish poisoning is the result of consuming marine fish that have become contaminated via the food chain with toxins produced by a benthic species of dinoflagellate (*Gambierdiscus toxicus*). According to Lange *et al.* (1992: 2049), 'this organism flourishes as a consequence of environmental insult to tropical and subtropical reef ecosystems'. Minerbi (1992) has associated ciguatera poisoning with inappropriate tourism development which has damaged coastal ecosystems, and coral reef in particular (see Chapter 5). Ciguatera fish poisoning is endemic in the South Pacific (Edmonds 1978; Bagnis *et al.* 1979; Ruff 1989), although 'the condition is not reportable to public health authorities either nationally or internationally, so its incidence is not clearly known, and its epidemiology is incompletely understood' (Lange *et al.* 1992: 2049). Many species of tropical and sub-tropical fish are affected by ciguatera poisoning with neither freshness nor cooking having any bearing on fish toxicity. Edmonds (1978) recommends that large, carnivorous fish be avoided, particularly as ciguatera poisoning occurs sporadically and unpredictably, and may gradually spread from one area to another. There is no sure way of avoiding ciguatera poisoning apart from not eating fish. Somewhat humorously Edmonds (1978: 169) suggests to 'try out a sample on the neighbour's cat, and observe for a few hours', while another approach 'is to feed the older members of the family first, and if they remain unaffected after several hours, the fish may be fed to the children with safety. Some cultures may reverse this process'. Despite such a comic approach, Edwards does have a significant point to stress in terms of the health of the international traveller. Many divers and visitors to more remote communities and islands will be staying in an environment in which fish is part of the staple diet. Furthermore, for many divers part of the experience in visiting these places will be the possibility of eating the fish they have caught. Ciguatera is therefore potentially a major problem for special interest travel health and as Lange *et al.* (1992: 2052) concluded, 'international travel is an important risk factor for [ciguatera fish poisoning], and . . . the health risk might even be comparable to that of acquiring hepatitis A, a threat against which specific precautions are routinely recommended and administered'.

CONCLUSIONS

At present few potential health problems exist if travellers contain their sightseeing and experiences to the more popular Pacific destinations and engage in safe sex and drug practices, although there is some evidence to suggest that increased resistance of some diseases to either treatment or spraying of vectors may lead to their becoming a health risk even in the larger resort areas. Nevertheless, for the growing number of special interest tourists who are intent on being off the beaten track in the South Pacific numerous health problems abound. Armed with comprehensive medical insurance, prophylactics, and a well-stocked medical kit, many feel that they are safe. However, the sheer isolation of many of the regions that they are travelling in is itself a health risk, particularly as many tropical diseases such as malaria and dengue fever are re-emerging as health threats.

Special interest travel is a rapidly emerging form of tourism marked by a desire of its participants to avoid many of the traditional tourist locations. However, the search for novel, 'tourist free' destinations and activities does in itself represent a health threat to participants. By being in relatively remote destinations, special interest travellers from Australia and New Zealand, as elsewhere around the world, are also exposing themselves to diseases and health risks that are not normally to be found in recreational tourism resorts. While risk is an essential element of the excitement of travel for many special interest tourists, tourist operators, travel agents and government tourist agencies have often not been providing an honest appraisal of some of the health risks. Given a better understanding of the health risks involved in visiting some of the destinations where tourism is being promoted, it may well be the case that tourists will reevaluate the risks and select an adventurous, yet not so potentially dangerous, form of leisure taking.

REFERENCES

Alleyne, G. (1990a) 'The health/tourism interaction', *The Courier*, 122: 67–8.
—— (1990b) 'Health and tourism in the Caribbean', *Bulletin of the Pan American Health Organization*, 24(3): 291–300.
Asia Travel Trade (1990) 'AIDS problem menaces tourism', *Asia Travel Trade*, 22: 56–7.
Australian Associated Press (1991) 'Tourists warned of malaria', *The Dominion* 9 December.
Australian Doctor (1995) 'Health message needs a united stand', *Australian Doctor* 12 May: 63.
Bagnis, R., Kuberski, T. and Laugier, S. (1979) 'Clinical observations of 3009 cases of ciguatera (fish poisoning) in the South Pacific', *American Journal of Tropical Medicine and Hygiene*, 28: 1067–73.
Barer, M. (1989) 'Diarrhoea and intestinal infections', in R. Dawood (ed.) *Travellers' Health: How to Stay Healthy Abroad*, 2nd edn, Oxford: Oxford University Press, pp. 21–42.
Bennett, J.A. (1987) *Wealth of the Solomons: A History of a Pacific Archipelago, 1800–1978*, Honolulu: University of Hawaii Press.
Chinn, J. (1988) 'HIV and international travel', in A. Fleming, M. Carballo, D. Fitzsimons, M. Balley and J. Mann (eds) *The Global Impact of AIDS*, New York: Alan Liss, pp. 61–5.
Clift. S. and Page, S.J. (eds) (1996) *Health and the International Tourist*, London: Routledge.
Colfelt, D. (1985) *100 Magic Miles of the Great Barrier Reef: The Whitsunday Islands*, Rose Bay: Windward Publications.
Commonwealth Department of Health, Housing, Local Government and Community Services (1992) *Travel Safe: An HIV/AIDS Education Campaign for Travellers*, Canberra: AIDS/Communicable Diseases Unit, Department of Health, Housing, Local Government and Community Service.
Commonwealth Department of Health, Housing, Local Government and Community Services (DHHCS) (1993) *National AIDS Campaign 1986–1992*, Submission by

AIDS/Communicable Diseases Branch for the Evaluation Panel Review of National HIV/AIDS Programs, Canberra: Department of Health, Housing, Local Government and Community Services.

Cook, G.C. (1992) 'Malaria: An underdiagnosed and often neglected medical emergency', *Australia and New Zealand Journal of Medicine*, 22: 69–82.

Department of Health (1993) *Fare Well: Health Aspects of International Air Travel*, Wellington: Department of Health/Te Tari Ora.

De Schryver, A. and Meheus, A. (1989) 'International travel and sexually transmitted diseases', *World Health Statistics Quarterly*, 42: 90–9.

Economic and Social Commission for Asia and the Pacific (1994) *Review of Tourism Development in the ESCAP Region*, ESCAP Tourism Review No. 15, New York: United Nations.

Edmonds, C. (1978) *Dangerous Marine Animals of the Indo-Pacific Region*, Diving Medical Centre Monograph on Identification, First Aid and Medical Treatment, Newport: Wedneil Publications.

Edmonds, C., Lowry, C. and Pennefather, J. (1992) *Diving and Subaquatic Medicine*, 3rd edn, Oxford and Sydney: Butterworths.

Ellis-Pegler, R.B. (1992) Travel to the tropics: Going away and coming home, *Communicable Disease New Zealand*, 92(12): 109–11.

Evening Post (1993) 'Warning on new cholera strain issued', *Evening Post*, 19 October.

Godlee, F. (1991) 'Cholera pandemic', *British Medical Journal*, 302: 1039–40.

Guadalcanal Province (1991) *The State of Health of the People of Guadalcanal Province*, Honiara: Guadalcanal Province.

Gyaneshwar, R., Nsanze, H., Singh, K., Pillay, S. and Seruvatu, I. (1987) 'The prevalance of sexually transmitted disease agents in pregnant women in Suva', *Australia and New Zealand Journal of Obstetrics and Gynecology*, 27(3): 213–5.

Hall, C.M. (1994a) 'Ecotourism in Australia, New Zealand and the South Pacific: Appropriate tourism or a new form of ecological imperialism?', in E.A. Cater and G.A. Bowman (eds) *Ecotourism: A Sustainable Option?*, Chichester/London: John Wiley/ Royal Geographical Society, pp. 137–58.

—— (1994b) *Tourism in the Pacific: Development, Impacts and Markets*, South Melbourne: Longman Cheshire.

—— (1994c) 'Nature and implications of sex tourism in South-East Asia', in V.H. Kinnaird and D.R. Hall (eds) *Tourism: A Gender Analysis*, Chichester: John Wiley, pp. 142–63.

—— (1995) 'Tourism prostitution: The control and health implications of sex tourism in South-East Asia and Australia', in S. Clift and S.J. Page (eds) *Health and the International Tourist*, London: Routledge, pp. 179–92.

Hall, C.M. and Rudkin, B. (1993) Ecotourism as Appropriate Tourism?: A Case Study from the Solomon Islands, Paper presented at the 13th International Congress of Anthropological and Ethnological Sciences, Symposium on Tourism as a Determinant of Culture Change, 30 July.

Hall, C.M. and Weiler, B. (1992) 'Introduction: What's special about special interest tourism?', in B. Weiler and C.M. Hall (eds) *Special Interest Tourism*, London: Belhaven Press, pp. 1–14.

Hay, J.E. (ed.) (1992) *Ecotourism Business in the Pacific: Promoting a Sustainable Experience, Conference Proceedings*, Environmental Science Occasional Publication No. 8, Auckland: Environmental Science, University of Auckland.

Honimae, J. (1992) 'Malaria research tracks down a killer', *The Solomons Voice*, 29 April: 9.

Howarth, A. (1992) 'Take your malaria medicine', *The Dominion*, 22 September: 13.

Isaacs, R. and Ellis-Pegler, R.B. (1987) 'Plasmodium falciparum resistance to quinine and sulfadoxime-prymethamine in the Solomon Islands', *Medical Journal of Australia*, 146: 449–50.

Karel, S.G. and Robey, B. (1988) 'AIDS in Asia and the Pacific', *Asian Pacific Population Forum*, 2(1–2): 1–14, 18–29.

Lange, R. and Dax, E. (1987) 'HIV infection and international travel', *American Family Physician*, 36(3): 197–204.

Lange, W.R., Snyder, F.R. and Fudala, P.J. (1992) 'Travel and ciguatera fish poisoning', *Archives of Intern Medicine*, 152: 2049–53.

Lewis, N.D. (1989) *AIDS and Tourism: Implications for Pacific Island States*, Honolulu: Pacific Islands Development Program, East-West Center.

Lombange, C. (1984) 'Trends in sexually transmitted disease incidence in Papua New Guinea', *Papua New Guinea Medical Journal*, 27(3–4): 145–57.

McMenamin, B. (1993) 'Sex tours of Asia breed corruption.' Letter to the editor from national coordinator, End Child Prostitution in Asian Tourism (ECPAT) Australia, *The Age*, 23 October: 20.

Mills, G.D. (1991) 'Clinical spectrum of dengue fever in travellers', *New Zealand Medical Journal*, 104: 228–30.

Minerbi, L. (1992) *Impacts of Tourism Development in Pacific Islands*, Greenpeace Pacific Campaign, San Francisco.

Mulley, S. (1995) 'Gonorrhoea strains show resistance', *Australian Doctor*, 12 May: 61.

National Evaluation Steering Committee (1992) *Report of the Evaluation of the National HIV/AIDS Strategy*, Report to the Minister for Health, Housing and Community Services and the Intergovernmental Committee on AIDS by the National Evaluation Steering Committee, Canberra: Australian Government Publishing Service.

Newsweek (1993) 'Mosquitoes on the comeback killer trail', *Newsweek*, 15 September, section 2: 14.

New Zealand Herald (1993a) 'Travellers catch typhoid', *New Zealand Herald*, 4 August, section 1: 24.

—— (1993b) 'Guard chickens', *New Zealand Herald*, 3 November, section 2: 2.

New Zealand Medical Journal (1991) 'Cholera rampages on', *New Zealand Medical Journal*, 26 June: 274.

Nicholls, D. (1992) 'Sea anemone sting while SCUBA diving', *New Zealand Medical Journal*, 24 June: 245.

Panos Institute (1989) *AIDS and the Third World*, London: Panos Institute.

PATA Advisory Council – Development Committee (1992) *Position Paper – Tourism and Health*, Woollahara: Dain Simpson Associates.

Ruff, T.A. (1989) 'Ciguatera in the Pacific: A link with military activities', *Lancet*, 1989, 1: 201–5.

Shannon, G. and Pyle, G. (1989) 'The origin and diffusion of AIDS: A view from medical geography', *Annals of the Association of American Geographers*, 79(1): 1–24.

Shaw, M. (1993) 'Catching the travel bug', *GP Weekly*, 10 March: 28–9.

Sinclair, D.P. (1992) 'The distribution of *Aedes aegypti* in Queensland, 1990 to 30 June 1992', *Communicable Diseases Intelligence*, 16, 19: 404–7.

Sofield, T. (1992) 'The Guadacanal track ecotourism project in the Solomon Islands', in J.E. Hay (ed.) *Ecotourism Business in the Pacific: Promoting a Sustainable Experience, Conference Proceedings*, Auckland: Environmental Science, University of Auckland, pp. 89–100.

The Economist (1993) 'One bite is one too many', *The Economist*, 21 August: 31–2.

Tiffany, M. (1995) 'Typhoid scare in New Zealand', *Pacific Islands Monthly*, February: 51.

Tourism Council of the South Pacific (TCSP) (1990) *Solomon Islands Tourism Development Plan, 1991–2000*, Suva: Tourism Council of the South Pacific.

—— (1991) *Solomon Islands Nature Sites Development Project: Lauvi Lagoon*, Suva: Tourism Council of the South Pacific.

Townsend, K. (1993) 'New killer cholera', *New Zealand Herald*, 19 October, section 1: 1.
Turley, R. (1990) 'Worldwide search for solutions', *Geographical Magazine*, February: 22–7.
Wallace, E., Thomas, M.G. and Ellis-Pegler, R.B. (1992) 'Travel associated illness', *New Zealand Medical Journal*, 105: 315–16.
Wilcox, F. (1980a) 'Venereal diseases in the islands of the South Pacific', *British Journal of Venereal Disease*, 56(4): 204–8.
—— (1980b) 'Venereal diseases in the Pacific islands: Papua New Guinea', *British Journal of Venereal Disease*, 56(5): 277–81.
Wilson, B.R. and Gillett, K. (1971) *Australian Shells*, Sydney: A.H. & A.W. Reed.
Wilson, N. and Baker, M. (1992) 'Choosing vaccinations for the traveller', *New Ethicals*, October: 47–55.
World Health Organisation (1993a) *International Travel and Health: Vaccination Requirements and Health Advice Situation as on 1 January 1993*, Geneva: World Health Organisation, Geneva.
—— (1993b) 'World malaria situation in 1991, Part I', *Weekly Epidemiological Record*, 68(34): 245–52.
—— (1993c) 'World malaria situation in 1991, Part II', *Weekly Epidemiological Record*, 68(35): 253–59.

Chapter 10

Seeking quality in Pacific tourism

Chris Ryan

INTRODUCTION

Quality is emerging as a major factor associated with the development and competitiveness of tourism during the 1990s, and the Pacific Islands are no exception to this. Tourists are increasingly experienced, and this alone requires operators to ensure a 'quality product'. Other trends reinforce this, including, in some of the Western democracies, a middle class facing pressures on discretionary incomes due to political and social changes, that will make them more 'value for money conscious'. However, the concepts of quality and 'value for money' within tourism are complex. Tourists may have expectations of previously unvisited places based on fragments of truth, while suppliers of the tourist experience may be required to formulate perceptions of the needs of tourists derived from different cultures and often life experiences different to their own.

An additional consideration is that the search for quality requires first the meeting of more basic needs. Pearce (1988) has noted the importance of meeting basic physiological and safety needs in his concept of the 'travel career ladder'. Williams and Gill (1994) have observed that the impact of tourism requires an assessment of multifarious considerations grouped under the categories of the visitor experience, the resident experience, and the economic, political-administrative, physical and ecological systems. Each of these overlap in their concerns. For example, Williams and Gill include accommodation under the heading, 'physical', while such accommodation could be counted under the heading 'service quality' in the visitor experience classification. It should be noted that Williams and Gill (1994: 178) criticise this type of classification as being 'too . . . complex' and with 'interrelated limiting factors that hamper its use', but for the current purpose the model is sufficient to show that tourism is a social phenomenon that is holistic in its nature.

To discuss quality issues in tourism therefore requires a concern about questions that are often much wider than the training issues associated with *KiwiHost* and other similar programmes which look at the nature of the attraction/service provider-tourist interface. Furthermore, because of a need to define 'quality' in operational ways, this chapter will note definitions of quality derived from the International Organisation for Standardisation (ISO). It will briefly review the complexity of the notion of quality tourism and then describe some of the initiatives that seek to establish quality, including human resource management issues, such as staff training, which has been regarded by the tourism industry as being of critical importance in tourism in Australasia and the Pacific Islands (AMEX and PATA 1994; also see Chapter 18).

Quality in tourism – the ISO criteria

Lockyer (1986) has argued that basically there is no distinction between manufacturing and services for both are concerned with managerial decisions seeking to convert inputs into outputs in such way as to produce consumer satisfaction. Indeed, Ryan (1991) has argued that in marketing, regardless of whether the product is tangible or a service, the basic decisions for marketing managers are the same – for example, how to develop the highest exposure per dollar spent on advertising requires the same analytical techniques whether the item is a service or a good. Other authors disagree. Murdick *et al.* (1990) sustain a more conventional view by arguing that services possess 12 distinct characteristics, as shown in Table 10.1, that make them different from goods.

However, the debate has two implications. Quality and total quality management as understood in manufacturing, may have lessons to teach services such as tourism, but the application of the lessons may be more complex in a service environment. Within manufacturing industry any discussion of

Table 10.1: Characteristics of services

- Services produce intangible output
- Services produce variable, non-standard output
- A service is perishable, i.e. it cannot be carried in inventory, but is consumed in production
- There is high customer contact throughout the service process
- The customer participates in the process of providing a service
- Skills are sold directly to the customer
- Services cannot be mass produced
- High personal judgement is employed by individuals performing the service
- Service firms are labour intensive
- Decentralised facilities are located near the customers
- Measures of effectiveness are subjective
- Pricing options are more elaborate

Source: After Murdick *et al.* 1990.

quality quickly leads to discussions of performance criteria, their development, implementation, management and processes of inspection and review. The Standards Association of New Zealand provides a series of definitions that relate to the ISO 9000 series of awards. These awards (ISO stands for the International Organisation for Standardisation) originally commenced with the need for internationally recognised standards of technical performance so that equipment manufactured in one country could perform just as well in another. However, the standards quickly developed processes for intra-company performance evaluation and blueprinting by which companies identified targets and criteria to judge their success in meeting customer requirements. Interest is high, and growing, as evidenced by Quality Assurance Services, a subsidiary of Standards Australia, receiving approximately 160 to 200 applications per month in 1994 from Australian and New Zealand companies. Many of the large international management consultancy companies such as Deloitte Touche Tohmatsu and KPMG are not only so certified, but offer quality certification processes to companies, including those in the tourism industry.

The Standards Association of New Zealand provide a number of definitions of quality and related concepts (Table 10.2), which tend to follow international ISO practice. Hence, 'quality' is identified at company level and processes of goal identification, measurement, implementation and review to achieve 'quality' are thus established.

Table 10.2: Definitions of quality and related concepts

Quality	the total features and characteristics of a product or service that bear on its ability to satisfy stated or implied needs
Quality management	that aspect of the overall management that determines and implements the quality policy
Quality policy	the overall quality intentions and direction of an organisation as regards quality, as formally expressed by top management
Quality system	the organisational structure, responsibilities, procedures, processes and resources for implementing quality management
Quality control	the operational techniques and activities used to fulfil requirements for quality
Quality assurance	all those planned and systematic actions necessary to provide adequate confidence that a product or service will satisfy given requirements for quality
Inspection	activities such as measuring, examining, testing and gauging one or more characteristics of a product or service and comparing these with specified requirements to determine conformity

Source: Standards Association of New Zealand.

Conceptual approaches to quality in tourism: gap analysis

It might be argued that the ISO criteria are product attribute related, whereas if tourism is an experience, there is a need for criteria to be client orientated. There is a rich literature on consumer orientated perceptual analysis emanating initially from both sides of the Atlantic (e.g. Gronroos 1982, 1988; Parasuraman *et al.* 1985, 1988, 1993), but which is being applied to companies in the Pacific region (e.g. Cliff and Ryan 1996). Reviews of this literature and the concepts involved are provided by Berry and Parasuraman (1993), Gilbert and Joshi (1992), with critiques by researchers such as Carmen (1990) and Brown *et al.* (1993) to mention but a few. From this perspective quality or service performance is defined as a congruence between client expectation and client perception of the service provided. For example, the SERVQUAL model (Parasuraman *et al.* 1985), identifies five gaps of importance:

- between consumer expectation and management perception;
- between management perception and service quality specifications;
- between service quality specifications and service delivery;
- between service delivery and external communications; and
- between perceived service and delivered service.

Thus, three parties are identified in the process, namely customer, management and employee. A number of criticisms have been made of the model. The model tends to be consumer and manager orientated in its view of service. There is no reference to any gaps between client behaviour and the expectations of the immediate service provider, or the employees' expectations of management and their performance. It can be argued that as players in the system, clients too have roles to fulfil. At a technical level of measurement, are clients utilising criteria of the 'ideal' level of service, or an 'acceptable' level based upon experience or other determinants? The SERVQUAL model is based upon five factors: tangibles, reliability, empathy, responsiveness and assurance. Other researchers have not been able to replicate these (e.g. Carmen 1990; Cliff and Ryan 1996). However, such studies have often been able to identify similar dimensions, and it might be that the exact number and components of the dimensions are partly situation and question specific (Carmen 1990; Ryan and Saleh 1991).

Quality – what does it mean in tourism?

Thus, quality in tourism is complex for a number of reasons. Tourist destinations are multi-products in that they are sold to different market segments. Additionally, tourists seek to experience a destination or country – an activity which is different to the purchase of an individual consumer good. The tourist is purchasing an experience from a large number of commercial bodies, not all of whom are in the destination zone. Purchase begins in the tourist generating country. Additionally, the total tourist experience is judged not only by the interaction with the commercial sector of the tourist industry in the tourist receiving country, but also through contact with those from non-commercial organisations. As MacCannell (1976) noted, the tourist may feel that they have failed as a tourist if they have not penetrated the 'back-stage'; have not been able to establish a rapport with the 'ordinary'. It might be contended that while this is much more true of the independent, non-package, tourists who establish their own itinerary, and who increasingly wish to avoid areas they categorise as being 'too touristy', other tourists have different 'back-stages' they wish to access. These latter include the experience of sharing a place with others.

Any consideration of quality within tourism therefore involves a complexity of concerns which pose many challenges to tourist boards and operators who are faced with competing and possibly incompatible demands. There are the components, both tangible and intangible, that create the quality of benefits that the tourist wants, the systems that create the means of 'delivering the desired satisfaction' (Kotler 1991: 365). These components can be identified as occurring at different points in the delivery system, for example, from *micro-concerns*, for instance at the specific site level, in the care and consideration given to actual site planning, from the architecture of buildings to the lay out and design of footpaths and car parks, to *macro-concerns*, for example, the national planning mechanisms which seek to achieve a balance between the needs of local communities and those of the tourist – not forgetting the need to maintain the natural environment, the sites of historic interest and heritage significance, while at the same time generating the desired levels of economic impact.

Quality in tourism therefore encompasses a whole range of issues, of which the following are only a partial listing:

- site aesthetics;
- managing visitor flows to avoid overcrowding;
- the provision of an accommodation stock that meets tourist demand for value for money;
- the training of staff in customer handling skills;
- the management of natural scenic areas considered to possess aesthetic value or specific biological, scientific value on the basis of uniqueness or contribution to eco-systems;
- the meeting of demands to recognise cultural integrity from minority cultures, even while, in many cases, permitting social evolution, economic gain and political self-control of their own futures;
- the demands of host communities to control their own destiny, to determine the levels of tourism they see as appropriate, and to develop their own relationships with international businesses; and
- the development of national plans which permit processes of consultation, determination of priorities, protection of those areas and peoples identified as needing protection, and a legislative framework which enforces the processes so determined.

While, in the above listing, a transition from specific site issues to the national interest can be identified, in reality a complex socio-economic-political process is in operation which is fuzzy, lengthy and often uncertain. Many of the issues that relate to the broad context within which tourism takes place are well discussed in the first section of this book (Chapters 1–9). It is therefore not the purpose of this chapter to define a holistic model of quality at all scales of tourism development, but by indicating some case studies of quality, and pointing to human resource issues in particular, various themes might be identified which may highlight some of the quality issues facing the Pacific Islands.

Quality through training staff who have contact with customers

While nature cannot be tamed, it is possible for management to exercise control over other variables contributing to 'quality'. Many countries now have in place training programmes for staff who come into contact with tourists, and which permit the organisation to display a symbol that indicates that their staff have been trained and certified (e.g. New Zealand's *KiwiHost* Programme). The KiwiHost programme has been in operation since February 1991, and by June 1994 over 55,000 individual staff belonging to over 2500 businesses had been through the programme. The programme was introduced by the New Zealand Tourism Board to address the problem of a variation in service standards in tourism and its related industries. Arthur (1994), national coordinator of the programme, has commented that historically, in New Zealand, there used to be apathy and an amateur approach to customer service. This, she argues, is being replaced by a distinctly different attitude that seeks to generate repeat business. Reichheld and Sasser (1990), in a study of sales staff, found that businesses lost the most customers because of indifferent attitudes by sales staff. It is claimed that training sales staff to be receptive to customers is a profitable exercise, for attracting back just an additional 5 per cent of existing customers can mean an additional improvement of profits by up to 25 per cent. *KiwiHost* programmes are of seven hours duration, and are usually run on a single day led by trained facilitators. The programme focuses upon basic communication, active listening and handling complaints skills, but seeks to reinforce the message that sales and service staff do make a difference. From a theoretical viewpoint, the programmes are about generating the positive critical incident as described by Bitner *et al.* (1990). Following the success of the original *KiwiHost* programme, two further programmes have been added, these being *KiwiHost Super Service* and *KiwiHost for Managers*. *KiwiHost Super Service* is a follow up to *Kiwihost*, and is also of one day's duration. It examines serving customers from diverse backgrounds and indicates the preferences of different groups and nationalities of visitors, builds up telephone skills, analyses body language, and shows ways in which complaints, by prompt action, can be turned into customers having positive perceptions of the supplying organisation.

As Bitner *et al.* (1990) demonstrate, the ability of front-line staff to respond positively to customer complaints requires managerial action to devolve authority to these front-line staff, yet also to train them so that their reactions are appropriate to the situation. Any organisation that responded to customer complaints by an automatic reduction of prices would soon find itself in financial difficulty! 'KiwiHost for Managers', again a one-day course, has a number of concerns. One is to show that the customers of managers include not only the paying guests, but also the staff – the internal customer. Discussions are initiated about the responsibilities and authority of staff dealing with clients. In part the programme is an explanation for managers about the skills staff gain from 'KiwiHost', and how best organisations can benefit from those skills. Upon completion of each of the courses participants are graded, and if successful, as most are, are certified and given a pin that can be worn.

As indicated above, the programme has been widely accepted. Some organisations have made it an inherent part of their staff training. For example, the George Hotel of Christchurch, a large, five-star hotel, requires all staff to undertake the 'KiwiHost' programme within the first 500 hours of employment, and all front-line staff take the 'Super Service' programme within the first 2500 hours of employment. All management are expected to attend the Manager's Workshop. The Southern Pacific Hotel Corporation also require each of their Hotel Human Resource Managers to train as leaders in KiwiHost so as to best be able to train their own staff. Other users of the programme include internationally known New Zealand based tourist operators like the Shotover Jet (jet boat operators), A.J. Hackett Bungy (bungy jumping), Kelly Tarlton's UnderWater World (part of the Helicopter Line) and the North Island ski resorts of Whakapapa and Turoa. The motivations for joining these schemes include those of marketing. The overseas market is important to New Zealand tourism. In 1995, 1.4 million overseas visitors spent approximately $NZ3.7 billion dollars, and accounted for approximately half the total tourist spending in the country. The marketing activities of the New Zealand Tourism Board outside of New Zealand are thus vital to the continued success of the growth story of New Zealand tourism, as the Board is often the first point of contact for both operators and potential tourists seeking information about tourism in New Zealand. It is increasingly Board policy to only recommend those organisations that have trained staff. Additionally, through its influence on the Visitor Information Network (VINs), it is increasingly becoming the norm that the VIN will only recommend organisations that are Qualmark (see below) rated and who have staff trained in KiwiHost.

However, what is an appropriate staff training scheme for a Pacific nation such as New Zealand may not work in another, quite different political and economic environment elsewhere in the Pacific. The 1994 PATA conference in Bali highlighted a concern over a shortage of skilled staff in its consideration of a report by AMEX and PATA (1994). This report noted that:

There is an acute shortage of qualified managerial and professional workers among small and medium sized firms in the Asia-Pacific Travel and Tourism industry. Approximately 63 percent of the firms are experiencing moderate-to-serious difficulties in finding managerial workers, and approximately 54 percent are experiencing moderate-to-serious difficulties in finding professional workers.

(AMEX and PATA 1994: iv)

Given such a shortage, it must inevitably mean that a threat to the quality of tourist experiences exists – a threat which implies continual difficulties in seeking business from new and existing clients.

Quality through rating

Some tourist related businesses are expressing interest in quality rating schemes or similar approaches developed by consumer protection groups. The first travel agent in Australasia to be granted ISO 9001 accreditation was Signature Travel in Wellington, a member of the Gulliver's Pacific group of agencies. In a study of New Zealand agencies Cliff and Ryan (1996) applied the SERVQUAL questionnaire developed by Parasuraman *et al.* (1988) and found that the major negative gaps between expectations and perceptions occurred on the reliability dimension, which included items such as the need to maintain error free records. Signature Travel's (NZ) general manager, Tim Thodey, identified error reduction as its most important objective, stating that the procedures required in obtaining ISO 9001 'meant setting certain procedures in place, documenting them and then ensuring everyone in the back office was working by them . . . It has allowed us to target 100 percent error-free processing as a realistic objective' (Thodey 1994: 21).

These procedures also include recording every contact made between customer and agency, with details of the matters discussed. It is also interesting to note that Thodey believes many business customers are experienced travellers, and as such know as much as many travel consultants. Hence, there is a continuous need to provide staff training to retain product knowledge, and the inspections required by ISO 9001 are an important part of the process of retaining an ability to survive in business – quality being 'no longer a competitive weapon in itself, but . . . a requisite for survival' (Thodey 1994: 21).

Quality measured by not only an assessment of 'objective', tangible components, but by customer involvement and through repeated processes of examination is also a feature of the Qualmark system introduced in New Zealand in 1993. Qualmark New Zealand Ltd is a grading company established by the New Zealand Tourism Board and The New Zealand Automobile Association Inc. It is voluntary, and by 1994 had extended to motels, hotels, holiday accommodation parks, camping grounds and caravan parks. Assessors visit the premises at times previously agreed by the operator and assessor, and the facilities are inspected. For motels the checklist falls into three sections relating to reception, accommodation and other facilities (Table 10.3). A fourth section consists of a customer questionnaire of a sample of visitors, who have previously agreed to be questioned, by a telephone survey by completing cards at the accommodation – the motelier or hotelier being able to provide the names and addresses from these cards. The assessor undertakes the survey. The final rating thus depends upon scores relating to facilities and standards of quality, which form the coordinates to arrive at the final rating.

Another area where quality is demonstrated is that of the air industry, where maintenance schedules are carefully plotted, and adhered to, in a continuous process of checking. However, outside of the major airlines, it has been found that maintenance scheduling is, in practice, more haphazard, and unfortunately action is perhaps only taken after serious accidents involving a loss of life. One

Table 10.3: Sections A and B of the Qualmark rating system

Part A
- The reservations system, tariff information and cancellation procedures
- The reception, check-in and check out, complaint procedures
- Staff presentation and training
- The telephone system and procedures
- Security and first aid facilities
- Housekeeping and laundry
- Parking and walkways
- The buildings, grounds and overall appearance

Part B
- Accommodation units of each type provided, including
- Lounge areas
- Kitchen facilities
- Dining facilities
- Bedrooms and bedding
- Bathrooms/ensuite facilities
- Other items provided
- Extra facilities
- Room service
- Service kitchens
- Conference facilities
- Restaurants/lounges
- Licensed bars
- Recreational facilities (e.g. pools, play areas)
- Others

such example is the case of scenic trips by light aircraft and helicopters. Even before the second accident in 1994 involving the loss of life of six tourists and their pilot over the Franz Josef glacier in South Island, New Zealand, the New Zealand Civil Aviation Authority (CAA) had come to the conclusion that simply requiring certification of airworthiness of the aircraft used, proper certification of pilots, and agreement of flight paths was, in fact, insufficient. Kevin Ward, NZCAA director is, in effect, seeking a quality management requirement of all such scenic airlines, where procedures as to quality assurance have to be in place, and have to meet the requirements of safety audit officers to be appointed by the CAA. These officials will not only visit the companies at agreed times, but also at other, unspecified times.

This procedure is becoming increasingly common, and under health and safety legislation and its interpretation by the courts in many countries, the lack of properly documented and adhered to specifications of safety checks is being held as *prima facie* evidence of negligence, and hence any tourist who is injured will have grounds for a successful claim against a company for injury or harm if such procedures are shown not to exist. This applies to adventure tourism operations as much as to manufacturing processes.

Quality through competition

Almost every country has tourism awards made to attract owners, operators and accommodation providers. It is easy to see this as simply an opportunity for the industry to indulge in self-congratulation, but this is not the whole of the story. Award winners present success stories, and often the basis of that success is the attention given to detail, planning and concern about the client experience. They form models for others to emulate, they are the 'leaders' within the industry. Often the motivation for such awards is to increase quality through the dissemination of good practice, and the publicising of success. The thinking is that competitors will 'try harder', on the premise that winning awards attracts business. Certainly award winners are quick to include such feats in their advertising as evidence of external assessments of quality.

In many countries awards are given to categories which include airlines, hotels and site operators, and for those concerned with the general impacts of tourism, an important question is the criteria being adopted by judges. Such criteria include consumer satisfaction, but other evaluations are increasingly being made including the adaptation of environmentally friendly operating procedures. Can such criteria include the social, cultural and environmental impacts of tourist attractions? There is little reason to believe why this cannot be the case, and if this suggestion was to be widely adopted it would create some changes in policies as the industry does value these awards. Certainly the worldwide British Airways awards for environmentally friendly tourist initiatives is one such high profile example. Indeed, even being short-listed for these awards is itself promoted in an attempt to attract even more visitors.

CONCLUSIONS

Quality in tourism is a complex issue, and the needs of a number of stakeholders must be satisfied, namely:

• the tourist
• the host community – i.e. the social and cultural environment
• the service providers and their employees
• the physical environment.

While it might be claimed that the main stakeholder is the tourist in that without the tourist there is no tourist industry, such a claim in no way simplifies the task about what quality in tourism means. Tourists are not homogeneous, and what satisfies one may be anathema to another.

Thus, any narrow consideration of quality will no doubt develop operational criteria of success – but strategic thinking about quality requires consideration of the wider context. This cliché is not restricted to the Pacific area, but as noted in the above discussion, the issues of quality in the Pacific must take note of the very different cultures, locations and geography of the Pacific nations. Linked together by numerous ties, the differences between the Polynesian microstates and the industrial powers of the USA and Japan, between the past colonial nations of Australia and New Zealand and the newly industrialised economies of south east Asia – such differences might lead to the conclusion that no commonality in quality can be found. Hopefully, this chapter has indicated some fundamental truths about the achievement of quality in tourism. It requires painstaking trouble over the details – whether it be the cleanliness of the hotel room, the location of the sewage disposal plant or the view from the bedroom window. But it also requires a vision of what is occurring in a wider world, and an awareness of the continuous processes of change.

REFERENCES

AMEX and PATA (1994) *Gearing up for Growth II: A Study of Human Resources Issues in Small to Medium Sized Enterprises in Asia-Pacific Travel and Tourism*, Honolulu: AMEX-PATA.

Arthur, M.(1994) *Bringing the Customer Back*, Wellington: New Zealand Tourism Board.

Berry, L.L. and Parasuraman, A. (1993) 'Building a new academic field – the case of services marketing', *Journal of Retailing*, 69(1): 13–59.

Bitner, M.J., Booms, B.H. and Tetreault, M. (1990) 'The service encounter: diagnosing favorable and unfavorable incidents', *Journal of Marketing*, 54, January: 71–84.

Brown, G. and Bacchieri, P. (1992) 'Planning for growth in the Asia-Pacific region: A case study of Club Med's human resource strategy', in J. Ruddy (ed.) *Direction 2000*, Hong Kong: Hong Kong Polytechnic.

Brown, T.J., Churchill Jr, G. A. and Peter, J.P. (1993) 'Improving the measurement of service quality', *Journal of Retailing*, 69(1): 127–39.

Carmen, J. (1990) 'Consumer perceptions of service quality: An assessment of the SERVQUAL dimensions', *Journal of Retailing*, 66, Spring: 33–55.

Cliff, A. and Ryan, C. (1996) 'Do travel agents measure up to consumer expectation – an application of the SERVQUAL model to New Zealand travel agents', *Journal of Travel and Tourism Marketing* (in press).

Gilbert, D.C, and Joshi, I. (1992) 'Quality management and the tourism and hospitality industry', in C.P. Cooper and A. Lockwood (eds) *Progress in Tourism Recreation and Hospitality Management, Vol. 4*, London: Belhaven, pp. 149–67.

Gronroos, C. (1982) *Strategic Management and Marketing in the Service Sector*, Helsinki: Swedish School of Economics and Business Administration, Helsinki.

Gronroos, C. (1988) *Assessing Competitive Edge in the New Competition of the Service Economy: The Five Rules of Service*, Working Paper No 9, Phoenix: First Interstate Centre for Services Marketing, Arizona State University.

Kotler, P. (1991) *Marketing Management, Analysis, Planning, Implementation and Control*, 7th edn, Engelwood Cliffs: Simon and Schuster.

Lockyer, K. (1986) 'Service – a polemic and a proposal', *International Journal of Operations and Production Management*, 6(3): 5–9.

MacCannell, D. (1976) *The Tourist – A New Theory of the Leisure Class*, New York: Schocken Books.

Murdick, R. G., Render, B. and Russell, R.S. (1990) *Service Operations Management*, Boston, Allyn and Bacon.

Parasuraman, A. Zeithaml, V.A. and Berry, L.L. (1985) 'A conceptual model of service quality and its implications for future research', *Journal of Retailing*, 49, Fall: 41–50.

Parasuraman, A., Zeithaml, V.A., and Berry, L.L. (1988) 'SERVQUAL: A multiple-item scale for measuring consumer perceptions of service quality', *Journal of Retailing*, 64(1): 12–37.

Parasuraman, A., Berry, L. and Zeithaml, V.A. (1993) 'Research note: More on improving service quality measurement, *Journal of Retailing*, 69(1): 140–7.

Pearce, P. (1988) *The Ulysses Factor: Evaluating Visitors in Tourist Settings*, New York: Springer-Verlag.

Reichheld, F. and Sasser, W. (1990) 'Zero defections: Quality comes to services', *Harvard Business Review*, 68(5): 105–13.

Ryan, C.A. (1991) *Recreational Tourism – A Social Science Perspective*, London: Routledge.

Ryan, C. and Saleh, F. (1991) 'Conviviality – a source of satisfaction for hotel guests: An application of the servqual model', in P. Johnson and B. Thomas (eds) *Choice and Demand in Tourism*, London: Mansell, pp. 107–22.

Thodey, T. (1994) 'Accreditation drawcard for customers', *The Dominion*, October 18: 21.

Williams, P.W. and Gill, A. (1994) 'Tourism capacity management issues', in W. Theobald (cd.) *Global Tourism: The Next Decade*, Oxford: Butterworth Heinemann, pp. 174–87.

Part II
Destination Cases

Chapter 11

Australia's and New Zealand's role in Pacific tourism: aid, trade and travel

C. Michael Hall and Stephen J. Page

INTRODUCTION

The development of tourism in most countries is a conscious decision to pursue an expansionist strategy to facilitate a growth in foreign exchange earnings derived from visitor expenditure, and to promote employment growth in this service sector activity. A prerequisite for the successful development of tourism in any context is the availability of capital, entrepreneurs and the ability of the public and private sector to ensure infrastructure, accommodation, attractions and associated facilities are provided (Pearce 1989). However, as Chapter 1 indicated, there is a comparative absence of indigenous capital and a pool of entrepreneurs in most Pacific Islands able to coordinate and facilitate tourism development without a degree of external assistance from the state, international funding agencies (e.g. the World Bank and, Asian Development Bank) and aid donors (e.g. the United Nations Development Programme). Although the development studies literature (Mabogunje 1980) and recent syntheses of tourism research in less developed countries (LDCs) (Harrison 1992) have indicated the comparative disadvantages which LDCs suffer, the situation for small islands (Lockhart *et al.* 1993) in the Pacific is more problematic in view of the role of aid as a catalyst for tourism development. To date, few studies have addressed the issue of aid and tourism development beyond the highly publicised role of Japanese foreign aid policy (Rix 1993) and the repercussions for tourism policy and development (Rimmer 1994). Therefore, this chapter considers the role of two influential actors in the South Pacific – Australia and New Zealand – and their role in aiding tourism development. It should be emphasised, however, that the major aid donors to the Pacific Island countries include France, the USA, Japan, the UK and other countries besides the coterminous states of Australia and New Zealand (Thakur 1991). The chapter commences with a discussion of aid as a development mechanism, followed by a review of travel and trade flows between Australia and New Zealand and the Pacific Islands. The provision of aid by each country is then considered in relation to its impact on tourism development followed by a review of the implications for Pacific Island tourism.

AID AS A DEVELOPMENT MECHANISM: ALTRUISM OR POLITICAL SELF-INTEREST?

There are two basic types of aid: multilateral (aid channelled to the recipient government by the donor government through a multigovernment and/or international agency, for example United Nations Economic and Social Commission for Asia and the Pacific (ESCAP) or the United Nations Development Programme (UNDP)), or bilateral aid (direct aid from a donor government to a recipient government). Crocombe (1992) also discusses the importance of voluntary aid and different organisations which assist in giving aid. According to White and Woestman (1994), there are four principal issues which need to be addressed in any analysis of aid (which is also referred to as development assistance):

(1) Volume – the amount given;
(2) Concessionality – the financial terms and conditions under which it is given;
(3) Tying – the extent to which a recipient country is required to use aid to purchase goods from the donor country to promote trade;
(4) Allocation – the geographical distribution of aid to recipients.

These four issues are a useful starting point for any critical analysis of aid and its role in the economic development of LDCs or developing countries because it highlights the range of political issues and agendas which sometimes underpin aid policies of donor countries. For example, Tarte (1989) argues that regionalism in the South Pacific will be determined largely by the strategic and economic interests of Western developed states with a stake in the region, often related to former colonial relationships and continued trade and geopolitical concerns. Gounder's (1995) recent survey of the motivation that underlies Australia's bilateral aid to developing countries recognises that it has a humanitarian concern compared with the United States aid allocation, which is based on donors' interests rather than recipients' needs.

In this context, aid can still be interpreted as serving the collective interests of the metropolitan powers, such as Australia and New Zealand, and may even reinforce existing neo-colonial interests when defence issues are involved. As Gounder (1995) observes, even Australia's aid programmes are motivated by a range of factors, though self-interest is not always readily apparent. Thakur's (1991) analysis of changing forces in South Pacific international relations provides a good introduction and background to the

> growing international sensitivity to the emerging reality of increasingly complex and diverse international relations in the South Pacific . . . Countries of the region are no longer content to accept being pawns in a great game being played out by others. They have their own priorities, and they are prepared to evaluate outsiders' actions on the basis of their responsiveness to regional aspirations.
>
> (Thakur 1991: 41)

Therefore, the Pacific Islands continue to receive substantial development assistance from a variety of countries and development agencies, each with their own motives and political objectives. Governments of Pacific Island states are, however, increasingly questioning the motives and, where possible, seeking to align development assistance to their own development strategies (Grynberg 1995). Yet, as Connell (1993: 138) argues, 'though most island states, especially in the Pacific, have development plans, and even policies, which emphasise the need to achieve greater self-reliance, such statements are rhetoric rather than reality, a legacy of the post-independence optimism'. Since there are political and diplomatic advantages to small Pacific Island states arguing for their rights as self-governing territories, while ignoring the implications of the MIRAB model (see Chapter 1) for such countries. Thus, as Connell (1993: 133) suggests while foreign aid is a major source of income for many island states,

> there is little or no opposition to the principle of sustained and increased aid delivery. Overall per capita flows to IMS (island microstates) are exceptionally high by global standards; the IMS have long benefited from a widespread 'small-country bias' in aid delivery. States that have remained in some form of dependent relationship (such as Niue, Pitcairn, the Micronesian states or the French overseas departments and territories . . .) have been even more fortunate.

In fact, Connell (1993) explains the small island state bias in aid delivery as a function of their voting rights in the United Nations equivalent to those of large states. Consequently, in large regions such as the Pacific, the strategic significance of island states has resulted in traditional donors increasing their aid while new donors, such as Japan (Muqbil 1995), have entered the arena. As Wendt (1987) observed in the context of Western Samoa,

> Over half our annual budget is from foreign aid (direct and indirect). Like most other Pacific countries, we've become a permanent welfare case. I can't see us ever getting out of a hole. Many of our leaders don't want to: foreign aid is now built into their view of development, into their way of life. It is also in the interests of foreign powers (our supposed benefactors) to keep us hooked on their aid.
>
> (Wendt 1987: 15, cited in Connell 1993)

While such observations indicate some of the effects of aid dependency, aid levels have not declined dramatically post-independence for Pacific Island states due to the overriding political and strategic arguments in its favour. In only one or two island states has a significant political independence movement developed to challenge the aid dependency relationship because of the continued advantages of political incorporation and mechanisms of a free association. Consequently, aid dependency has been used as a mechanism by some Pacific Island states to achieve self-sufficiency. But what are the motives for giving and receiving aid among donor countries?

Giving and receiving aid

Where governments provide aid, it is in relation to a perceived need which may provide a psychological, economic or political benefit to the donor country and it will normally be based on an existing relationship. There is, however, the concept of altruistic giving where the donor has no connection, no thought of a return or sense of obligation. While this may be an important philosophical basis for aid in human transactions, it is not the main explanation for aid giving. According to Crocombe (1992: 70):

> What determines the level, recipients and nature of . . . aid to the . . . [Pacific] Islands? I doubt that anyone knows in any precise way. The humanitarian element is present, larger in voluntary aid than in official, and to some extent dependent on media and other communications . . . This is particularly apparent in the case of spectacular disasters like hurricanes, earthquakes and tsunamis. But they also have good public relations and leverage spin-offs at a political and security level at both ends.

Crocombe (1992) argues that most governments tie aid in some way: the USA, Japan, China and France tie aid closely to their own resources and personnel compared to Scandinavian countries which do so the least. One explanation of this tying is that it is less costly for the donor country and White and Woestman (1994) cynically argue that it is easy to give money if you do not give too much. The United Nations goal of countries allocating 0.7 per cent of GDP to foreign aid has not been met by New Zealand, equating to 0.51 per cent of GDP in 1991. The OECD Development Assistance Committee annual report monitors the details given by all OECD countries as Table 11.1 illustrates. The aid from OECD countries is closely tied to spheres of influence (the USA north of the equator; Australia in PNG and to a lesser extent in other parts of Melanesia; the UK in its former territories and New Zealand with its territories and countries with close political links). While the European Union, China and Japan have also become major players in the 1980s, this has had a weakening effect on some of the spheres of influence. The majority of aid to Pacific nations has been directed towards a wide range of projects designed to improve the quality of life of the population (education and health programmes), to improve transport and communications as 'in the South Pacific communications have always been a problem and a lively issue. Because of the vast distances involved, air transport assumes a special importance' (Ministry of Foreign Affairs 1972: 9).

In addition, aid for productive economic activities such as agriculture and forestry has occurred, particularly through the development banks of some countries. For example, in the late 1980s Kiribati (the former UK Gilbert Islands), received aid from different sources and for different purposes which typifies the situation among many Pacific Islands. Australia, New Zealand and the European Union provided:

Table 11.1: Aid from OECD Development Assistance Committee Donors to Pacific Islands, 1973–91

Country or territory	1973*	1984	1985	1986	1987	1988	1989	1990	1991
					$US million				
Cook Islands	4.25	8	10	26	11	12	13	12	13
Fiji	14.65	31	32	42	36	54	43	45	46
Kiribati	5.97	12	2	13	18	16	17	20	22
Nauru	–	–	–	–	–	–	–	–	–
New Caledonia	74.64	131	145	207	283	261	282	301	327
Niue	1.65	3	4	4	7	5	6	7	9
Pacific Islands (Trust Territories)	65.61	185	159	232	186	152	159	63	16
Papua New Guinea	194.98	322	259	263	322	380	339	376	381
Polynesia (French)	50.35	172	172	248	294	331	289	261	311
Solomon Islands	11.63	19	21	30	57	58	49	44	40
Tokelau	0.44	2	2	2	2	4	5	5	4
Tonga	1.34	16	14	15	21	19	25	29	27
Tuvalu	–	5	3	4	26	14	7	6	5
Vanuatu	–	24	22	24	51	39	40	49	48
Wallis and Futuna	0.33	2	0	0	1	1	0	0	2
Western Samoa	2.99	20	19	23	36	31	31	49	52
Total	428.83	974	900	1159	1412	1436	1361	1341	1372

Note: *1973 is the only year between 1971 and 1974 with virtually complete data for each country.

Source: OECD Development Cooperation: Efforts and Policies of the Members of the Development Assistance Committee Reports 1974–1992, OECD, Paris.

- capital aid to finance construction and engineering projects;
- technical aid to provide personnel and finance for training and higher education;
- aid in kind (equipment and materials).

Japan entered into a fishing agreement and in return provided aid for the national fishing industry. The European Development Fund and Asian Development Bank supported a number of programmes including the upgrading of Bouriki Airport. In addition, the upgrading of a sewerage plant was supported by funds from AIDAB (the Australian International Development Assistance Bureau).

TOURISM, AID POLICIES AND AID PROVISION

According to Fallon and Karabalis (1992), structural changes in the economies of Pacific Islands and the reform of their public sector to make them more responsive and service-orientated has focused attention on tourism. In the absence of any major form of domestic or indigenous tourism in most Pacific Islands, access to major metropolitan markets and the capital of large tourism organisations (e.g. hotel chains and airlines) are critical to the development of this activity. Even though tourism may be a fickle industry, subject to the whim of the travelling nations of the northern hemisphere and the emergent Pacific Rim nations (Hall 1994), Pacific Island nations do have comparative advantages in terms of their resource base, if developed in a sensitive and sustainable manner. Most Pacific Island countries have acknowledged the growth prospects for tourism as a form of international business. However, to understand tourism as a form of international business requires an analysis of the two components of tourism: the travel flows between Australia, New Zealand and the Pacific Islands; and trade and aid flows, since tourism is a form of foreign exchange.

Travel flows between Australia and the South Pacific

Australia has experienced massive growth in inbound travel in recent years. In 1980 inbound tourism resulted in less than one million visitors. In 1990 the figure was over 2.2 million. By the year 2000, the Australian Bureau of Tourism Research forecasts that Australia will be receiving nearly 7 million visitors per annum, while the Australian Tourism Industry Association has estimated that the figure will be 7.5 million (Hall 1994; 1995). Apart from visitors from New Zealand, visitor flows from elsewhere in the South Pacific are of only minor importance in terms of the overall number of inbound tourists to Australia (Table 11.2). However, multi-destination travellers who visit Fiji and/or New Zealand before coming to Australia are increasingly being targeted by the Australian Tourist Commission (Hall 1994).

Although the focus of international tourism in Australia has been on inbound tourism, it has only been since 1987 that the number of short-term arrivals to

Table 11.2: Short-term visitors arriving in Australia from Oceania

Country of residence	1985	1988	1989	1990	1991	1992	1993
Fiji	12,400	19,300	17,500	16,000	16,800	16,300	17,300
New Caledonia	8,200	17,200	13,400	14,400	15,200	18,000	18,400
New Zealand	245,300	534,300	449,300	418,400	480,600	447,500	499,300
Papua New Guinea	27,700	37,800	34,800	34,600	35,200	37,000	40,400
Solomon Islands	1,800						
Tonga	2,300						
Vanuatu	2,300	3,200	3,000	2,600	2,600	3,200	3,200
Other	5,600	16,600	15,400	14,600	15,300	15,800	17,700
Total Oceania	304,900	628,200	533,500	500,700	565,700	537,900	596,300

Note: As of 1991, Australian arrival figures for Oceania include Antarctica.

Source: Australian Bureau of Statistics 1986, 1989, 1990, 1991, 1992, 1993, 1994.

Australia has outnumbered the short-term departure of Australian residents overseas (Hall 1995). The Australian outbound market is of great importance to the South Pacific island nations because although it attracts only a small proportion of the total Australian outbound market (Table 11.3), Australian visitors are the major inbound market for most of the South Pacific destinations. Table 11.4 records the number of Australian residents travelling to destinations in the South Pacific.

Trade flows between Australia and the South Pacific

In 1992–3 Australia's exports to the South Pacific (including Papua New Guinea) were valued at $1658.4 million (2.7 per cent of total exports) and imports at $A1,512.4 million (2.5 per cent of total imports). Gold accounts for 57 per cent of imports from PNG and Fiji, and 26 per cent of imports is coffee from PNG. The 1992/93 figure for Australia's exports to the region represented just over 20.2 per cent increase on the previous financial year. Although trade with the region is relatively small for Australia compared with other trading partners such as New Zealand, ASEAN, and Japan, 'the South Pacific region remains an important destination for manufactured products from Australia and has been accorded some priority in Austrade's market development strategy' (Department of Foreign Affairs and Trade 1994: np).

Unfortunately, due to the means by which tourism is included in national account figures for the various countries in the region, the flow of revenue derived from tourism services is extremely difficult to ascertain as it is generally included within a 'services' category. Australia's current account balance in 1991/92 showed a $A7 million deficit with PNG and a $A311 million surplus

Table 11.3: Short-term departures of Australian residents by region, 1992–3 ('000s)

Region	1992	% of total	1993	% of total
Africa	24.8	1.1	29.0	1.3
North America	366.9	16.1	330.4	14.6
Other America	16.2	0.7	16.8	0.7
Asia	782.5	34.4	812.6	35.8
UK/Europe	491.0	21.6	479.9	21.1
Middle East	44.0	1.9	46.9	2.1
Fiji	86.7	3.8	78.0	3.4
New Zealand	340.7	15.0	350.4	15.5
Other Oceania	119.2	5.2	115.5	5.1
Total	2,276.3	100	2,267.2	100

Source: Adapted from Australian Bureau of Statistics in Hall 1995.

Table 11.4: Australian residents departing for short-term stay in Oceania, 1985–93

Country of intended stay	1985	1988	1989	1990	1991	1992	1993
Cook Islands	2,500	4,100	4,000	3,700	4,100	5,800	4,600
Fiji	82,100	73,200	93,900	102,200	90,000	86,700	78,400
French Polynesia					3,700	4,400	5,100
New Caledonia	5,000	10,300	14,500	14,900	17,400	15,500	16,300
New Zealand	279,200	247,100	297,300	320,200	318,300	340,700	347,200
Norfolk Island	20,400	15,000	12,200	14,200	16,900	18,000	15,400
Papua New Guinea	25,800	32,700	34,400	34,400	37,000	37,600	35,500
Solomon Islands	3,100						
Tahiti	4,800	5,100	6,800	5,800			
Other	16,400	19,600	29,400	35,100	35,000	37,800	38,800
Total Oceania	439,300	407,100	492,400	529,900	522,400	546,600	541,200

Note: As of 1991 Australian resident departure figures for Oceania include Antarctica.

Source: Australian Bureau of Statistics 1986, 1989, 1990, 1991, 1992, 1993, 1994.

with the rest of the region. According to the Australian Department of Foreign Affairs and Trade (1994: np):

These figures take into account tourism flows and services trade and more accurately reflect the degree of balance in the overall economic relationship Australia has with the countries of the region. In the area of services trade, the limited statistics available show that Australia has a surplus of $155 million in 1991/92 with PNG and a surplus of $52 million with the rest of the region.

Australian investment in tourism in the South Pacific is also extremely hard to ascertain. Apart from mention in the media of investment in specific hotel or tourist projects, little publicly available information is held by governments on tourist investment activity. Australian investment in PNG has traditionally been associated with mining or agricultural projects. Investment activity by Australian companies in tourism-related projects in the South Pacific is usually associated with countries such as Fiji, Vanuatu and the Solomons. In 1992/93 the level of Australian investment in Fiji was $A314 million as compared with $A105 million the previous year. The value of Australian investment in the rest of Oceania in 1991/92 was $A123 million. However, it should be noted that tourism is specifically identified by the Australian Department of Foreign Affairs and Trade as a potential investment area, as the Department noted:

The development of exports of services (tourism, aviation, medical, telecommunications, banking, insurance) and some construction opportunities offer the main avenues for the expansion of Australia's overseas earnings from the South Pacific.

(Department of Foreign Affairs and Trade 1994: np)

Australia's aid programme in the South Pacific

Australia's overseas development programme makes a substantial contribution to the South Pacific island economies. In the early 1990s, Australia accounted for over a quarter of all foreign aid in the South Pacific (Pacific Economic Bulletin 1992) (Table 11.5). Although the former Australian protectorate of Papua New Guinea receives the largest proportion of Australia's aid in the region, other countries, and Fiji, Kiribati, Tonga, the Solomon Islands, Vanuatu and Western Samoa in particular, also receive aid contributions in the millions of dollars (Table 11.6). Despite the significance of tourism to the island economies, aid assistance in this sector is only a very small proportion of Australia's total project assistance in the South Pacific (Table 11.7). Australia has also provided aid for tourism development through cooperative programmes with other aid agencies. For example, under the Fourth Cycle (1987–91) of the Pacific Regional Programme of the United Nations Development Programme, Australia co-financed a South Pacific regional tourism development planning and training project, with the UNDP providing $US616,000 and AIDAB $US225,000 over the four-year period. The project, consisting of a range of advisory services, individual consultancies, workshops, training and fellowships, had the objective:

> To improve the quality and standards of living of the people of Pacific islands nations by diversifying their economies (e.g. generating increased income, employment and foreign exchange earnings) through creating greater self-sufficiency in, and promoting orderly and controlled expansion of, tourism.
> (United Nations Development Programme 1990: 27)

Unfortunately, as far as can be ascertained, no evaluation of the success of this programme is available.

However, to isolate Australia's contribution to the tourism industry just through aid specifically listed under the 'tourism' heading would be very misleading. As with the nature of tourism itself, Australia's aid contributes to a diverse number of sectors that assist in the development of tourism infrastructure and the tourist product of many of the countries in the region. Table 11.8 records the substantial amount that Australia has contributed in overseas development cooperation assistance for transport and navigation. Although this heading is not strictly limited to tourism infrastructure, many of the projects recorded as transport and navigation are very significant for tourism in the region. For example, Australia has been contributing aid for civil aviation projects in the region including the development of international airports and regional airfields, such as Bauerfield Airport in Vanuatu. Similarly, Australia has been contributing to training and education, a South Pacific Cultures Fund, and has assisted in the development of conservation programmes in the region, through such activities as the development of conservation management plans (Australian International Development Assistance Bureau 1994).

Table 11.5: Australian overseas aid as a percentage of total aid flows for Pacific Island countries

Country	Total aid flows 1990 ($USm)	Australian aid flows 1990/91 ($USm)	Australian aids as % of total aid
Cook Islands	12	1.58	13.20
Fiji	45	17.86	39.70
Kiribati	20	3.12	15.58
Papua New Guinea	376	261.59	69.57
Solomon Islands	44	10.04	22.82
Tonga	29	8.46	29.17
Tuvalu	6	1.91	31.83
Vanuatu	49	10.99	22.34
Western Samoa	49	9.68	19.76
South Pacific Total	1,277	347.72	27.23

Source: After *Pacific Economic Bulletin* 1992.

Table 11.6: Australian Overseas Development Cooperation, 1989/90 to 1993/4 ($A)

Country	1989/90	1990/91	1991/92	1992/93	1993/94
Papua New Guinea	338,034,570	331,728,149	335,986,374	333,679,185	338,957,222
Cook Islands	1,677,535	2,016,780	2,480,840	2,339,649	2,406,604
Fiji	29,995,010	29,270,852	27,465,063	25,113,955	23,406,975
Kiribati	5,406,631	3,815,336	5,070,151	5,367,366	7,062,759
Nauru	162,582	292,764	294,923	210,496	2,848,138
New Caledonia	331,587	1,041,814	865,239	1,457,759	1,313,922
Niue	644,156	620,282	860,911	945,260	801,570
Pacific Islands (US)	1,250,243	1,832,928	2,020,228	1,838,546	
Palau					233,989
Marshall Islands					838,954
Federated States of Micronesia					1,510,521
Polynesia (French)	9,157	21,362	–	51,044	236,007
Solomon Islands	12,813,476	13,034,297	14,258,452	14,137,807	13,930,718
Tokelau	54,086	21,197	6,300	46,541	26,374
Tonga	10,524,986	10,237,454	11,271,080	10,904,529	10,789,675
Tuvalu	2,007,367	2,425,874	2,982,833	2,312,439	2,821,122
Vanuatu	12,421,450	12,499,814	13,286,837	13,781,801	16,163,825
Wallis & Fatuna	25,000				
Western Samoa	10,091,983	12,532,450	15,919,811	11,981,709	11,986,893
South Pacific Regional	20,596,670	19,629,757	23,081,569	28,321,855	29,190,260
Total Pacific Island Countries	104,991,599	109,217,114	119,863,045	117,676,383	125,568,306
Total Oceania (including PNG)	443,026,169	440,945,263	455,849,419	451,355,568	464,525,528

Source: Australian International Development Assistance Bureau 1994.

Table 11.7: Australian Overseas Development Cooperation for Tourism, 1989/90
to 1993/4 ($A)

Country	Year	Amount	Project
Fiji	1989/90	412,262	Tourist industry development
	1991/92	117,850	Tourist industry development
	1992/93	41	School of Hotel and Tourism
Solomon Islands	1989/90	71,226	Sasape Marina
	1990/91	17,023	Tourism Training Centre
Western Samoa	1993/94	200,000	Visitor's Bureau Development Fund

Source: Australian International Development Assistance Bureau 1994.

NEW ZEALAND'S ROLE IN PACIFIC TOURISM

New Zealand, like Australia, has maintained a close political relationship with many of the neighbouring Pacific Islands in Polynesia and to a lesser degree with those in Micronesia and Melanesia. The historical ties New Zealand has with many Pacific Islands can be dated back to the nineteenth century (Britton 1987). This colonial legacy was closely aligned to Britain's global strategic concerns during the heyday of the British Empire, while New Zealand's immediate geopolitical concerns were to secure shipping routes and refuelling stations for its Commonwealth trade. Britton (1987) and Crocombe (1992) explain how many of the Pacific Islands were aligned to New Zealand, and as Britton (1987: 283) argues,

> From the time of discovery by Europeans, New Zealand was considered part of a wider arena of geopolitical interest. For both the governments and agents which directed the events of colonisation, and the settlers who established and were the substance of the new antipodean society, the earliest days of occupation were inextricably linked with international affairs: the global empire of Great Britain, rivalry between colonial powers for new spheres of influence, and the geographical extension of capitalist relations of production throughout the Pacific. These historical events were responsible for shaping New Zealand's relations with its island neighbours. They were also driving forces for an unfolding geography of postcontact island societies.

The implication here is that, in a tourism context, it is the period of decolonisation which swept the Pacific after the UN Committee on Decolonisation required New Zealand to prepare its territories for independence in the 1960s which is of significance. This coincided with a political realignment in the Pacific, as Britain's role as a world power waned and its later decision to join the EC. Therefore, in a tourism context, a number of major changes have occurred since the 1960s in New Zealand's relationship with Pacific Islands including:

Table 11.8: Australian Overseas Development Cooperation for Transport and Navigation, 1989/90 to 1993/94 ($A)

Country	1989/90	1990/91	1991/92	1992/93	1993/94
Papua New Guinea	4,364,536	3,691,209	4,914,744	7,991,881	3,317,781
Cook Islands	146,625	312,248	50,624	18,080	7,144
Fiji	227,085	655,515	14,602	–	24,980
Kiribati	649,156	791,893	986,962	1,409,152	1,321,066
Niue	25,341	11,391	136,466	7,500	–
Solomon Islands	789,128	288,173	253,164	59,933	475,985
Tonga	2,859,250	353,375	44,523	73,976	162,299
Tuvalu	241,172	20,661	48,966	–	–
Vanuatu	1,123,755	2,786,745	68,151	87,234	2,440,000
Western Samoa	629,287	445,589	542,174	1,234,724	934,284
South Pacific Regional	500,000	156,000	500,000	603,333	371,000
Total Pacific Island Countries	7,190,799	5,821,590	2,645,632	3,493,932	5,736,758
Total Oceania (including PNG)	11,555,335	9,512,799	7,560,376	11,485,813	9,054,539

Source: Australian International Development Assistance Bureau 1994.

- a number of islands have gained independence (e.g. Western Samoa)
- former colonies under formal New Zealand political influence (e.g. Tokelau, the Cook Islands, and Niue) have moved from colony status to self-governing territory, becoming semi-autonomous regions within the New Zealand polity (Britton 1987)
- Pacific Island economies have had to reposition themselves in the world trading system
- aid has become a major component of Pacific Island economic status – termed 'economic assistance', with the overt political purpose of securing the political and economic stability of the South Pacific.

In this respect, France, Australia and New Zealand have assumed the role of political policemen in the South Pacific as the United States has concentrated on North Pacific strategic defence concerns. Indeed, despite the furore surrounding French nuclear testing in the Pacific in 1995, both Australia and New Zealand made it clear that they still desired the French presence in the region as a mechanism for maintaining political stability. Therefore, the Pacific has become a location for maintaining political influence, with New Zealand continuing its sphere of influence over former colonies and territories for geopolitical, economic and strategic purposes. As Britton (1987: 290) argued:

In the last 20 years significant changes have taken place in New Zealand's relations with the islands. Flows of trade and investment between New Zealand and the islands have increased, partly because unprecedented steps taken by newly independent states to expand their economies have provided opportunities for New Zealand suppliers, investors and distributors. In addition, New Zealand enterprises have been encouraged to go offshore to boost foreign exchange earnings and to gain access to island and possibly other markets such as the European Community. A parallel development has been the creation of ever larger units of capital in New Zealand (epitomized by Fletcher Challenge, Air New Zealand and the New Zealand Insurance Corporation) which are systematically expanding operations around the Pacific basin.

For the independent states of the Pacific, contemporary New Zealand economic links have taken at least two forms. The first is the extension and diversification of commercial power by New Zealand firms previously active in former colonies (for example mercantile, finance and tourism capital) which represent neo-colonial economic linkages. The second are new forms of investment which are incorporating independent islands into a new economic order as major restructuring occurs in the dominant metropolitan countries of the Pacific Rim (such as mining, forestry, and finance corporations). Island economies increasingly rely on enterprises and institutions that not only may be of greater economic size than themselves but also may operate at regional and global scales, whereas previous links were largely geographically and politically constrained within bilateral colonial relationships.

Britton's insights raise a number of issues in relation to aid and development, mostly notably that 'by freely choosing development strategies which enable the manipulation of metropolitan national policies' (Connell 1993: 142), Pacific Island politicians and bureaucracies have recognised the advantages of 'a special relationship' with metropolitan powers, given the opportunity cost of not pursuing such a policy. In addition, Connell (1993) notes the retreat from self-reliance for some Pacific Island nations. It is notable that such features have occurred in relation to tourism. This is particularly pertinent in the case of New Zealand where the 'special relationship' persists with many island states and is reflected in both travel and trade flows together with the aid flows and policy.

Travel flows between New Zealand and the South Pacific

New Zealand, like Australia has received a major growth in international arrivals, now in excess of 1.3 million visitors a year. This is part of a sustained growth since the 1980s. By the year 2000, the New Zealand Ministry of Tourism had optimistically forecast a target of 3 million arrivals, which has now been replaced by tourist expenditure forecasts in the event that three million arrivals seemed unattainable given infrastructure constraints. Australia remains the main market for international arrivals with Pacific Island arrivals a minor component due to low average incomes. The main inbound visitors from Island states are from Fiji, the Cook Islands, New Caledonia and Tahiti mainly visiting friends and relatives, with many often seeking short-term jobs. Due to overstaying, entry visas for many visitors are limited term (except for Kiribati, Nauru and Tuvalu) and similar sentiments exist in Pacific Island nations who restrict New Zealand overstaying. It is difficult to identify the main origin of international visitors from the Pacific Islands since the international statistics do not distinguish between 'Other Pacific Islands' (except in the case of Fiji, French Polynesia, New Caledonia and Papua New Guinea) (Crocombe 1992).

Conversely, New Zealanders visiting the Pacific contain a range of visitor types. For example, ethnic Samoans returning to visit friends and relatives comprise almost a third of all arrivals, with 10 per cent of ethnic Cook Islanders. However, the main category of visitor from New Zealand is the visitor seeking a 'south seas holiday', often a short-term visit based in a resort enclave orientated to:

- the coral coast of Fiji
- Anse Vata in New Caledonia
- the islands of Raratonga
- Aitutaki in the Cook Islands
- Vanuatu.

For example, in 1990 some 82,000 New Zealanders visited the Pacific Islands with the main destinations in descending order of importance being: Fiji, the Cook Islands, Western Samoa, New Caledonia, Tahiti, Tonga, Papua New

Guinea, Vanuatu, together with Niue, the Solomon Islands, Micronesian countries and Norfolk Island, which is constitutionally part of Australia. In addition to these trends, there are multidestination travellers from other parts of the Pacific-Asia region who are visiting New Zealand and other parts of the region as part of a wider Pacific itinerary who also depart to Pacific destination from gateways in Auckland and Christchurch.

Trade flows between New Zealand and the South Pacific

Although tourism is a component linking the economies of the Pacific region, trade flows indicate some of the crucial linkages and trade relationships which New Zealand has developed. Since 1961, New Zealand exports to the Pacific basin (including Australia) have increased from 25 to 70 per cent in 1989 (Henderson 1991). The South Pacific now accounts for 3.5 per cent of New Zealand exports, Fiji, Papua New Guinea and French Polynesia are the main markets. In 1991–2, Fiji accounted for $NZ624.1 million of exports to the region in 1991–2. The main importing countries are those near to New Zealand or with whom a special relationship exists. In terms of imports of Pacific Island goods into New Zealand, the South Pacific Regional Trade and Economic Co-operation Agreement (SPARTECA), launched in 1981, provides duty-free access to New Zealand on a non-reciprocal basis, which also extends to Australia (subject to meeting rules on the origin of goods). This agreement applies to all South Pacific Forum Island countries, with special treatment for smaller island nations. The main imports into New Zealand in 1991–2 were from Fiji ($NZ63.5) which is mainly clothing, Nauru ($NZ29.2 million) in the form of phosphates for agriculture out of a total value of $NZ110.9 million (also see Crocombe 1992 for a more detailed discussion). Crocombe (1992) points to the imbalance in the ratio of New Zealand exports to imports of almost 6 to 1, although caution must be exercised for two major reasons. First, approximately 22 per cent of exports to the Pacific Islands are re-exports which are being transhipped from New Zealand. Second, New Zealand tourism expenditure in the Pacific Islands helps offset the trade imbalance. For example, Crocombe (1992) estimated this expenditure to be $NZ64 million a year together with the benefits of official aid, voluntary aid and remittances of approximately $NZ50 million a year.

New Zealand's aid to the South Pacific

Hoadley's (1991) analysis of New Zealand's international aid programme outlines the historical development of its aid after it assumed colonial responsibility for Niue (1901), Western Samoa (1949) and Tokelau (1925) where aid was disbursed periodically in response to disasters or for administrative purposes. In 1945–6, the Department of Island Territories was established to administer programmes in dependent territories, and the functions of the Department are now based in the Ministry of Foreign Affairs and Trade.

Crocombe (1992) points to the relative decline in New Zealand aid to dependent territories, since from the 1950s to the 1980s, island government departments sought assistance from their New Zealand counterparts, often on an informal basis. Such aid comprised advice, training, personnel and resources, though after 1986 such links were diminished due to restructuring and stringencies on government spending. The informal aid was replaced by making aid visible and subject to normal aid project criteria in relation to the development aid strategy designed in consultation with each recipient country.

Aid giving by New Zealand is subject to official principles which Hoadley (1991: 201) outlined as a list of working objectives:

- Aid is directed primarily to the Island states of the South Pacific; the second area of concentration is the countries belonging to ASEAN.
- Aid is provided in accordance with New Zealand's capacity and in response to specific requests made by recipient governments.
- The principal purpose of aid is to help promote the economic and social development of the recipient countries by expanding their capabilities to raise the living standards of their peoples.
- Aid is normally provided from New Zealand itself; New Zealand goods and services are used wherever this is compatible with the principal purpose.
- A project should have specific development objectives that are to be achieved within a specified time and with specified resources and then be carried on by the recipient country from its own resources.
- Priority in project selection is to be given to
  - increasing productive capacity;
  - improving living conditions and welfare especially of people on lower incomes and in rural areas;
  - safeguarding the interests of vulnerable groups and increasing their capacity to contribute to development;
  - encouraging popular participation and support of the project.

In addition to these principles, practical considerations affecting aid decisions include:

- staff workloads and personnel availability to administer specific schemes;
- aid as an instrument of foreign policy to improve countries' profile;
- encourage trade with New Zealand.

These practical issues were also evident in a survey by Applied Research Consultants (1987) on public attitudes to aid giving in New Zealand where:

- 77 per cent of respondents felt that morality was important grounds for giving, but;
- 63 per cent agreed with the premise that aid helps to reduce political instability;
- 70 per cent felt aid assisted with international relations;

- 81 per cent felt that New Zealand would gain if the less developed world became stronger.

New Zealand aid policy is published in the Ministry of Foreign Affairs and Trade Project Profiles while debates in parliament and parliamentary questions provide another source of information. Table 11.9 outlines New Zealand's official Development Assistance Programme for 1994/95 and the breakdown of countries receiving aid and other regional programmes outside of the Pacific. While the Pacific dominates the pattern of aid, Crocombe (1992) illustrates the priority areas for aid being:

- forestry;
- transport and communications (to assist accessibility and tourism);
- human resource development;
- education, especially University-level programmes;
- assistance following natural disasters;
- an increasing tourism element.

Not surprisingly, Table 11.9 indicates that those countries with the closest relations with New Zealand receive the most aid, since it is not related to per capita incomes. Polynesian islands nearest to New Zealand are major beneficiaries while considerably less aid is destined for Melanesia, with the exception of Fiji. The importance of Fiji as a pivotal location in the Pacific helps explain New Zealand's aid policy towards the country, despite having a per capita income four times that of Tonga, Western Samoa, Tuvalu, Kiribati, Vanuatu and the Solomon Islands. Aid to Micronesia (with the exception of Kiribati) receive only small-scale aid from New Zealand. Thus those island states with a constitutional relationship with New Zealand (Western Samoa, Cook Islands, Niue and Tokelau) benefit the most while former British territories closest to New Zealand (Fiji and Tonga) also receive favourable treatment followed by the more distant areas (Tuvalu, Kiribati, Vanuatu and Solomon Islands). But how does tourism feature in these patterns of aid?

New Zealand official aid for tourism projects

To assess the extent to which New Zealand development assistance has been targeted at tourism for specific Pacific nation states, a number of data sources exist:

- New Zealand Overseas Development Assistance Programme Profiles;
- Annual Reports of the Ministry of Foreign affairs;
- *Ad hoc* government reports, such as *New Zealand Aid in the South Pacific 1973–74, South Pacific Policy Review Group: Towards a Pacific Island Community,* published in 1990;
- Entries on aid by country published in the *Pacific Island Yearbook.*

Table 11.9: New Zealand's Offical Development Assistance Programme 1994–5, bilateral assistance

Assistance programme	$(000)
South Pacific Country Programmes	
Cook Islands	13,000
Budget Support	8,100
Projects and Training	4,900
Niue	10,000
Budget Support	5,000
Projects and Training	2,000
Airport development	3,000
Tokelau	5,200
Budget Support	4,300
Projects and Training	900
Kiribati	3,100
Tonga	5,600
Tuvalu	2,100
New Caledonia	300
Micronesia +	300
(+ Federated States of Micronesia, Marshall Islands, Palau)	
French Polynesia	100
Wallis and Futuna	25
Fiji	5,000
Solomon Islands	4,500
Vanuatu	4,200
Western Samoa	7,300
Papua New Guinea	5,900
South Pacific Country Programmes Total	66,625
South Pacific Regional Programmes	
Forum Secretariat	2,500
South Pacific Commission	2,500
South Pacific Regional Environment Programme (SPREP)	750
Forum Fisheries Agency	660
South Pacific Applied Geoscience Commission (SOPAC)	425
University of the South Pacific	2,400
South Pacific Board for Educational Assessment	290
Pacific Regional Sectoral Programmes	800
Pacific Islands Private Sector Development (include PIIDS)	500
Development Assistance Facility	350
South Pacific Regional Programme Total	11,175
South Pacific Head of Mission Funds	510
South Pacific Total	**78,310**
Asia and other programmes	22,420
Other bilateral	27,191

Source: New Zealand Overseas Development Assistance Programme Profiles 1994/95, Ministry of Foreign Affairs and Trade, Wellington.

Despite the existence of these data sources, comparatively little is written on the role of tourism in relation to aid. The official policy statements make only a passing reference to tourism as a mechanism to assist dependent countries to diversify their economic base.

As a result, the period 1981–95 was identified as the most salient to observe the emergence of a support for tourism. However, as Table 11.10 shows, the entire list of projects aided by year are largely transport-related where tourism will be a component. It is not until 1983–4 that Niue features as a destination where hotel upgrading and visitor promotion are specifically targeted. Aid projects with a tourism focus have typically taken the following format:

- feasibility studies/impact studies;
- cash grants to assist with marketing activities;
- environmental tourism projects;
- transport/infrastructure projects with a tourism component (e.g. coastal defence works);
- establishing a World Heritage Site with some tourism potential.

Table 11.10:   New Zealand government aid to Pacific Island tourism-related projects, 1981–95

Financial year	Country	Programme description	$NZ assistance
1981–2	Cook Islands	Installation of power supply for Akitua resort complex	75,000
	Kiribati	Provision of six transceivers to assist with airline bookings	26,000
		Civil aviation study	8,000
	Niue	Assistance with promotional activities to boost visitor arrivals	20,000
		Airport equipment	120,000
		Runway resealing	146,000
	Tonga	Airport runway lighting	600,000
	Tuvalu	Provision of aircraft beacons to assist with seaplane service	7,000
	Western Samoa	Airport communications re-equipment programme	220,000
		Technical assistance with Faleola International Airport	250,000
		Civil aviation training (including 2 advisors)	100,000
	Pacific Region	Calibration flights for checking aviation equipment in the Pacific Islands (Tonga, Kiribati, Western Samoa and Niue)	120,000
	Total aid for 1981–2		1,692,000

. . . *continued*

Financial year	Country	Programme description	$NZ assistance
1982–3	Cook Islands	Installation of power supply for Akitua resort complex	35,000
	Niue	Installation of navigational aids at Hanan International Airport	90,000
	Tonga	Fuaíamotu airport lighting project	435,000
	Western Samoa	Advisers and equipment for Faleolo International Airport	250,000
		Civil aviation training adviser	50,000
	Pacific Region	Calibration flights for checking aviation equipment in the Pacific Islands	100,000
		Short-term technical visits to island airports in Western Samoa, Tonga, Kiribati, Niue and the Cook Islands for aviation	40,000
	Total aid for 1982–3		1,000,000
1983–4	Niue	Visitor promotion and development of special-interest tourism	10,000
		Niue hotel upgrading	34,000
		Provision of civil aviation equipment Tonga	36,500
	Fuaíamotu	Airport runway lighting project	33,000
		New control tower for Fuaíamotu airport	98,000
	Western Samoa	Provision of a civil aviation manager Faleolo International airport	110,000
		Provision of essential airport vehicles	100,000
		Electrical upgrading of airport telecommunications	290,000
		Airport telecommunications	150,000
		Provision of a civil aviation instructor	55,000
	Pacific Region	Calibration flights	100,000
		Regional transport study in cooperation with the United Nations Development Programme	100,000
		Civil aviation inspection visits	30,000
	Total aid for 1983–4		1,146,500
1984–5	Vanuatu	Bauerfield airport safety equipment and training	160,000
	Tonga	New control tower at Fuaíamotu airport	190,000
	Western Samoa	Provision of a civil aviation manager and telecommunications technician at Faleolo International airport	180,000
		Equipment to establish a new communications link between Faleolo International airport and Apia	180,000
	Pacific Region	Calibration flights in the Pacific Islands, expanded to include the Solomon Islands, Vanuatu and Tuvalu	190,000
		Regional transport study in cooperation with the United Nations Development Programme	25,000
	Total aid for 1984–5		865,000

. . . continued

Financial year	Country	Programme description	$NZ assistance
1985–8	Vanuatu	Bauerfield airport safety equipment	60,000
		Trade, banking and tourism development Bank Grant	50,000
	Western Samoa	Provision of a civil aviation manager telecommunications technician and electrical officer	180,000
		Airport extension project	1,684,000
	Pacific Region	Calibration flights in the Pacific Islands	240,000
	Total aid for 1985–6		2,214,000
1986–7	Cook Islands	Cash grant to Cook Islands tourist authority for promotional campaign to boost Australian and New Zealand arrivals	75,000
	Tonga	New control tower at airport	370,000
	Vanuatu	Bauerfield airport – training and safety/rescue programme	12,000
		Upgrading and maintenance of outer island airports damaged by heavy rain	50,000
	Pacific Region	Calibration flights	350,000
	Total aid for 1986–7		857,000
1987–8	Tokelau	Airstrip development	No costing
	Tonga	Civil aviation assistance (training, funding, technical assistance, control tower construction and provision of equipment)	50,000
		Tourism impact study to recommend tourism strategy	80,000
	Vanuatu	Bauerfield airport safety training programme	25,000
	Western Samoa	Civil aviation assistance	350,000
	Total aid for 1987–8		505,000
1988–9	Cook Islands	Rarotongan hotel loan for Cook Islands government to purchase equity and to support tourism	502,834
	Tonga	Civil aviation assistance	60,000
	Vanuatu	Bauerfield airport safety training programme	15,000
	Western Samoa	Promotion of Western Samoa as a tourist destination and development of a Visitor Information Centre in Apia to encourage tourists to visit different places	70,000
		Civil aviation assistance	171,000
	Pacific Region	Checking and repairing airport equipment and facilities	20,000
	Total aid for 1987–8		838,834
1989–90	Cook Islands	Rarotongan hotel loan	502,844
	Fiji	Environmental tourism project	150,000
	Tonga	Civil aviation assistance	60,000

. . . continued

Financial year	Country	Programme description	$NZ assistance
	Vanuatu	Outer island airstrip development	530,000
	Western Samoa	Civil aviation assistance	115,000
		Tourism promotion cash grant to promote the cultural heritage and natural environment as a renewable resource	130,000
	Pacific Region	Calibration flights	400,000
	Total aid for 1989–90		1,887,844
1990–91	Cook Islands	Ministry of Works Development Programme to facilitate the growth of tourism (3-year programme)	600,000
		Tourism expansion programme (technical expertise and assistance with grants and tourism promotion	300,000
		Rarotongan hotel loan	800,000
		Coastal defence unit on the beachfront in front of the Rarotongan hotel	15,000
	Kiribati	Appraisal of Line and Phoenix group tourism development options for wildlife tourism and other future projects	20,000
		Provision of flight beacons	150,000
	Fiji	Environmental tourism project	100,000
	Papua New Guinea	Conservation and environmental project to investigate the establishment of a World Heritage Conservation site	200,000
	Solomon Islands	Rennell Island and Maroro Lagoon Sustainable Rural Development Programme to preserve the cultural heritage and develop ecotourism in a sustainable context	80,000
	Vanuatu	Outer island airstrips	500,000
	Western Samoa	Civil aviation assistance	50,000
		Tourism development and promotion	165,000
	Pacific Region	Calibration flights	470,000
	Total aid for 1990–91		3,450,000
1991–2	Cook Islands	Coastal defence for beachfront of the Rarotongan hotel	10,000
		Rarotongan hotel loan	500,000
		Technical assistance with tourism promotion	400,000
		Ministry of Works programme	385,000
	Fiji	Environmental tourism project	80,000
	Kiribati	Calibration of airport navigation equipment	60,000
	Solomon Islands	Ecotourism project – World Heritage Site	100,000
		Calibration flights	100,000
	Tonga	Civil aviation assistance	200,000
		Assistance with tourism marketing, training, infrastructure and development	50,000

. . . continued

Financial year	Country	Programme description	$NZ assistance
	Vanuatu	Civil aviation engineering	70,000
		Outer island airstrip development	300,000
	Western Samoa	Tourism development in Western Samoan forest and coastal development Construction of Visitor Bureau	175,000
	Civil aviation assistance		230,000
	Total aid for 1991–2		2,660,000
1992–3	Cook Islands	Civil aviation assistance	190,000
		Tourism marketing and human resource development assistance	400,000
	Fiji	Nature tourism development in conjunction with local landowners (policy oriented)	50,000
	Kiribati	Airport service provision	70,000
	Niue	Tourism development and promotion assistance to market the destination to Australian/New Zealand visitors/staff for National Tourism Organisation/ establishment of a research and statistical database for tourism	240,000
	Solomon Islands	Ecotourism project – World Heritage site	150,000
	Vanuatu	Outer island airstrip development	105,000
	Western Samoa	Tourism development programme	100,000
	Pacific Region	Calibration flights	25,000
	Total aid for 1992–3		1,330,000
1993–4	Cook Islands	Five-year programme to assist with tourism projects to the private sector	489,000
		Civil aviation assistance	85,000
	Fiji	Nature tourism project	100,000
	Kiribati	Airport service provision and calibration of navigation equipment	100,000
	Niue	Tourism development and promotion assistance to enhance the quality of tourism services and to upgrade the National Tourism Organisation while increasing awareness of Niue as a tourism destination	180,000
	Solomon Islands	Ecotourism project – World Heritage Site	150,000
	Tonga	Project identification and appraisal	100,000
		Civil aviation assistance	320,000
	Tuvalu	Air navigation calibration	45,000
	Vanuatu	Outer island airstrip development	150,000
	Western Samoa	Technical assistance for tourism development, promotion and policy development	100,000
	Total aid for 1993–4		1,819,000

. . . continued

Financial year	Country	Programme description	$NZ assistance
1994–5	Cook Islands	Funding of tourism development projects in the Tourism Master Plan	609,000
		Civil aviation assistance	85,000
	Fiji	Nature tourism project/Integrated Conservation and Development Plan	100,000
	Kiribati	Airport service provision	30,000
	Niue	Tourism promotion campaign to attract the Australian and New Zealand market/Compilation of a tourism statistics database and tourism training	155,000
	Solomon Islands	Ecotourism project – World Heritage Site/ appointment of a manager to implement the project	200,000
	Tonga	Tourism project identification and assistance	100,000
		Civil aviation assistance	230,000
	Tuvalu	Airport service provision	30,000
	Total aid for 1994–5		1,539,000
Total aid for tourism-related projects 1981–95			21,394,168

Source: New Zealand Bilateral Aid Programme – Project Profiles 1981–6; New Zealand Bilateral Assistance Programme – Project Profiles 1987–90; New Zealand Official Development Assistance Programme Profiles 1991–5; Development and Cooperation Division, Ministry of External Relations and Trade, Wellington.

Beyond these official projects, New Zealand investment in the Pacific is difficult to pinpoint apart from the announcement of specific projects in the media and the *Pacific Island Monthly*. No published statistics exist to assess commercial investment related to aid projects, making the issue a largely unknown and unresearched area. Yet the fact that Pacific Island states are lobbying New Zealand's Development Assistance Programme decision-makers to fund tourism projects is a belated change in official aid policy from a traditional focus on items related to improving existing economic sectors (e.g. primary production). In the absence of official data on the number of tourism projects proposed for aid assistance, it is apparent that the criteria for funding is consistent with aid policy to encourage community-related projects and assist with sustainability and nature-related tourism projects rather than funding those projects which the private sector can normally be expected to develop.

CONCLUSION

The aid policies of Australia and New Zealand do not occur out of altruism. Undoubtedly, there may be a sense of responsibility borne out of colonial ties and, particularly in the case of New Zealand, potential powerful domestic political constituencies which will influence aid flows. As the New Zealand South Pacific Policy Review Group (1990: 111) observed, 'New Zealand's Official Development Assistance (ODA) programme underpins our relations with the Pacific. Our mana as a people of the Pacific is maintained through our ODA because it gives substance to our relationships'. However, foreign aid is a mechanism by which Australia and New Zealand can continue to exert influence over the politics of the South Pacific in order to meet national diplomatic, political, trade and economic interests. As Hughs (1990: 25–26) recognised, 'Strategic and economic leverage can be better exerted through bilateral programmes . . . very often linked to preferential access to the recipient's natural resources . . . markets or sites for military bases. The South Pacific region offers shining examples of such linkages.'

The contribution of aid from one government to another is clearly not without influence, particularly in the case of the South Pacific where Australia and New Zealand are the dominant aid donors in the region. As Henderson (1991: 143) argues,

> the relationship between the New Zealand, Australian, and Pacific Islands economies is important for two reasons . . . Firstly, . . . both New Zealand and Australia have a special responsibility to assist with the economic development of a region of which they are a part. Both provide substantial development assistance, and any failure to generate economic development will further increase and extend the need for this assistance. Secondly, the Pacific Islands are important trading partners in their own right.

Nevertheless, while aid and development assistance clearly helps assist Australian and New Zealand goals with respect to ensuring political and economic stability in the South Pacific, such aid programmes are increasingly coming under pressure from domestic political concerns. In the case of both Australia and New Zealand there are increasing signs of 'aid fatigue' from both the governmental and community level. Savenaca Siwatibau, the Vanuatu-based head of ESCAP, observed that 'the unconditional budget aid, for example, to most independent island countries has ended and the competing demand for the limited aid resources from various claimants around the globe make it unlikely that such aid will be restored in the foreseeable future' (quoted in Decloitre 1995: 47). Similarly, Grynberg (1995: 34) noted, there is 'a sense that given the failure of the islands to develop a climate that would aid inward investment, all that aid was doing was propping up political structures that refused to reform and deal with their problems'. However, what are the alternatives to the current range of aid programmes?

One suggestion has been to allow Pacific islanders to sell their labour services in Australia as an alternative to aid (Grynberg 1995). Such a suggestion may make economic sense given that most Polynesian and Micronesian countries earn the majority of their foreign exchange from the remittances of nationals living abroad, but it is highly unlikely that Australian governments would risk domestic concerns over the perceived importation of cheap labour at a time of high domestic unemployment. Therefore, it is probable that, in both Canberra and Wellington, policy settings for the South Pacific will continue to be set on their existing courses.

Aid programmes, combined with the encouragement of Australian and New Zealand corporate investment, will likely be the mainstay of the two countries influence in the region well into the next century. Domestic political factors will likely rule out the complete opening of the Australian and New Zealand labour markets to South Pacific workers, nor will increased immigration be possible given concerns over economic development and unemployment. Aid will therefore remain of central importance. Given the development potential of tourism in some parts of the region and the already substantial involvement of Australian and New Zealand companies, it may be predicted that tourism and related infrastructure development will become an increasingly important component of the Australian and New Zealand aid dollar in the South Pacific in the next decade. Furthermore, it is likely that both countries will attempt to use aid to try to provide a basis for corporate investment in market orientated solutions to the development problems of the Pacific islands economies. In this policy setting, emphasis will be placed on those areas where the South Pacific islands may have some comparative advantage, mining, fisheries, specialised agricultural products and, perhaps most significantly in the long run, tourism.

REFERENCES

Applied Research Consultants (1987) *Overseas Aid and Development: The New Zealand Publics Attitudes and Beliefs*, Auckland: Applied Research Consultants.
Australian Bureau of Statistics (1986) *Overseas Arrivals and Departures Australia 1985*, Catalogue No. 3404.0, Canberra: Australian Bureau of Statistics.
—— (1989) *Overseas Arrivals and Departures Australia 1988*, Catalogue No. 3404.0, Canberra: Australian Bureau of Statistics.
—— (1990) *Overseas Arrivals and Departures Australia 1989*, Catalogue No. 3404.0, Canberra: Australian Bureau of Statistics.
—— (1991) *Overseas Arrivals and Departures Australia 1990*, Catalogue No. 3404.0, Canberra: Australian Bureau of Statistics.
—— (1992) *Overseas Arrivals and Departures Australia 1991*, Catalogue No. 3404.0, Canberra: Australian Bureau of Statistics.
—— (1993) *Overseas Arrivals and Departures Australia 1992*, Catalogue No. 3404.0, Canberra: Australian Bureau of Statistics.
—— (1994) *Overseas Arrivals and Departures Australia 1993*, Catalogue No. 3404.0, Canberra: Australian Bureau of Statistics.
Australian International Development Assistance Bureau (1994) *Australian Overseas Development Cooperation 1989 to 1993/94: Official Expenditure by Country, Region and Sector*, Canberra: Australian International Development Assistance Bureau.
Britton, S. (1987) 'New Zealand in the South Pacific: Towards a regional geography of colonial and capitalist relations', in P. Holland and W. Johnston (eds) *Southern Approaches: Geography in New Zealand*, Christchurch: New Zealand Geographical Society, pp. 283–304.

Connell, J. (1993) 'Island microstates: Development, autonomy and the ties that bind', in D. Lockhart, D. Drakakis-Smith and J. Schembri (eds) *The Development Process in Small Island States*, London: Routledge, pp. 117–50.

Crocombe, R. (1992) *Pacific Neighbours: New Zealand's Relations with Other Pacific Islands*, Christchurch and Suva: Centre for Pacific Studies, University of Canterbury and Institute of Pacific Studies, University of the South Pacific.

Decloitre, P. (1995) 'In the red', *Pacific Islands Monthly*, June: 46–7.

Department of Foreign Affairs and Trade (1994) *Australia's Trade Relations in the South Pacific*, Canberra: Department of Foreign Affairs and Trade.

Fallon, J. and Karabalis, C. (1992) 'Current economic trends in the South Pacific', *Pacific Economic Bulletin*, 7(2): 1–18.

Gounder, R. (1995) *Overseas Aid Motivations – The Economics of Australia's Bilateral Aid*, Aldershot: Avebury.

Grynberg, R. (1995) 'Immigration vs aid', *Pacific Islands Monthly*, May: 34–6.

Hall, C.M. (1994) *Tourism in the Pacific Rim: Development, Impacts and Markets*, South Melbourne: Longman Australia.

—— (1995) *Introduction to Tourism in Australia: Impacts, Planning and Development*, 2nd edn, South Melbourne: Longman Australia.

Harrison, D. (1992) (ed.) *Tourism and the Less Developed Countries*, Belhaven: London.

Henderson, J. (1991) 'New Zealand, CER and Pacific economic co-operation', in R. Kennaway and J. Henderson (eds) *Beyond New Zealand II: Foreign Policy into the 1990s*, Auckland: Longman Paul, pp. 140–50.

Hoadley, S. (1991) 'New Zealand's international aid', in R. Kennaway and J. Henderson (eds) *Beyond New Zealand II: Foreign Policy into the 1990s*, Auckland: Longman Paul, pp. 198–210.

Hughs, A.V. (1990) 'Back to first principles: project design as the best defence against aid addiction', *Pacific Economic Bulletin*, 5(1): 20–8.

Lockhart, D., Drakakis-Smith, D. and Schembri, J. (eds) (1993) *The Development Process in Small Island States*, London: Routledge.

Mabogunje, A. (1980) *The Development Process: A Spatial Perspective*, London: Hutchinson.

Ministry of Foreign Affairs (1972) *Annual Report*, Wellington: Ministry of Foreign Affairs.

Muqbil, I. (1995) 'Financial services: Japanese aid and investment assistance for Asia-Pacific tourism', *EIU Travel and Tourism Analyst*, 3: 54–65.

Pacific Economic Bulletin (1992) 'Statistical Annex', *Pacific Economic Bulletin* 7, 2: 53–5.

Pearce, D. (1989) *Tourist Development*, Harlow: Longman.

Rimmer, P. (1994) 'The Japanese bubble economy and the Pacific: The case of EIE International Corporation', in D. Hawke (ed.) *Inaugral Joint Conference New Zealand Geographical Society and Institute of Australian Geographers Proceedings*, Vol. 2, New Zealand Geographical Society Conference No. 16, Chritchurch: New Zealand Geographical Society, pp. 648–59.

Rix, A. (1993) *Japan's Foreign Aid Challenge: Policy Reform and Aid Leadership*, London: Routledge.

South Pacific Policy Review Group (1990) *Towards a Pacific Island Community, Report of the South Pacific Policy Review Group*, Wellington: South Pacific Policy Review Group.

Tarte, S. (1989) 'Regionalism and globalism in the South Pacific', *Development and Change*, 20(2): 181–201.

Thakur, R. (1991) 'Changing forces in South Pacific international relations', in R. Kennaway and J. Henderson (eds) *Beyond New Zeland II: Foreign Policy into the 1990s*, Auckland: Longman Paul, pp. 27–42.

United Nations Development Programme (1990) *Pacific Regional Programme 1987–1991*, Canberra: United Nations Development Programme/Department of Foreign Affairs and Trade.*

Wendt, A. (1987) 'Western Samoa 25 years after: Celebrating what?', *Pacific Islands Monthly*, 58: 14–15.

White, H. and Woestman, L. (1994) 'The quality of aid: Measuring trends in donor performance', *Development and Change*, 25(3): 527–34.

Chapter 12

Hawai'i

Luciano Minerbi

INTRODUCTION

The myth of paradise which has characterised so many of the images of the South Pacific has been a characteristic of the marketing and promotion of Hawai'i since the 1850s (see Chapter 2). Indeed, to many tourists, particularly from North America and Japan, Hawai'i *is* the South Pacific (see Figure 12.1). However, behind the tourist image lies substantial problems with respect to the islands' economy, environment and culture (Plates 12.1 and 12.2). As the following discussion indicates, while Hawai'i's economic growth and physical development is due to the extraordinary growth of the tourism industry, it has resulted in an uneven distribution of wealth. Tourism was grafted upon the existing plantation economy for the benefit of outsiders and the local elite (Hall 1994). Furthermore, foreign investment has adversely impacted on many facets of the island cultural and natural environment and brought many immigrants to the state, often to the disadvantage of the indigenous population. Although alternatives to the previous pattern of tourism development are now being sought, the chapter concludes by noting that the excessive dependence on tourism makes it difficult to move toward economic diversification, local ownership, and affordable living conditions in a sustainable manner.

FOREIGN INVESTMENT, HEGEMONY AND SOVEREIGNTY

The impacts of foreign tourism investment has been a major issue in previous research on tourism in Hawai'i and colours much of the thinking which surrounds discussion on tourism in the state. Kelly (1994), in examining foreign investment in Hawai'i, concluded that trading, plantation agriculture, and tourism developments have all been destructive to the island ecology and to traditional land and ocean food sources. Kent (1983) explained that Hawai'i's development has been a reflection of the alliance between the elite in the metropole and the elite in Hawai'i. Descendants of traders and missionaries established five big companies, known as the 'Big Five', that controlled all facets of the local economy. Interlocking directorates, pattern of joint financing

Plate 12.1: Sunbathing on Waikiki Beach, one of the classic tourist images of Hawai'i (Michael Hall)

Plate 12.2: Back from the beach at Waikiki. Tourism development has turned Waikiki into an urban environment little different from that which many of the tourists have escaped (Michael Hall)

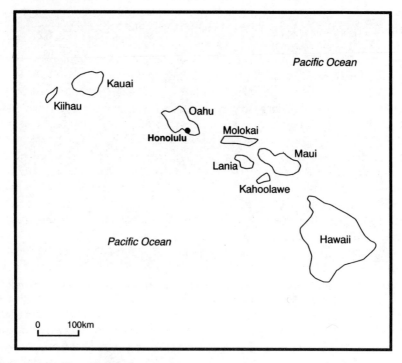

Figure 12.1: Hawai'i: location map

and ownership, and family intermarriages ensured their economic hegemony. With the stagnation of sugar and pineapple in the 1950s, the Big Five underwent a corporate transformation forming medium-sized transnational corporations by linking their land assets with overseas financing, external resort management, and foreign construction companies. The result was a tourism and land dependent development economy wholly supported by the state Republican administration until 1963 and by the Democratic administration afterward. The subsidies of tourism consisted of physical infrastructure and monetary policies resulting in borrowing and debt service well beyond what the state could really afford (Kent 1983).

The development of tourism led to substantial debate over the most appropriate direction of the state's economy and the impact of foreign and mainland investment on the indigenous culture. Farrell (1982) concluded that Hawai'i needed to slow mainland cultural encroachment, immigration and land speculation. He advocated a limit to the tourism industry and recognised the importance of the '*aloha* spirit' (Farrell 1982). However, Aoude (1994) argued that a diversification of the Hawaiian economy away from tourism was politically rather impossible to achieve. Indeed, Hitch (1992) saw tourism in a positive light and argued that Japanese investment did not constitute a threat to Hawai'i because of sufficient legal control over foreign investment and foreign immigration. Hitch recognised that tourism jobs are lower-skilled and lower-paying, and underlined that the tourism sector generates additional and better paying jobs created by the direct and multiplier effect of visitor spending.

The problematic nature of foreign investment was also reinforced by Kim (1994) who concluded that there is a need for improving the data collection on foreign exchange so that fiscal impact assessment establishes cost and benefits of development. Kim argued that tax policies and corporate responsibility needed to improve if social development goals were to be realised. Kim called for a social contract between stakeholders to address the social-economic impacts of tourism in Hawai'i and observed that the failure of the United States to protect the people and land in Hawai'i, and the increasing economic colonisation of the islands by the Japanese, has led to people thinking about greater political independence for the Hawaiian islands (Kim 1994).

The search for development alternatives was also evident in the work of Minerbi (1991), who explored whether 'responsible and alternative tourism' was possible in Hawai'i by assessing how alternative tourism models met desirable community objectives including tourist plant being locally owned; small-scale enterprises; minimal dollar leakage outside the economy; a reduction in negative social impacts such as crime; higher wages; and greater use of local labour, local produces, and services. Minerbi concluded that, if Pacific island nations would like a type of tourism different from the Hawaiian case, they will have to carefully plan for it by keeping tourism:

- small;
- locally owned;
- eco-cultural orientated (Minerbi 1991; Rother 1992).

However, as the following discussion indicates, the achievement of such goals will be fraught with difficulty.

TOURISM MARKETS

Since 1953 visitor arrivals to Hawai'i have grown at nearly an exponential rate. Total visitors' arrival surpassed one million in 1967 and continued to grow, approaching the 7 million mark in 1990. Beginning in 1991 the total arrivals began to decline to 6.2 million in 1993, a total decrease of 12.1 per cent (Hawai'i Department of Business Economic Development and Tourism 1992, 1994) (Table 12.1). This decline created substantial apprehension in the industry and led to demands for greater state financing for an aggressive advertising campaign. However, tourist numbers rebounded in 1994 with a 5 per cent increase in arrivals.

East-bound growth rate outstripped West-bound rate after the mid-1970s. Tourist arrivals briefly levelled off during recessions, airline strikes, the Middle

Table 12.1: Visitor arrivals in Hawai'i, 1987–94

Year	Total
1984	4,855.6
1985	4,884.1
1986	5,606.0
1987	5,800.0
1988	6,142.4
1989	6,641.8
1990	6,971.2
1991	6,873.9
1992	6,513.0
1993	6,124.6
1994	6,455.1

Source: Hawai'i Visitors Bureau, PATA.

East Gulf crisis, and during the 1992 air fare increase. The trend in foreign and domestic visitor arrival to Hawai'i since 1984 indicates that the share of mainland visitor has been declining and the share of the foreign visitors has been increasing reaching more than 44 per cent in 1993. Between 1988 and 1993 foreign visitors' growth was accounted for by Canada (14 per cent), Europe (22 per cent), Asia (56 per cent) with Japan accounting for 48 per cent alone. Mainland visitors outnumber the Asian visitors and stay longer, but spend less (Hawai'i Visitor Bureau 1994).

The economic impact of tourism in Hawai'i is substantial (Tables 12.2–12.5). Gross visitor expenditures increased every year and peaked at $US10.6 billion in 1991. Annual visitor personal expenditures have increased 71 times and the annual number of visitors 24 times between 1960 and 1990. Visitor expenditures decreased to $US8.7 billion in 1993. The decrease is due to American visitors because the Japanese expenditures have remained relatively constant since 1988 (Hawai'i Department of Business and Economic Development and Tourism 1994). Japanese investment and Japanese tourism spending was estimated at 15 per cent of total 1988 income (La Croix and Mak 1989). A transit accommodation tax (TAT) which largely goes to the county governments raised almost $US50 million in 1994.

The expansion in visitor numbers was made possible because of the extensive airline service, which supplanted the passenger ships of the pre-Second World War period (see Chapter 2). Pan American Airways started a passenger clipper plane service from San Francisco opening up visitors' arrivals by air in 1936. It monopolised the Hawai'i air route until after the Second World War (Kent 1993). In 1959 jet airplanes opened up a new era of mass travel to Hawai'i. The Civil Aeronautics Board awarded routes to Hawai'i to seven airlines from 35

Table 12.2: Visitor accommodation in Hawai'i by type and geographic area, Spring 1992

Type of accommodation	Properties			Units		
	State total	Oahu	Other islands	State total	Oahu	Other islands
All types	671	211	460	73,779	37,279	36,500
Apartment-hotel	18	11	7	360	303	57
Bed and breakfast	97	2	77	411	38	373
Condominium	233	36	197	14,363	3,289	11,074
Condo and hotel	64	25	39	8,282	4,844	3,438
Cottage	53	20	33	279	60	219
Hotel	163	86	77	49,324	28,500	20,824
Other	43	13	30	70	245	515

Source: Hawai'i Visitors Bureau, State of Hawai'i.

Table 12.3: Visitor expenditure in Hawai'i by direction of travel, country of residence and islands, 1990 and 1991 ($US '000)

Year and direction of travel or island	Country of residence*			
	Total	United States	Japan	Other countries
1990				
All visitors	9,409,772	5,661,847	2,500,138	1,247,787
Westbound	6,224,829	5,276,369	169,026	779,434
Eastbound	3,184,943	385,478	2,331,112	468,353
Oahu	5,441,149	2,533,197	2,111,416	796,536
Maui	2,023,032	1,553,008	211,640	258,384
Molokai	58,985	45,340	4,274	9,371
Lanai	15,165	11,283	129	3,753
Kauai	945,777	787,304	68,915	89,558
Hawai'i	925,664	731,715	103,764	90,185
1991				
All visitors	9,920,902	5,751,981	2,796,973	1,371,948
Westbound	6,403,885	5,395,710	134,950	873,225
Eastbound	3,517,017	356,271	262,023	498,723
Oahu	5,353,171	2,061,652	2,454,310	837,209
Maui	2,225,228	1,744,280	188,593	292,355
Molokai	89,838	69,181	2,540	18,117
Lanai	57,166	42,983	1,835	12,348
Kauai	1,104,896	937,471	66,520	100,905
Hawai'i	1,090,603	896,414	83,175	111,014

Note: *Additional business expenditures by MCI (meetings, conventions, and incentive) visitors are included with 'other countries'.

Table 12.4: Estimated direct visitor-related expenditure in Hawai'i, 1988–91 ($US millions)

Year	Total[1]	Visitors	MCI[2] visitors	Airline and ship crews	Airlines[3]
1988	8,587.0	7,849	36.1	22.0	716.0
1989	9,628.0	8,785	37.4	24.0	819.0
1990	10,357.0	9,407	46.5	27.0	921.0
1991	10,955.1	9,921	100.6	29.0	1,005.1

Notes: [1] Total has been rounded off
[2] MCI (meetings, conventions, and incentive) visitors
[3] Includes payroll, fuel taxes, and landing fees.

Source: Unpublished 1981–91 estimates based on the DBED Input-Output Model and Hawai'i Econometric Model.

mainland cities. Meanwhile Japan Airlines attained 51 per cent control of the International In-Flight Catering Co. However, concern now exists that with the changes in the technology of travel long-range flying jets may bypass Hawai'i as Qantas has done in the case of Fiji for example.

TOURISM DEVELOPMENT ISSUES AND IMPACTS

Tourism has been established in Hawai'i for over 150 years. In the 1840s, with a population of 8000, Honolulu town had five hotels and six boarding houses in order to meet the needs of the developing plantation economy (Farrell 1982). However, the modern phase of tourism development can be said to have begun with the attainment of statehood in 1959 and the desire for economic development. By 1967, 27 per cent of Hawai'i's tourists were arriving on package tours, and many hotels were dependent upon tour groups (Kent 1993). At the end of the 1970s there were eleven major resorts in the planning or construction stage, valued at over $US2 billion (Kent 1993). Japanese investment poured into Hawai'i when the Japanese government relaxed controls on foreign exchange in the early and middle 1970. The second wave came in the mid-1980s, when the yen appreciated dramatically against the US dollar (Hitch 1992). Additional factors in the growth of Japanese investment was the high price of urban land in Japan, which made land in Hawai'i appear as a bargain, and the many Japanese visitors coming to Hawai'i (Kim 1994). Japanese investment in all sectors of the Hawaiian economy grew from $US1.5 billion in 1984, to over $US9.3 billion in 1990, and accounted for the main share of the $US10.6 million in total foreign investment (Kim 1994). In the 1990s Japanese investment has been reduced markedly, with a number of Japanese properties, golf courses, and hotels being sold at discounted prices and a number of companies going bankrupt.

Table 12.5: Economic activity generated by visitor-related expenditure in Hawai'i, by industry, 1991

	Direct visitor-related expenditures[1] $US millions	Total sales or output[2] $US millions	Total household income[3] $US millions	Jobs (1000) industry total[3]	Jobs (1000) direct only
All industries	10,955.1	19,375.9	6,542.7	250.9	140.1
Agriculture	35.5	238.8	85.7	2.9	0.4
Manufacturing	407.1	1,924.6	295.6	8.7	1.8
Air transportation	1,269.1	1,327.0	435.1	12.4	11.8
Other transportation	560.2	894.1	354.0	13.3	8.3
Wholesale trade[4]	201.2	650.6	301.5	9.5	2.9
Eating and drinking places	1,543.3	1,949.7	569.8	40.0	31.7
Other retail trade[4]	1,249.1	2,070.5	820.8	41.2	24.8
Hotel services	2,979.6	3,045.0	957.0	41.2	40.3
Other services	1,047.4	3,305.1	1,685.3	55.3	17.5
Other industries	59.8	3,969.6	1,037.9	26.4	0.5
Imports	1,602.8	–	–	–	–

Notes: [1] Direct expenditures by visitors, airline and ship crews, and overseas airlines.
[2] Direct, indirect, and induced sales.
[3] Direct, indirect and induced jobs.
[4] Expenditure figure refers to mark-up earned, not total sales revenue.

Sources: *Hawai'i State Department of Planning and Economic Development, The Economic Impact of Tourism in Hawai'i: 1970 to 1980*, Research Report 1983–2 (April 1983), and revised 1970–91 estimates based on the DBED Input-Output Model and Hawai'i Econometric Model (Department of Business, Economic Development and Tourism 1993).

Population growth and migration

Population growth by immigration has been a feature of the plantation economy era and the tourism economy. However, population growth has been a cause for concern. Nordyke (1978) argued that,

- two out of three jobs were being planned for immigrants by the state population projections;
- tourism and population growth were related;
- the state should hold the growth of tourism at 3.5 million annually to avoid the adverse effect of excessive population growth by immigration, the decline of per capita income, the increase of welfare costs, and the depletion of natural resources.

However, net migration accounted for 48 per cent of the overall civilian growth in 1980–90 (Minerbi 1994) and has continued to contribute to population growth since (Lind 1994).

Economic dimensions

The economy of the State of Hawai'i has grown substantially in the modern tourism era. The gross state product (GSP) has increased 14 times between 1960 and 1990, but only 3.7 times in constant dollars. It reached a level of $US29 billion in 1992 corresponding to a GSP per capita of $US25,288 in current dollars and of $US16,458 in constant dollars. State tax receipts reached $US4 billion in 1990. Per capita personal income increased 8.8 times to the 1990 level of $US20,552 and median family cash income 6.7 times (Hawai'i Department of Business and Economic Development and Tourism 1992). However, the GSP per capita measured in current dollars increased 91 per cent between 1980 and 1990, the GSP per capita measured in constant dollars showed an increase of only 24 per cent. Meanwhile, the consumer price index increased 66 per cent and the state and county public bonded debt increased 138 per cent in the same period, reaching more than $US5 billion in 1991. The median household and family income measured in constant dollars actually decreased 3 per cent and 1.4 per cent respectively between 1970 and 1980s. The per capita personal income between 1981 and 1991 increased 85 per cent in current dollars, but only 14 per cent in constant dollars, while the Honolulu Consumer price index increased 60 per cent in the same years.

Hawai'i's growing economy is associated with a deteriorating quality of life and inequalities among social classes. The labour force changed from a craft to a service base resulting in the long-term fall in wages (Pai 1989). In 1991 the hypothetical intermediate budget for a family of four reached $US55,833, being 37.7 per cent higher than the US national average, 80.5 per cent higher for personal income tax and 60 per cent higher for shelter cost. The result of this tourism economy is that:

- Hawai'i has one of the highest rates of multi-wage earner families with a high proportion of women in the labour force, particularly in service occupations; and
- many residents must leave, while foreign immigrants come into the islands.
(Minerbi 1994)

The distribution of household income has deteriorated over the years with lower and medium income families increasing and upper income families declining. The cost of living in Hawai'i grew six times faster in the 1980s than did household income. The poverty status of persons has increased 3 percentage points between 1980 and 1990 reaching a level of 121,000 people or 11 per cent in 1990. There are also ethnic concerns: civilian unemployed among ethnic groups was greater than among the total resident population for Hawaiians and Filipinos (Hawai'i Department of Labor 1994). One conclusion is that Hawai'i has experienced increasing relative poverty with unprecedented wealth. The aggregate wealth has increased but the distribution of that wealth has deteriorated (Pai 1989; Matsuoka 1991). Yet the state of Hawai'i continues to plan for 11 million tourists, 56,300 additional hotel rooms, and a 1.5 million population target for the year 2010.

Currently, there are 700 hotels and condominiums in Hawai'i providing over 70,000 accommodation units, mainly concentrated in specific resort areas, mostly controlled by large landowners. In 1966 almost 80 per cent of the units were located on Oahu and 20 per cent of the units in the neighbouring islands. That proportion continued to change over the years until the percentage of the units in the neighbouring islands equalled Oahu in 1991. The rapid growth of hotels and condominiums and the recent decline in visitor stay and expenditures resulted in many resorts experiencing a negative cash flow, particularly on the neighbouring islands. Properties have been resold at low rates. The result is a lower property tax revenue, a lower transient accommodation tax collection and lower county revenues. Hotel jobs steadily increased in Hawai'i from 25,000 in 1980 to just over 40,000 in 1991. However, employment decreased to 7 per cent from 40,982 to 38,000 in 1993. Employment in eating and drinking establishments neared 35,000 in 1980 and surpassed the 48,000 mark in 1992, but declined to just above 45,000 in 1993.

DIRECTIONS FOR HAWAIIAN TOURISM?

The above discussion indicates the somewhat problematic nature of contemporary tourism development in Hawai'i. The optimism of the late 1880s which has continued for much of this century that 'The tourist travel to these islands is capable of an almost indefinite expansion' (Kuykendall 1930: 110), clearly cannot hold any longer.

In the 1980s a cacophony of newspaper advertising revealed that the stakeholders in Hawaiian tourism were not talking to each other about a common vision for tourism. Major hotels advertised Hawai'i in an insensitive way as the perfect escape, proclaiming luxury, and up-scale living: 'the ultimate playground'. Indigenous Hawaiians fighting geothermal development and the destruction of sacred rainforest on the big island counter-advertised: 'Come to Hawaii: Swim in polluted Water, Breath toxic fumes, See [the] ugly electric tower'. Similarly, native Hawaiians opposing new resorts in West Oahu placed an advertisement stating 'West Beach – An Island of Luxury in an Ocean of Pollution and Poverty'. The Hawai'i Visitor Bureau's advertising invited tourists to rediscover aspects of Hawai'i that the first time visitor – captive of the resort – might have missed: 'How to Avoid Hawaii's 283 Beautiful Beaches – Part III', while the unions, fighting deteriorating employment conditions, paid for a one-page advertisement against the new Japanese hotel owners (Minerbi *et al.* 1988; Minerbi 1992).

Cultural tourism was perceived as one mechanism of bringing together the various stakeholders in tourism development. However, the state government and industry approach to cultural tourism was narrow in scope and promoted Hawaiian culture abroad as a 'new marketing tool'. Few hotels started employee instruction on Hawaiian indigenous values or produced brochures identifying cultural areas in Hawai'i, although the state community colleges did initiate an *Interpret Hawai'i Program* to strengthen Hawaiian cultural values in the hospitality sector. In 1989 the state proposed to start a data base of cultural events and allocated $US500,000 to establish a state tourism arts company as a promotional showcase of the Native Hawaiian heritage abroad with the hope of attracting new visitors and prolonging the stay of the existing market (Hawai'i Department of Business Economic Development and Tourism 1989).

Ecotourism was also perceived as a new tourism opportunity. However, the first state of Hawai'i conference on ecotourism in 1994 was conceived as a way to learn how 'to diversify the Hawai'i's travel product' rather than an opportunity to restructure the tourism economy (Hawai'i Department of Business Economic Development and Tourism 1994). In 1994 the Hawai'i Visitors Bureau focused on international geographic targeting, public relations, monitoring, and increasing the number of visitors by 6 per cent. These initiatives, by and large, failed to recognise the substantial conflicts which exist between the tourist industry and Native Hawaiians and the steps that must be taken to evolve a genuine community based, small-scale cultural approach to tourism in Hawai'i.

The extent to which tourism development has become the subject of debate within Hawai'i is indicated by the 1989 Hawai'i' declaration on tourism. This declaration, by a group of Hawaiians and local church leaders, stressed that a state of emergency existed for Hawaiian people and for the fragile island environment and emphasised that tourism did not benefit the poor and native Hawaiians, that tourism was a new form of exploitation, and that it was not an indigenous practice. The proposed actions included: return of the public and private lands held in fiduciary trust to the Native Hawaiian people, an immediate ban on new resort development in Hawaiian rural communities, and assistance to foster a community-based economy (Hawai'i Ecumenical Coalition on Tourism 1989).

The temporary downturn of international tourism, the recession affecting American and Japanese economies, and the devastating Iwa Hurricane on Kauai encouraged a brief dialogue in 1993 among tourist officials and Hawaiian grass root groups exploring the rebuilding of the Kaua'i visitor's industry from a community-based perspective. The proposed plan called for the establishment of a Native Hawaiian community development corporation and the establishment of a Native Hawaiian cultural centre to involve Hawaiians in the industry (Hui Ho'Okipa o Kaua'i 1993: 6). However, while demands for alternative, 'responsible' forms of tourism have continued to come from native Hawaiian and church groups (Hawai'i Ecumenical Coalition 1993), the ability of such organisations to substantially affect the future direction of tourism development in the state remains problematic.

PROSPECTS FOR THE 1990S: TOWARDS ECO-CULTURAL TOURISM?

Alternative policy implementation requires an understanding of the impacts of tourism in Hawai'i. Initially, construction for tourism brings hotels, luxury housing and condominiums; gradually new residents settle resort areas. Affluent newcomers drive up the cost of living to unaffordable levels and displace local people. Immigrant workers, attracted by low paying jobs, create additional stress on social services and on ethnic relations.

Carefully matching new job creation with the local labour force to avoid excessive immigration is a way to manage the amount and pace of development and population growth. This can be done by:

- not oversizing infrastructure and facilities;
- reserving land for use by local people, by zoning to protect the integrity of the natural ecosystem;
- training the local labour force for the new jobs being envisioned.

The construction and real estate industries should be kept in check and controlled. Excessive construction and real estate activity lead to an unbalanced, growth-led environmentally unsustainable and economically unaffordable development path. There is a relationship between the high proportion of foreign ownership of the tourism industry, the immediate and excessive leakage of the tourist dollar outside the local economy and the increasing number of tourists needed to attain desirable levels of income in the local economy. Indeed, the direct and indirect subsidies of local government for the provision of facilities, infrastructure and services to build up the tourism industry can be so great that they saddle the local people for decades and preempt alternative economic options to tourism.

There is plenty of tourism data, but statistics that really assess the performance of this industry are quite inadequate. More can be done to assess:

- *diversion*: how much money is made and remains elsewhere because of the hotels in the locality;
- *leakage*: how much money comes into the locality and leaves it immediately;
- *multiplier effect and equity*: how much of the money that remains and circulates in the community reaches the various groups of the society.

When current information is available to the community on economic changes, cost of living, profit and loss from tourism, it is easier to plan the appropriate size of the tourism sector and arrive at fair management and labour relations and adjust wages upward, avoiding disruptive and prolonged labour strikes and move toward equitable profit sharing and co-ownership schemes.

A recent survey indicated residents' support for tourism but also a desire to control its growth. Substantial concerns exist that the island is being 'run for tourists at the expense of the local people' (Community Resources 1993: 2). When new resorts are planned in a locality, community-based corporations should ideally be established in order to monitor the provision of essential services and affordable housing and support employment training. These community organisations are needed to ensure that the terms of the agreements between resort developers, government and the community are carried out.

Tourism and construction should not be the preponderant industries in a locality, otherwise local people's livelihoods remain unprotected, particularly those of indigenous peoples. This requires fostering community-based indigenous development. Certain native ancestral land should be zoned and protected from tourism encroachment to allow for the exercise of basic indigenous rights and the retention of a land base suitable for traditional practices. Therefore, community-based management of historic, cultural, sacred and scenic sites should be encouraged so that interaction with tourists is managed by government supervised curatorships and grass roots-based guardianships.

A desirable prospect for the future – but not necessarily politically likely – is the restructuring of tourism leading to a form of eco-cultural tourism that meet the needs of Native Hawaiians, other residents, and of the fragile island ecosystem. Local communities should be in good cultural and economic health for eco-cultural tourism to take place in their localities. Sustainable tourism takes places where local people have homes, own, lease, or directly manage lands, take care of nature, and feel positive enough about themselves and their culture, that they are willing to share – with proper protocols – what they have with invited guests.

Eco-cultural tourism requires restructuring conventional mass tourism away from foreign corporate control and back to local communities. Required strategies should address:

- Hawaiian trust lands;
- government decentralisation and co-management;

- voluntary private land reform and partnership;
- *ahupua'a* (district) planning or restoration and access of subsistence resource *mauka-makai* (from the mountain to the sea) within each district.

With the implementation of these strategies the economic, sociocultural, environmental and political concerns of indigenous Hawaiians could be addressed within a social contract that binds guest, host, and industry. This is the setting in which ecocultural tourism will flourish and the local residents benefit for the longer-term, sustainable development of Hawai'i.

REFERENCES

Aoude, I. (1994) 'Tourism attraction: Hawai'i's locked-in economy', in P. Manicas (ed.) *Social Process in Hawaii: A Reader, Vol. 33*, Honolulu: Department of Sociology, University of Hawai'i, pp. 218–35.

Community Resources Inc. (1993) *A Brief Survey of Hawai'i Resident Attitudes About Tourism and Product Development*, Honolulu: Community Resources.

Farrell, B. (1982) *Hawai'i The Legend That Sells*, Honolulu: The University Press of Hawai'i.

Hall, C.M. (1994) *Tourism in the Pacific Rim: Development, Impacts and Markets*, Melbourne: Longman Australia.

Hawai'i Department of Business and Economic Development and Tourism (1989) *A Report on Cultural Tourism*, Honolulu, Hawai'i.

Hawai'i Department of Business and Economic Development and Tourism (1992) *Hawai'i Data Book*, Honolulu, Hawai'i.

Hawai'i Department of Business, Economic Development and Tourism (1993) *Hawai'i Data Book*, Honolulu, Hawai'i.

Hawai'i Department of Business and Economic Development and Tourism (1994) *The 1994 Hawai'i State Tourism Congress*, Honolulu, Hawai'i.

Hawai'i Department of Labor (1994) *Labor Force Information by Age and Sex*, Honolulu, Hawai'i.

Hawai'i Ecumenical Coalition on Tourism (1989) *The 1989 Hawai'i Declaration of the Hawai'i Ecumenical Coalition on Tourism Conference. Tourism in Hawai'i: Its Impact on Native Hawaiians and its Challenge to the Churches*, Honolulu: Hawai'i Ecumenical Coalition on Tourism.

Hawai'i Ecumenical Coalition (1993) *Action Alert: Responsible Tourism: A 10–Point Hawaiian View. Kaua'i: HEC /Ho'Okipa*, Honolulu: Hawai'i Ecumenical Coalition on Tourism.

Hawai'i Visitor Bureau (1994) *Hawaiian Beat*, 8, 4(April).

Hitch, T. (1992) *Island in Transition*, Honolulu: First Hawaiian Bank.

Hui Ho'Okipa o Kaua'i (1993) *Staring Over: Rebuilding Kauai's Visitor Industry From a Community Development Perspective*. Kauai, Kapa'a: Hawai'i Ecumenical Coalition.

Jennings, H. and Swindler, W. (1978) *Chronology and Documentary Handbook of the State of Hawai'i*. Dobbs Ferry: Oceania Publishers.

Kelly, M. (1994) 'Foreign investment in Hawai'i', in I. Aoude (ed.) *Social Process in Hawai'i, Vol. 35*, Honolulu: Department of Sociology, University of Hawai'i, pp. 15–39.

Kent, N. (1983) *Hawai'i Islands Under the Influence*, Honolulu: University of Hawai'i Press.

Kim, K. (1994) 'The political economy of foreign investment in Hawai'i', in A. Ibrahim (ed.) *Social Process in Hawai'i*, Honolulu: Department of Sociology, University of Hawai'i, pp. 40–55.

Kuykendall (1930) *The Hawaiian Kingdom*, 3 vols, Honolulu: The University of Hawai'i Press.

La Croix, S. and Mak, J. (1989) *Honolulu Advertiser*, 25 April.

Lind, I. (1994) 'US finds a lag in Hawai'i growth', *Star Bulletin* 28 December.

Matsuoka, J. (1991) 'Differential perceptions of the social impacts of tourism development in a rural Hawaiian community', *Social Development Issues*, 13(2): 55–65.

Minerbi, L. (1991) *Alternative Forms of Tourism in the Coastal Zone: Searching for Responsible Tourism in Hawai'i: A Summary*, Newport: National Coastal Research and Development Institute.

Minerbi, L. (1992) *Impact of Tourism Development in Pacific Islands*. San Francisco: Greenpeace Pacific Campaign.

Minerbi, L. (1994) 'Sustainability versus growth in Hawai'i', in I. Aoude (ed.) *Social Process in Hawai'i*, Vol. 35, Honolulu: Department of Sociology, University of Hawai'i, pp. 145–60.

Minerbi, L., McGraw, R., Johnston C., and Yukio Ohashi, Y. (1988) *Alternative Forms of Tourism in the Coastal Zone: Searching for Responsible Tourism in Hawai'i*, Newport: National Coastal Research and Development Institute.

Nordyke, E. (1978) 'Tourism and population: Their growths are related', *The Sunday Star Bulletin and Advertiser*, 5 March: G-3.

Pai, G. (1989) *Long Term Changes in the Structure of the Hawaiian Economy and Their Impact on Social and Economic Welfare in Hawai'i*, Honolulu: Church of the Crossroads.

Rother, I. (1992) *A Green Hawai'i Sourcebook for Development Alternatives*, Honolulu: Na| Ka|ne O Ka Malo Press.

Chapter 13

Fiji

Nii-k Plange

INTRODUCTION

Bula! This word, addressed to tourists in a semi-exclamation form is a welcome greeting to Fiji, and is the enduring signifier of contemporary tourism and the tourism product and its development in Fiji. Substantively, the mass tourism product is dominated by expatriate investments, with emphasis on the culture and friendliness of Fiji's people as a draw card, and the naturally tropical climate; long white sandy beaches and extensive coral reefs as the natural facilities for leisure and relaxation (see Figure 13.1). It is along these shores of these sandy beaches, and recently on remote islands that Fiji's tourism resorts have sprung up to service the over 300,000 visitors who arrive annually. On the contrary, the origins of tourism in Fiji was based on culture, flora and fauna and hotels away from sandy beaches to cater for transit passengers on the long and arduous North American-Pacific sea route (see Chapter 2). These hotels, by the 1900s, included the Melbourne Club, Club Hotel, Viti House, and a few boarding houses. Increased passenger traffic by the Union Steamship Company led to the design and building of the then international hotel in 1914, The Grand Pacific Hotel. With its imperious Victorian architecture it now symbolises the real beginnings for tourism in Fiji. Tourism now stands as a number one foreign exchange earner for Fiji. It contributes about 15 per cent of national GDP and provides direct employment for about 15,000 persons which is almost 15 per cent of total estimated employment. These impressive contributions to the national economy of Fiji and the intended economic development strategies notwithstanding, tourism has faced problems in its growth, development and direction. This chapter reviews some of these.

THE DEVELOPMENT OF TOURISM IN FIJI

The steamship route through Fiji and its transit passengers provided the earlier initiatives by local Europeans in colonial Fiji to establish a tourist product for consumers. By the 1920s there had emerged a few hoteliers in Fiji whose intentions according to Sutherland (1992: 73) were the need for more

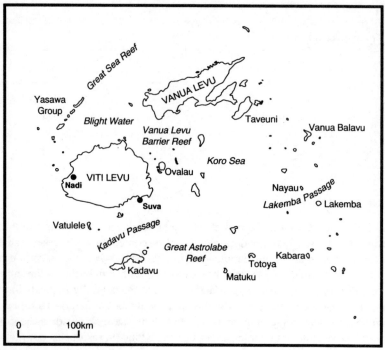

Figure 13.1: Fiji: Location map

coordination and planning for the tourism industry. This initiative resulted in the formation of the Suva Tourist Board in 1923 which later in 1925 became the Fiji Publicity Board and Tourist Bureau (the forerunner of the current Fiji Visitors Bureau). The problems encountered by this organisation in its attempts to establish tourism as a viable economic industry were not only financial but also lacked favourable recognition of the economic viability of tourism in the midst of an overarching sugar industry. Indeed, the colonial administration was never convinced of tourism's economic significance let alone its long-term viability and profitability, as in the case of sugar. There was thus no direct assistance by the colonial administration and local hoteliers had to bear the cost of development and maintenance, as well as marketing Fiji as a destination. The Bureau's marketing attempts were directed at Australia, New Zealand and North America – geographical areas which then lay on the steamship route and produced the smaller number of transit tourists. This trinity of source markets have since remained the dominant source of tourists for Fiji. Early marketing strategies included advertisements in selected newspapers in these countries. With a small budget of £500 the Bureau undertook these advertisements and other activities which were geared to assisting potential visitors wishing to enter Fiji. Perhaps one of the few positive contributions to the infant industries at this period by the colonial administration was the immigration policy, which withdrew all passport requirements for inbound ship passengers in 1935 (Francis 1995).

These bleak economic circumstances for tourism, however, changed with time to augment not only an interest in the development of the industry, but the provision of needed infrastructure to encourage investors. Some of these changes were chanced ones which did not particularly have tourism as its purpose. Primarily among these was the building of Nadi Airport to contribute airline activities during the Second World War. This opened a gateway for Fiji and the Pacific for international tourism. As an international-sized airport it was, after the war, a jet aircraft refuelling station for the Honolulu–Sydney and the Honolulu–Auckland route. The location of the airport also prompted many trans-Pacific carriers to use Nadi as a refuelling stop for their propeller aircraft and by 1951 Pan-American, Canadian Pacific Air, and Air Pacific were using the airport. Accommodation facilities also grew with local European investments to cater for the increasing traffic. There was the Royal Hotel in Levuka, Grand Eastern Hotel in Labasa, the Northern Hotel Chain at Raki Raki, Tuvua, Ba, Lautoka, Nadi and Sigatoka and road works on Viti Levu linked some of the hotels to Suva (Britton 1983).

These developments were accompanied by the increasing numbers of tourist (or visitor) arrivals in Fiji. In 1926 there were 3733 visitors. Ten years after in 1937 there was almost a 70 per cent increase to over 21,000 visitors. This phenomenal growth appeared to have finally convinced the colonial adminis-tration of the significant probability of tourism which local European settler investors have identified earlier. A change of perception inevitably followed, with a little influence from local capital. This was shown in the *Report of the Economic Review Committee of 1953* which observed, positively, that 'the tourist industry is one of which can be of considerable economic value to the colony . . . and government should consider ways and means of assisting the industry (without necessarily taking part) particularly in questions of finance' (Sutherland 1992: 76). This new interest could not have come at a better time given the extensive damage to the tourist facilities including hotels/boarding houses caused by the combined forces of the 1952 hurricane and an earthquake in 1953. But the intended financial assistance was not immediately forthcoming to local investors and hoteliers as they sought to rebuild and refurbish. Meanwhile, foreign investors had, since the beginning, been reluctant to invest in Fiji's inchoate tourism industry, and remained so inspite of requests for assistance by local European interests. In the midst of these uncertainties the Publicity Bureau was renamed the Fiji Visitors Bureau and it immediately sought financial assistance from other sources including the Commonwealth Development Corporation, but in vain. It also became a member of Pacific Travel Area Association (PATA).

Most significantly before the end of the 1950s, which is usually recognised as the beginning of the tourism industry in Fiji, a significant impetus was provided to the establishment of a firm basis for tourism; a basis which would now entice international investors into Fiji's tourist product. This was the Hotel Aids Bill, 1958, which has offered considerable concessions to attract foreign capital in the same way as the colonial administration had done by the turn of the century to entice and sustain the sugar industry. In other words, the colonial administration saw the growth of tourism in Fiji as a viable economic sector in the hands of expatriate capital with relevant resources including skills of all sorts needed by the industry. This perception as expressed in the Hotel Aids Bill, 1958 was damaging to local investors and entrepreneurs who had nurtured the tourism industry from the beginning. They felt the danger of being marginalised and 'cautioned about the danger of the tourist industry monopolised "by just a few"' (Sutherland 1992: 76). Some recognition was given to their fears in the final bill of the Hotel Aid Ordinance, 1958. This lowered the minimum capital expenditure to qualify for state concessions. With the ordinance and its soft concessions to investors, however, international tourism capital recognised an environment for profit. Though the threshold for assistance was lowered, the total package of the Bill still favoured foreign (multinational) capital with access to considerable resources.

It appeared then that by the end of 1950s, the scene was set for local European capital in tourism: it was now to occupy a secondary position in the industry. The ownership structure of the industry was thus laid. International capital occupied the commanding heights followed by local European capital and some Indo-Fijian interests, with indigenous Fijians way behind.

THE TAKE-OFF OF TOURISM IN FIJI

An amended version of the Bill of concessions was finally introduced as the Hotel Aid Ordinance, 1960. Among other things it opened the way for foreign investment in Fiji's tourism, especially the accommodation sector. In doing this it satisfied the colonial government which had felt that 'we need urgently something really big, a major step forward in hotel accommodation' (Sutherland 1992: 78). Fiji Visitors Bureau membership of the internationally reputable Pacific Area Travel Association also brought Fiji into the context of international tourism and led to the first comprehensive survey of Fiji's tourism development potential. This report known as the Cheechi Report, called on international capital to invest through a positive presentation of Fiji as a bonanza for investors (Cheechi & Co. Ltd 1961).

Another dimension of the development of tourism at this time was the duty-free provisions allowed by the colonial government. This encouraged local firms to import and wholesale, as well as distribute and retail different kinds of electrical, jewellery and other products. Local Indian capital entered this sector of the developing tourism industry. Among these were D. Gokal, Narseys Ltd and Cains Janiff. But they were not alone. Some local entrepreneurs also entered the duty-free sector of Fiji's tourism.

Investments in the accommodation sector and corresponding growth of the duty-free shopping made tourism in Fiji an attractive option. Small wonder then that the 1960s witnessed a gradual increase in visitor arrivals. By 1960 four sizable hotels catered for about 40 per cent of visitor rooms. Indeed, to the extent that the Cheechi Report 'marketed' Fiji it produced significant returns to the growth of the tourism industry.

All these subsequently produced a boom in visitor arrivals in Fiji. Between 1967 and 1969 a remarkable sixfold increase was recorded from all source countries for Fiji, Australia, New Zealand, the United States and Canada recorded twelvefold, fivefold, fivefold, and tenfold increases of their visitors respectively. These increases depended primarily on the availability of transportation, either airplanes or cruise ships, from these source countries; but more importantly the airplane whose own technological improvements have by now produced the jet airliners which reduced time and gave travellers some reasonable comfort. The important elements of tourism development in Fiji began to appear: accommodation and transportation, including internal linkages.

Since the 1960s the accommodation sector has grown remarkably to include international standard hotels with foreign investments like the Regent, Sheraton, Hyatt (now Warwick), The Fijian and the Mocambo (of the Shangri-La group) and the Travelodge and Best Western. These are all representatives of the extent of foreign capital in Fiji's tourism development.

NATIONAL INDEPENDENCE AND TOURISM

The independent government of Fiji inherited an economy built upon the twin pillars of sugar and tourism. Different as they may be, they share some characteristics of concern to all sovereign governments. First is foreign domination and second the role of local people. Tourism had its own third characteristic – the pressing of traditional Fijian culture into the service of tourism. While sugar concerns were dealt with soon after independence, those of tourism lingered on. Small wonder then that repeatedly at national tourism conventions, keynote speakers, usually government ministers, called attention to tourists' potential impact on culture, tourism as a new form of colonialism, the lack of local representation at the higher echelons of the industry, and the issue of profits and leakage. Indeed, all these were candid expressions of the dilemma that the industry presented to the newly independent national government: it recognised and appreciated the economic returns while at the same time it remained uncomfortable with potential influence on culture and tradition.

This dilemma has indeed remained an enduring characteristic of the industry and has polarised local perception and the reception of tourism (Plange 1985). Notwithstanding the dilemma, development plans for the 1970s endeavoured to sustain tourism and encourage its growth albeit with caution to its real and potential impact. Meanwhile the 1970s also witnessed an increase in tourism employees, from a total of 2059 in 1970 to 3180 in 1975. Nevertheless, the oil crisis produced its own shock effect on the travel industry internationally and contributed to a lowering of room occupancy rates in Fiji from 73 per cent in 1970 to 52 per cent in 1975 (Varley 1978: 58).

TOURISM IN CRISIS

With the basis of the industry laid and the consequent boom of the mid-1960s and 1970s – the oil crisis and its impact notwithstanding – tourism development settled sown to an expected performance in the 1980s. However, devastating cyclones in 1983 and 1985 again affected tourism fortunes. Accompanying this was the apparent weakening currencies of Australia and New Zealand in the late 1980s and aggressive, pro-active marketing strategies by other Pacific and south east Asian destinations. Meanwhile, short-haul, single destination visitors from Australia and New Zealand declined in favour of long-haul multi-destination visitors. Though this produced an increase in visitor arrivals in the 1980–85 period, the average length of stay declined from 9.5 days in 1981 to about 8.4 days in 1985. This also produced a decline in real average expenditure per visitor from $F576 in 1980 to $F31 in 1985, a decline of 7.6 per cent. Meanwhile gross tourism receipts increased steadily from $F109.5 million in 1980 to $F169 million in 1985. An expected increase in these figures due to marketing efforts took a tumble in 1987 as a result of the political events and crisis of mid-1987 with drastic social consequences for tourism workers. What ensued was an urgent and 'crisis marketing' plan to polish the apparently tarnished image caused by the events and advertised in the international media. This was sustained and a revival was realised soon after. Since then, a steady increase has been maintained by the industry especially from European and Japanese sources, with a spectacular and much applauded increase, especially in 1990 to 278,996 visitors, from that of the previous year of 250,565. Corresponding to this, tourism earnings had also been increased between 1987 and 1993 (Tourism Council of the South Pacific 1994)

TOURISM RESEARCH

With the post-1960s development in tourism in Fiji there has been accompanying research on the various aspects of the industry and their influence on Fiji's society as a whole. These researches include those that can be described as economic, sociocultural and environmental and the researches on socio-cultural aspects have been both from academics and non-academics. Among the earliest were a collection published by the University of the South Pacific's Institute of Pacific Studies (Rajotte 1980). In one of these studies the author examined local workers share in tourism receipts and concluded that they received on the whole 'crumbs from the table', with there also being a social danger in terms of the sociopsychological impact that hotel/resort work would have on locals from 'relatively unsophisticated backgrounds' (Samy 1980: 67).

While this was a remarkable conclusion, some of the anticipated consequences have only recently been explored in a research thesis which examined the impact of resort and hotel work on Fijian mothers (Auger-Andrews 1995). Within the same period other more localised research examined the impact of tourism on urban Fijian villages (Niukula 1980) and the relationship between tourism and the Fijian philosophy and practice of hospitality (Vusoniwailala 1980). This localised destination research was taken a step further when another study examined 'Tamavua Village', which had apparently been established as 'an attempt to give tourists a chance to see how Fijian people lived in the past' (Salato and Ilaiu 1980: 89). This research concluded rather sadly that the experiment, if it can be called that, failed and 'today [the village] demonstrates how many Fijians have to live in a world of halves: half-traditional, half-modern, half-adapted, but also all too real' (Salato and Ilaiu 1980: 91). In the same book another contributor, Bolabola (1980), concluded after her research on the impact of tourism on Fijian woodcarving that increasingly the art had been commercialised yet 'Fijian woodcarving could be a forgotten art if it was not for tourism and its demand for souvenirs'. A positive influence of tourism was thus presented.

Bolabola's (1980) conclusions addressed one of the issues of enduring debate on the impact of tourism on society and culture. While some applaud tourism as having the capacity to revitalise cultures and traditions, others see the industry as destructive of values and practices. Indeed, most of the sociocultural research on Fiji as a destination falls between these two poles. These positions, together with other local attitudes towards tourism and the tourism product of Fiji, were subject of a nationwide population-based research project undertaken in the country between 1983 and 1985 (Plange 1985). The survey was commissioned by the Fiji Visitors Bureau as part of its attempt to undertake visitor awareness education. The survey of a large representative sample of about 2000 respondents covered a wide area of the industry including environmental impacts, use of ancestral locations as tourist attractions, tourism's economic contribution to Fiji and positions occupied by locals in the structure of the industry. This study was perhaps the first of its kind in terms of breadth of coverage, and it concluded by noting the dilemma that exists within the public about the tourist industry. While there was unanimous appreciation of the economic contributions of the industry to Fiji, there were also corresponding misgivings about its influence on culture and religion and its tendency to 'commercialise' ancestral sites as well as its domination by expatriates. In a 1987–8 study commissioned by the newly established Tourism Council of the South Pacific some of these difficulties were still being expressed (Plange 1988).

THE ECONOMICS OF TOURISM

Extensive coverage of the economics of tourism especially with respect to macro-economic aspects like employment, gross national product, investments and contribution to national per capita income were provided through research undertaken by Britton (1983). Prior to this, however, similar terrain had been covered by Varley (1978) with his monograph of *Tourism in Fiji: Some Economic and Social Problems*. Britton's work, however, remained the more comprehensive of the two. As an extension of his analysis, Britton also explored the investments and development on tourism in Fiji and its contribution to the underdevelopment of Fiji.

The core of Britton's argument is aptly summarised by his observation that

> when a Third World country uses tourism as a development strategy it becomes entrenched in a global system over which it has little control . . . the international tourism industry is a product of metropolitan capitalist enterprise . . . the industry, because of the commercial power held by foreign enterprise, imposes on peripheral destinations a development mode which reinforces dependency on, and vulnerability to, developed countries.
>
> (Britton 1983: 22)

This political economy-orientated observation notwithstanding, research observes the economic contributions of tourism, even if these are 'Leftovers from Pacific Tourism', as Le Fevre titled his article as far back as 1975. In that year tourism produced about 7000 jobs and contributed $F15.5 million GDP in terms of value added. The picture then, as other research shows, has been that of steady growth – the fluctuations notwithstanding. By 1984, research identified the industry as a strategic sector on which the future growth of Fiji's economy can be based; and by 1985 Fiji hosted a total of 240,000 visitors which produced a total earning of $F169.4 million and soon came to rank second to sugar as the largest income earner, number one in employment growth and the generation of foreign exchange (Bureau of Statistics 1994). It took little time after this for tourism to become the number one sector of Fiji's economy.

Accompanying these had been the expansion and investments in the accommodation sector. From about 10 hotels/boarding houses in 1960 (with about 520 rooms) the hotel industry jumped to 104 establishments with about 4000 rooms in 1984. These establishments and available rooms together cater for the diversity of visitors, from up-market to the budget-orientated visitor, to the foot-loose traveller seeking a basic room. Increasing expansion of the accommodation industry appears to be due to the growth of tourism in the 1990s: a $F300 million 4–5 star hotel investment at Denaru in Nadi, another $F300 million project to build three hotel/resorts at Natadola Beach in Sigatoka, a $F260 million at Vulani and another 100 million 5-star hotel promised for urban Suva. Meanwhile, a Disneyland amusement park is due soon in the Nadi area. This political economy-orientated analysis illustrates that despite the economic benefits which tourism contributes to Fiji, they are still the 'leftovers from Pacific tourism' as Le Fevre titled his article back in 1975.

TOURISM MARKETS

Destination Fiji has maintained Australia, New Zealand and North America as its prime markets. Recently, Japan and Europe have also emerged as important markets. The increase in visitor arrivals from these markets have been sustained both by continued marketing efforts by Fiji and particularly also from increased air transportation, air routes and the flexibility that this provides for potential visitors. Additionally, the emergence of tour wholesaling sometimes with variable destinations has also contributed to this growth. In 1960 as research shows, about 60 per cent of visitors arrived on pre-paid package tours compared to 80 per cent of the same in 1984.

Meanwhile the 1980s saw a decline in the United States and New Zealand markets of about 13 and 12 per cent respectively. This was offset by a growth in the Japanese market of about 9 per cent. The concern for the industry, however, was the apparent dependence of the industry on rather narrow base in Australia, New Zealand and United States. In the 1980s these three produced almost 80 per cent of total arrivals. While there has been observable changes in this picture (by 1989, 63 per cent came from these traditional markets and in 1992 56 per cent), there is still a concern to tap the European and other Asian markets (Table 13.1).

This has led to a new market drive for Europe and Asia. The Fiji Visitors Bureau has expressed interest in intensifying its promotional activities in Japan and Korea, and the government is in the process of seeking flight arrangements to allow a penetration of the Korean market.

Growth of tourism source markets cannot be examined without due respect to the national carrier Air Pacific. Blazing with colourful decorations its penetration from the 1980s of the American market has been a contributory factor to the development of the industry. With flights to Australia, New Zealand, Japan and other South Pacific island states, Air Pacific has since the beginning of the 1990s, bounced back from the red into the profit column. It has recently purchased new jet liners and, with its young pilots and enterprising Chief Executive, has remained one of the backbones of tourism development in Fiji. With its own extension and development it has relocated to Nadi and subsequently turned Nadi into the gateway to the South Pacific.

DEVELOPMENT ISSUES AND IMPACTS

Tourism development issues, and planning, have not been lacking in the industry. Between 1973 and 1990 six Development Plans based on examination of the existing product have been produced. The first of these, now commonly referred to as the Belt–Collins Report (1988), recommended more cultural activities to be included in the tourism product in order to distribute the economic benefits of the industry, together with educational programmes to prepare local residents to deal with and take up relevant positions on the industry. A 1988 report, the Cleverdon Report (Cleverdon and Brook 1988),

Table 13.1: Visitor arrivals in Fiji by major market, 1987–92

Market	1987	1988	1989	1990	1991	1992	% change 1991/92
Australia	65,382	75,264	96,992	103,535	86,625	87,395	0.09
New Zealand	16,197	21,507	28,128	29,432	30,631	37,227	21.5
USA	47,037	42,144	34,425	36,928	31,842	34,802	9.3
Canada	16,819	16,883	16,536	18,438	15,242	12,602	–17.3
United Kingdom	8,511	8,464	11,4041	16,773	16,555	16,795	1.4
Germany	(a)	(a)	(a)	(a)	(a)	9,809	65.3
Other Europe	14,726	20,498	23,916	27,211	16,456	13,294	–19.2
Japan	5,487	3,425	13,840	21,619	27,802	35,960	29.3
Other Asia	(b)	(b)	(b)	(b)	7,420	7,664	3.3
Pacific Islands	11,217	14,219	18,064	17,528	16,227	15,627	–3.7
Other countries	4,490	5,751	7,260	7,532	741	949	28.1
Total	189,866	208,155	250,565	278,996	259,350	278,534	7.4

Notes: (a) included under Other Europe
(b) included under other countries.

Sources: Bureau of Statistics, Fiji and TCSP.

funded by the United National Development Programme (UNDP) and the World Tourism Organisation (WTO) recommended, as a strategy of tourism recovery from the 1987 slump, some consideration of what is described by government of a Department of Tourism to coordinate tourism-related activities and provide a one-stop shop for potential tourism investors. In a comprehensive exercise, the report identified the full responsibilities of the department. Alongside this report and recommendation was the Fiji Government's own Contingency Marketing Plan for Recovery of Tourism Industry (Government of Fiji 1987) which was prepared in June 1987. Its focus was an aggressive advertising and promotion of Fiji in its traditional markets to counter what was felt as the negative coverage the country received after the military coup of May 1987.

With the exception of the 1987 Contingency Plan, neither the Belt–Collins nor the Cleverdon Report saw any action upon their recommendations. This notwithstanding, another plan was commissioned in 1989, the Fiji Islands Tourism Masterplan prepared by Coopers and Lybrand (1989). The recommendations of this plan were similar to the earlier Belt–Collins Report in that it emphasised the recharging of Fiji's tourism with more cultural input, environmental concerns and consideration for their relevant and appropriate inclusion of local people at all levels of the industry. The core of this report is 'to restore and build visitor confidence . . . to build on Fiji's distinctive advantage in natural, cultural and other resources . . . and to attract additional value-adding tourists to Fiji' (Coopers and Lybrand Associates 1989: 20). This was followed by yet another plan prepared in 1990 by the Native Land Trust Board (NLTB). This board is the custodian at large of all native land in Fiji and it acts as broker with potential investors on behalf of indigenous Fijians. Since most of the land for tourism development is within the category of native land the NLTB finds itself in the midst of tourism development policies, planning and investment in the country. The NLTB report also underlined the necessity of including culture and heritage in the tourism product, in response to what appears to be changing visitor interest. Once again the report reiterated the need for an increasing level if indigenous Fijian participation in all aspects of the tourism industry. In mid-1992 another report (Ayala 1992) presented by an American academic emphasised the same development issues, and by 1993 the Fijian government began to undertake steps towards a slight shift of Fiji's tourism away from the traditional sun, sand and surf towards what it described as eco-tourism (Ministry of Tourism 1994). To date clarity is still needed, so that the new approach provides a product whose consumption will reproduce the essential principles of ecologically sustainable tourism (Plange 1995), and maintain a healthy symbiosis with the environment as has been recommended by other research on environment and tourism in Fiji (King and Weaver 1993).

MARKETING AND PROMOTION

The Fiji Visitors Bureau leads the way in marketing and promotion of Fiji's international tourism product, despite a budget of under $F5 million. For this it has offices in Los Angeles, Auckland, Sydney and Tokyo, which remain as the agencies through which information on and about Fiji's attractions are provided to both individuals and travel agents as well as tour operators. In addition, the Bureau also organises trips for cultural groups and Fiji's famous police/military band to perform at some of these locations. World trade shows and fairs have also provided occasions for a concerted effort from industry representatives to put Fiji on show. All these have gathered favourable results.

Another level of promotion and marketing is undertaken by the four- and five-star hotel resorts through their own international linkage. Thus the Regent, Sheraton, Wakaya and the Shangri-La Groups provide relevant promotional and marketing information.

Since 1987 the European Union funded regional tourism organisation, the Tourism Council of the South Pacific, has also been instrumental in designing and implementing marketing strategies. Through its funding and presence at European trade and other fairs it puts the whole South Pacific region on show. Additionally, its 'Visit South Pacific Year', launched in 1993 was meant as an aggressive pro-active marketing/promotional strategy for the region.

FUTURE RESEARCH

The possibilities and potential for future tourism research are enormous. New directions in ecologically sustainable tourism chartered by government remain an open field for both economic and sociocultural impact research, especially on indigenous Fijian villages where the bulk of sustainable tourism resources will be derived. Additionally, small-scale management of tourism enterprises and their significance for village-based development consequent upon involvement in tourism will become relevant. Issues in sustainable tourism development remain vague so their final crystallisation and definition will profit from sustained research. One area of tourism development which remains under-studied is local attitudes, perceptions and acceptability of the industry and its pervasive interaction with society, culture and politics. Future research in this area cannot be overlooked, especially since the Fiji tourism product is always marketed as including friendly and enduring hospitable people. The extent to which tourism as an economic phenomenon has constructed a culture of its own will be an interesting and challenging area of research for students of anthropology and sociology interested in cultural studies.

PROSPECTS FOR THE 1990S

For the remainder of the decade, Fiji's tourism industry will grow. Elements of this growth are already in sight, as the statistics show. With a contribution now of 15 per cent of GDP, more than 35 per cent of total employment (through direct and indirect employment) and the government's obvious readiness to throw its weight behind the industry, growth can be assured. This is also underlined by current investor interest as shown in the ready-to-start Disneyland type of investment in Nadi, the interest shown by Koreans in purchasing a five-star hotel, and the national airline's remarkable growth and profits. The 1990s has heralded Fiji's tourism product as the nation's number one economic sector, ahead of sugar which is beginning to face its own crisis.

REFERENCES

Auger-Andrews, M. (1995) 'The human dimension of tourism: impact of resort work on Fijian mothers.' Unpublished MA Thesis, Suva: Department of Sociology, The University of the South Pacific.

Ayala, H. (1992) *A Masterplan for Fiji's Leadership in New Tourism with Strengthened Opportunities for Wellbeing*, Suva: Government of Fiji.

Belt Collins (1988) *A Tourism Development Maunal for Fiji*, Suva: United Nations Development Program.

Bolabola, C. (1980) 'The impact of tourism on Fijian woodcarving', in F. Rajotte (ed.) *Pacific Tourism: As Islanders See It*, Suva: Institute of Pacific Studies, pp. 93–6.

Britton, S.G. (1983) *Tourism and Underdevelopment in Fiji*, Development Studies Centre, Monograph No. 31, Canberra: Australian National University.

Bureau of Statistics (1994) *Republic of Fiji*, Suva: Bureau of Statistics.

Cheechi & Co. Ltd. (1961) *The Future of Tourism in the Pacific and Far East*, Washington, DC: US Department of Commerce.

Cleverdon, R. and Brook, M. (1988) *Secondary Tourism Activity Development in Fiji: Opportunities, Policies and Control*, Suva: United Nations Development Program.

Coopers and Lybrand Associates (1989) *Government of Fiji Tourism Master Plan*, Suva: Government of Fiji.

Fiji Trade and Investment Board (1993) *Opportunities for Growth*, Suva: Fiji Trade and Investment Board.

Francis, J. (1995) 'Rethinking Fiji's tourism: Ecotourism in Fiji.' Unpublished MA thesis, Suva: Department of Sociology, The University of the South Pacific.

Government of Fiji (1987) *Contingency Plan for Recovery of Tourism Industry*, Suva: Government of Fiji.

King, B. and Weaver, S. (1993) 'The impact of the environment on the Fiji tourism industry: A study of industry attitudes', *Journal of Sustainable Tourism*, 1(2): 97–111.

Le Fevre, T. (1983)˙ 'Making do with the leftovers from Pacific Tourism', in S. Tupoumiua, R. Crocombe and C. Slater (eds) *The Pacific Way: Social Issues in National Development*, Suva: South Pacific Social Science Association, pp. 215–21.

Ministry of Tourism (1994) *Master Plan for Eco-Tourism Development*, Suva: Ministry of Tourism.

Native Land Trust Board (1990) *Policy for Tourism Development on Native Land 1990–1995*, Suva: Native Land Trust Board.

Niukula, P. (1980) 'The impact of tourism of Suvavou Village', in F. Rajotte (ed.) *Pacific Tourism: As Islanders See It*, Suva: Institute of Pacific Studies, pp. 83–6.

Plange, N-K. (1985) *Tourism in Fiji: How People See it and What They Think of it*, Suva: Fiji Visitor Education Council.

—— (1988) *Tourism Awareness: A Manual for Tourism Education in the South Pacific*, Suva: Tourism Council of the South Pacific.

—— (1995) 'Sustainable tourism development: Views from the Pacific.' Paper prepared for the World Conference on Sustainable Tourism Development Conference, Lazarote, Canary Islands, Spain, May.

Rajotte. F. (ed.) (1980) *Pacific Tourism: As Islanders See It*, Suva: Institute of Pacific Studies.

Salto, R. and Ilaiu, M. (1980) 'Tamavua Village: For tourists only', in F. Rajotte (ed.) *Pacific Tourism: As Islanders See It*, Suva: Institute of Pacific Studies, pp. 89–92.

Samy, J. (1980) 'Crumbs from the table: the workers share in tourism', in F. Rajotte (ed.) *Pacific Tourism: As Islanders See It*, Suva: Institute of Pacific Studies, pp. 67–82.

Sutherland, W. (1992) *Beyond the Politics of Race: An Alternative History of Fiji*, Canberra: Australian National University.

Varley, R.C.G. (1978) *Tourism in Fiji: Economic and Social Problems*, Cardiff: University of Wales Press.

Vusoniwailala, L. (1980) 'Tourism and Fijian hospitality', in F. Rajotte (ed.) *Pacific Tourism: As Islanders See It*, Suva: Institute of Pacific Studies, pp. 101–6.

Chapter 14

The Cook Islands

Philip Buck and C. Michael Hall

INTRODUCTION

The Cook Islands are a group of fifteen islands and atolls that extend south from 10° south, 160° west to 22° south 161° west. Scattered over an area of 2 million square kilometres of ocean but with a land area of only 237 square kilometres, and situated almost midway between Tonga and Tahiti, the Cook Islands lie virtually at the centre of the Polynesian triangle of the South Pacific. The islands fall into the same time zone as Hawai'i and Rarotonga, the most populous island, is approximately the same distance south of the equator as Hawai'i is north. Tourist guidebooks often describe the Cook Islands as comparable to Hawai'i of the 1950s, before the onset of mass tourism. For example, Smith (1991: 9) wrote 'Paradise has been found, alive and well, hidden deep in the exotic South Pacific'. The Cook Islands Tourism Authority in one of its brochures state 'Welcome to the Cook Islands Holiday . . . to a necklace of islands in the sun and a way of life so relaxed that stress and worry vanish in the first hours of your spellbound stay in the South Pacific's most unspoiled paradise.' Undoubtedly, to many people the Cooks provide the image of what the Pacific is meant to be in terms of sun, sand and sea.

The islands vary dramatically in their geography. The northern group comprising of Penrhyn, Rakahanga, Pukapuka, Manihiki, Nassau and Suwarrow are true coral atolls with a lagoon and very little, if any, high ground. These northern islands have only minimal tourist facilities. The northern atolls are extremely exposed during severe cyclones. The southern group of islands take a variety and combination of forms – Palmerston is an atoll, Aitutaki is a combination of coral atoll and eroded volcanic peak. The other southern group islands are raised coral atolls. The result of this volcanic uplifting is a very harsh coastal fringe that once represented a living coral reef. In its exposed state, this jagged limestone is called the *makatea*. The central regions of these islands often contain lake and swamp areas and very fertile soils. The *makatea* is home for a variety of birdlife (some are extremely rare) and limestone caves that are increasingly being seen as a significant nature-based tourism attraction (Smith 1991). The main island is Rarotonga with over 50 per cent (9700) of the population of about 17,200, and is the centre of government and transport, including the international airport. Rarotonga has what is described as a high island appearance with central volcanic peaks rising to over 640 metres.

The first settlers to these islands were Polynesians who arrived almost 1500 years ago. European missionaries arrived first in Aitutaki in 1821 and in Rarotonga in 1823. The islands were declared part of the British dominions on 26 October 1888. New Zealand was permitted annexation on 11 June 1901, after discussion with the paramount chiefs, Makea and Ngamaru Ariki and others. The Cook Islands became a self-governing state on 4 August 1965, although the country still maintains a special relationship with New Zealand. The New Zealand dollar is the main unit of currency while more than 20,000 Cook Island Maoris live in New Zealand.

International tourism is currently confined to Rarotonga and the larger islands of the Southern Group, as they offer accessible transport options via domestic air and shipping services. However, the most significant element in Cook Island tourism is the development of international aviation linkages.

THE IMPORTANCE OF AVIATION LINKS

The Cook Islands have remained an isolated region once serviced only by sea, and this irregularly due to the small population and long-haul distances involved. As Hall (1994: 8) observed: 'Transportation – both sea and air – has possibly been, and still remains that largest [development] constraint of all . . . Less than viable cargo volumes and passenger numbers, relative to the numerically small population, has made transportation inherently very expensive.' As with many other Pacific Island nations, the Second World War changed the outlook and the destiny of the Cook Islands. Most significantly, their strategic position encouraged the construction of three major airstrips. In 1944–5 the New Zealand Government constructed a 5000-foot runway in Rarotonga. During the same period the United States Army Corps built strips on Aitutaki and Penryhn. A regular fortnightly service from New Zealand was commenced by the New Zealand Air Force in 1944. This service was taken over by New Zealand National Airlines Corp in 1947.

While the Rarotonga airstrip was a valuable communication and transport link to the rest of the Pacific, 'the operation of the strip . . . was devoid of any long-term purpose and without due regard for the developing needs of the country' (Hall 1994: 19). However, the reconstruction of the airport by the New Zealand Government for international jet aircraft paved the way for the development of the country's tourism industry. Although the agreement between the Cook Islands and the New Zealand Government over the airport was fraught with substantial difficulties, the civil aviation agreement between the two countries does reveal something of the country's dependence on New Zealand capital:

Article 1: The Government of New Zealand shall develop, maintain, manage and operate an International Airport at Rarotonga.

Article 9: The Government of New Zealand shall have sole control of air traffic rights into and out of the Cook Islands during the continuance of the Agreement but shall CONSULT the Government of the Cook Islands before granting any other Government the rights necessary for the conduct of air services to, from or through the Cook Islands.

Article 10: The Government of New Zealand shall ensure that the provision of such services shall be adequate to foster the growth of tourism and commercial activity together with the reasonable requirements of Cook Island residents.

Article 15: The Agreement to stay in force for a period of twenty-one years or until financial aid from the Government of New Zealand to the Government of the Cook Islands is restricted to loans or grants for specific capital purposes, whichever period is the longer.

(Agreement dated 14 February, 1969, in Hall 1994: 21)

The comments of the Premier of the Cook Islands, Hon. A.R. Henry, at the commencement of work ceremony on 11 June 1970, highlighted the reasons for New Zealand's enthusiasm for the new airport:

We are opening our doors to a dangerous future, and I don't think that tourism alone will enable this small country to live . . . but we know that New Zealand needs an international airport here because of her involvement in the international air race, and that the Cook Islands is the only territory in the Pacific which is in a position to let New Zealand build such an airport. This is why Rarotonga Airport has been accorded priority over other proposed airports in New Zealand.

(in Hall 1994: 28)

Although the airport officially opened in January 1974, substantial tourism development did not occur until the opening of the Rarotongan Tourist Hotel in May 1977 (Hall 1994; Burns and Cleverdon 1995). The dependence of the Cook Islands on foreign capital and expertise was indicated by the hotel being jointly owned by the New Zealand Tourist Hotel Corporation, the Cook Islands government and Air New Zealand. The importance of the expansion of accommodation facilities for aviation was also indicated by the September 1977 inauguration of the Air New Zealand DC10 Auckland–Rarotonga–Honolulu– Los Angeles service which provided for the arrival of ten DC10 services a week (Hall 1994).

Throughout the late 1970s and the early 1980s the Cook Islands' tourism fortunes were entwined with Air New Zealand's decisions regarding route services and aircraft purchases. For example, when in 1982 Air New Zealand announced the replacement of the once-weekly terminal DC10 flights between Auckland and Rarotonga by 737 services via Nadi and/or Tonga. 'There was some Cook Island concern over this eventuality. It meant not only a reduction in seat capacity, with obvious detrimental effects on the tourist industry, but would drastically cut freight space availability which would severely affect the country's two biggest and most promising export industries, namely, fresh produce and textiles' (Hall 1994: 63). A further example of the dependency of the Cook Island on Air New Zealand was the effects of a strike by airline staff over Christmas 1985 which left the Cook Islands isolated. However, as a result of the strike, the Cook Islands Government sought and obtained control of its airport and air rights. The 1986 Agreement on Civil Aviation still provided for a significant New Zealand role in country's aviation but it meant that 'The Cook Islands would have sole control of all international air traffic rights into and out of the Cook Islands', while 'the New Zealand Government would ensure the [Air New Zealand] service was adequate to foster tourism and commercial activity in the Cook Islands, and provide for the reasonable requirements of the Cook Island residents' (in Hall 1994: 67).

Since the 1986 aviation agreement Cook Island tourism has continued to grow and diversify. The significance of the development of aviation links for tourism in the Cook Islands cannot be over-emphasised. As with the other Pacific Island nations, tourism in the Cook Islands is dependent on the partnerships it can establish with the aviation sector. The following section highlights the growth of tourism in the Cook Islands and the changing tourism market.

THE CHANGING TOURISM MARKET

The opening of the international airport and the completion of the Rarotongan Resort Hotel were the two most significant milestones in the development of tourism in the Cook Islands (Okotai 1980). As Chris Wong, Director of Tourism, Cook Islands, commented:

> These developments heralded a conscious move by the Government of the day to use tourism as a viable alternative towards economic development . . . At the end of 1974, visitor arrivals stood at 6,477. This increased 59% to 10,962 by the end of 1975, which was when the airport facilities became fully operational. The next significant increase in arrivals was at the end of 1977, after the opening of the Rarotongan Resort Hotel, when visitor arrivals rose to 14,584, an increase of 58% of the previous year, also reflected the importance of the accommodation component of the industry.
>
> (in Hall 1994: 75)

Table 14.1 illustrates the growth in tourist arrivals in the period 1976–94. While the Cook Islands account for only approximately 2 per cent of total arrivals in the South and Central Pacific (excluding Hawai'i), the Cook Islands have experienced a rapid growth rate in arrivals over this period in excess of other competing Pacific destinations with declines in visitor arrivals only occurring in three years (Tourism Council of the South Pacific 1993). The substantial decline in 1981 and 1982 can be attributed to a reduction in air services and overall capacity during this period while the marginal decline in 1989 may also possibly be related to airline services and general economic conditions in tourism generating areas.

One of the most notable features of Cook Island tourism has been the increased diversification of the market (Table 14.2). Since 1984 New Zealand visitor arrivals to the Cook Islands have remained virtually static. By 1994, New Zealand market share had dropped to approximately 20 per cent of total visitor arrivals compared with almost 60 per cent a decade earlier. Almost every other market has experienced growth in the same period, with the most substantial growth occurring in the Australian, the United States, Canadian and European markets. In 1992 European and British arrivals exceeded those of New Zealand for the first time, with Europe now being the market leader at approximately 35 per cent of total visitor arrivals.

According to Wong (in Hall 1994: 76) and Milne (1995), a number of factors have worked in favour of the Cook Islands in terms of encouraging tourism growth:

Table 14.1: Cook Islands tourist arrivals

Year	'000 tourist arrivals	% change over previous year
1976	9.9	8.6
1977	14.6	47.3
1978	17.0	16.6
1979	19.7	16.0
1980	21.1	6.7
1981	18.6	−11.7
1982	17.5	−6.2
1983	19.8	13.4
1984	25.6	29.2
1985	28.8	12.5
1986	31.2	8.6
1987	32.1	2.8
1988	33.9	5.5
1989	32.9	−2.9
1990	34.2	4.0
1991	40.0	16.8
1992	50.0	25.0
1993	52.7	5.4
1994	57.3	8.4

Source: Cook Islands Tourist Activity, various.

Table 14.2: Visitor arrivals to the Cook Islands: total visitors by market, 1983–94

		1983	1984	1985	1986	1987	1988	1989	1990	1991	1992	1993	1994
New Zealand	Number	8,958	10,366	11,884	11,384	11,640	12,077	11,543	10,976	11,260	13,365	10,919	11,581
	% of Change	19.97	15.72	14.64	-4.21	2.25	3.75	-4.42	-4.91	2.59	18.69	-18.30	6.06
Europe/UK	Number	1,808	2,084	1,987	3,185	5,287	5,493	5,649	6,015	8,417	13,702	17,524	20,310
	% of Change	16.72	15.27	-4.65	60.29	66.00	3.90	2.84	6.48	39.93	62.79	27.89	15.90
USA	Number	1,898	3,069	3,030	3,298	2,890	3,330	3,304	4,376	4,411	5,969	7,790	7,744
	% of Change	40.8	62.75	-1.91	8.84	-12.37	15.22	-0.78	32.45	0.80	35.32	30.51	-0.59
Australia	Number	2,125	3,217	4,147	5,112	4,975	5,439	5,282	4,918	5,703	5,326	5,256	4,663
	% of Change	127.03	51.39	28.91	23.27	-2.68	9.33	-2.89	-6.89	15.96	-6.61	-1.31	-11.28
Canada	Number	2,480	3,091	3,092	2,907	2,292	1,975	1,684	2,386	3,914	3,747	4,026	3,963
	% of Change	122.02	24.64	0.03	-6.68	-21.16	-13.83	-14.73	41.69	64.04	-4.27	7.45	-1.66
Cook Islanders in New Zealand	Number	1,573	2,020	2,324	2,887	3,303	3,778	3,401	3,371	3,569	3,235	3,358	3,386
	% of Change	–	28.42	15.05	24.23	14.41	14.38	-9.98	-.088	5.87	-9.36	3.80	0.83
Cook Islanders in Australia	Number	–	–	–	–	–	–	282	310	370	365	550	473
	% of Change	–	–	–	–	–	–	–	9.93	19.35	-1.35	50.68	-14.00
Other Pacific Islanders	Number	344	888	1,501	1,489	937	1,027	985	1,023	1,072	2,281	1,433	1,277
	% of Change	-36.53	157.56	69.41	-0.80	-37.07	9.61	-4.09	3.86	4.79	112.78	-37.18	-10.89
Tahiti	Number	266	397	510	603	340	401	388	441	642	1,350	1,180	3,151
	% of Change	-41.92	49.25	28.46	18.24	-43.62	17.94	-3.24	13.66	45.58	110.28	-12.59	167.03
Asia	Number	205	191	208	223	325	280	327	291	510	496	652	474
	% of Change	-20.54	-6.83	8.90	7.21	45.74	-13.85	16.79	11.01	75.26	-2.75	31.45	-27.30
Other countries	Number	142	127	99	157	121	86	62	111	116	173	180	299
	% of Change	129.03	-10.56	-22.05	58.59	-22.93	-28.93	-27.91	79.03	4.50	49.14	4.05	66.11
Total	Number	19,799	26,488	28,782	31,245	32,110	33886	32,907	34,218	39,984	50,009	52,688	57,321
	% of Change	13.37	28.63	13.01	8.56	2.77	5.53	-2.89	3.98	16.85	25.07	5.36	8.42

Source: Cook Islands Tourist Authority.

- a firm recognition by government of the importance of the tourism industry to the economy;
- quality additions to the accommodation sector;
- new restaurants with consistent standards;
- a concerted marketing effort aimed at diversifying the market base of Cook Islands visitors;
- a favourable exchange rate for most currencies against the New Zealand dollar;
- the introduction of B747 and B767 services by Air New Zealand;
- the introduction of Hawaiian Airlines services to the Cook Islands;
- increased awareness of the Cook Islands in long-haul markets;
- a realignment of tourist traffic in the wake of the Fijian political coups.

Despite the strong pattern of growth of the early 1990s, a general decline in visitor arrivals began to be experienced in mid-1994 and appeared to be continuing well into 1995. This has been caused by a complex variety of reasons:

- Air Polynesia withdrawing from connections in Los Angeles;
- the damage to Air Polynesia's Aircraft during a stowaway incident resulting in a two-week delay in service (Air Polynesia was carrying approximately 10 per cent of arrivals at the time of the incident);
- the increasing value of the New Zealand dollar thereby increasing the costs to international visitors, particularly the European and North American markets;
- short-term financial uncertainty surrounding the Cook Islands;
- the relatively high cost of accommodation and airfares compared to other South Pacific destinations;
- the return of international tourists to Europe and the Middle East following the cessation of the Gulf conflict and a decrease in terrorism activity in Europe.

One further factor affecting visitor arrivals in the Cook Islands may be publicity surrounding French nuclear testing in the South Pacific (see Chapter 6). Indeed, the most noticeable fallout of the French testing may be that of a decline in visitor arrivals for years to come. Concerns over contamination make little sense given the vast distances in the South Pacific but their effect on tourist perceptions of a destination may be considerable. The Cook Island government and population are now strongly committed to environmental protection but, unfortunately, the greater the media attention surrounding the nuclear tests and associated protests the higher will be the level of international awareness of the Cook's relative proximity to the test site and French Polynesia (Cook Islands News 1995).

Many of the factors affecting tourist arrivals in the Cook Islands are beyond the immediate control of the Cook Island government. However, government does have the capacity to influence a number of factors with respect to tourism development and these issues will be examined in the next section.

TOURISM DEVELOPMENT ISSUES

Since the upgrading of the airport in 1974 tourism has dominated the non-aid revenues of the country. Tourism is the principal source of foreign exchange and employment (Milne 1987, 1992, 1995; Short 1992). Direct and indirect revenues are believed to bolster the national economy by over $NZ32 million dollars annually. This compares to approximately $NZ13 million in development assistance funding from New Zealand.

Tourism has been perceived as a major development mechanism for the Cook Islands since the early 1960s (Hall 1994). However, one of the ongoing issues facing tourism is the extent to which tourism development is compatible with the country's culture. Therefore, it should not be surprising that government plays an extremely active role in tourism planning and development. As the policy statement of the Democrat Party for the 1978 general election stated:

> The beauty of our Islands are a major asset to our people. The people of our Islands are a major asset to our country. Both assets and resources must be preserved and nurtured. Tourism has been introduced to our country; it is to work for us and not against us. It is a good friend but a generous enemy. Thus, emphasis should be on planned tourism. This will ensure that the disadvantage of tourism in the other countries do not arise in the Cook Islands. The Cook Islands government will pursue an overall tourism policy of *balanced and controlled development.*
>
> (1970 Democrat Party Manifesto in Okotai 1980: 49)

By 1989 the government's emphasis had shifted to more of an economic and market-orientated perspective. According to Geoffrey Henry, Prime Minister of the Cook Islands:

> My government's commitment to tourism development will be reflected in increases in expenditure within this sector over the coming years. We are also mindful of the increasing competitiveness of our regional neighbours, that my government will do everything possible to ensure that appropriate steps are taken to protect the overall profitability and viability of our industry.
>
> (quoted in Short 1992: np)

One of the chief mechanisms by which the Cook Islands government encourage tourism development is the Cook Islands Tourist Authority (CITA). Under the Tourist Authority Act 1968 which established CITA, the Authority was accorded a wide range of powers related to tourism development, promotion, planning and regulation. For example, the first mentioned function of CITA under the Act is 'to promote and encourage the tourist industry in the Cook Islands and to promote and increase tourist and other traffic from overseas and within the Cook Islands' (Cook Islands 1968: 4). However, the Act then went on to give the Authority powers to:

- 'license, regulate, and control hotels, accommodation premises, restaurants and tourist and public accommodation of all kinds';
- 'promote the establishment of hotels and all other forms of accommodation for tourist and public purpose';
- 'provide services and amenities for tourists';
- 'regulate and control the use and development of scenic attractions and recreational facilities in the Cook Islands'.

(Cook Islands 1968: 4)

In 1989 the Act was amended, and CITA restructured, to give the private sector a greater role in tourist development and promotion. Under the Tourist Authority Amendment Act 1989 membership of the Authority was adjusted to appoint members 'on the recommendation of the Cook Islands Chamber of Commerce' which 'in the opinion of the Minister represents the interests of owners and/or operators of hotels, accommodation premises, restaurants and tourist related services and facilities' (Cook Islands 1989a: 2). The functions of the Authority to issue licences was also abolished with a General Licensing Authority established to undertake such a role (Cook Islands 1989b). The increased corporate emphasis of CITA on promotion and marketing activities and the reduction of its regulatory role to an advisory capacity is a reflection of an increased commercial emphasis to tourism planning and development in the Cooks which, perhaps not coincidentally, reflects the changed priorities of national tourism organisations in New Zealand and elsewhere in the region (Hall and Jenkins 1995).

Several other government institutions also impact on tourism development in the Cook Islands. The Cook Island Monetary Board, established under a 1981 Act, has broad powers with respect to the control and regulation of money supply, monetary stability, banking, finance and the stabilisation, control and adjustment of goods and services, rents, interest rates and wages and salaries (Cook Islands 1981, 1986). More specifically with respect to tourism development the Board has the objective 'to promote and foster the establishment of sound business activities in the Cook Islands, to facilitate the channelling of investment into those business activities and to regulate foreign investment' (Cook Islands 1981: 4).

The broad framework for foreign investment in the Cook Islands for much of the past two decades has been set by the Cook Islands Development Investment Act 1977 (Cook Islands 1977a) and the Investment Code established under the provisions of the Act (Cook Islands 1977b). Tourism has been one area of 'desired investment' identified under the Code. One of the most noteworthy aspects of the Code is the extent to which it encouraged Cook Island involvement in economic development. The 'operative guidelines' of the Code state:

(1) There should be the maximum practicable use and expansion of facilities and services available from existing enterprises owned and controlled by Cook Islanders (namely Cook Islands Maori and permanent residents).

(2) The creation of desirable new enterprises owned or controlled by Cook Islanders should be encouraged as far as practicable.
(3) Small-scale enterprises owned and controlled by Cook Islanders should be encouraged as far as practicable.
(4) Foreign enterprises must make an important positive contribution to the development of the Cook Islands.
(5) Foreign enterprises that may endanger the Cook Islands' national integrity, political sovereignty or economic stability should be discouraged.
(6) Generally, provision should be made in the case of new foreign investment for the acquisition of equity by or on behalf of Cook Islanders, or for joint ventures with enterprises owned or controlled by Cook Islanders.
(7) In respect of (6) above, the traditional owners of a site or land used for or by the enterprises should participate effectively in such equity and control.

(Cook Islands 1977b: 1)

Although interpretation of some of the guidelines has changed over the past 20 years, it should be noted that the focus on indigenous development which the Code advocates has been an important concept in tourism development in the Cook Islands. At present foreign investors in the Cook Islands require a local partner who must control 10 per cent of the investment or 50 per cent in the case of new tourism ventures. The new 50 per cent policy is in place to maximise the benefits of tourism to the local population. However, its effect on foreign investment is yet to be measured.

Accommodation

There has been a substantial growth in the accommodation sector in recent years. Tourists can expect a large range of accommodation services which may all be described as being of mid-range or lower level quality. Table 14.3 illustrates the approved room stock for the Cook Islands. There are currently over 800 rooms available on the Cook islands and approval has been issued for up to 1412 rooms (this includes the former Sheraton site with over 200 rooms and two large developments on Aitutaki).

The 1991 Cook Islands Tourism Masterplan recommended that no further large-scale development be encouraged on Rarotonga and that the focus of development should shift to the outer islands and Aitutaki in particular (Rendell, Palmer and Tritton–Economic Studies Group (RPT–ESG) 1991; Hall 1994; Burns and Cleverdon 1995). However, the plan is now becoming dated and the growth rates experienced in the early 1990s substantially exceeded the visitor targets that had been set (RPT–ESG 1991). Projections of 69,900 visitors by the year 2000 would require development of substantial infrastructure to accommodate so many tourists (Hall 1994). Approval has been given for five-star properties on Rarotonga and Aitutaki but due to various financial delays these have failed to come onstream. The Cook Islands Sheraton Resort has still

Table 14.3: Approved room stock, 1990–95

Room type	1990	1991	1992	1993	1994	1995
Budget accom.	87	99	114	134	173	173
Self-catering	148	121	150	188	228	246
Luxury villas	0	0	0	0	23	27
Hotels	82	84	86	86	106	217
Resorts	368	367	384	364	399	399
Luxury resort	0	0	0	0	0	350
Total rooms	685	671	734	772	929	1412
Total properties	35	33	39	50	65	70

Note: Most of the newly licensed properties have not been commenced with the exception of the former Sheraton site and are unlikely to until at least mid-1996.

Source: General Licensing Authority, various.

to be fitted and, after three years of debate, the proposed Sheraton franchise has been withdrawn. Originally due to open in mid-1993, the promotion of the Sheraton Resort still continues (mid-1995) through some travel agents with people being booked and then later being transferred to a lesser quality property.

Accommodation occupancy averages in the 80 per cent range with the better properties such as Lagoon Lodges, Pacific Resort, Sokala Villas, Rarotongan Sunset and the Muri Beachcomber running consistently at over 90 per cent. The two largest properties, the Rarotongan Resort Hotel and the Edgewater, experience a large variance in occupancy and tend to bear the brunt of fluctuations in passenger arrivals. The higher quality hotels which operate at an average of over 90 per cent occupancy charge a high rack-rate as a means of controlling demand. Unfortunately, their price movements are often copied by other operators regardless of their individual occupancy or return on investment. This has, at times, promoted the image of an expensive destination with only the better operators delivering value for money. However, this situation will likely start to break down as more accommodation comes on stream and properties begin to establish their own markets with a broader price structure more relevant to the services offered and reasonable return on investment.

Customer service in the Cook Islands tends to be of a good quality and the opening of a Hospitality and Tourism Training centre with the support of the World Tourism Organisation (WTO) and the United Nations Development Program (UNDP) will no doubt strengthen the human resource dimension of tourism development. The Pacific Resort was recently voted the best resort in the South Pacific at the world's largest travel show. This resort is locally managed and is one of the few that are not managed by foreign interests. Foreign ownership in the accommodation sector is concentrated on larger properties. According to Short (1992: np), 'As a consequence, while one-quarter of all units are foreign owned, they together account for around 59% of all tourist rooms.' Short goes on to note:

While the government is applying restrictions on the areas in which non-Cook Islanders can own tourism-related businesses, it realises that the imbalances which at present exist can only be addressed over time through the more active participation of Cook Islanders in the provision of future accommodation and ancillary services. It realises also that the import requirements of the tourism sector are bound to remain considerable, but policies in respect of agriculture and import-substitution industrialisation are designed to contribute to a reduction over a period of time.

(Short 1992: np)

Transport infrastructure

As noted above, transport links are a critical element in Cook Island tourism development. Air New Zealand and Air Polynesia are the major carriers to the islands. New Zealand is the only market source which has a reasonable degree of flexibility in flight arrangements. One possibility for the further expansion of tourist numbers, particularly in the off-season, could be the development of charter flight services (Burns and Cleverdon 1995), an option which had to be utilised during the Air New Zealand strike in 1985 (Hall 1994).

Airline and inter-island trading vessels are currently enjoying the least competition for many years. Air Rarotonga is the only inter-island airline with short-haul high-yield destinations such as the resort island of Aitutaki compensating for the non-profitable legs to the Northern group. Though they have no competition, flight prices have not increased in many years.

No local cruise boats operate but international vessels of up to 800 persons sometimes call for day tours and day shore breaks. This form of tourism has seen considerable expansion in recent years although from a very low base. Transport services are stretched with a sudden influx of ship passengers, but the economic benefits to the community may be considerable. There are no port facilities for vessels of this size, so overnight or two-day stopovers seldom occur.

Tourism impacts

Although Milne (1987, 1992, 1995) has undertaken research on the economic dimensions of tourism in the Cook Islands, little systematic research has been undertaken of the social and environmental impacts of tourism in the islands. Short, a Cook Islander, has discussed various aspects of the social impacts of tourism on the islands. According to Short (1992) tourism-related prostitution has become increasingly evident over the last decade and expressed concern that 'Tourism advertising for Tahiti openly plays on sex and generally implies a certain promiscuity of the Tahitian female . . . There is a fear that the advertising done by the Tahitian Tourist Board may have reflected on the way that tourist[s] view all of the Pacific Islands' (1992: np). Similarly, Short also identified an increase in tourism-related crime.

The cultural impacts of tourism are regarded as being mixed. While tourism is encouraging heritage preservation, arts and crafts, and cultural display through the presentation of traditional foods and dance for tourists, concerns have been expressed about the authenticity of the cultural experience. For example, in order to provide tourists with different dances during their stay, dances have been featured from other Pacific Island nations. The Cook Island people take great pride in their traditional dancing. Dancing teams form a very important part of the local tourism experience with a performance every night of the week somewhere on Rarotonga. However, according to Short 'it is now difficult for tourist[s] to distinguish between some dances such as Tahitian and Cook Islands "hula" dance. The local people who have noticed this change have expressed their concern for this loss of individuality and uniqueness of each islands culture' (1992: np). Nevertheless, the development of the National Cultural and Arts Centre and a programme of cultural education in schools will undoubtedly help to reinforce Cook Islands cultural identity.

FUTURE PROSPECTS

The Cook Islands have some of the finest natural resources of any of the Pacific Islands. The people recognise the importance of their own language and culture, both of which play a paramount role in daily life as well as in the tourist industry. The Cook Islanders are well educated and have generally sought to encourage indigenous tourism development in a manner which seeks to maximise the benefits of tourism. Nevertheless, while the image of paradise is used to lure tourists, substantial problems exist in the long-term tourism development of the Cook Islands.

A current point of debate in the Cook Islands is the need to promote greater linkage between tourism and other economic sectors. Approximately 80 per cent of goods on sale in Rarotonga are imported, with many of these being imported to satisfy visitors or the recently acquired western tastes of Cook Islanders. This trend could be significantly altered by the further development of local products and foodstuffs. One proposal being discussed by locals is to establish a 'buy Cook Islands' style promotion campaign that would aim at identifying indigenous Cook Island business people and their ideas, and market Cook Islands produce. The proposed project would centre around promotion of logo and key phrases such as 'Produce of Paradise–Cook Islands' with the addition of individual island identification when necessary. Such a promotion might assist many small businesses that currently lack a marketing strategy or company image of their own. Those operations with a well-established marketing image would be encouraged to add a small version of the 'Produce of Paradise–Cook Islands' logo to their existing labels as an indication of their level of support for the programme.

At the local level such a programme would aid in identifying those products that are made or produced in the Cook Islands. This local branding is especially important in the tourism industry where visitors are often keen to purchase locally produced products and souvenirs. With significant numbers of Cook Islanders living in New Zealand and Australia, it is also anticipated that a significant level of purchasing support would be derived from promotional activities in these markets. A sense of national pride may then be carried internationally by those Cook Islanders who choose to live and work abroad.

While the government can undertake a number of measures to encourage appropriate tourism development the future destiny of the Cook Islands will largely be determined by external factors. In discussing tourism in the Cook Islands, Burns and Cleverdon (1995: 226) referred to the 'follies' of tourism development, 'because of the absence of reasoned government policies and practices related to tourism', including 'the Government's uncritical embracing [of] Air New Zealand's substantial contribution to tourist flows'. Such a statement perhaps not only reflects a case of Western experts notions of tourism planning (see Chapter 7) but also demonstrates a gross lack of knowledge of the history and context of tourism in the Cook Islands. As has been discussed above, the relationship between the Cook Islands and New Zealand, and Air New Zealand as a national carrier, has not been unproblematic and the statements of various Cook Island Prime Ministers have indicated that the Cook Islands Government are not unaware of the difficulties they face with respect to tourism development (Hall 1994). Furthermore, it would be foolish of European 'experts' to ignore the close economic, cultural and political ties that exist between the Cook Islands and New Zealand and which must undoubtedly provide much of the context for aviation and tourism development in the Cook Islands.

Burns and Cleverdon (1995: 227) described the Cook islands as

a 'destination on the edge', not only in terms of geographic location but, more importantly, on the edge of its physical and social capacity to carry more tourists. The reality for many microstates is that whatever the level or quality of planning, the tourism profile, growth patterns and systems are all fundamentally determined by the *realpolitik* of international carriers; the volume of passengers carried and their ability to reach the destination rests ultimately on the quality of the relationships between the microstate governments and the metropolitan carriers.

Unfortunately, Burns and Cleverdon's comments do not reflect some of the more recent advances in understanding tourism in either the Cook Islands or in Pacific microstates as a whole. Poon (1990), for example, has highlighted the capacity of microstates to adopt competitive market strategies. As Milne (1995: 17) observed, 'tourism development is not "unidirectional" and . . . local governments and communities can play an important role in defining a course for tourism development which meets broader economic, societal and economic objectives'. The Cook Islands are reliant on Air New Zealand as the major international carrier and there is a perceived need for additional international carriers, perhaps regionally based, with high seat availability in terms of further diversification of both markets and aviation links (Hall 1994). Nevertheless, both the Cook Islands and Air New Zealand appear to benefit from their relationship. The activities of the Cook Islands with respect to tourism development, as with other Pacific microstates, 'represents a rational response to the economic realities of the region . . . [They] are not forced to adopt tourism out of an overwhelming sense of economic desperation and appear to be well aware of the negative consequences of compromising broader development goals in the hope of attracting large scale foreign investment and mass tourism development' (Milne 1995: 18).

The Cook Islands have placed a great deal of emphasis on tourism as a mechanism for economic development and employment generation. Despite their close dependency on New Zealand in terms of aid, trade and aviation links, they have generally managed to follow a path of indigenous tourism development which has sought to maximise the benefits of tourism to Cook Islanders. Undoubtedly, the Cook Islands will have to make decisions with respect to the acceptable economic, sociocultural and environmental impacts of tourism. However, choices over which direction tourism will take in the Cook Islands will be a blend, as in any destination, of endogenous and exogenous decisions and forces. Up until the present, the Cook Islanders appear to be relatively pleased with the path they have chosen, and it is to be hoped that they will continue to be the ones who set their development goals and control the means to achieve them.

ACKNOWLEDGEMENTS

The authors would like to acknowledge the assistance of the many members of the Cook Island community who assisted the stay of Philip Buck during his period as a WTO/UNDP small business consultant. The contents of the chapter reflect the personal opinions of the authors and do not reflect the opinions of the Cook Island Tourist Authority, World Tourism Organization or the United Nations Development Programme.

REFERENCES

Burns, P. and Cleverdon, R. (1995) 'Destination on the edge? The case of the Cook Islands', in M.V. Conlin and T. Baum (eds) *Island Tourism: Management Principles and Practice*, Chichester: John Wiley, pp. 217–28.
Cook Islands (1968) *Tourist Authority Act 1968* (1968, No. 9), Rarotonga: Cook Islands Legislative Assembly.
—— (1977a) *Development Investment Act 1977* (1977, No. 21), Rarotonga: Cook Islands Legislative Assembly.
—— (1977b) *Investment Code*, Rarotonga: Cook Islands Legislative Assembly.
—— (1981) *Cook Islands Monetary Board Act 1981* (1981, No. 18), Rarotonga: Cook Islands Legislative Assembly.

—— (1986) *Cook Islands Monetary Board Amendment Act 1986* (1986, No. 10), Rarotonga: Cook Islands Legislative Assembly.

—— (1989a) *Tourist Authority Amendment Act 1989* (1989, No. 6), Rarotonga: Cook Islands Legislative Assembly.

—— (1989a) *General Licensing Authority Act 1989* (1989, No. 10), Rarotonga: Cook Islands Legislative Assembly.

Cook Islands News (1995) *Cook Islands News*, 22 July.

Cook Islands Tourism Authority (nd) *Visit Heaven While You're Still on Earth* (brochure), Rarotonga: Cook Islands Tourism Authority.

Hall, C. (1994) *Coming in on a Jet Plane: A Pictorial History of the Cook Islands International Airport Rarotonga 1944–1994*, Rarotonga: Airport Authority, Cook Islands and Colin Hall.

Hall, C.M. and Jenkins, J. (1995) *Tourism and Public Policy*, London: Routledge.

Milne, S. (1987) *The Economic Impact of Tourism for the Cook Islands*, Occasional Publication 21, Auckland: Department of Geography, University of Auckland.

—— (1992) 'Tourism and development in South Pacific microstates', *Annals of Tourism Research*, 19: 191–212.

—— (1995) 'Tourism, dependency and South Pacific microstates: Beyond the vicious cycle?', in D.G. Lockhart and D. Drakakis-Smith (eds) *Island Tourism*, London: Mansell: author's manuscript.

Okotai, T. (1980) 'Tourism in the Cook Islands', in F. Rajotte (ed.) *Pacific Tourism: As Islanders See It*, Suva: Institute of Pacific Studies, pp. 49–56.

Poon, A. (1990) 'Flexible specialization and small size: The case of Caribbean tourism', *World Development*, 18(1): 109–23.

Rendell Palmer and Tritton – Economic Studies Group (RPT–ESG) (1991) *Cook Islands Tourism Master Plan*, London: Rendell Palmer and Tritton – Economic Studies Group.

Short, S. (1992) 'What tourism is doing in the Cook Islands.' Unpublished graduate report, Department of Management Systems, Massey University, Palmerston North.

Smith, E. (1991) *Cook Islands Companion: The Visitor's Guide to Rarotonga and the Outer Islands*, Emeryville: Pacific Publishing.

Tourism Council of the South Pacific (1993) *Annual Report*, Suva: Tourism Council of the South Pacific.

Chapter 15

Vanuatu

Charles de Burlo

INTRODUCTION

Place

Vanuatu is a small island nation in the region of Melanesia of the southwest Pacific. It is a Y-shaped archipelago of 80 islands and islets between 12° and 21° S latitude and 166° and 171° E longitude (see Figure 15.1). There are twelve 'high' volcanic islands of large size where most of the indigenous (ni-Vanuatu) population resides. The capital of Port Vila is located on Efate in the central region of the group. Port Vila is the main commercial centre and port town. The tourist industry is enclaved in and around Port Vila.

Vanuatu achieved a hard-won political independence in July 1980. It was formerly the colonial Condominium of the New Hebrides, jointly administered since 1906 by France and Britain. However, this unique colonial territory was extremely poorly administered. With many administrative functions separately performed by each colonial power, there existed no unified planning and each government contested the other for the support of the indigenous (ni-Vanuatu) population. Even as late as 1957, when a great many less developed colonies were independent, local councils were only just being implemented in Vanuatu (Predmas and Steeves 1984).

Independence was achieved by the Vanua'aku Party under considerable tension from a population whose loyalties had been split, and a colonial administration which did not plan for political independence (Predmas and Steeves 1984). Vanuatu, consequently, inherited persistent economic, political and social problems. These problems include:

- an inefficient dualistic administrative structure;
- a weak system of local government;
- a dualistic educational system;
- an economy reliant on one primary export (copra); and
- a dependence on foreign aid and capital. (Douglas and Douglas 1989; Sturton and McGregor 1991; World Bank 1991).

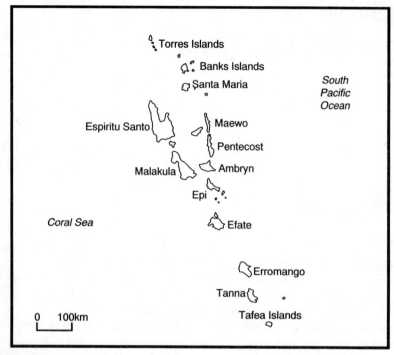

Figure 15.1: Vanuatu: location map

Tourism in Vanuatu, as in other island microstates, has appeared to be a sector of comparative advantage due to climate, distinctive cultures and geography, and clean beaches (Wilkinson 1989; Connell 1993). In the 1970s expatriate business interests in Vanuatu initiated tourism development, and it has remained largely in foreign control (de Burlo 1984; Milne 1990; Hall 1994). Nevertheless, tourism is of major significance to the national economy, and may be described as a 'tourism country' in that at least 15 per cent of foreign exchange is from tourism (Cater 1987). Tourism ranks first among all 'commodity exports' for Vanuatu (WTO 1994: 50). International tourism receipts for Vanuatu in 1991 were $US30 million (WTO 1993: 168).

As Wilkinson (1989) and Connell (1993) conclude, however, tourism and other service sector strategies (such as Vanuatu's tax haven and finance centre) offer limited ability to achieve economic development because of domination by external decision-makers, and capital creates a 'structural dependency' on foreign states (especially former colonial states). Current international tourism development in Vanuatu (as in other island microstates), is *not* development for the needs and values of local communities (Wilkinson 1989), or in terms of an environmentally sustainable and 'people-centred' social process (Korten 1990: 4).

People

The population of Vanuatu is 170,000, with a population density of 30 per square mile (Reedy 1994). Over 90 per cent of which are ni-Vanuatu (Douglas and Douglas 1989). Vanuatu has a wide linguistic and cultural diversity, with some 100 indigenous languages spoken. This cultural diversity is a main attraction to tourists, making it more than merely a tropical island destination for sun and sand (de Burlo 1984; Jayaraman and Andeng 1993). Ni-Vanuatu live primarily in rural areas of the archipelago.

The rural populace lives by subsistence and semi-subsistence agriculture. Under the Constitution, land is now under the tenure of indigenous 'custom owners', and all alienated lands have been given back to custom owners under leasing arrangements (Van Trease 1987; Douglas and Douglas 1989). People produce root crops such as taro, yams and manioc, as well as fruits and, in the peri-urban area, European-type vegetables. Copra and cocoa are produced primarily by smallholders, and copra is the main export (Sturton and McGregor 1991; World Bank 1991).

Economy

The economy of Vanuatu has been described as 'dualistic' because the majority of the populace practices traditional subsistence agriculture, while a 'modern sector' includes the government services, tourism industry, and the finance centre located in Port Vila. Rural ni-Vanuatu are engaged in a 'simple commodity' economy rooted in domestic production organised by households and kin groups, based on subsistence agriculture of root crops (such as taro and yams) (Rodman 1990). In so doing, ni-Vanuatu have retained a cultural resilience that has enabled local economic diversity (de Burlo 1984; Rodman 1990).

Vanuatu's economy is similar to those of other island microstates, in that it is limited in infrastructure, has a local resource base, is small in size and geographically peripheral (with high transport costs to distant markets), has extremely high expenditures on administration, dependence on external (metropolitan assistance), and unstable political systems (Wilkinson 1989; Connell 1993; Hall 1994). Other significant constraints to economic development for Vanuatu are:

- significant alienation of prime agricultural land by colonial expatriates requiring a long time to return to 'custom owners';
- human resources limitations in access to schooling, with adult literacy 'far below the regional average' (World Bank 1991: 279);
- vulnerability to cyclones causing economic, infrastructural, and social damages (World Bank 1991).

Vanuatu's GNP was $US130 million in 1988. The per capita GDP in 1989 was is $US415 for ni-Vanuatu population, placing it as 'one of the least developed island economies of the Pacific' (Sturton and McGregor 1991: 1). GDP growth has fallen from a high of 5.2 per cent in 1990 to 1.9 per cent in 1993 (Vanuatu 1993; Economic and Social Commission for Asia and the Pacific 1994). Services amount to some 70 per cent of GDP, and the retail/wholesale trade and tourism comprise one-third of GDP (World Bank 1991). Agriculture is another 25 per cent, and copra is the most significant commodity export (World Bank 1991).

Vanuatu has experienced a recurrent deficit in overseas trade with a corresponding negative balance of payments of 39.8 million vatu in 1988 (World Bank 1991). There was an overall decline in the standard of living during the 1980s due to declines in copra prices, damages from severe cyclones, contraction in budgetary support, political instability and low foreign investment, fluctuations in tourist arrivals, and a 2.9 per cent population growth rate (Sturton and McGregor 1991). Foreign aid has remained 'a dominant feature of the balance of payments and the economy', in which 95 per cent of all development spending is financed through external aid (World Bank 1993: 282).

The strength of the economy was shaky during the 1980s. Vanuatu's GDP went from a growth rate of 3 per cent in 1983 to 7 per cent in 1984, and a plunge to zero growth in 1985–7, with a recovery of 4.5 per cent during 1989 (Sturton and McGregor 1991). Both a rise in the price for copra and a recovery of the tourism sector at the end of the decade assisted a return of investment and foreign exchange earnings for the finance centre in Vila. Return from a zero to a 2 per cent growth in 1992–3 was attributable to cyclone damage to crops and infrastructure (World Bank 1991; UNCTAD 1994). Tourism suffered in the cyclone damages of 1987, 1989 and 1992, but the 1990 budget and the Government's emphasis on tourism development has helped economic recovery (Economist Intelligence Unit 1990; World Bank 1993; Hall 1994).

Air services has been a key aspect of this recovery in tourism and the economy. After losing a direct connection by UTA services to Noumea in 1987, Vanuatu lost a large Japanese market for tourism (Hall 1994). With the non-renewal of Ansett Airlines' contract to operate the national carrier, Air Vanuatu, led quickly to a loss of regular flights to Australia which had supplied 57 per cent of all tourist arrivals (*Pacific Islands Monthly* 1991). The 1989 purchase of a Boeing 727 from Australian Airlines, together with a new advertising and public relations effort brought recovery (*Pacific Islands Monthly* 1991; Hall 1994).

The most significant feature of these economic trends, however, is that the real standard of living dropped some 24 per cent for most ni-Vanuatu who live in rural areas and depend on agricultural production (such as copra) for their income needs. Vanuatu is, by several indicators, such as health, infant mortality, value of exports, access to safe water, a 'least developed' nation (UNCTAD 1993/94). Infant mortality in Vanuatu is 68 per 1000 live births, compared to 28 per 1000 for the neighbouring Solomon Islands (UNCTAD 1993/94). Only 64 per cent of the rural population has access to safe water and 33 per cent adequate sanitation (UNCTAD 1993/94:A-77). Malaria debilitates 47 per cent of the populace, and 40 per cent of children two years old and under suffer from malnutrition. Adult literacy is a low 30 per cent (World Bank 1991).

Although the government has stated its desire to have more local participation in tourism, ni-Vanuatu do not directly benefit from tourism as a positive force for rural development. Foreign ownership, urban enclave resorts, and high economic leakage hinder its ability to positively affect the lives of the people. As Hiller (1977) noted, the tourist industry 'rejects the integrity of the local area', and tourists and islanders relate only through a 'limited range of commercial contacts'. The main resort hotels and restaurants in Port Vila are entirely expatriate or foreign owned and operated (Jayaraman and Andeng 1993). Ni-Vanuatu only participate as employees, or through tour transportation, and the informal sector of handicraft selling and small guest house operations (de Burlo 1984, 1989, 1995) (Plates 15.1 and 15.2).

REVIEW OF RESEARCH

Research on tourism in Vanuatu has grown significantly in recent years. Academic and non-academic research on tourism in Vanuatu has been mainly orientated to economic development issues or marketing. In addition, both UNDP and PATA have published planning documents on Vanuatu's tourism sector. However, few studies have directly addressed social and environmental issues.

Plate 15.1:   Markets at Port Vila provide an opportunity for tourists to purchase local produce (Michael Hall)

Plate 15.2:   The interplay of local and foreign commercial interests is seen in the availability of secondary tourist activities in Port Vila (Michael Hall)

Planning-based research

An early planning document for tourism was completed during the colonial regime. In 1972, SCET-COOP/International conducted research on developing tourism in Vanuatu (then the New Hebrides) for the Condominium government (SCET 1973). This research covered both the supply and demand sides of tourism in Vanuatu, including the cruise ship sector. The study calculated that tourism would diversify the economy, and add employment and public revenue benefits. What was needed was infrastructure development around the port towns of Vila and Santo. The study primarily proposed the development of a series of 'village hotels' on the islands of Efate and Santo of a Club Med style to accelerate tourism in Vanuatu (SCET 1973). It is significant that the SCET study included Eugene Peacock, the American real estate developer who attempted to buy up land on Santo for an a real estate scheme that the British government abruptly stopped because it was both fomenting political strife on the eve of independence and alienating ni-Vanuatu lands (de Burlo 1984). The SCET study, moreover, argued that it is necessary to change local attitudes if tourism development was to be successful.

Just prior to independence, a UN Development Advisory Team studied the prospects for international tourism development in Vanuatu (Bergerot 1979). The report was guided by the goal of suggesting how a tourism development plan should be made to fit within the overall national development plan to come after independence. Two key propositions were made by the study. First, that community-based tourist guest houses be encouraged for the explorer tourism market. This strategy was conceived to generate revenue for rural ni-Vanuatu communities for general development purposes (e.g. health, education). Second, a 'Cultural Recreation Centre' be established in Vila to fill the need of both entertainment and educating tourists about ni-Vanuatu cultures (Bergerot 1979).

The 1979 UNDAT study is remarkable in its focus on culture and environment. The study makes it clear that, for Vanuatu, local economies and lifeways are bound to local environments, and that tourism development depends on maintaining this quality of life. To achieve a market niche and genuine local development with tourism, a 'qualitative image' of Vanuatu must be planned for by the Government. This research on tourism underscores the critical importance of both cultural and environmental integrity for development.

PATA (1985) conducted a post-independence advisory mission study of tourism for the Government of Vanuatu. This advisory team report focused on the creation of a National Tourism Office and its funding, and the linking of the Chamber of Commerce as a statutory body to the National Tourism Office. Improvements to the airport runway and facilities, and the regularising of air links to New Zealand were also recommended. These recommendations were acted upon by the Government. The National Tourism Office was enacted in 1982, and a national tour operator – Tour Vanuatu – came into being the following year. The PATA and UNDAT studies both had a direct effect on restructuring tourism, and influenced the new Government of Vanuatu's role in tourism and planning.

Economic research

Milne (1990) indicated that the economic multipliers for Vanuatu are low compared to other Pacific Island nations, and that economic leakage in Vanuatu's tourism industry is significant due to weak linkage with the economy. Milne concluded that ni-Vanuatu enterprises in tourism will have high direct impacts for employment and income in the local economy, and should be supported in strategic planning for tourism.

The PIDP economic report, *Vanuatu: Toward Economic Growth* by Sturton and McGregor (1991), demonstrated the importance of international tourism for the economy of Vanuatu. Tourism was recognised as being at the core of Vanuatu's economic development plagued, as it is, by a recurrent negative trade balance, and loss of development budgetary aid. With substantial instability in copra export earnings, tourism growth has supported the national economy since 1989 (Sturton and McGregor 1991). Tourism is the leading economic sector (16 per cent of GDP), earning 4500 million vatu in 1990. However, development for Vanuatu remains dependent on its agricultural sector from which the large majority of the population make their living.

The tourism economy of Vanuatu was also examined by Jayaraman and Andeng (1993). The study analysed variables of tourist demand, supply of rooms, tourism revenues as part of gross domestic product and trends in annual growth rates relative to investment, promotions, and tourist expenditures. The report concluded that the significant variables having a negative effect on international tourism in Vanuatu were cyclones and perceived political unrest. Improved air access to Vanuatu, improved infrastructure, and promotional spending were all regarded as having a positive impact on tourism in Vanuatu (Jayaraman and Andeng 1993). However, the economic modelling of tourism does not, by itself, give empirical information on how ni-Vanuatu groups and individuals are involved in tourism, nor its consequences for the lives of urban and rural ni-Vanuatu.

Cultural research

Tourism planning advisers and the government of Vanuatu have all expressed the views that indigenous culture is at the heart of the role of tourism in development. Tourism is seen as the sector in which ni-Vanuatu should have a larger share of local participation, and a knowledge of the potential adverse effects of tourism on indigenous society.

The real position that tourism takes in the lives of ni-Vanuatu, and its meaning for local communities, however, has only been directly researched (to date) by de Burlo (1984, 1995). This field research on tourism and ni-Vanuatu groups indicated that tourism does often have a positive benefit for local groups *if* it is managed by ni-Vanuatu within the *context* of local social organisation and the limited commodity economies of most communities. De Burlo (1989) also demonstrated that the alienation of land for tourist developments by expatriates remains a major issue for ni-Vanuatu which denies the traditional and constitutional resource tenure rights of ni-Vanuatu. As Baines (1987) observed, both private and government tourist developers have 'manipulated' landowning groups and denied them the opportunity to make informed decisions on proposed tourist projects.

De Burlo (1984, 1991) revealed many of the problems associated with tourism for ni-Vanuatu communities. It has often been a socially divisive force; especially over rights to 'tradition' in the case of ethnic tourism, or over resources (such as land). For urban communities near Vila, tourism provides employment, but also has social costs in childcare, lack of access to skilled work, and a tightening dependence on cash income with associated loss of marine and land resources to resorts (Philibert 1981).

Tourism plays a vital role in the Vanuatu economy. However, it is not without economic and cultural costs. The participation of ni-Vanuatu in tourism remains a crucial area to be addressed in planning and policy on tourism. In particular, very little attention has been paid to the environmental contexts and effects of tourism.

TOURISM MARKETS AND DEVELOPMENT

Tourism is the 'most important generator of foreign exchange earnings on the service account' and amounted to one quarter of the total 1990 receipts (Sturton and McGregor 1991: 31). Tourism contributed 14.3 per cent of GDP in 1981, and (after a 1985–7 downturn) increased to 25.1 per cent of GDP by 1990 (Jayaraman and Andeng 1993). With the strong growth in tourism since 1988, however, imports have also risen sharply as a reflection of tourist demand. As exports remain low, and copra prices fall, the terms of trade may also deteriorate. Therefore, tourism and external aid are crucial to Vanuatu for stabilising these deteriorating economic trends (Sturton and McGregor 1991; World Bank 1991).

International visitors

Tourism in Vanuatu depends on international visitor arrivals. Tourists on both package tours and travelling independently come mainly from Australia, New Zealand, New Caledonia, and Japan. It is in competition with other regional destinations, such as Fiji and Bali. There is a substantial volume of cruise ship passengers who stop for a day, but this 'excursionist' type of visitation does not have as much economic or social impact because of their short stay and limited spending (Milne 1990; Jayaraman and Andeng 1993).

The dramatic declines (and upswings) in visitor arrival figures, such as the 18 to 35 per cent in air arrivals and 27 to 30 per cent drops in cruise ship arrivals during 1985–7, depict the serious instability in tourism to Vanuatu (Table 15.1). The sharp downturns in arrivals recorded in 1985–7 were a direct result of both severe cyclone damage to tourist hotels and infrastructure, uncertainties in the political Vanuatu's political scene, and disruptions in air service (Strurton and McGregor 1991; Jayaraman and Andeng 1993). For example, in 1988 all the hotels in Port Vila were undergoing extensive renovations following the cyclones of the year before, and small ni-Vanuatu owned/operated bungalows were especially severely damaged.

Vanuatu depends heavily on mass tourism and its operators who direct the flow of tourists to the islands and its resort hotels (de Burlo 1984). Australia, New Zealand, New Caledonia, and Japan are the main markets for Vanuatu. Some 52 per cent of all tourists to Vanuatu are independent travellers, but 48 per cent are package tourists (Jayaraman and Andeng 1993). Of tourists on package tours in the late 1980s, 74 per cent were from Australia, which contributed some 72 per cent of all tourists (Vanuatu 1987).

Many visitors from Asia and other Pacific island countries are in Vanuatu on business; for example, 81 per cent from Asia and 75 per cent of those from Fiji are on business. In contrast, 21 per cent of European tourists are visiting friends and relatives (Jayaraman and Andeng 1993).

Investment in tourism promotion and infrastructure has driven the recent strong growth in tourism (Sturton and McGregor 1991; Jayaraman and Andeng

Table 15.1: Visitor arrivals to Vanuatu, 1982–94

Year	Visitor arrivals ('000)	Year	Visitor arrivals ('000)
1980	22.0	1988	17.5
1981	22.1	1989	23.9
1982	32.2	1990	35.0
1983	32.4	1991	39.8
1984	31.6	1992	42.6
1985	24.5	1993	44.4
1986	17.5	1994	42.1
1987	14.6		

Sources: Hall 1994; Page 1996.

1993). Both the second and third five-year development plans have targeted tourism as a major sector for investment.

The Second National Development Plan targeted the following tourism development goals:

• maximise the economic benefits of tourism through increased local participation in the tourism industry and reduced leakages of tourist expenditure from the country;
• encourage the future expansion of tourism facilities in the preferred locations of Efate, Espiritu Santo and Tanna;
• develop Vanuatu and promote its image as a high class tourist destination, attracting visitors from the upper income groups from widespread tourist originating countries;
• plan and implement projects with explicit attention to the conservation of fragile or vulnerable aspects of the country's environmental and cultural heritage.

(Hall 1994: 178)

The goals of increased local participation in the tourism industry and conservation of ecological and cultural heritage will be significant challenges. The development of Vanuatu as a high-class, upper income end, destination, for example, may be counter in the participation of ni-Vanuatu in the industry because, except for the urban elite, they have neither the financial resources nor inclination to invest in being full-time tourist business owner-operators (de Burlo 1984; Milne 1990).

Regular Air Vanuatu services from Australia and New Zealand have also supported tourism growth since the government and Australian foreign aid money (of 1,500 million vatu) funded the purchase of a Boeing 727 aircraft by Air Vanuatu. Nevertheless, tourism in Vanuatu remains 'sensitive to the perception of domestic political developments, flight availability, and the state of the Australian economy' (Sturton and McGregor 1991: 8).

Tourism development

There is currently a variety of tourist developments in Vanuatu, with new foreign and Government investment in infrastructure and resorts (Jayarman and Andeng 1993). In recovering from severe tropical hurricanes in 1986–7, and political unrest in 1988, the government invested in an upgrading of the runway and air terminal at Port Vila, while the national carrier settled a dispute with Ansett Airlines. Hotel occupancy rates rose 52 per cent in 1989 (Economist Intelligence Unit 1990: 50), and room-night capacity rose from 41 per cent in 1988 to 60 per cent in 1990 (Jayarman and Andeng 1993).

Although there is a variety of types of accommodation, most tourists stay in Port Vila where the resorts are located (Hall 1994). Accommodation developments in Vanuatu run a spectrum from a few capital intensive, large-scale, international class resorts to many small guest houses built and operated by ni-Vanuatu (de Burlo 1984, 1989). By 1988 there were 464 rooms available in Vanuatu, and 521 by 1990, with occupancy at 59.6 per cent (Jayaraman and Andeng 1993).

In 1987 Japanese private corporation and government investments increased the room capacity at Iririki Island Resort in Port Vila (MacDermott 1995). In 1990–91, the Radisson Royal Palms Resort was upgraded and a casino built. By 1993, total hotel capacity in Vanuatu stood at 666 rooms; 83 per cent were located in Port Vila environs (Jayaraman and Andeng 1993). The Radisson Royal Palms Resort is owned by HPL Pty Ltd of Singapore, and the Le Lagon Resort by the Tokyu Hotel Chain Company of Tokyo, Japan (MacDermott 1995). These foreign owned resorts dominate the tourism sector.

Small-scale guest houses and bungalows owned and operated by ni-Vanuatu sprang up in both urban and rural areas (de Burlo 1984, 1989, 1995). They form an informal sector of the foreign-dominated tourism system in Vanuatu (cf. Crick 1994). Tourism planning advice (Bergerot 1979) and economic analysis (Milne 1990) both have supported the idea that the government of Vanuatu give special attention to indigenous ventures for their ability to increase local participation in development, provide income retained within the local economy, and support linkages with the agricultural sector (Milne 1990). However, at present, Vanuatu is becoming further committed to large-scale resort tourism. As Hall (1994: 182) stated, although a few accommodations are ni-Vanuatu owned and managed, 'the majority are overseas owned and managed'.

Marketing and promotion

Direct investment in tourism promotion has also assisted the renewed growth in Vanuatu's international tourism. This has been largely possible due to the restructuring of tourism following independence. The creation of the national tour operations in 1985 – Tour Vanuatu and the National Tourism Office (under the Ministry of Finance, Commerce, Industry and Tourism) – have enabled the

Vanuatu government to promote inbound tourism (Sofield 1991; Jayaraman and Andeng 1993). The Vanuatu Hotels and Resorts Association (also created in 1985) acts as liaison with the NTO in Vanuatu's tourism promotion and marketing. The National Tourism Office (NTO) promotes tourism directly in its marketing and development, and receives foreign assistance funds for promotions in Europe at trade shows (PATA 1985; Jayaraman and Andeng 1993). For example, in 1990 the government of Australia provided funding to market Vanuatu in Australia (*Pacific Island Monthly* 1991). Tourism promotions by the NTO were 46.42 million vatu (VT) in 1988, and VT41.52 million in 1990, or between 0.31 and 0.23 per cent of gross domestic product (Jayarman and Andeng 1993).

Vanuatu stands in competition with regional destinations such as Fiji and Bali. It has attempted to promote its physical and recreation attractions of sun, sea and diving to the package tourist market. The former colonial heritage of French and British society in the urban areas has also been marketed. However, the indigenous cultural landscape has always been a key to tourism promotion to position Vanuatu in the region (Bergerot 1979; PATA 1985; Hall 1994). From the early colonial era to the present, ni-Vanuatu cultures and 'custom' have acted as an attraction for travellers and tourists. Just as for adventurers, such as Martin and Osa Johnson (1944) or Kal Muller (1970), images of 'primitive' people and 'cannibals' continue to draw travel writers such as, David Attenborough (1976), Paul Theroux (1992), or Michael Krieger (1994) to Vanuatu. These are the image makers who bring many other tourists in their wake. The government has also taken a direct role in marketing ethnicity. In some instances, the state has manipulated 'statements' and images about 'custom' and national identity (Wood 1984). This is dangerous ground. It reduces the diversity of ni-Vanuatu cultures in the archipelago into a few stereotypes palatable to tourists. Some groups, such as those with 'tradition' (*kastom*) moreover, bear both the advantage of touristic attention and the burden of its impacts (de Burlo 1984; Wood 1984).

Marketing indigenous cultures is advantageous in terms of positioning, but it is a very serious cultural issue for tourism. The government has been cautious towards developing mass tourism because of its potential negative effects for ni-Vanuatu communities and their cultures. However, this policy may change with the new government led by the Union of Moderate Parties. Tourism has been a divisive force in those communities in Vanuatu in closest contact with tourists (such as on Tanna, Pentecost and Efate) (de Burlo 1984). For example, the renowned 'Land Dive' ritual of South Pentecost, which has became a tourist spectacle in the 1980s, has been discontinued for tourist viewing by the government because of the commercialisation of this unique part of local culture.

One of the main problems for Vanuatu has been making itself known to international markets in Australia, Japan, Europe, and North America (Bergerot 1979; PATA 1985). Nevertheless, the prospects for the 1990s remain positive.

Japan is investing in the region in both foreign aid for tourism development, such as infrastructure, and in corporate investment. Vanuatu has also marketed itself in Japan in an effort to diversify away from market dependence on Australia. Its linkage to its traditional markets can still be observed, however, in the establishment in 1990 of National Tourism Office branch offices in Sydney, Auckland, and San Francisco, and the hosting of its first tourism convention (Economist Intelligence Unit 1990).

TOURISM DEVELOPMENT: ISSUES AND IMPACTS

Tourism in Vanuatu presents both immediate and long-term issues for development. Each will be addressed in turn. Tourism in Vanuatu has serious cultural and environmental impacts which both the industry and Government must ameliorate or solve.

Economic impacts and issues

Tourism is having a direct and positive benefit on the national economy. In 1984 gross tourism revenue was estimated at $US20 million, with a total of $US213,000 in government revenue (PATA 1985). By 1989, following the 1986–7 declines in tourist arrivals, tourism revenue had risen to VT2659 million ($US265,900) (Milne 1990; Jayaraman and Andeng 1993). It was the highest earner of foreign exchange for Vanuatu in 1990 accounting for 25 per cent of the service account (Sturton and McGregor 1991). As tourism grew in the 1988–90 period, so did Vanuatu's GDP; with tourism at 25 per cent of GDP by 1990 (Jayaraman and Andeng 1993).

Milne's (1990) study calculated a range of (1987) visitor spending earnings from VT520 million in the accommodation sector, VT190 million for restaurants, to VT61 million in tours and VT35 million in taxi rentals, down to VT10 million for handicraft sale. Accommodation contributed VT293 million, and VT603 in 'standardised' employment; while the taxi sector generated an income of VT19.6 million with VT19.6 'standardised' and VT24.9 'unstandardised' jobs (Milne 1990). The major sectors of visitor expenditure revenue are accommodation, duty-free shopping, and clothing. The disparities are significant between sectors. Duty-free goods and souvenirs, clothing, internal air transport, and large hotels all show the highest percentages of spending for imports on the first round. It is these sectors that have 'the weakest linkages within the local economy' and achieve the lowest levels of employment and income creation in Vanuatu (Milne 1990: 20). Accommodation and restaurants are dominated by foreign ownership. Taxis and handicrafts are the formal and informal domains of locals. In these sectors, however, the multiplier effects are most strong, even if the totals on earnings and employment are low (Milne 1990).

For handicrafts, tours, and taxi services use of local labour is great, and leakage of visitor spending is much less than for shopping and large hotels which depend heavily on imports and repatriation of revenue. Handicrafts, moreover, generates a very high amount of informal job creation (Milne 1990).

A critical problem in tourism for Vanuatu is the high level of economic leakage. PATA (1985) estimated this at 60 per cent of gross revenue. Milne's (1990) analysis indicated about a 50 per cent leakage. Hall (1994) reported an approximate 55 per cent leakage in payment for imports. The large foreign firms that dominate the tourist industry in Vanuatu rely on foreign imports and send profits overseas. In addition, these businesses are managed by expatriate labour who command high salaries, some of which is also repatriated (Sturton and McGregor 1990).

Vanuatu's Second National Development Plan (1987–91) expressly stated the goal of maximising economic benefits from tourism by reducing leakage through an increase in local participation in the industry (EIU 1990; Hall 1994). The problem remains, however, that ni-Vanuatu are not sufficiently supported in tourist business entrepreneurship (e.g. in operating guest-houses or bungalows).

Ethnographic research on tourism in Vanuatu by the author (de Burlo 1984) supports Milne's (1990) analysis. In peri-urban villages of Port Vila, handicraft production and selling is practised in a part-time manner by most households as a means to supplement household income. Only, a few women, including residents from other Pacific Islands, specialise in clothing and craft production for the tourist market. Producing and selling crafts for tourists allows households to earn cash income *and* continue to practice home gardening. For example, for villagers of Ifira Island, whose garden land is scarce, taken up by Vila urban seafront and Iririki Island (now with a resort on it) (Van Trease 1987), tourist trade in handicrafts has become an important source of cash.

The handicraft sector is the domain of women, and tourism propelled them into making the market a regular aspect of the household economy. This gender dimension is absent in most discussions of the impact of tourism in Vanuatu. Earnings are meagre, and amount to what women term 'pocket money'. This pocket money is, however, saved by women, and has funded special social obligations, and even their own travel outside Vanuatu. However, there remain social and environmental costs for households and communities in tourist work.

Environmental impacts

The 1985 PATA report on tourism advised that environmental impact research be undertaken for all proposed tourist developments. Pacific island ecology is especially vulnerable to tourism in its demands on land, foreshore, fresh water supply, lagoons and mangroves, and capacity for waste disposal (Baines 1977). Ecological integrity has not usually been discussed in regard to tourism development in Vanuatu except in terms of site selection for resorts (PATA 1985). The PATA report merely recommends that environmental impact assessment be conducted for developments, but does not specify damages already extant in Vanuatu or what kinds of ecological indicators are most important.

Baines (1977, 1987) reports that in the Solomon Islands, Vanuatu, and Fiji, the development of coastal areas has meant that traditional rights to land and marine resources have been usurped by 'ad hoc decisions' in favour of tourism developers who see these countries as an environmentally 'soft option'. In Vanuatu, ni-Vanuatu have violently contested tourist access to beaches and reefs, demanding 'rent' and using force in the absence of regular legal processes to secure their rights to resources (Baines 1987). Ni-Vanuatu have also employed regular legal channels to reclaim their lands before and since independence (Van Trease 1987). Working out a system of resource tenure based on the Constitution's declaration that all lands belong to traditional owners is a priority for Vanuatu.

Much land has already been alienated in Vanuatu for tourist development (de Burlo 1989; Van Trease 1987). Environmental impacts and control remains a critical area for tourism research. Ni-Vanuatu of peri-urban villages around Vila comment on the loss of marine resources, such as fish and molluscs, as well as a loss of beach access. An important part of this problem is that ni-Vanuatu perceive and value the environment in ways much different than Western ideology, and even within Vanuatu there is great variation in cultural construction of the environment.

Vanuatu, fortunately, has begun to establish an institutional framework for environmental conservation. In 1984 it established an Environment Unit within the Ministry of Lands, Energy, and Rural Water Supply, in order to respond to the environmental issues raised by development of tourism and other industries (Chambers *et al.* 1989). Vanuatu has also begun the development of a National Conservation Strategy (NCS) through the assistance of the South Pacific Regional Environment Programme. The NCS is designed to assist in achieving national 'sustainable development, conservation of national heritage and self-reliance' (Chambers *et al.* 1989: 26). The long-term goal is to establish a strategy that will meet the national planning goals of sustainable economic growth and conservation of environmental and cultural heritage. The National Tourism Office is responsible for reporting on environmental problems relating to tourism, such as 'pollutants, subsistence versus commercial resources, conservation of species and critical habitats' (Chambers *et al.* 1989: 27).

Social and cultural issues

Tourism has created many sociocultural problems in Vanuatu in both its resource use and its reliance on ethnic tourism in rural areas. Both resource use and ethnic tourism impinge directly on the lives of ni-Vanuatu, and carry cultural and political weight for tourism's use of 'tradition' (de Burlo 1984, 1989; Jolly 1994).

Land carries great cultural value for ni-Vanuatu, beyond its productive capacity. It symbolises personal and group identity, and encapsulates the idea of 'tradition' (*kastom*) in contemporary Vanuatu (Van Trease 1987; de Burlo 1989). The use of land for tourist industry developments has created many social and political conflicts in Vanuatu since resorts were established.

In the colonial era, developers succeeded in building resorts, such as the Intercontinental (now Radisson) when ni-Vanuatu rights to land were suppressed (Baines 1987; Van Trease 1987; de Burlo 1989). The 1980 Land Reform Regulation secured ni-Vanuatu traditional tenure rights. The value of land as a source of identity is a strong element in ni-Vanuatu cultures which has resisted intrusions of outsider directed change, such as tourism. It is *not* to be considered something to be changed; cultural integrity has secured ni-Vanuatu lifestyles and values in the face of foreign intrusions, leaving open the potential of sustainable development.

On Tanna, for example, people have contested outside control of tourism and prevented foreign domination of tours and access to natural attractions (de Burlo 1984; Bonnemaison 1994). The main reasons for this success has not been economic incentive. Tannese, like other rural ni-Vanuatu, are not primarily interested in tourism for its economic benefits – political and social considerations take precedence. It is here that the impacts of ethnic tourism are most strongly felt.

Ni-Vanuatu culture is a primary attraction in Vanuatu's tourism industry, especially in tours to rural areas such as Tanna or South Pentecost (de Burlo 1984; Sofield 1991; Lindstrom 1993; Jolly 1994). For many communities, such as *kastom* villages on Tanna and South Pentecost ethnic tourism has rendered culture a commodity. Tourists indulge in 'cozy stereotypes' of the 'primitive' (Lindstrom 1993). Tourism's imposed change has singled out specific 'markers' of 'tradition', such as 'Land Diving', 'cargo cult' or penis-wrapper wearing *kastom* people for sale to outsiders (Farrell 1979; Wood 1984; Wilkinson 1989). For ni-Vanuatu the effect has been to promote 'reconstructed' traditions for tourist spectacle (Jolly 1994; de Burlo 1995). This tourism-driven construction of 'tradition' has had the negative impact of producing intense conflict among and within communities over the 'ownership' of 'custom', as a commodity, not as a living pattern of values and world view that guide social life (de Burlo 1984). The political value of 'tradition' in Vanuatu is so strong that ethnic tourism becomes a vehicle of contesting political power through demonstration of rights to tradition (Crick 1989). This is recently demonstrated by the cancellation of 'land dives' (*gol*) for tourists because of local conflicts on South Pentecost over the 'custom ownership' of this ritual (Margaret Jolly, 1995, pers. comm.).

Both the government and the industry play a central role in marketing tradition for profit (Wood 1984; Sofield 1991). This puts the government in the role of being an arbiter of culture (Wood 1984), with the potential to manipulate the perceptions of both tourists and locals about national culture. What is especially insidious in Vanuatu is that this process reduces the integrity of its diversity of cultures. At present, there is some effort being made to examine this issue and form national cultural policy (Jolly 1994).

Other social and cultural impacts of tourism in Vanuatu abound. Many, however, are obscured by the more general effects of other commercial changes. In urban villages, for example, mothers who work in hotels must rely on relatives for child care, and are increasingly dependent on cash income (Philibert 1981).

PROSPECTS FOR THE 1990S

The prospects for Vanuatu's international tourism for the 1990s look positive from the perspective of benefits to the national economy (Sturton and McGregor 1991). Tourism is taking a larger role as a source of revenue and is targeted as a key growth sector by the national development plans.

The continued success of tourism in Vanuatu will depend on:

- integrating tourism directly into national and local planning in a manner which accommodates and rests on traditional natural resources management systems. This especially applies to achieving sustainable development through policy and practice which places tourism within the guidelines of the framework of the National Conservation Strategy;
- evaluating all tourism development projects in terms of ecological and sociological design, not merely economic feasibility;
- maintaining Air Vanuatu's regular flight connections to main markets. The government owned domestic airline, Vanair, will also contribute to tourism development (Economist Intelligence Unit 1990);
- continued funding for promotions by the NTO and regional association in marketing (e.g. with PATA);
- serious attention and support given by Tour Vanuatu, the National Tourism Office, and government ministries concerned with commerce, agriculture, land, water, environmental planning *to ni-Vanuatu owned/operated* small-scale tourism ventures such as tourist transport, handicrafts, and guest houses/ bungalows;
- integration of tourism as a supportive aspect of broad based development based on local ni-Vanuatu needs and values.

Tourism is ultimately about international political economy and power to control natural and economic resources, not local development (Hiller 1977; Britton 1987; Crick 1989; Enloe 1990; Connell 1993; Johnston 1994). As Britton (1987: 132) argued, the tourist industry in the small island nations of the Pacific aims to 'satisfy the commercial imperatives of overseas interests and only partially, and too often inappropriately, meet the needs of local development'.

In the long term, it will be the challenge of Vanuatu to control and use tourism to achieve a pattern of development based on people and land. Tourism often alienates the basic resources of land, water, and labour from Pacific island peoples, devastates agriculture, promotes nutritional problems, and deepens economic dependence (Thaman 1982). A moderate or small-scale tourism, based on local participation will be difficult to achieve, but may likely be the most stable path to sustainable development (Wilkinson 1989; Hall 1994). The present trends in Vanuatu toward large-scale tourist developments are the antithesis of sustainable development (Crick 1989). It will be up to the government of Vanuatu to guide tourism development to meet its national development needs in agriculture, health, the environment (and other areas) for its rural and urban populace.

The most essential element of 'sustainable development' is that 'a community's and a nation's basic stock of ecological capital should not decrease over time' (MacNeill 1990: 114). In a nation with a majority rural population practicing subsistence horticulture, and for whom land is the most valued cultural, as well as economic, resource, the agricultural sector is the crux of sustainable development. Sturton and McGregor (1991) correctly assert that agricultural diversification is the most important sector for development in Vanuatu.

Cultural diversity and integrity is an essential element for development (de Kadt 1990: 4). The goals and values of ni-Vanuatu communities must be placed first. *Genuine* indigenous participation in tourism in Vanuatu remains rhetoric. For indigenous tourism to fit into local economies and social organisation, local cultural perspectives must be placed first by both ni-Vanuatu elites and outsiders (Baines 1989; de Burlo 1995).

Sustaining the growth of tourism in Vanuatu will not necessarily generate development. In spite of twenty years of international tourism growth, Vanuatu and its people face serious economic, environmental and social troubles. Growth is not development. There is now widespread recognition that past Western models of development as growth are obsolete and inappropriate for small developing countries (Korten 1990; Connell 1993). Development is guided by the principles of social justice, ecological systems' sustainability, and inclusiveness (of persons and power to create social change) (Korten 1990). Control over resources must rest with people and their communities (Baines 1989; Korten 1990).

As Baines (1989: 290) observed, there is a basic 'development dilemma' for Pacific island nations in their pursuit of economic growth in the 'free market' system form, and the simultaneous rhetoric in support of indigenous cultures and traditional institutions. International tourism in Vanuatu exemplifies this dilemma. Government and private sector strategy for tourism in Vanuatu follows standard tourism based on large international hotels and resorts (Hall 1994). Yet, Vanuatu's Second National Development Plan called both for increased local participation, and conservation of environmental and cultural heritage (Hall 1994).

If tourism is going to be part of development planning for Vanuatu, there will need to be a genuine commitment to altering the growth model to include one based on a form in which local rights to resources and power in decision-making about resource use are supported. Tourism in Vanuatu has provoked many disputes and social tensions for many communities (de Burlo 1988, 1995). This need not occur. Local participation in tourism, and tourism's role in promoting development in Vanuatu, would be best served by working with local 'customary' groups and assisting them in decision-making about whether to embrace tourism at all, what type, and how to design tourism projects to best conserve local resources and provide an educational (as well as economic) component.

REFERENCES

Attenborough, D. (1976) *The Tribal Eye*, New York: Norton.

Bergerot, J. (1979) *New Hebrides Guidelines for the Development of Tourism: Its Significance and Implications*, Suva: UNDAT.

Baines, G.B.K. (1977) 'The environmental demands of tourism in coastal Fiji', in J. Winslow (ed.) *The Melanesian Environment*, Canberra: Australian National University Press.

—— (1987) 'Manipulation of islands and men', in S. Britton and W.C. Clarke (eds) *Ambiguous Alternative: Tourism in Small Developing Countries*, Suva: University of the South Pacific, pp. 16–24.

—— (1989) 'Traditional resource management in the Melanesian South Pacific: A development dilemma', in F. Berkes (ed.) *Common Property Resources: Ecology and Community-based Sustainable Development*, London: Belhaven, pp. 273–95.

—— (1991) 'Asserting traditional rights: Community conservation in Solomon Islands', *Cultural Survival Quarterly*, 15(2): 49–51.

Bonnemaison, J. (1994) *The Tree and the Canoe: History and Ethnography on Tanna*, Honolulu: University of Hawai'i Press.

Britton, S. (1987) 'Tourism in small developing countries: Issues and research needs', in S. Britton and W.C. Clarke (eds) *Ambiguous Alternative: Tourism in Small Developing Countries*, Suva: University of the South Pacific, pp. 167–89.

Butler, R.W. (1991) 'Tourism, environment, and sustainable development', *Environmental Conservation*, 18(3): 201–9.

Cater, E. (1989) 'Tourism in the least developed countries', *Annals of Tourism Research*, 14(2): 202–26.

Chambers, M., Bani, E. and Esrom, D. (1989) 'Developing a NCS for Vanuatu – a model for the South Pacific', in *Proceedings of the Fourth South Pacific Conference on Nature Conservation and Protected Areas*, Vol. 2, *Case Studies*, Port Vila: South Pacific Regional Environmental Programme.

Connell, J. (1993) 'Island microstates: Development, autonomy and the ties that bind', in D.G. Lockhart, D. Drakakis-Smith and J. Schembri (eds) *The Development Process in Small Island States*, London: Routledge, pp. 117–47.

Crick, M. (1989) 'Representation of international tourism in the social sciences: Sun, sex, sights, savings, and servility', *Annual Review of Anthropology*, 18: 307–44.

—— (1994) *Resplendent Sites, Discordant Voices: Sri Lankans and International tourism*, Chur: Harwood.

de Burlo, C. (1984) 'Indigenous response and participation in tourism in a southwest Pacific island nation, Vanuatu.' Unpublished PhD dissertation, Syracuse: Syracuse University.

—— (1989) 'Land alienation, land tenure, and tourism in Vanuatu, a Melanesian island nation', *GeoJournal*, 19(3): 317–21.

—— (1991) 'Neglected social factors in tourism project design: The case of Vanuatu', in T.V. Singh, M. Fish, V.L. Smith, and L.K. Richter (eds) *Tourism Environment – Nature, Culture, Economy*, New Delhi: Inter-India Publications, pp. 286–95.

—— (1995) 'Indigenous environment, tourism, and eco-development in island Melanesia.' Paper presented at the annual meeting for The Society for Applied Anthropology, Albuquerque, New Mexico.

de Kadt, E. (1990) *Making the Alternative Sustainable: Lessons From Development for Tourism*, Discussion Paper 272, Brighton: Institute of Development Studies, University of Sussex.

Douglas, N. and Douglas, N. (eds) (1989) *Pacific Islands Yearbook*, 16th edn, Sydney: Angus and Robertson.

Economic and Social Commission for Asia and the Pacific (1994) *Review of Tourism Development in the ESCAP Region*, ESCAP Tourism Review No.15, New York: United Nations.

Economist Intelligence Unit (1990) 'Pacific Islands', *EIU Country Report*, No. 3: 46–52.

Enloe, C. (1990) *Making Feminist Sense of International Politics: Bananas, Beaches, and Bases*, Berkeley: University of California Press.

Farrell, B.H. (1979) 'Tourism's human conflicts: Cases from the Pacific', *Annals of Tourism Research*, 6(2): 122–36.

Hall, C.M. (1994) *Tourism in the Pacific Rim: Development, Impacts, and Markets*, Melbourne: Longman Chesire.

Hiller, H. (1977) 'Industrialism, tourism, and changing values', in B.H. Farrell (ed.) *The Social and Economic Impact of Tourism on Pacific Communities*, Santa Cruz: Center for South Pacific Studies, University of California, Santa Cruz, pp. 115–21.

Jayaraman, T.K. and Andeng, J. (1993) *Tourism Sector in Vanuatu, 1981–90: An Empirical Investigation*, Economics Division Working Papers, South Pacific, 1, Canberra: Research School of Pacific Studies, Australian National University.

Johnson, O. (1944) *Bride in the Solomons*, Boston: Houghton Mifflin.

Johnston, B.J. (1994) 'Environmental alienation and resource management: Virgin Islands experiences', in B.R. Johnson (ed.) *Who Pays the Price?: The Sociocultural Context of Environmental Crisis*, Covelo: Island Press, pp. 194–205.

Jolly, M. (1994) 'Kastom as commodity: The land dive as indigenous rite and tourism spectacle in Vanuatu', in L. Lindstrom and G. White (eds) *Culture, Kastom, Tradition: Developing Cultural Policy in Melanesia*, Suva: University of the South Pacific, pp. 119–34.

Krieger, M. (1994) *Conversations with the Cannibals: The End of the Old South Pacific*, Hopewell: Ecco Press.

Korten, D.C. (1990) *Getting to the 21st Century: Voluntary Action and the Global Agenda*, West Hartford: Kumarian Press.

Lindstrom, Lamont (1993) *Cargo Cult: Strange Stories of Desire from Melanesia and Beyond*, Honolulu: University of Hawai'i Press.

MacDermott, K. (1995) 'Australia: Investors combine fun and business in island resorts – tourism', *Australian Financial Review*, January 18. (On line.) (Available from Lexis Library: ASAIPC File: ALLNWS.)

MacNeill, J. (1990) 'Strategies for sustainable development', in *Managing Planet Earth: Readings from Scientific American*, New York: W.H. Freeman.

Milne, S. (1990) 'Tourism and economic development in Vanuatu', *Singapore Journal of Tropical Geography*, 11(1): 13–26.

Muller, K. (1970) 'Land diving with the Pentecost Islanders', *National Geographic Magazine*, 138(6): 799–817.

Pacific Islands Monthly (1990) 'Vanuatu's revival as untouched paradise', *Pacific Islands Monthly*, 60(3): 37–9.

—— (1991) 'Safe bet on tourism', *Pacific Islands Monthly*, 61(7): 25–6.

Page, S.J. (1996) 'Pacific Islands', *EIU International Tourism Reports*, 1: 67–102.

PATA (1985) *Vanuatu*, Sydney: Pacific Area Travel Association, South Pacific Regional Office.

Philibert, J.M. (1981) 'Living under two flags: Selective modernization in Erakor Village, Efate', in M. Allen (ed.) *Vanuatu: Politics, Economics and Ritual*, Sydney: Academic Press, pp. 315–36.

Predmas, R.R. and Steves, J.S. (1984) 'Vanuatu: The evolution of the administration and political context of decentralization', *Public Administration and Development*, 4: 231–48.

Reedy, M. (1994) *Statistical Abstracts of the World*, New York: Gale Research.

Rodman, M. (1990) 'Constraining capitalism? Contradictions of self-reliance in Vanuatu fisheries development', *American Ethnologist*, 14(4): 712–26.

SCET-International (1973) *Le Development Touristique Aux Nouvelles-Hebrides*, Paris: SCET.

Sofield, T.H.B. (1991) 'Sustainable ethnic tourism in the South Pacific: Some principles', *The Journal of Tourism Studies*, 2(1): 56–72.

Sturton, M. and McGregor, A. (1991) *Vanuatu: Toward Economic Growth, Pacific Islands Development Programme*, Economic Report No. 2, Honolulu: East-West Center.

Thaman, R.R. (1982) 'The impact of tourism on agriculture in the Pacific Islands', in F. Rajotte (ed.) *The Impact of Tourism Development in the Pacific*, Peterborough: Environmental and Resources Studies Programme, Trent University.

Theroux, P. (1992) *The Happy Isles of Oceania: Paddling the Pacific*, Hamish Hamilton: London.

UNCTAD (1993/94) *The Least Developed Countries, 1993–1994 Report*, New York: United Nations.

Van Trease, H. (1987) *The Politics of Land in Vanuatu: From Colony to Independence*, Suva: University of the South Pacific.

Vanuatu (1987) *Statistical Indicators, Second Quarter*, Port Vila: Government of Vanuatu, National Planning and Statistics Office.

—— (1993) *Third National Development Plan, Republic of Vanuatu*, Port Vila: National Planning and Statistics Office.

—— (1995) in KCWD (Online) Available: LEXIS Library:ASAIPC, File: PROFIL.

Wilkinson, P.F. (1989) 'Strategies for tourism in island microstates', *Annals of Tourism Research*, 16(2): 153–77.

Wood, R.E. (1984) 'Ethnic tourism, the state, and cultural change in Southeast Asia', *Annals of Tourism Research*, 11(3): 353–76.

World Bank (1991) *Pacific Island Economics: Toward Higher Growth in the 1990s*, Washington, DC: World Bank.

World Tourism Organization (1993) *Compendium of Tourism Statistics*, Madrid: World Tourism Organisation.

—— (1994) *Tourism Market Trends: East Asia and the Pacific: 1980–1993*, Madrid: World Tourism Organisation.

Chapter 16

Papua New Guinea

Ngaire Douglas

INTRODUCTION

'Like every place you've never been' (Papua New Guinea publicity slogan)

Papua New Guinea (PNG) is a little-known tourist destination in the Pacific, yet its glossy promotional posters, an award winning inflight magazine, an extensive domestic air network, an efficient international carrier, sophisticated inbound operators, comfortable, even occasionally luxurious, hotels, lodges and resorts in the designated tourist locations do not illustrate the realities of the tourism industry in the 1990s. Thus, while PNG has the necessary components of a viable tourism industry, appearances can be deceptive. Although it has by far the largest land area, the biggest population and the most varied geography in the South Pacific, PNG has one of the regions most insignificant tourism industries in economic terms (Economist Intelligence Unit 1989; Douglas 1994; Milne 1991). Yet PNG has been on the itineraries of people seeking leisure, pleasure and recreation since 1884 when Burns Philp & Co Ltd (BP) first advertised tourist cruises in the *Sydney Morning Herald* (Douglas 1994), giving it a much longer period of exposure than a number of other, considerably more successful Pacific destinations. Up until 1970 when BP retired the last of its coastal ships, PNG was more accessible by sea from Australia than any other Pacific nation. It had one of the first domestic airlines in the world and certainly in the South Pacific. The first guide books were appearing by 1899. An eclectic collection of hotels and guest houses had been operating since the late 1880s, primarily to accommodate the ever increasing number of administrators, missionaries, opportunists and traders but also for the convenience of the occasional tourist who managed to negotiate their way to this colonial outpost. In short, while the opportunities were there, other factors have seriously impacted upon the development of a successful tourism industry (Douglas 1994).

In 1965 the World Bank pronounced that tourism in PNG could have greater economic prospects than mining (International Bank for Reconstruction and Development (IBRD) 1965) and it has since attracted more international tourism planning expertise than many other Pacific destinations. But the dilemma of PNG tourism has been created by administrative indifference, social mobilisation and modernisation (MacNaught 1982; Sofield 1990), the international media and extremely high cost of production. The purpose of this chapter is to plot the erratic path of tourism in one of the region's most well-endowed destinations and to position the industry within the overall economic, social, planning and political context of tourism in the Pacific.

THE DESTINATION: CULTURAL, ECONOMIC, SPATIAL AND SOCIAL ISSUES

Papua New Guinea includes the eastern half of the island of New Guinea, the world's second largest island of which the Indonesian province of Irian Jaya occupies the western half, as well as many smaller islands including the Bismarck Archipelago (see Figure 16.1). It extends from the equator to 12° S latitude and from 141° to 160° E longitude and has a land area of 461,690 square kilometres. It is part of the Pacific region known as Melanesia which also includes the Solomon Islands, Vanuatu and New Caledonia. Fiji, long regarded a part of Melanesia, is now considered by an increasing number of scholars to be geographically, culturally and historically peripheral (Routledge 1985; Thomas 1989; Tui'malaeli'ifano 1990).

The land is characterised by high and rugged ranges peaking at over 4500 metres which sweep in a northwest to southeasterly direction across the mainland as well as bisecting the larger islands of New Britain, New Ireland and

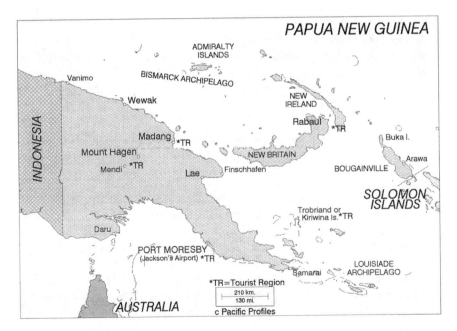

Figure 16.1: Papua New Guinea: location map

Bougainville. These mountains shape and directly influence the weather and vegetation patterns as well as transport, economic development and cultural diversity. They also conceal extensive plateaus and valleys which have become known collectively as the Highlands although geographically, administratively and linguistically they are divided into Eastern, Southern and Western Highlands, Enga and Chimbu. These areas were first explored by Europeans as recently as the 1930s and their discoveries have been well documented (see for example Hides 1936, 1939; Connolly and Anderson 1987; Jones 1990).

Culturally, PNG is as diverse as it is geographically. The population is rapidly approaching 4 million and over 800 languages have been identified, most of them mutually unintelligible. This communication barrier, coupled with the geographical features, has assisted in the development and maintenance of a multitude of cultural variations. Over 80 per cent of the population live in rural communities practising subsistence agriculture, their contact with urban life and its accoutrements minimal or non-existent. However, like many developing nations, PNG is experiencing the rural-urban drift which places considerable strain on the infrastructure of the town areas and on the resident family members (MacNaught 1982; Sofield 1990). The country has extensive and rich resources of minerals and oil and although many of the deposits are in difficult terrain, multinational companies continue to invest heavily in extraction processes. Exports of crude materials account for more than half of total figures; it is one of the few Pacific nations that actually maintains a positive balance of trade (see Table 16.1). But the overall economy is in an extremely poor state. The national debt has reached $US6 billion. Real GDP per person is less than half that of the average for developing countries identified by the United Nations while foreign aid is ten times higher per head of population. Only 9 per cent of the active labour force is paid a wage and nearly 50 per cent of the 2 billion kina national budget is consumed by the public service wage bill. To many observers, PNG is approaching anarchy (McGeough 1995).

TOURISM'S HISTORICAL DEVELOPMENT IN PAPUA NEW GUINEA

Transport

Turn of the century advertisements for BP cruises to Papua New Guinea promised passengers the opportunity to meet 'real live cannibals', 'savages' and 'people from the stone age' while appreciating beautiful island scenery and enjoying balmy tropical weather (Douglas 1994). So popular were these itineraries that by 1914 the canny Messrs Burns & Philp had recognised the potential of this type of 'cargo' and had already published several guide books to the region, leased the Hotel Papua and were offering escorted tours from their newly established Tourist Department in their Sydney Head Office. P&O, Matson, and the Bergen shipping lines began calling at PNG ports, albeit infrequently, from the beginning of the 1930s. Cruise ship arrivals peaked in the

Table 16.1: Economic profile of Papua New Guinea, 1993 (exchange rate $US = 0.979 kina)

Population	3.9 million
Urban population as % of total	16.0
Population estimate for year 2000	5.0 million
Gross Domestic Product (kina million)	4,880.0
Real GDP per capita	1,140.0
Government revenue (kina million)	1,331.0
Foreign grants (kina million)	197.5
Exports (kina million)	2,434.4
Minerals	1,809.2
Imports (kina million)	1,335.0
Overall Balance of Payments (kina million)	−135.0
Real minimum wage (kina per week)	
urban	25.8
rural	9.6

Source: author.

mid-1970s and have declined sharply ever since. In the 1990s it is possible to get only estimates of cruise ship passenger (excursionists) statistics from the Tourism Promotion Authority and the National Statistics Office denies having any such category in its statistical categories.

The first commercial domestic air route was established in 1927 to service the goldfields and by 1938 it was possible to fly from Sydney to Rabaul on the Sunshine Route, although tourists were given very low priority in seat allocation. Following a period when all civil air services had been abandoned because of the Second World War, Qantas resumed the service in 1945 until 1960 when it was replaced by Ansett-Australia National Airlines (ANA) and Trans Australian Airlines (TAA), both Australian domestic airlines. Finally, in 1973, in keeping with approaching political independence, Air Niugini became the national air carrier. As the year 2000 looms, air transport continues to be the only form of access to many areas in PNG: indeed, many people have long been more familiar with aircraft than with cars and in many remote townships the airport and its activities are the centre of development and entertainment.

But while the mode of travel has changed over the last 100 years, the marketing images used by tourism promoters have not. The glossy brochures and posters continue to portray Papua New Guineans as 'savages' and 'primitives' living in 'the land that time forgot' and that the country itself is 'like every place you've never been', whatever that is supposed to mean. Papua New Guineans run corporations, graduate from university and attempt to deal with the same economic, social and environmental problems that confront developing countries worldwide. The paradox is further compounded in that while the tourism industry has a vested interest in maintaining the promotional images of primitive and stone-age behaviour, it must also cope with the widely held perception in its main market areas that it is an extremely unsafe destination. This belief is reinforced by both brochure pictures of fierce tribesmen wielding axes and spears and media reports of tribal violence and social unrest.

Tourists and their souvenirs

Australians, as administrators, public servants, traders, planters, opportunists, explorers and missionaries have been travelling to PNG since the late 1880s. Their primary purposes for going there were to govern, control, convert and exploit the resource base and the indigenous population. The Second World War saw a further influx of foreigner visitors, this time Allied and Japanese troops who fought over the territory as the gateway to Australia and the South Pacific. Nelson (1982) gives an excellent account of the attitudes and behaviours of these distinctly different groups of arrivals and their impact upon the indigenous people.

Many Melanesians quickly learned to accommodate the requirements of the over one million troops occupying the area. De Burlo (1989) attributes the demands of soldiers seeking souvenirs to be an important factor in mass artefact production, one of the few areas in the tourism industry where Melanesians have autonomy (Douglas 1994). During the 1970s PNG artifacts were the focus of heated debate on whether indigenous artisans' attempts to meet tourists' demands for portability were debasing traditional art forms. May (1975) declared tourism's impact as ambiguous; MacKenzie (1977: 84) saw airport art as the 'prostitution of the symbols of the people'; Graburn (1976) acknowledged that missionisation,[1] blackbirding[2] and massive colonisation[3] had had a far greater effect on style than tourism; and Abramson (1976) and de Kadt (1979) agreed that transformation did not necessarily mean loss of meaning. Academic discussion notwithstanding, PNG artefacts continue to be highly prized by professional collectors and souvenir seekers and for many villages in areas like the Sepik the trade is the mainstay of their economy (see Plate 16.1).

Apart from creating a huge pool of potential tourists and stimulating artefact production, the war impacted upon PNG tourism in other ways. Locations like the Kokoda Trail, Bougainville and Rabaul became candidates for MacCannell's (1989) 'sight sacrilisation'[4] process the moment they became battlegrounds. Over fifty years later the locations and relics of war are still among the major attractions promoted by tourism entrepreneurs. The 1992 Spirit of Kokoda event in which people were encouraged to walk the rugged Kokoda Trail in memory of its wartime role is an interesting example of how practically any event or resource, regardless of how dangerous or horrific it may have been, can be coopted or institutionalised into becoming a feature in an industry which is associated primarily with leisure and pleasure.

Plate 16.1:   A village on PNG's flood prone Sepik River. Tourist vessels cruise
the river regularly (Norman Douglas)

Accommodation

Accommodation is certainly a miscellaneous collection. By 1975 PNG claimed
to have ninety resorts, hotels and guesthouses (Reid Ross and Farrell 1975), the
majority established not with tourists in mind but to accommodate the ever-
increasing army of administrators, business people and opportunists who filed
through the country. There had been a flurry of activity after the release of the
1965 World Bank report with several large hotels opening in Port Moresby and
Lae, followed by the first multinational development, the Port Moresby
Travelodge in 1978. Proposals by the multinational Oberoi and Sheraton chains
in 1980 and 1986 respectively have never eventuated. By 1993 PNG claimed to
have 132 hotels (Tourism Council of the South Pacific (TCSP) 1994). However,
a major problem with this figure is that they have not been rated in terms of
quality in any way, therefore, the most fundamental local resthouse rooms are
counted alongside those of the Travelodge and similar facilities. This factor
contributes considerably to inaccurate profiles of tourism infrastructure. The
general manager of the largest hotel group, the Coral Seas hotels, part of the
Steamships trading company, claims that holiday tourists contribute to only
about 6 per cent of occupancy (pers. comm., 17 October 1994), a useful insight
into the current state of tourism in PNG. Infrastructure ownership is
predominantly in the hands of PNG citizens and companies, while the
government has only indirect participation. For example, the Public Officers

Superannuation Fund Board and the Investment Corporation of PNG are shareholders in Travelodge PNG Ltd. Foreign investment in tourism is concentrated on small, individual developments, usually with significant local participation to both comply with national and regional regulations and to ensure local cooperation and support.

PAPUA NEW GUINEA'S TOURISM MARKET

In terms of natural resources, PNG is abundantly supplied with the attributes of the identified 'pleasure peripheries' of Western industrialised societies (Turner and Ash 1975: 11): the climate is tropical – although in the mountains the temperature can fall below freezing – the vegetation primarily pristine tropical rainforest, the surrounding seas warm, clear and clean, and its geographical features range from challenging mountains, to huge, navigable rivers to classic coral atolls, thereby providing a wide variety of environments for tourism. The prerequisites of cultural or ethnic tourism (Harron and Weiler 1992), educational tourism (Schwaninger 1989; Kalinowski and Weiler 1992), nature-based tourism (Valentine 1992), and adventure travel (Hall 1992) are prolific. It is the closest South Pacific island nation to the region's traditional major tourist generating market – Australia, and to the area's fastest developing generating market – Japan, and yet it receives less than 10 per cent and 2 per cent of these markets respectively (TCSP 1994).

Unlike industrialised Western countries, where domestic tourism accounts for by far the largest market share, PNG's domestic tourism is relatively insignificant. Internal travel for recreation is primarily undertaken by expatriates on short-term work contracts. Melanesians, unlike Polynesians, rarely travel. The exception is for the annual gathering at the festivals and agricultural shows. These have become major exhibitions for the culture and customs of an area with groups practising all year to compete in tribal displays. Although thousands of people participate, their economic impact upon the area is minimal with most bringing with them everything they need and staying with *wantok* (clan group) members in the Melanesian way. Executives of Air Niugini, the national carrier, claim that expatriate participation in domestic tourism has also declined considerably recently as contracts become shorter and rascal (criminal) behaviour more widespread, violent and publicised (pers. comm., 8 November 1994).

For this reason, the discussion of tourism development in PNG focuses on international tourism. However, statistics must be considered cautiously. It is necessary to look at the purpose of visit categories with some understanding of the country to appreciate the situation (Table 16.2). The number of visitors who claim to be in PNG for pleasure is generally less than 30 per cent. However, even this figure must be regarded with some caution. Major inbound operators estimate a more accurate figure would be less than 20 per cent as it is recognised that a considerable number of arrivals for other purposes categorise themselves as pleasure tourists to avoid high visa charges and form filling, a not uncommon international practice (Douglas 1994; Economist Intelligence Unit 1989). Secondly, the categories of 'business' and 'other' include people who are arriving for a period of up to twelve months and incorporating large numbers of people who come on short-term work contracts and consultancies. Those in the visiting friends and relatives (VFR) category are also increasingly staying within the relative 'protection' of expatriate compounds, and thus departing the country without having experienced its diversity at all. This category continues to contribute 14 per cent of total arrivals compared to other major Pacific destinations such as the Cook Islands and Fiji which record 5 and 6 per cent respectively (TCSP 1994). This is confirmation of PNG's continued reliance on expatriate skills. While nearly 50 per cent of total arrivals are from Australia (see Table 16.3), it is the American and European visitors, primarily Germans because of that country's colonial connections, who comprise the majority of holiday makers.

TOURISM POLICIES AND PLANNING IN PAPUA NEW GUINEA

Since 1993 tourism development has been under the auspices of the Tourism Promotion Authority, the government's latest in a long line of attempts to establish a national tourism organisation to meet private sector expectations. Its predecessors are numerous and given the government's record of lack of commitment to tourism as a potentially viable economic sector, its future is uncertain. The first PNG Tourist Board was established in 1966 as a response to a World Bank report (IBRD 1965). Since then there have been six variations on the theme (Table 16.4), each one memorable only for its lack of achievement. Broad policies have remained unchanged:

- the government is to direct and control the growth of tourism;
- tourism growth rate is not to be disruptive to the environment;

Table 16.2: Tourist arrivals in Papua New Guinea by purpose of visit, 1990–93

Purpose	1990	1991	1992	1993
Pleasure	13,022	8,861	14,815	8,677
% share	32.0%	23.2%	34.6%	21.5%
Business	17,269	16,592	18,088	15,793
% share	42.4%	44.4%	42.2%	39.0%
VFR	6,812	6,174	6,351	5,599
% share	16.7%	16.5%	14.9%	13.8%
Other	3,639	5,919	3,562	10,407
% share	8.9%	15.8%	8.3%	25.7%
Total	40,742	37,366	42,816	40,476

Sources: TCSP 1994; PNG National Statistics Office 1994.

Table 16.3: Short-term visitor arrivals in Papua New Guinea by major markets, 1985–93

Market	1985	1987	1989	1991	1993
Australia	13,920	17,163	23,590	15,324	18,803
New Zealand	1,544	1,444	2,184	1,825	2,076
USA	3,238	4,278	4,907	5,051	3,951
UK	3,137	1,793	2,161	2,450	2,323
Germany	844	1,083	1,795	866	985
Other Europe	1,458	1,255	2,574	2,822	1,991
Japan	1,670	2,036	1,906	1,766	1,623

Source: TCSP, Suva, 1994; PNG National Statistics Office, Port Moresby, 1994

Table 16.4: Milestones in tourism development in Papua New Guinea since 1965

1965	World Bank report declares tourism to have potential
1966	PNG Tourist Board formed
1968	Burns Philp withdraws its last passenger vessel *Bulolo*
1971	First tourism statistics study
1972	*Analysis of Papua New Guinea Tourist Potential* Launch of Sepik River houseboats.
1973	*Tourism in Papua New Guinea,* *Tourism Development Plan Papua New Guinea* Air Niugini established
1974	PNG Tourist Board becomes PNG Tourist Authority PNG Tourist Authority becomes PNG Office of Tourism
1975	First Tourism Act Melanesian Tourist Services, becomes largest the inbound operator Tourism Advisory Council established Tourism Coordinating Committee established
1978	Port Moresby Travelodge opens First all indigenous crew on Air Niugini
1980	*The National Tourism Plan: A Summary released* PNG Office of Tourism closed
1982	PNG National Tourism Authority (NTA) established
1984	*Medium Term Development Strategy* prepared
1986	Tourism given official economic status by PNG's government
1987	Second Tourism Act *Five Year Tourism Development Plan 1987–1991* launched
1989	*Tourism Development in Papua New Guinea* produced
1990	*Papua New Guinea, Evaluation and Development Needs* prepared *Five Year Tourism Development Plan 1990–1994* launched NTA becomes PNG Tourism Development Corporation (TDC)
1992	Steamships Coral Seas hotel group launched
1993	TDC become PNG Tourism Promotion Authority (TPA) TPA *Corporate Plan, 1994–1996* produced

Source: author.

- tourism development is not to disrupt the people and their cultures;
- tourism development is not to be at the detriment of overall national development.

Responsibility for the Office of Tourism has been passed from department to department, successively passing through commerce, information, labour and industry, science and culture and civil aviation and culture. In the early 1980s it was abandoned altogether for several years.

In 1986 the national budget finally acknowledged the potential of the tourism sector (see Figure 16.2) and by 1994 the budget allocation had increased from 500,000 kina to three million kina. However, 80 per cent of the Tourism Development Corporation's (TDC) budget was going on salaries for its 175 staff rather than promotion. In another of its regular reshuffles, the government abolished the TDC in 1993, reassembling it as the Tourism Promotion Authority (TPA). This most recent office, reduced to a staff of 25, was in a state of confusion in early 1995, the result of the national government's own financial crisis.

The frequent manifestations of tourism's public office is mirrored in its development plans. The eternally optimistic nature of these was set by the World Bank report (IBRD 1965), which was deemed to be the blueprint for economic development in PNG by the Australian government. Although tourism was mentioned on only six of the 450 pages, it was endowed with greater prospects than mining, which was viewed as having only limited potential (see the

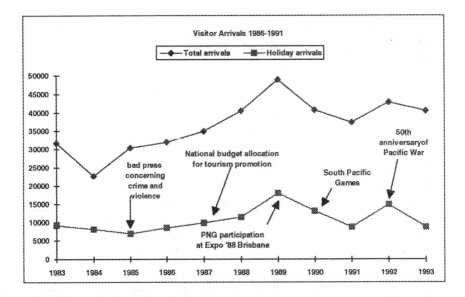

Figure 16.2: Visitor arrivals to Papua New Guinea, 1986–91

Source: National Statistics Office, Port Moresby, 1983/4; TCSP, Suva, 1994

economic contribution of mining in Table 16.1). In 1972 a study on tourism's potential predicted that from a base of 10,164 holiday visitors in 1968 there would be over half a million people visiting the country by the mid-1980s.

Peat, Marwick, Mitchell and Company, a firm identified as 'specialists in tourism plans for corporate developers' (Ranck 1984) produced the first officially designated tourism development plan in 1973. In accordance with their obviously vested interests the plan was extremely optimistic in its predictions although it hedged its bets by providing both high and low estimates of expected arrivals. By 1978, with active government support, 99,988 international visitors would be arriving. If no government support was forthcoming, 83,527 arrivals could be expected (Peat *et al.* 1973). Tourism receipts were expected to reach $US40 million by the same year. In fact there were only 32,388 visitor arrivals. Receipts, even with the most generous calculations, amounted to only $US13 million (Office of Tourism 1980).

The next official plan was compiled in 1978 although only a 45-page summary was publicly released (Ranck 1984). It avoided the obvious pitfall of forecasting visitor arrivals. A flurry of policy documents and planning strategies appeared throughout the 1980s and early 1990s (see Table 16.4) but none have been effectively implemented. In 1993, the TPA rejected the former policies and adopted its own corporate strategy for 1994–96. Its implementation is based on an annual budget of 3.5 million kina and tourism revenue of 120 million kina, both of which would seem wildly optimistic. The mission statement claiming to 'increase the number of overseas and domestic travellers thereby stimulating strong economic growth in the sector' merely repeats claims made in all the past plans with little regard given to the extremely low base consistently recorded over the past 30 years from which this 'strong economic growth' is supposed to eventuate.

PROBLEMS AND PROSPECTS FOR TOURISM IN PAPUA NEW GUINEA

Despite the ongoing production of policies, plans, predictions and promotions, tourism in PNG remains an enigma. The validity of the published data is questionable because of unreliable measuring tools, although the TPA hopes this will be rectified by 1995 when more reliable collection methods are implemented. TPA's manager admits that claims of 1993 tourism receipts reaching $US45 million and total employment of 5,500 could be grossly over-estimated or perhaps, he suggests hopefully, underestimated (pers. comm., 26 October 1994). Whatever figures are accurate, tourism employment opportunities for Papua New Guineans at management level remain very limited and there is a high turnover of expatriate management. Ambua Lodge, for example, one of the nation's premier accommodations in the Highlands, has had ten managers in two years, a problem largely attributed to their inability to understand their Melanesian workforce (see Plate 16.2). When compared to

Plate 16.2:   Ambua Lodge, a resort in the Southern Highlands region of PNG
(Norman Douglas)

other Pacific destinations, tourism's significance in the PNG economy is very marginal (see Table 16.5) and seems unlikely to change given the problems with which it must contend.

Perhaps the most significant of these is the law and order situation which has been perceived as very dangerous by the main source markets for many years. Certainly there is a high crime rate, traditionally in Port Moresby where there is high unemployment and associated social problems, although crime is widespread throughout the country.

Occasionally in the Highland areas, where tribal battles are still fought with bows and arrows, deaths occur. But rarely is crime perpetrated on tourists, although the international media would imply otherwise. Well publicised incidents of exposed government corruption coupled with the frequent overthrow of ruling political factions support perceptions of an unstable political environment, an acknowledged deterrent to tourists (Fletcher and Snee 1989; Gee and Cain 1986; Lea and Small 1988; Scott 1988). Inconsistent government support for tourism promotion compared to aggressive policies promoted by other Pacific destinations ensure that tourism's international profile remains low. Papua New Guinea's reputation is one of being a very high cost destination. Inflated prices for airfares, accommodation, food and beverages and ground transport are maintained by the high value of the kina and the fact that these services are, in the main, directed at business travellers with company accounts. All these disincentives to tourism development have been regularly reiterated in

Table 16.5: Comparative tourism indices for Papua New Guinea and other Pacific destinations, 1993

Country	Tourism receipts $US million	Tourism earnings as % of GDP	Growth rate %	% pleasure tourists of total visitation
PNG	45	0.91	−20.1	29.1
Vanuatu	31	17.93	+31.8	70.8
Fiji	251	61.80	+0.9	81.1
Cook Islands	31	36.79	+27.9	85.0
French Polynesia	164	5.47	+28.7	85.0
New Caledonia	95	26.80	0.0	73.0

Source: TCSP 1994.

plan proposals but solutions are no closer at hand in 1995 than they were in 1965.

The TPA is currently focussing on small-scale, soft adventure, decentralised developments which could contribute to local economies with minimal environmental and social impacts (see Plate 16.3). However, Ranck (1987), Iowa (1989, cited in Sofield 1990), and Sofield (1990) provide case studies of low key indigenous developments and these are usually fraught with problems caused by:

Plate 16.3: A Huli Wigman of the Southern Highlands demonstrates his technique for tourists (Norman Douglas)

- isolation (the very thing which is supposed to be a major pull factor);
- poor management;
- lack of funds;
- lack of access to target markets;
- clan jealousy.

Tourism development continues to be concentrated in the Sepik River region, the Highlands, Madang, the Trobriands and, more recently, the Milne Bay area. Sepik River cruises have been a major attraction in PNG since 1972 and the two operations have been promoting sustainable tourism practices since well before they became the fashionable catchcry of the 1990s. Negligible impact, high yield, quality experience, sustainability and community consultation typifies this aspect of PNG tourism but its success is an isolated pocket in this country of contrasts.

With its cultural and scenic diversity PNG is well suited to accommodating special interest tourism requirements. This market was identified in 1987 as the one least likely to cause disruptive social impacts as well as the one probably less likely to be influenced by the international medias' 'horror headlines' (Millett 1987). But until the problems discussed in this chapter have been addressed it seems extremely unlikely that the TPA's target of 70,000 pleasure tourists by the year 2000 will be reached. These include:

- significantly improved law and order throughout the country but in the. Highlands and Port Moresby in particular;
- more favourable international media reporting on PNG;
- more competitive international airfares;
- better value for money in accommodation, food, and local tours;
- developing a better image within its potentially best market, Australia.

Tourism in PNG, to be or not to be, is the question that continues to confound operators and observers alike.

ENDNOTES

1 The Melanesian Mission was established in 1849 but already the founder was lamenting the fact that beachcombers, whalers and traders had preceded its arrival. Shineberg (1967) and Whiteman (1983) agree that one of the greatest impacts of the missionaries was the introduction of Western material goods into Melanesian society.
2 'Blackbirding' is the term given to the South Pacific labour trade of the late nineteenth century in which Islanders were recruited by both legitimate and illegitimate means to work in the sugarcane fields of North Queensland, Australia.
3 All the island countries which make up Melanesia were colonised in the late nineteenth century. The Australians and British occupied Papua, the Germans took over New Guinea until the end of the First World War, the British administered the Solomon Islands, the British and French jointly administered Vanuatu and the French took over New Caledonia. All have since achieved independence except New Caledonia.
4 Site sacrilisation has five identified stages; naming, whereby the site is marked off as

worthy of preservation; framing and evaluation incorporates the protection and enhancement of the site; enshrinement occurs when the material used to frame the site is itself identified by markers; mechanical reproduction and social reproduction see the site being copied and perpetuated.

REFERENCES

Abramson, J.A. (1976) 'Style changes in an Upper Sepik contact situation', in N.H.H. Graburn (ed.) *Ethnic and Tourist Arts: Cultural Expressions from the Fourth World*, Berkeley: University of California, pp. 249–65.

Australian International Development Assistance Bureau (1993) *The Papua New Guinea Economy: Prospects for Sectoral Development and Broad Based Growth*, Canberra: Australian Government Printer.

Boutilier, J.A. (1981) 'The nature, scope and impact of the tourist industry in the Solomon Islands', in R.W. Force and B. Bishop (eds) *Persistence and Exchange: Papers from a Symposium on Ecological Problems of the Traditional Societies of the Pacific Region*, Honolulu: University of Hawai'i Press, pp. 37–50.

Connolly, B. and Anderson, R. (1987) *First Contact*, New York: Viking Penguin.

de Burlo, C. (1989) 'Islanders, soldiers and tourists: The war and the shaping of tourism in Melanesia', in M.G. White and L. Lindstrom (eds) *The Pacific Theater Island Representation of World War II*, Honolulu: University of Hawai'i Press, pp. 299–325.

de Kadt, E. (ed.) (1979) *Tourism: Passport to Development?* Oxford: Oxford University Press.

Department of Trade and Industry (1972) *Analysis of Papua New Guinea Tourist Potential*, Waigani, Papua New Guinea: Department of Trade and Industry.

Department of Civil Aviation, Tourism and Culture (1987) *Five Year Tourism Development Plan 1987–1991*, Boroko: Government of Papua New Guinea.

—— (1990) *Five Year Tourism Development Plan 1990–1994*, Boroko: Government of Papua New Guinea.

Douglas, N. (1994) 'They came for savages: A comparative history of tourism development in Papua New Guinea Solomon Islands and Vanuatu, 1884–1984'. Unpublished PhD thesis, Brisbane: University of Queensland.

Douglas, N. I. and Douglas, N. (eds) (1989), *Pacific Islands Yearbook 16th Edition*, Sydney: Angus & Robertson.

Economist Intelligence Unit (1989) 'The Pacific Islands', *EIU Travel and Tourism Analyst*, 4: 70–99.

Fletcher. J. and Snee, H. (1989) 'Tourism in the South Pacific islands', in C. P. Cooper (ed.) *Progress in Tourism, Recreation and Hospitality Management, Vol. 1*, London: Belhaven, pp. 114–24.

Gee, C.Y. and Cain, C. (1986) 'Coping with crisis', *Travel and Tourism Analyst*, June, 3–12.

Gibbings, M. J. (1973) *Tourism in Papua New Guinea: A Report Prepared for the Department of Foreign Relations and Trade*, Brisbane: University of Queensland, Brisbane.

Graburn, N.H.H. (1976) *Ethnic and Tourist Arts: Cultural Expressions from the Fourth World*, Berkeley: University of California Press.

Hall, C.M. (1992) 'Adventure, sport and health tourism', in B. Weiler and C. M. Hall (eds) *Special Interest Tourism*, Belhaven: London, 141–58.

Harron, S. and Weiler, B. (1992) 'Ethnic tourism', in B. Weiler and C.M. Hall (eds) *Special Interest Tourism*, Belhaven, London, pp. 83–94.

Hides, J. (1936) *Papuan Wonderland*, Glasgow: Blackie and Son.

—— (1939) Beyond the Kubea, Sydney: Angus & Robertson.

International Bank of Reconstruction and Development (IBRD) (1965) *The Economic Development of the Territory of Papua and New Guinea*, Baltimore: Johns Hopkins University Press.

Iowa, B. (1989) 'An examination of low cost tourism accommodation development. Papua New Guinea's indigenous village based guest house industry.' Unpublished research paper, James Cook University, Townsville.

Jones, D.E. (ed.) (1990) *Michael J. Leahy: Exploration into Highland New Guinea 1930–1935*, Tuscaloosa: University of Alabama Press.

Kalinowski, K. M. and Weiler, B. (1992) 'Educational travel', in B. Weiler and C.M. Hall (eds) *Special Interest Tourism*, London: Belhaven, 15–26.

Lea, J. and Small, J. (1988) 'Cyclones, riots and coups: Tourist industry responses in the South Pacific', in B. Faulkner and M. Fagence (eds) *Frontiers of Australian Tourism: the Search for New Perspectives in Policy Development and Research*, Canberra: Bureau of Tourism Research, 305–15.

MacCannell, D. (1989) *The Tourist: A New Theory of the Leisure Class*, 2nd edn, New York: Schocken Books.

MacNaught, J.J. (1982) 'Mass tourism and the dilemmas of modernisation in Pacific Island communities', *Annals of Tourism Research* 9: 359–81.

MacKenzie, M. (1977) 'The deviant art of tourism: Airport art', in B. H. Farrell (ed.) *The Social and Economic Impact of Tourism on Pacific Communities*, Santa Cruz: Centre for South Pacific Studies, pp. 83–4.

McGeough, P. (1995) 'PNG in crisis: Our troubled neighbour', *Sydney Morning Herald*, 14 January.

May, R.J. (1975) 'Tourism and the artifact industry in PNG', in B. Finney and K.A. Watson (eds) *A New Kind of Sugar: Tourism in the Pacific*, Honolulu: East West Centre/Santa Cruz: Centre for South Pacific Studies, pp. 125–32.

Millett, J. (ed.) (1987) *The Role of Tourism in Development*, Port Moresby: Institute of National Affairs.

Milne, S. (1991) 'Tourism development in Papua New Guinea', *Annals of Tourism Research*, 18(3): 508–11.

National Planning Office of Papua New Guinea (1984) *Medium Term Development Strategy*, Waigani: National Planning Office of Papua New Guinea.

Nelson, H. (1982) *Taim Bilong Masta: The Australian Involvement with Papua New Guinea*, Sydney: Australian Broadcasting Company.

Office of Tourism (1980) *Tourism Data Bulletin*, Port Moresby: Office of Tourism.

Office of Tourism and Department of Labour and Industry (1980) *The National Tourism Plan: A Summary*, Waigani: Office of Tourism.

Peat, Marwick, Mitchell and Company (1973) *Tourism Development Plan Papua New Guinea 1973*, Port Moresby: Peat, Marwick, Mitchell.

Ranck, S. (1980) 'The socio-economic impact of recreational tourism on Papua New Guinea', in D. Pearce, (ed.) *Tourism in the South Pacific: the Contribution of Research to Development and Planning. Proceedings of UNESCO Tourism Workshop*, Christchurch: University of Canterbury, pp. 55–68.

—— (1984) 'Plans and projections for tourism in Papua New Guinea: Who is being served?', in Department of Geography, *Contemporary Issues in Australian Tourism*, Sydney: University of Sydney, pp. 60–6.

—— (1987) 'An attempt at autonomous development: The case of the Tufi guesthouses in Papua New Guinea', in S. Britton and W. C. Clarke (eds) *Ambiguous Alternatives: Tourism in Small Developing Countries*, Suva: University of the South Pacific, pp. 154–67.

Reid Ross, D. and Farrell, B. (1975) *Source Materials for Pacific Tourism, Basic Statistics, Policy, Pacific Researchers, Selected Bibliography*, Santa Cruz: Center for South Pacific Studies.

Routledge, D. (1985) *Matanitu: the Struggle for Power in Early Fiji*, Suva: University of the South Pacific.

Scott, R. (1988) 'Managing crisis in tourism: A case study of Fiji', *Travel and Tourism Analyst*, 6: 57–71.

Schwaninger, M. (1989) 'Trends in leisure and tourism for 2000–2010: Scenario with consequences for planners', in S.F. Witt and L. Moutinho, (eds) *Tourism Marketing and Management Handbook*, 1st edn, New York: Prentice-Hall, pp. 599–605.

Shineberg, D. (1967) *They Came for Sandalwood: A Study of the Sandalwood Trade in the Southwest Pacific, 1830–1856*, Melbourne, Melbourne University Press.

Sofield, T.H.B. (1990) 'The impact of tourism development on socio-cultural values in the South Pacific: Conflict, coexistence and symbiosis', in M.L. Miller and J. Auyong (eds) *Proceedings of the 1990 Congress on Coastal and Marine Tourism, 25–31 May 1990, Honolulu, Hawai'i*, National Coastal Resources Research and Development Institute, 49–66.

Statistical Digest (1991) *Department of Trade and Industry*, Papua New Guinea.

Thomas, N. (1989) 'The force of ethnology: Origins and significance of the Melanesian/Polynesian division', *Current Anthropology*, 30(1): 27–34.

Tourism Council of the South Pacific (TCSP) (1990) *Papua New Guinea: Evaluation and Development Needs*, Suva: Tourism Council of the South Pacific.

—— (1994) *South Pacific Regional Tourism Statistics 1993*, Suva: Tourism Council of the South Pacific.

Tourism Promotion Authority (1993) *Corporate Plan 1994–1996*, Port Moresby: Tourism Promotion Authority.

Tui'maleali'ifano, M. (1990) *Samoans in Fiji: Migration, Identity and Communication*, Suva: University of the South Pacific.

Turner, L. and Ash, J. (1975) *The Golden Hordes: International Tourism and the Pleasure Periphery*, London: Constable.

Valentine, P.S. (1992) 'Nature-based tourism', in B. Weiler and C. M. Hall (eds) *Special Interest Tourism*, London: Belhaven, pp. 105–27.

Whiteman, D.L. (1983) *Melanesians and Missionaries: An Ethnohistorical Study of Social and Religious Change in the Southwest Pacific*, Pasadena: William Carey Library.

Chapter 17

The Pacific Islands: Markets, development and planning issues

Stephen J. Page and Glenda Lawton

INTRODUCTION

A number of chapters within this book have emphasised the issue of tourism in island microstates (IMS). There is a growing academic interest in the analysis of these IMS in relation to development issues, and belatedly, tourism. For example, Lockhart *et al.* (1993) included two chapters on tourism in their review of the development process in small island states, while Conlin and Baum's (1995) review contains a more focused assessment of the issue of island tourism (though only two chapters examined the Pacific region). The limited literature base on island tourism consistently reiterates a number of common issues which makes it a worthwhile area for study. Scale, which is highly visible on small islands, is one such key issue whereby the effects and impact of tourism can be assessed more easily. The discrete and almost closed economic systems on small islands offer the opportunity for detailed research to gauge tourism effects. Scale also plays a key role in relation to the international organisation and management of tourism on small islands, since IMS often have a dependency upon outside interests to develop and maintain the local tourism industry in the absence of indigenous supplies of capital. Furthermore, the issues of scale and dependency also means that island destinations are dependent upon the highly volatile and fickle nature of international tourist arrivals to supply the visitor market with its lifeblood. As Britton's (1982) research implied: the shackles of colonialism have often been broken on many small island states in the Pacific region, but a new post-colonial order and dependency has replaced the export of primary produce with an alternative dependence on importing international visitors. As emphasised in Chapter 1, the development of tourism in IMS displays many of the characteristics of the MIRAB model (Wilkinson 1989; Milne 1992a) although a number of common themes also characterise tourism in IMS. These include the significance of tourism planning and development to manage the sustainability of the resource base in order to support tourism activities, the growing competitiveness of the international tourism markets and the growing significance of marketing activities to attract, develop and expand visitor arrivals thus maintaining the economic dependence upon tourism.

Although the previous chapters in this book have examined many of the aforementioned issues in relation to the patterns and processes shaping tourism in the Pacific Islands, no one book can adequately convey the situation in each of the 30,000 or more islands dispersed across the Pacific Ocean. While the principal destinations in the region are Guam, Saipan, Fiji and Tahiti in terms of visitor arrivals, many other Pacific Island states are predisposed towards a growth in visitor arrivals as a route to economic development. For this reason, this chapter provides an overview of tourism markets, planning and development in the Micronesian, Melanesian and Polynesian tourism destinations not dealt with elsewhere in the book. In view of the scale and diversity of tourism destinations involved, the chapter can offer only a cursory examination of many countries though it does seek to further develop a range of common issues emphasised in part one of the book. These issues, now affecting many of the island destinations, are the diversity of tourism markets, infrastructure constraints, investment opportunities and the economic contribution of tourism. Even so, one theme notably absent from this chapter is the fact that as early as 1982, governments were obviously cognisant of some environmental problems, but the concept of the South Pacific as a 'paradise' which increasingly attracted tourism and its associated economic benefits was rarely questioned (Wendt 1992: 187). Wendt (1992) reiterates many of the criticisms raised by Hall in Chapter 5 as the South Pacific is marketed as a tourist paradise. The development of mass tourism in very developed destinations, such as Saipan in Micronesia, has led to large-scale tourist resorts, the erosion of the environment and the sale of local land to overseas investors for construction and spatially concentrated tourist development. However, it should be noted that economic development in general has also caused less visible but more destructive impacts. The tendency in some Pacific Islands is for the consequences of tourism to be overlooked as a political trade-off against economic growth and development. Thus the destinations discussed in this chapter should not be viewed in isolation from the issues developed in the first part of this book. However, prior to any discussion of individual destinations it is pertinent to consider the data constraints facing tourism researchers in the Pacific region and the most accessible sources.

DATA SOURCES ON PACIFIC ISLAND TOURISM MARKETS

The most widely accessible data source on international arrivals for individual Pacific Island destinations is the World Tourism Organisation's (WTO) annual publication, *World Tourism Statistics*. The major weakness with this data source is that it contains only limited information on arrivals by destination. The data is also dated, being two years old on publication. Other sources of data are:

- The Pacific Asia Travel Association's (PATA) *Visitor Arrival and Outbound Statistics* which include origins of Pacific-Asia arrivals by major regions and countries. They also contain statistics on outbound travel of residents and nationals of selected PATA countries as well as a limited range of tourism-related statistics for some countries.

- The *Pacific Islands Yearbook*, which appears rather sporadically, often on a three- to five-year basis and which contains a range of data for individual islands.
- The individual visitor bureaus and tourism offices of particular Pacific Islands.

The users of such data sources should also be wary, since discrepancies exist between each source, posing certain problems of comparability for researchers. In short, the Pacific Islands are among the most difficult tourism destinations to research due to the inherent problems of accessing accurate, up-to-date and reliable tourism data beyond that supplied to WTO. In fact the competitive nature of Pacific tourism has meant that some destinations are reluctant to release up-to-date data that may give competitors an advantage.

VISITOR ARRIVALS IN THE ASIA–PACIFIC REGION

Within the Asia–Pacific region, the number of arrivals recorded by PATA have more than doubled between 1983 and 1994. However, Guam, Fiji and the Northern Marianas account for a significant proportion of this growth. In contrast, arrivals in North East Asia trebled in the same period while the expanding South East Asia region has grown seven-fold over the same period (Table 17.1).

During the mid to late 1980s, the Pacific Island destinations depended upon three origin markets which were Japan, the USA and Australia/New Zealand, the exception being New Caledonia and Tahiti with proportionally more European visitors. The level of dependence on these markets changed in the early 1990s, as the new Pacific Rim nations (Hall 1994) and the expanding outbound markets in South and North East Asia emerged (Hitchcock *et al.* 1993).

One of the major impediments to Pacific Islands developing a tourism product is accessibility and the availability of air transportation. While the majority of flights to Pacific Islands radiate from a number of major hubs and sub-regional hubs (ie. Auckland, Brisbane, Guam, Honolulu, Nadi, Noumea, Pago Pago, Papeete and Sydney), inter-island transport is slow and costly. A number of island states have their own airlines, but they are often under-equipped/under-capitalised, and heavily subsidised. Many of the aircraft are small (e.g. Boeing 737 or smaller) and growth in the future is probably related to the acquisition of larger aircraft with code-sharing or cooperative agreements. As Bywater (1990) rightly acknowledges, Air New Zealand is the major carrier in the region (Figure 17.1). With air travel a major component of most tourist packages in the region, receipts from travel comprise a key element of the tourism economy in Pacific-Asia but assessing the economic impact of tourism for individual Pacific Islands and the region remains an intractable problem.

Table 17.1: Visitor arrivals in Guam by origin, 1990–94

Country	1988	%	1989	%	1990	%	1991	%	1992	%	1993	%	1994	%
Japan	493,543	84.25	55,748	83.09	637,569	81.70	582,270	78.98	676.659	77.18	549,343	70.07	773,349	71.16
Korea	2,044	0.35	4,514	0.69	7,645	0.98	19,008	2.58	39,121	4.46	68,604	8.75	118,538	10.91
US[1]	37,092	6.33	42,678	6.38	51,544	6.60	50,258	6.82	59,558	6.79	61,169	7.80	66,847	6.15
Taiwan	774	0.13	966	0.14	2,189	0.28	8,574	1.16	12,443	1.42	23,562	3.01	38,791	3.57
CNMI[2]	22,990	3.44	19,322	3.30	30,649	3.90	27,860	3.78	24,291	2.77	26,455	3.37	29,635	2.73
Micronesia	14,546	2.17	12,533	2.14	17,999	2.31	19,020	2.58	24,456	2.45	20,142	2.57	26,343	2.42
Phillipines	3,761	0.64	3,960	0.59	4,424	0.57	5,484	0.74	8,189	0.93	7,914	1.01	6,811	0.63
Hong Kong	1,440	0.25	1,990	0.30	2,161	0.28	3,019	0.41	8,608	0.98	6,613	0.84	2,390	0.22
Canada	715	0.11	593	0.10	655	0.08	639	0.09	884	0.10	726	0.09	315	0.03
Europe	2,793	0.42	2,125	0.36	2,643	0.34	1,998	0.27	2,643	0.30	2,278	0.29	911	0.08
Nauru	329	0.05	243	0.04	387	0.05	562	0.08	624	0.07	473	0.06	405	0.04
Australia	5,194	0.78	820	0.14	7,784	1.0	6,040	0.82	6,660	0.76	4,403	0.56	922	0.08
Thailand	0	0	0	0	0	0	0	0	780	0.09	1,747	0.22	469	0.04
All Others	2,539	0.38	1,860	0.32	4,407	0.56	3,990	0.54	1,158	0.13	1,685	0.21	10,711	0.99
Total Air Arrivals	576,170		658,962		769,876		728,722		863,074		775,115		1,076,437	
Total Arrivals	585,799		668827		780,404		737,260		876,742		784,018		1,086,720	

Notes: [1] Includes Hawai'i
[2] Commonwealth of the Northern Mariana Islands.

Source: Guam Visitor's Bureau.

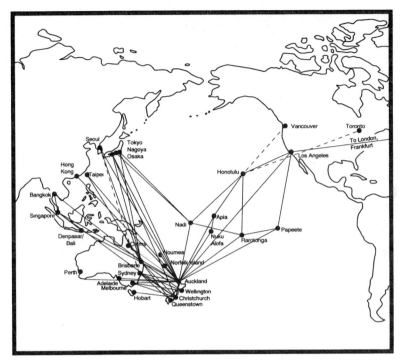

Figure 17.1: Air New Zealand route network in the South Pacific and international connections

Source: Reproduced courtesy of Air New Zealand Limited, Auckland

THE ECONOMIC CONTRIBUTION OF TOURISM IN PACIFIC ISLAND STATES

Despite impediments to tourism development and the associated economic problems in some Pacific Island states, the economic benefits derived from tourism have been viewed by many island governments as a way of reducing dependence on uncertain aid income. Milne (1992a) recognised that if aid payments are excluded, most governments received at least 7 per cent of their revenue as a result of tourism. In the Cook Islands, this figure rose to 25 per cent of government revenue (e.g. from taxes, duties and licence fees from the tourism industry). Tourism also provides an important source of employment. Although Kiribati and Niue each had less than 10 per cent of their labour force employed in tourism, Vanuatu and the Cook Islands had over 20 per cent of their workforce employed in this sector.

The dominant tourist destinations in Micronesia are Guam and the Northern Marianas, followed by the Federated States of Micronesia, the Republic of the Marshall Islands and Palau. According to the WTO, 1,402,000 arrivals were recorded for Micronesia in 1992, with 89.18 per cent originating from within the East Asia–Pacific region. The accommodation capacity in Micronesia comprised approximately 11,000 bed spaces and 9,000 rooms with an average receipt of $US1,507 per arrival for the region. According to the World Tourist Organization, tourism receipts for Micronesia increased from $US909 million in 1988 to 2,113 million in 1992 thus more than doubling the receipts in a five-year period.

Guam

Guam is the largest island group between Hawai'i and the Philippines, mainly comprising one large island of 549km². As a self-governing territory of the USA, tourism is the most important private sector industry in terms of revenue generation after federal state spending (e.g. the military). The island was occupied by the Japanese during the Second World War for two and a half years and now the Japanese tourist is the backbone of the tourism economy. The inauguration of flights from Tokyo to Guam in 1967 led to the expansion of the Japanese tourism market and in 1994, arrivals topped the one million mark. According to Wendt (1992: 190):

> the island of Guam has become a regular visiting spot for many thousands of tourists from Japan; so too has Saipan in the Northern Marianas, the economies of both these areas being heavily dependent on continuing tourist development. The result is large-scale tourist resorts. This large-scale development has resulted in busy roads, and certainly a less than pristine environment, with traditional aspects of the local culture proving difficult to retain and land ownership increasingly being forfeited through sale to overseas interest.

This large-scale nurturing of the mass tourist is largely a 1970s and 1980s phenomenon. However, not only did arrivals double between 1979 and 1988, but this impressive growth has continued throughout the late 1980s and early 1990s with a further doubling by 1994. The figures up to August 1995 indicate that visitor arrivals are showing strong signs of growth, with forecasts of nearly 1.2 million arrivals looking likely.

Estimates of tourism employment indicate that some 13,000 people are employed as a result of tourism activity with 5090 full-time and 281 part-time employees working in the hotel sector. An additional 800 people are employed in tour operations or travel agencies. As a gateway to Micronesia, Guam has been assisted by military investment in infrastructure (e.g. the airport), but in recent years inward investment in tourism has been funded by Japanese commercial interests which now own a sizable proportion of the island's hotels in the Tuman Bay area. The majority of construction activity in Guam is related to the building of new hotels as the demand for accommodation has resulted in a building boom. In addition, since it is cheaper to fly to Guam to play golf than pay the fees in Japan, the development of golf courses marketed to the Japanese visitor has also seen a major growth as a leisure activity. There were five golf courses in 1992 and there are now plans for a further 21. According to KPMG (1993: 28) 'Guam is primarily a service-based economy with the hospitality industry providing the bulk of non-government income. Total tourism generated revenue approximates $US1 billion per annum.'

The number of hotel rooms has expanded from 3974 in 1988 to 7526 rooms in 1994 and there are plans for a further 1109 rooms to be built. Hotel occupancy rates are recorded by the Guam Hotel and Restaurant Association. The high occupancy rates of 90 per cent experienced in 1988 fell to 79 per cent in 1991 during the Gulf War and in February 1994 an all-time high of 109,187 visitor arrivals contributed to an 88 per cent hotel occupancy rate. The occupancy rates are relatively enviable by international standards, a feature assisted by Guam's strategic advantage of being a Micronesian hub with a regional airline – Continental Air Micronesia. One notable feature is that tourism seasonality is irregular, although arrivals have tended to occur in the northern summer holiday months (June to September) and in the northern winter months (January to March) when visitors are seeking an overseas break from their own weather. One feature which has helped Guam to spread arrivals is event tourism. This has undoubtedly assisted Guam in extending the length of stay among tourists and in 1994, Japanese and Korean visitors stayed an average of four days, while Taiwanese visitors stayed an average of five days.

Given the volume of Japanese investment in Guam and the frequency of air services, it is not surprising to find that the dominant visitor market is Japan yet a comparison of arrivals by air and country of residence for 1988 and 1994 illustrates that the Japanese market has declined from 84 per cent of arrivals to 71 per cent in 1994. Despite this proportional decline, the absolute numbers of Japanese visitors has increased from 493,543 in 1988 to 773,349 in 1994 and reflects the direct air links to Fukuoka, Nagoya and the Tokyo region. In 1994 the Kinki (Osaka) region experienced growth as a result of the opening of Kansai International Airport in September 1994 (Page 1994), and the region now ranks third after Tokyo and Nagoya. At the same time, arrivals from the South East Asia region have recorded impressive growth from 0.35 per cent of arrivals in 1988, to 2.58 per cent in 1991 to nearly 11 per cent in 1994. The Korean and Taiwanese markets have assisted Guam in diversifying its traditional appeal away from the Japanese market.

The government levies an occupancy tax on hotels of 11 per cent amounting to $US12,360,311 in 1994 but the Guam Visitors Bureaus' exit surveys indicate that in 1994 Taiwanese visitors spent $US670 per trip locally while in 1995, Japanese visitors spent $US916 and Korean visitors spent $US450 per trip locally.

However, these economic benefits have to be considered in the context of Guam's requirement to import food and materials and the repatriation of profits by Japanese investors. As KPMG (1993: 28) point out, 'The Government of Guam, through the Guam Economic Development Authority, is authorised by law to allow tax rebates to qualified investors. These incentives are aimed primarily at manufacturers, commercial fishing companies, agricultural, aqua culture, mariculture, and tourism development entities'. Those companies eligible to receive grants may receive:

- 75 per cent of income tax rebated for up to 20 years;
- 100 per cent abatement on real property tax for up to a decade;
- 75 per cent rebate on corporate dividend tax up to five years;
- abatement of gross receipts tax for a decade.

It is these extremely attractive conditions for investors that create the appeal of Guam for Japanese inward investment.

The Guam Visitors Bureau, a public-private sector partnership funded by government and private sector interests is responsible for overseas marketing and promotion. Much of the marketing has been undertaken in conjunction with the Northern Marianas and Continental Air Micronesia, with promotion being focused on the USA, Germany, South Korea, Taiwan and Australia.

The Northern Marianas Islands

The Northern Marianas are a 685 kilometre chain of four islands extending north of Guam comprising 'high' volcanic islands which are covered with limestone. They were formerly a district in the Trust Territory of the Pacific Islands administered by the USA and since 1978 they have become the self-governing Commonwealth of the Northern Mariana Islands. The largest island is Saipan (116.5 km^2) where 90 per cent of the population live while other islands of note are Rota (83 km^2) and Tinian (101 km^2) with Rota, comprising a secondary tourist destination, and Tinian a less developed area. The appeal and attraction of the Islands is largely related to its Second World War heritage, particularly the battlegrounds, suicide cliff and the old Japanese prison. The Islands' beaches, diving and rocky landscape together with the reefs and lagoons also add to the attraction.

In locational terms, Saipan is 5280 kilometres west of Honolulu and 2400 kilometres South East of Tokyo. There are direct air routes to Japan and routes to the USA via Honolulu. Continental Air Micronesia and Japan Airlines are two of the major carriers, with Continental Air Micronesia and Air Nauru connecting Saipan with other parts of Micronesia. Air Nauru also provides links to Australia and New Zealand. Additional connections to Guam exist on Philippine Airlines and smaller airlines, while charter operations exist between Japan and the northern islands. According to KPMG (1993: 4) 'foreign investment has provided many of the facilities for the major industry, tourism'. This is reflected in the development of casinos on the island of Tinian with five licences issued to promote this activity. In contrast to Guam, Article XII of the Covenant to Establish a Commonwealth of the Northern Mariana Islands in Political Union with the United States of America outlined restrictions on the ownership of land by indigenous people while non-locals can lease land for up to 55 years. Yet despite these restrictions on investment, visitor arrivals have expanded. The period 1983–7 saw visitor arrivals expand by over 50 per cent and a growth of over 200 per cent occurred between 1987 and 1994. The Japanese market has continued to perform well in the late 1980s and early 1990s although the actual proportion of Japanese arrivals dropped from 74 per cent of all arrivals in 1987 to 65 per cent in 1994. At the same time, an attempt by the Marianas Visitors Bureau to diversify its existing market base from the USA and Japan is reflected in the recent expansion in North East Asia areas.

Tourism is now viewed by government sources as the sector of the Northern Marianas' economy with the best growth prospects. In 1991 tourism expenditure was estimated to be $US428.3 million. The rapid expansion of tourism has fuelled a growth in the construction of tourism infrastructure, with 2651 hotel rooms available in 1991 and rising to 3346 in 1994, with an enviable 73 per cent occupancy rate. A further 1425 rooms are under construction to meet tourism demand for accommodation. However, this growth has been accompanied by increased imports from the US mainland to service tourist needs, particularly in relation to foodstuffs as local production has declined (Douglas and Douglas 1994). Marketing is undertaken by the Marianas Visitor Bureau and although the focus is still largely on the Japanese market, there is a growing emphasis on the South East Asian markets as a consequence of the rapid growth experienced in nearby Guam. In 1994, the Marianas Visitor Bureau budget was $US3.8 million, which was spent in the Japanese market (75 per cent), the USA (10 per cent) and other markets.

Federated States of Micronesia and Palau

The Federated States of Micronesia (FSM) consists of approximately 600 islands and atolls, though only 40 are deemed to be of significance in terms of size and population. The islands are scattered over a distance of 2500 kilometres. The main islands which comprise the four states of the FSM are:

- Pohnpei (345.4 km^2)
- Kosrae (109.6 km^2)
- Yap (121.2 km^2)
- the Chuuk group (118k m^2) (Truk, formerly known as the Caroline Islands).

The FSM is associated with the USA in a Compact of Free Association up until the year 2001. Tourism is at a relatively low level of development, but it is being viewed by governments as a significant element of the state economy. Each state government has its own tourism department responsible for planning and developing tourism as emphasised by KPMG (1993: 11) in that 'there exists a desire to build a more vibrant tourism industry'. To facilitate such a desire, foreign investment is positively encouraged although foreign investment permits, which have to be approved by the FSM Foreign Investment Board, are needed (KPMG 1993). Like the Northern Marianas, the ownership of land is prohibited by foreign investors although there are attractive tax regimes. Among the most likely forms of tourism opportunities are sustainable and environmental tourism, though these need to be tempered by appropriate protection mechanisms. Most islands' would be keen to experience some growth in arrivals, but the major constraint is airlinks: the States are accessible via Continental Air Micronesia from Hawai'i, Guam, Australia and Japan, while Air Nauru provides links to Pohnpei and Chuuk. In each island, tourism infrastructure is strictly limited, with many hotels being family-owned and offering basic to standard types of accommodation. In 1991, Yap had 26 rooms, there were 144 in Pohnpei, 80 in Chuuk and 30 in Kosrae indicating the limitations on developing a visitor industry. The tourist commission or visitor bureau in each state promotes the unique features of the island(s) with each state emphasising cultural attractions, snorkelling and scuba diving. Because of the limited resources available to the FSM and in the absence of a major visitor market, the marketing of each state has occurred in joint initiatives with Guam and the Northern Marianas as well as in regional South Pacific promotions. Yap is the most well-documented tourism destination in the FSM and Figure 17.2 illustrates the recent expansion of visitor arrivals. According to Yap's Commerce and Industries Division, the last survey of visitor expenditure in 1991 found that the average length of stay was 4.3 days. The average expenditure per visitor was $US125 generating an estimated expenditure of $US689,750. The main visitor markets are the USA, Australia, Canada, Japan and Germany. Although the FSM are at a very limited stage of development, future growth will inevitably be related to improving air transport access.

Palau (Belau)

Palau comprises a group of 200 islands in the Western Carolines, though only eight are inhabited. Palau is a republic in free association with the USA, with over 65 per cent of revenue generated from aid assistance received from the USA. Tourism is viewed as a future growth area and arrivals have shown a marked increase from 12,092 in 1985 to 40,497 in 1993 and 40,548 in 1994 although an expected growth in 1993–94 did not materialise. In common with many other states in Micronesia, the main markets are the USA, Japan, Taiwan, the Philippines and Korea which dominate arrivals. Fletcher and Snee (1989) draw an important distinction between the Japanese visitors who are general holidaymakers who relax in Palau's scenic beauty and the American tourist who seeks 'special interest activities', particularly scuba diving and snorkelling, in the unique marine environment.

The move towards a more highly developed visitor industry was marked by the opening of the 100-room Palau Pacific Resort complex in 1984, then owned by the Tokyo Land Corporation of Japan and costing $US20 million to develop, illustrating that foreign investment is positively encouraged. A notable feature is

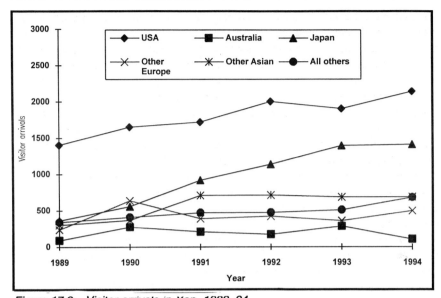

Figure 17.2:   Visitor arrivals in Yap, 1989–94

Source: Commerce and Industries Division, Department of Resources and Development, Yap

that 90 per cent of the workforce is comprised of local people and by 1991, 21 hotels/motels were in operation with 481 rooms, of which 78 were located outside the state administrative centre, Koror. Fletcher and Snee (1989) indicate that on the basis of input-output analysis, for every $US1 million of expenditure, 58.46 full time equivalent jobs are supported, while imports contribute to a leakage of 53 cents in every dollar during the first round of expenditure, and rising to 82 cents in the final analysis.

The Palau Visitors Authority coordinates and promotes tourism, using images and slogans that portray it as 'one of the seven underwater wonders of the world' and 'nature's pot of gold'. Visitor revenue is generated from a 10 per cent hotel room tax and $US3 departure tax in 1992. The majority of accommodation ventures remain small, but there is likely to be growth in foreign investment and development. For example, recent plans indicate that Outrigger Hotels Hawai'i, the largest Hawaiian hotel chain, plans to manage a 135-unit condominium complex to be built by the Micronesian Investment and Development Corporation, for completion in early 1997.

The Marshall Islands

The Marshall Islands is a republic, also in free association with the USA, comprising a chain of 31 atolls and four coral islands and a total land area of 171 square kilometres. The economy of the Marshall Islands is relatively underdeveloped with a strong reliance on grant assistance and lease payments from the USA. Tourism is in its infancy, although visitor numbers have increased from 1882 in 1984 to 6868 in 1991, with approximately 33 per cent originating from the USA. There are some indications that the government is actively considering the economic benefits which will accrue from tourism development. The WTO/UNDP have previously prepared tourism reports on the Marshall Islands' prospects and potential and government sources are actively targeting foreign investment in tourism, although tourist facilities are strictly limited (KPMG 1993). The natural attractions of the Islands are its marine environment (e.g. coral reefs, lagoons, diving and Second World War remains).

Hotel accommodation remains a continued impediment to an expansion of tourism. For example, in 1985, there were 100 rooms in the capital (Majuro) and ten on Mili, although by 1994 there were five main hotels in Majuro, with the largest containing 35 rooms. Another limitation is air transport. The national flag carrier, Air Marshalls, flies three times a week to the FSM, to Fiji via Kiribati and Tuvalu using a Hawker-Siddley 748 (HS-748). Since July 1995, the airline has acquired a new Saab 200 turboprop (with another on order) at a cost of $US30 million to replace its slower HS-748. It also plans to extend the airlines' network west through Micronesia, requiring only a 45 per cent load factor to be profitable. However, the major volume carrier is Continental Air Micronesia who fly from Majuro to Honolulu and then to Guam. Air Tungaru flies on a weekly schedule from Majuro to Tarawa in Kiribati. The implication here is that by acquiring a larger fleet to service the Japanese and North Asian destinations and the Fiji gateway directly, tourism will probably expand beyond its current level.

Kiribati and Tuvalu

Kiribati is an independent republic and comprises three small groups of islands, formerly known as the Gilbert and Ellice Islands. Tourism has the potential to contribute to the local economy, but limited international access (i.e. Air Marshalls provides services) and poor infrastructure are constraints to development. This reflects its designation by the UN in 1987 as a least developed country. In 1987, visitor arrivals were 2774, though almost 40 per cent were residents from Tuvalu and Nauru. By 1991, actual arrivals dropped to 2,100 and in 1992 this figure rose to 2,537. The limited number of international tourists are from Australia, New Zealand and the USA. The country's isolation continues to hinder expansion while tourism is virtually non-existent on the other Islands outside of Tarawa and Kiritimati. Government policy aims to protect the more fragile island environments from tourism's negative social and cultural effects where limited populations exist. A development plan has been produced by the Tourism Council of the South Pacific (TCSP) to control future tourism growth, with the Kiribati Visitors Bureau responsible for promotion and advising on suitable development. The fragile marine ecosystems and war relics around Kiritimati pose an interesting feature for visitors. Accommodation is limited, with two hotels on Tarawa and a number of government rest houses available for visitors.

Tuvalu is a set of five atolls and four coral islands comprising a total land area of 25.9 kilometres. Like Kiribati, tourism is limited by accessibility to major markets and the cost of air travel. Non-Tuvaluan arrivals in 1986 were 716 and this had increased to only 962 in 1992. While the government hopes to see tourism expand, limited accommodation and infrastructure compound the high cost of air travel which is among the most expensive per kilometre in the world. At present, there is no ministry or government department for tourism, but the TCSP has developed a Tourism Master Plan for the government to facilitate development to the year 2002. The number of visitors is thought to be approximately 400–500 per annum, with the balance either visiting for business purposes associated with aid assistance or Tuvaluans visiting friends and relatives. Most tourists' visits are orientated towards the island of Funafuki, and the government recognises that it has 'the potential to carve out a lucrative niche in the international tourism market'. Most tourism marketing is undertaken by the TCSP with accommodation being strictly limited in range.

MELANESIA

The Melanesian region comprises New Caledonia, Papua New Guinea (PNG), the Solomon Islands, Vanuatu and Fiji. Melanesia's share of East Asia-Pacific arrivals has fluctuated from 0.74 per cent in 1988 to 0.91 per cent in 1989 and dropping to 0.73 per cent in 1992. Receipts from East Asia-Pacific arrivals have also dropped from a peak of 1.03 per cent in 1989 to 0.87 per cent in 1992. At the same time bed spaces have increased from 23,000 in 1988 to 25,000 in 1992 and the number of rooms has also increased over the same period from 8000 to 10,000. International tourism receipts have risen consistently from $US236 million to $US399 million in 1992, although actual expenditure has been variable, rising from $US94 million in 1988 to a peak of $US101 million in 1991 and dropping to $US100 million in 1992.

New Caledonia

New Caledonia comprises one large and one small island and also includes the Loyalty and Huon group of Islands (see Figure 17.5, page 292). It is a French territory, and the main island is New Caledonia (La Grande Terre) with an area of 16,750 square kilometres and its capital is Noumea (Plate 17.1). Tourism is New Caledonia's second most important economic activity after nickel mining, but the 1980s were characterised by a steady decline in the main tourist markets following political unrest and poor diplomatic relations with New Zealand. Visitor arrivals have expanded from 56,627 in 1986 to 85,103 in 1994, although arrivals dipped slightly in 1991–2 due to the repercussions from political

Plate 17.1: Noumea city, reproduced courtesy of Destination New Caledonia, Auckland

problems. The growth in arrivals during the 1980s reflects a conscious decision by the government to diversify the economic base of the country following a slump in world nickel markets. During the period 1986–94 there has been little change in the composition of visitor arrivals, with a slight growth in Pacific Islanders visiting New Caledonia. The only major change has been a strengthening of the French market, as a response to declining visitor arrivals from Australia and New Zealand in the early 1990s. The degree of seasonality in visitor arrivals is not as marked as in other Pacific Island destinations and as Figure 17.3 shows, there is a considerable degree of consistency in the spread of visitors by season.

Visitors in the late 1980s were faced by a shortage of airline seats and accommodation, but investment in Air Calédonie International appears to have relaunched the airline as a regional carrier in the Pacific, with the introduction of new services. New Caledonia is also served by the French carrier UTA, while Air New Zealand operates a weekly service from Auckland using a Boeing 767. Air Calédonie International has plans to acquire a Boeing 767 to increase capacity and to penetrate new markets. There is evidence of new investment in New Caledonia in a number of small luxury beach resorts (see Plates 17.2 and 17.3). A new 253 room Le Meridien recently opened in Noumea and this expansion of accommodation capacity consolidates the development to 1992, when Japanese investment facilitated the opening of a second Club Méditerranée complex.

Noumea and the Isle of Pines are regular ports of call for cruise ships. One important development is the involvement of the indigenous Melanesian population in the ownership of tourism facilities, in the small rural gîtes sector and in some

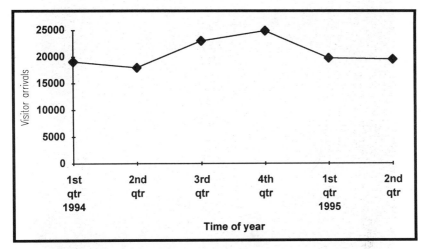

Figure 17.3: Seasonality in visitor arrivals in New Caledonia, 1994–5
Source: Destination New Caledonia

larger accommodation units (e.g. the Club Méditerranée in Hienghene and a major hotel in Noumea), a feature stressed as critical to the long term sustainability of Pacific tourism by many of the contributors in this book. There are no statistics on the economic contribution of tourism, though budgetary aid from France and other sources is a major component of the local economy.

Despite the absence of visitor expenditure statistics, Destination New Caledonia notes that for New Zealand visitors, approximately 50 per cent stay at either Club Méditerranée, Noumea or Hienghene (or on the cruise ship *Club Méditeranée 2* when it is in New Caledonian waters). The implication here is that the holiday is pre-paid in New Zealand dollars (i.e. the air fare, accommodation, food, wine with meals and activities) so local expenditure is minimal. Likewise, the majority of New Zealand visitors not staying at Club Méditerranée travel on a pre-paid package, with local expenditure on meals and activities only. It is likely that this holds true for other international markets, so that the distribution of economic benefits from tourism is dependent upon the linkages within the destination between the tour operator/airline/accommodation sectors and upon the degree of local participation in the tourism industry. Tourism promotion is undertaken by Destination New Caledonia which has offices in Australia, Japan and New Zealand.

The Solomon Islands

The Solomon Islands comprises a double chain of six islands and a number of smaller ones, with the capital, Honiara, located on the main island of

Plate 17.2:   Le Surf Novotel Hotel, Noumea illustrates resort hotel development in New Caledonia, reproduced courtesy of Destination New Caledonia, Auckland

Plate 17.3:   Kou Bungy Resort, Isle of Pines, illustrates small-scale beach hotel development in New Caledonia, reproduced courtesy of Destination New Caledonia, Auckland

Guadalcanal and is the third largest archipelago in the South Pacific. The Solomon Islands' attributes as a tourism destination are outlined in detail by Fletcher and Snee (1989) and Hall and Rudkin (1993) and need not be reiterated here. It is an independent state and one of the better documented Pacific Islands in relation to tourism statistics, with the Statistics Office publishing quarterly statistical bulletins on tourism. Recent research by Rudkin and Hall (1993) reviews the existing state of tourism development and planning in the context of eco-tourism development, particularly the politics of tourism development. Visitor arrivals are modest by comparison with other Pacific Islands. Visitor arrivals have grown only slightly from a base of 10,517 in 1980 to a peak of 12,446 in 1992 and stabilised at around 11,500 to 12,000 for 1993–4. The Solomon Islands are also a regular port of call for cruise ships, although the number of passengers visiting for less than 24 hours varies annually.

The main visitor market remains Australia, which has declined from 40 per cent in the late 1980s to 36 per cent in 1994. The New Zealand market accounted for 12 per cent of arrivals in 1994 followed by PNG (8 per cent), Japan (7 per cent), the UK (7.2 per cent) and the USA (5.3 per cent). The degree of seasonality in arrivals is not particularly marked, with arrivals in 1994 spread across the peak months of July, August and December to coincide with holidays in the USA and Australasia. Over 50 per cent of all visitors from the main markets are professional workers or people in managerial positions, highlighting the Solomon Islands' appeal to this market. In the first quarter of 1995, nearly 79 per cent of all visitors arrived on Solomon Airlines, 17 per cent on Air Niugini, and just over 4 per cent on Air Nauru, which are the main carriers serving the destination. In 1994, the average length of stay was between 10–20 days, depending on the actual period of arrival, though typically 13 days. In 1991, gross earnings from tourism totalled $US14.4 million. The Solomon Islands' estimated accommodation capacity was 260 rooms in 1991. The Government House was sold in 1991 to a Japanese company for future hotel development. The Islands' Hotel Group has also begun investing $US2.4 million in upgrading its properties and in 1995, an American and Malaysian Consortium intended to invest $US30 million in a beach resort at Poha, two kilometres west of the capital Honiara.

A Japanese grant of $US60 million together with European Aid has been used to redevelop the main Henderson airport. To facilitate local investment, the government has established a $US2 million budget to fund small-scale local hotel development and has provided incentives (e.g. tax free holidays) to encourage indigenous participation. Promoting the Solomon Islands as a destination bursting with discovery, the Solomon Islands Tourist Authority has increased its annual marketing budget from $US240,000 in 1994 to $US700,000 in 1995. Solomon Airlines is also promoting the destination by offering a 40 per cent reduction of air fares from Australia and New Zealand over a two-month period. However, in June 1995, *Pacific Island Monthly* reported that financial strains in 1994 had posed major problems for Solomon Airlines, though load

factors of up to 70 per cent were emerging. The appointment of a former Qantas
Executive as general manager has meant the airline now anticipates to be in
profitability by the end of 1995. Lack of market demand in relation to the
frequency of flights is one problem that has plagued the airline since it was
launched as the national flag carrier and to help offset losses, the Solomon
Airline Boeing 737–200 was leased to Royal Tongan Airlines a few times each
week prior to 1994.

The main document which sets out the Islands' tourism future is the Solomon
Islands Tourism Development Plan 1991–2000 commissioned by the TCSP. As
Figure 17.4 shows, the consultancy forecast the growth in arrivals based on a
number of assumptions related to infrastructure improvements, economic and
political stability, expansion in accommodation capacity and government policy.
The report states that 'tourism demand in the initial years of the plan . . . will
largely be supply-led, consequent to the initial impact of Solomon Airlines
operation and the additional accommodation capacity'. As Figure 17.4 indicates,
a low, medium and high projection was put forward but the forecasts, even at the
low projection, are far too optimistic even though Solomon Airlines has replaced
its Boeing 737–200 with a Boeing 737–400 on the Australia, New Zealand, Fiji,
Vanuatu and PNG services.

In June 1995, the *Pacific Islands Monthly* reported that the Solomon Islands

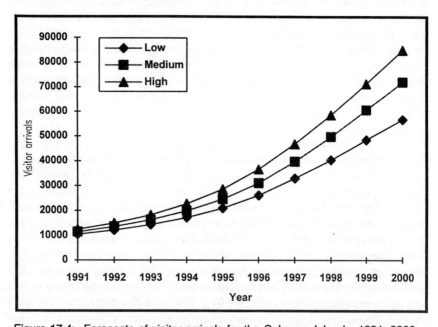

Figure 17.4: Forecasts of visitor arrivals for the Solomon Islands, 1991–2000

Source: Solomon Islands Tourism Development Plan 1991–2000, Ministry of Tourism and
Aviation, Government of the Solomon Islands and the Tourism Council of the South Pacific, 1990

asked PATA for technical assistance in drawing up a Tourism Act to govern operational issues related to diving, tours and hotel accommodation. The potential to attract the adventure tourist through ecotourism (e.g. snorkelling, scuba diving and visiting wilderness areas), has led the government (with New Zealand aid) to identify a World Heritage Site. As Hall and Rudkin (1993: 11) observe,

> in order to understand how development initiatives which maximise economic, environmental and social objectives can be affected, it becomes necessary to understand the cultural and political milieu in which tourism projects occur . . . In the case of the Solomon Islands . . . it is therefore essential that as a prerequisite to the funding of ecotourism projects . . . the politics of the tourism development process [is examined] . . . and . . . that the potential collective benefits of tourism are not destroyed by the individual interests of big-men and local elites.

In other words, given that the benefits of investment and aid may actually reinforce local inequalities in the social system, the political context of tourism is as important as the project. Expansion of tourism markets and development in the Solomon Islands will be a much slower process than that identified in the Solomon Island's Tourism Development Plan. Tourism earns approximately $US10 million for the Solomon Islands per annum, but it is less than 10 per cent of the total exports of goods. According to an Asian Development Bank Outlook, the Solomon Islands have a chronic fiscal deficit and dependence on external grants for finance. As emphasised in Chapter 5, it is only unsustainable logging exports that are supporting the economy and with the government intention to reduce the rate of logging, tourism will be looked at with renewed interest to supplement the largely agricultural economy.

POLYNESIA

Polynesia comprises the two dominant destinations – Fiji (see Chapter 13) and Tahiti, followed by American Samoa, Western Samoa, the Cook Islands (see Chapter 14), Tonga and Niue. Both Tahiti and Fiji initially developed major tourism industries because of their geographical locations as natural stopover locations on trans-Pacific flights. In contrast, tourism development in other Polynesian destinations has been hindered by poor airline connections. During 1995, Qantas announced its intention to withdraw all trans-Pacific flights via Fiji, except for a Qantas transit flight through Tahiti. This decision leaves Air New Zealand as the last major international carrier still servicing Polynesia on a regular basis and given Bywater's (1990) assessment of the prospects for airlines in the South Pacific, is not an unexpected outcome. However, Qantas still retains a 10 per cent stake in Air Pacific (a Fiji-based airline), and this still gives British Airways, with its 25 per cent share in Qantas, a stake in the region (see Bywater 1990 for a detailed review of air travel in the Pacific). Polynesia and other Pacific

Islands are therefore more dependent upon the existing carriers and thus, Tahiti's and Fiji's role as a gateway to Polynesia are no longer assured as they were in the past. Tourism receipts in the region, amounting to $US235 million in 1992 with arrivals of 294,000, fell between 1988 and 1992. This was not as much as Polynesia's market share of east Asia-Pacific arrivals which fell from 0.61 per cent in 1988 to 0.43 per cent in 1992.

French Polynesia

French Polynesia comprises five groups of 130 islands, with a land area of 3521 square kilometres, being dispersed across 5 million square kilometres of ocean. Tahiti is the main island in terms of tourism. Since the 1980s French Polynesia's economy has been dominated by tourism and nuclear testing on Muroroa atoll. Riots in Tahiti opposing French rule and nuclear testing in August 1995 are likely to have severely dented Tahiti's image as a tourist paradise. According to Marciano (1996: 3), the territory experienced 'major economic losses when thousands of tourists cancelled their visits before and after September's first nuclear test on Mururoa atoll and the riots in the capital, Papeete, that followed'.

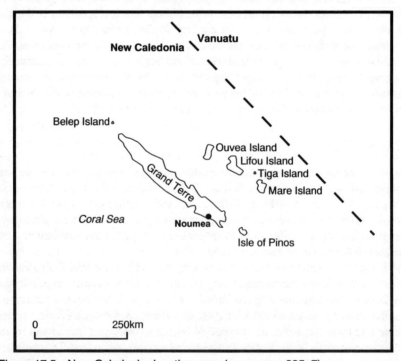

Figure 17.5:   New Caledonia: location map (see pages 285–7)

An estimated 14 per cent of visitors cancelled their visit according to French Polynesian government sources and Club Méditerannée estimated that the cancellation of tour groups, especially from Japan, led to a loss of $NZ8.97 million. The development of tourism in Tahiti is not a new phenomenon although the advent of mass tourism is comparatively recent with the opening of Faaa airport in 1961 acting as a catalyst for expansion. The foreign exchange earnings from tourism equate to almost a quarter of Tahiti's import bill and in 1994, tourism generated $US240 million in revenue. The island's economy is dominated by imports from France which has a self-favouring trade agreement, exporting consumer goods and fuel in return for primary products and as a result, over 70 per cent of goods purchased by tourists are imported, thus reducing the local spin-off for the tourism economy. However, tourism does constitute 15 per cent to GDP.

Up until 1987, visitor arrivals continued to grow, but after 1987 they recorded a sharp decline due to both the cost of the product and living costs in the destination. For the entire period 1980–92 visitor arrivals grew by only 2.8 per cent. But from 1992, visitor arrivals have risen again, to an all time high of 166,086 in 1994. The American and French markets account for over 51 per cent of arrivals, with Japanese and European markets also prominent. The European and Japanese markets have been major growth sectors for Tahiti, particularly during the late 1980s and early 1990s when American arrivals slumped. Australasia accounts for just under 8 per cent of arrivals.

There are currently two major carriers generating over 50 per cent of arrivals, emphasising the pattern of transnational companies operating and controlling Tahiti's tourism industry. Airlines, tour companies and major hotels in Tahiti are all under foreign control with the top eight hotel chains under the direct control of Japanese (the Beachcomer Park Royal, Hyatt Regency, Moana Beach and Kia Ora), French (Sofitel and Club Méditerranée) and American companies (Bali Hai). Traditionally, Qantas airlines have promoted Tahiti as a stopover destination during trans-Pacific flights. However, the dominance of foreign investment and control of the local tourism industry is now becoming an issue. During the 1990s there has been a backlash towards Japanese investment as the indigenous people question the efficacy of foreign ownership. Tahiti's residents voted against a $US94.3 million Sheraton and golf course project for Moorea proposed by Japanese investors for Moorea and opposed the development of a 330 room Meridien Hotel complex in Tahiti.

The average length of stay does not vary greatly among Pacific market with the typical 'one week package' being an important feature that shapes tourism patterns among these markets. In 1994, New Zealand visitors spent an average of 7.24 days compared with 8.03 for Australia and 8.22 for the USA. In contrast, French tourists stayed an average of 14.24 nights reflecting the impact of the Club Méditerranée complex in European holidaymaking habits. These patterns of holidaymaking contributed to the increase in visitor expenditure from $US168 million in 1993 to $US231 million in 1994.

With over 5000 people employed in various aspects of tourism and related services, the expansion of tourism on outer islands may offer long-term potential economic gains. The Tahiti Tourist Development Board encourages the geographical dispersion of visitors to some of the outer islands in French Polynesia and this policy has resulted in an expanding accommodation capacity on these islands. In 1993, there were 2955 rooms with a 57 per cent occupancy rate while according to Tahiti's Tourism's Asian/Pacific Manager, the optimum number of rooms is 5000 and 200,000 visitors are expected in 1995. This is probably a more realistic figure than the 300,000 visitors expected by the year 2000 although improved air links in the late 1980s undoubtedly assisted growth in the 1990s.

The national tourism organisation, the Tahiti Tourist Development Board, has branch offices in a number of countries including Australia, the USA, Europe, Japan, New Zealand and South East Asia. The USA has traditionally been the focus of tourism promotion, but overdependence on this market has led to more diverse marketing activities including targeting high-spending Japanese honeymooners. Tahiti's tourism budget, among the largest in the South Pacific, was $US11.24 million in 1995 with $US1 million for promotion and a $US116,000 to open a Tahiti Tourist Board office in New York. Despite this budget, French Polynesia is also planning a multi-million dollar international advertising campaign in 1996 to address the negative effects of nuclear testing.

American Samoa

American Samoa is comprised of five islands and two atolls of 197 square kilometres, with Pago Pago the administrative centre on the main island, Tutuila. Until 1951, American Samoa was run as a US naval base but following the closure of this naval outpost, US aid was used to develop a tuna canning industry to replace the former reliance on military expenditure. American Samoa receives approximately $US80 million in aid each year and the government still remains the main employer for 33 per cent of the population. In this context, tourism may offer an important opportunity to further diversify the local economy.

The visitor arrival statistics for American Samoa must be treated with caution since analysts point to the limited number of people travelling for the purpose of tourism. For example, visitor arrivals increased from 82,314 in 1988, to 99,804 in 1990 and declined to 81,827 in 1992. But of the 99,804 arrivals in 1990, approximately less than 10 per cent (8499 arrivals) were for tourism. In 1994, 39.5 per cent of arrivals were from the USA, 31.3 from New Zealand, 4.5 per cent from Australia and 6.8 per cent from North East Asia. However, within these statistics are a large number of Chinese, Korean and Filipino business travellers undertaking activities related to the commercial activities on the country. International tourism receipts are estimated to be $US10 million, but that is unlikely to be a realistic assessment of actual expenditure which is probably only 10–20 per cent of the figure.

The government promotes tourism but high air fares remain a major impediment to a growth in visitor arrivals and in fact, a succession of air carriers (including Pan Am, Continental and Air Samoa), operated for a few years and then withdrew. The current carriers include Polynesian Airlines, Hawaiian Airlines and Air Nauru and the existing Apia connection into Western Samoa is an important gateway for the Islands. American Samoa has only one major hotel, the government-owned Rainmaker Hotel which has been affected by management problems and unavailable rooms due to refurbishing. Prior to 1993, it had only made a profit in two years of its 25-year history. The planned development of a new 94–room hotel and the establishment of a National Park is expected to improve American Samoa's tourism appeal. During the summer season, cruise ships sometimes spend a few hours in Pago Pago harbour. The Islands are promoted under the slogan 'come share our world' and joint Western Samoa and American Samoa marketing initiatives have been undertaken.

Tonga

Tonga, an independent Kingdom and member of the Commonwealth, comprises three main island groups with a land area of 696.71 square kilometres. Thirty-six of the 150 islands in the group are inhabited, with two-thirds of the population living in the Tongatapu group of islands. The capital, Nuku'alofa, is on Tongatapu and tourism is a large contributor to the local economy though visitor numbers are relatively modest at 28,408 (air arrivals) and 10,757 (sea-borne arrivals in 1994). Tourism in Tonga is reviewed in Laws (1995) who emphasises cultural tourism and a number of recent developments. The most detailed and analytical review is contained in the classic study by Urbanowicz (1989) which is a critical discussion of the anthropological effects of tourism on the indigenous culture. Included within the air-arrivals statistics are business travellers, those on holiday and returning Tongans and for this reason, the actual number of tourists is probably only 50 per cent of the published statistics. A high proportion of visitors from New Zealand and the USA are Tongans returning to visit friends and relatives. Not surprisingly, visitor arrivals by air are dominated by New Zealand, the USA and Australia. Although seasonality is not particularly acute in Tonga, the main peak occurs at Christmas when Tongans return home to stay with friends and relatives.

The cruise ship market appears to be highly variable and unpredictable with arrivals fluctuating from 7536 in 1988 to 10,757 in 1994. Tonga's physical distance, considered by the cruise ship industry to be too far from Sydney for inclusion in 10–14 day cruises, is the main reason expansion of this market is limited. According to Milne (1990: 25):

the most recent Tongan development plan lists three central objectives in relation to the development of the tourism sector: to develop tourism into one of the major sectors of the economy; to ensure a planned sectoral growth with positive contributions to employment generation and foreign exchange earnings; and to ensure an equitable distribution of tourism earnings and activities throughout the Kingdom.

This is seen as critical for an economy characterised by large trade deficits, due to its dependence upon imports of consumer and capital goods (Milne 1990). However, remittances and aid payments help to offset some of the deficit while tourism offers potential to broaden the national economic base. Tonga's tourism industry is characterised by high levels of local ownership although Milne (1990: 40) observes that 'at present the linkages between the tourist sector and the rest of the economy are relatively weak and must be strengthened if the industry's potential to generate national income and employment is to be realised'. The tourism industry in Tonga was estimated to contribute $US10 million in 1989–90 and $US11 million in 1994, though this may include remittance receipts. The weakness of these linkages can be seen in the limited workforce (in excess of 1420 people), employed in the tourism sector. This reflects the predominance of visitors staying with friends and relatives rather than contributing to the local tourism economy through expenditure on accommodation and services.

Infrastructure is one factor constraining Tonga's tourism industry. Tonga has few large international standard hotels, although the Tongan government is keen to attract international investment for further hotel development. The majority of establishments are small, family-owned guest houses and the new airport hotel indicates that Tonga is as much a stopover point as a major tourist destination. A new terminal has recently been built at the main international airport at Fua'amotu and in 1991, Royal Tongan Airlines began flights to Suva and Auckland on a lease arrangement with other regional airlines. The Royal Tongan Airlines has a twinning arrangement with Air Pacific for the use of a Boeing 737–300 so that Air Pacific uses it 2000 hours a year and Royal Tongan Airlines 1000 hours a year in order to reach profitability. The airline was hoping for its first profitable year in 1995 and is actively discussing a similar twinning arrangement with Air Marshalls for its domestic routes.

One area of marine tourism currently being developed at Vava'u is whale watching, when the period June to October sees pilot, sperm and humpback whales visiting the area on their annual migration from the Antarctic to warmer calving areas. After October, the waters get too hot and the whales begin their journey south again. This offers a potential growth market for nature tourism following the international success of Whalewatch in Kaikoura, New Zealand.

Western Samoa

Western Samoa an independent state and member of the Commonwealth, comprises two large islands (Upolu and Savai'i) and a number of smaller islands with the capital Apia on the island of Upolu. Western Samoa has a largely agricultural economy with a huge trade deficit and tourism, together with international aid and overseas remittances is seen as one possible mechanism for addressing the deficit. In 1990, receipts from private payments were estimated to be $US34 million in the wake of a cyclone. Tourism in Western Samoa was reviewed by Fletcher and Snee (1989) and more recently Theuns (1994) in the academic literature, while a range of research studies commissioned to examine the Islands tourism potential and future have made it among one of the most researched Pacific Islands:

- In 1984 a UNDP/WTO *Samoa Tourism Master Plan 1984–93* was produced which outlined a planned, controlled development of a moderate-sized tourism industry, while preserving the nation's heritage, culture and environment.
- In 1988 KRTA Limited published a study entitled *Environmental Planning for Tourism in Western Samoa* which endorsed the existence of environmental resources to develop tourism.
- In 1989 the Pacific Islands Development Programme published a report on *Tourism Development in Western Samoa*.
- In 1990 the TCSP produced a report on *The Tourism Sector in Western Samoa – Evaluation and Development Needs*.
- In 1991, the results of the Dangroup consultancy for the Government of Western Samoa and the TCSP – *Western Samoa Tourism Development Plan 1992–2001* was released.

(Dangroup 1991)

It is the Dangroup (1991) study, a product of the European Development Fund in the Pacific Regional Tourism Programme, which provides the most comprehensive review of tourism in Western Samoa.

One feature which all these studies emphasise, is the island's cultural assets as an integral component of the island's tourism product. As the TCSP (1990) report emphasised, the four most important attractions which appealed to the majority of visitors were: the friendly people (75 per cent), relaxed atmosphere (61 per cent), natural scenery (58 per cent) and traditional Samoan villages (50 per cent). Visitor arrivals have grown from a base of 866 arrivals in 1967 to 20,342 in 1970 and subsequent growth has been fuelled by visitors from the USA, New Zealand, Europe and Australia. During the 1970s and early 1980s, arrivals almost doubled, but between 1986 and 1988 arrivals stagnated, dropping to 47,642 in 1990 and 34,953 in 1991 as a result of Cyclone Ofa (February 1990) and Cyclone Val (December 1991). The poor growth prospects between 1990 and 1992 were attributed, by the Dangroup report, to the following factors; a lack of a product range (especially a lack of beach resorts), an absence of international accommodation, inadequate marketing and promotion, constraints on air access in relation to seat capacity, a lack of promotional fares and the effects of short-term disruptions caused by cyclones in 1990 and 1991. The majority of international travel to Western Samoa comprises business travel and expatriates visiting friends and relatives, with only a small proportion of total arrivals being pleasure tourists on holiday (Theuns 1994). Because a significant proportion of the arrivals from American Samoa and New Zealand are visiting friends and relatives, this reduces the potential of these source areas to generate holiday traffic with a more substantial economic impact. The most recent data for 1990–91 indicates that only 15 per cent of New Zealanders visit for pleasure. In contrast 60 per cent of Australians, 68 per cent of visitors from the USA and 91 per cent from Germany visit for pleasure, while 85 per cent of other European and 68 per cent of Other origin markets visit for pleasure.

According to PATA the source areas for visitor arrivals in 1994 from American Samoa (27.6 per cent), from New Zealand (22.7 per cent), USA, (11.5 per cent), Germany (4.9 per cent), from the UK (2 per cent) and Other Pacific Islands (8.9 per cent). The majority of visitors arrive by air (95 per cent in 1990), with the largest proportion of sea-borne arrivals coming from American Samoa. The majority of visitors travel independently, with only 11 per cent, primarily pleasure seekers travelling on a package in 1990 (Theuns 1994). In 1990, the average length of stay was 7–9 nights and nearly 60 per cent of visitor nights in 1995 were spent outside hotels in non-commercial private or village accommodation. Western Samoa has suitable air access and Faleolo Airport has sufficient capacity for visitor arrivals to the year 2001.

Dangroup (1991) also points out that Western Samoa has the potential to raise the foreign exchange earnings through tourism from $WS41 million in 1992 to $WS112 million in 2001. This is expected to contribute $WS23.5 million to government revenue by 2001 and to generate up to 4700 jobs for Western Samoa from tourism activities. The forecasts used by Dangroup (1991) indicate that visitor arrivals could increase to 101,000 in 2001 (the population of the area was 158,000 in 1990), but this assumes a significant growth beyond the existing level of arrivals: a doubling in six years, with a growth in the Australian, USA, European and Japanese markets. The infrastructure requirements are that the forecast number of rooms will need to rise to 1120 by the year 2001. In 1990, the number of rooms totalled 432, 154 of which were in the island's main hotel – Aggie Grey's, with 85 per cent of current capacity located on the island of Upolu and geographically concentrated in and around the capital, Apia. Whether these targets are actually feasible and attainable is debatable given the existing constraints (see Dangroup 1991) which are unlikely to be rectified in the space of six years. In this respect and in view of past experience, such forecasts must be treated with some caution. According to Dangroup (1991), to achieve these targets, three specific types of arrivals are being sought which include family-based tourism (i.e. families), honeymooners and special interest tourists, especially nature tourism.

This growth will also necessitate the geographical redistribution of visitors from the current concentration on the two main islands of Upolu and Savai'i. The Dangroup (1991) report recommends that Upolu continues as the main destination, but 12 new development centres will be needed. However, no accommodation facilities will be developed on the small islands because the 'low volume high yield' policy advocated by Dangroup (1991) does not envisage Western Samoa becoming a mass destination with large-scale resorts or large-scale tourist facilities. As Theuns (1994: 6) argues 'Western Samoa has maintained a cautious attitude towards tourism, fearing that the Samoan way of life might be disrupted by an influx of foreign visitors'. To facilitate a cautious expansion of tourism, a rise in inward investment will be critical and will need to be supported by aid assistance for infrastructure projects to support the growth (see Chapter 11). To create the right environment for investment, the Enterprise Incentive and Export Promotion Act, 1990 will assist in the development of tourism and manufacturing, with local equity participation encouraged, but not perceived as mandatory (Theuns 1994). To support this investment, an institutional framework to assist in marketing and promotion is also essential.

Marketing and promotion is undertaken by the Western Samoa Visitors Bureau (WSVB) and if it is to meet the requirements of the tourism master plan, an expansion is required in its budget and activities. The current marketing of the destination by the WSVB is representative of the essential qualities of most Pacific Islands as Western Samoa is 'a jewel of extraordinary beauty in the South Pacific – of fragrant blooms, swaying palms, lush vegetation, cascading waterfalls and turquoise lagoons'.

Niue

Niue, a single uplifted coral island, is a self-governing country of 258 square kilometres, which suffers from the problem of geographical isolation, although this can be a much sought-after asset for some tourists. To date the only article published on tourism in Niue is by Milne (1992b). It has a population of approximately 2500 (though 12,500 Niueans are resident in New Zealand – since all Niueans are New Zealand citizens). Tourism is recognised as a future prospect, since Niue is probably the least developed and unspoilt island in the Pacific. Niue is one of the most dependent islands in the South Pacific, receiving $NZ10 million in aid a year. Remittance flows from New Zealand are also an important source of revenue, given that economic development is hampered by formal economic employment opportunities (Milne 1992b). Thus isolation and a limited resource base are not major obstacles to tourism given the island's ability to provide 'typical' palm tree and beach holidays. Milne (1992b) reviews the economic impact of tourism using late 1980s data and the linkages which exist between different sectors of the local economy.

Air access continues to limit the expansion of tourism in Niue, initially being dependent upon Air Nauru which had services suspended for some time and then stopped in 1988. In 1990, Niue Airlines was formed, but its certification was cancelled by the Niue government in late 1992 after defaulting on a fuel bill (Douglas and Douglas 1994). In 1994, Polynesian Airlines cancelled its Boeing 737 service which had called at Niue en route to the Cook Islands. The main carrier at present is Royal Tongan Airlines which replaced a weekly Air Nauru service from New Zealand in August 1995. The airport runway is currently being developed under a New Zealand government aid project so that it can accommodate Boeing 767 jets by the end of 1995.

Visitor arrivals in Niue have seen an increase from 361 arrivals in 1988 to 1047 in 1990 and 1668 in 1992. Figures for 1994 from the Niue Tourism Office indicate that arrivals have exceeded 4000 and Niue would like to see the number rise to 5000. The aim is to target eco-tourists with nature walks and whale watching. Although the island currently has only 100 beds, the opening of the Matavai Resort late in 1995 will add another 48 rooms. Despite having only a few beaches, the island has excellent scuba diving which is featured in its promotional literature. Yet Milne (1992b: 569) argues that 'while tourism will continue to be an important source of additional income and employment, Niue will remain dependent on public sector employment and international aid flows for the foreseeable future'.

IMPLICATIONS FOR SMALL ISLAND TOURISM IN THE SOUTH PACIFIC REGION

It is apparent from the visitor statistics and patterns of tourism activity reviewed in this chapter that there is great diversity in the levels and nature of tourism in the Pacific Islands ranging from 'mass destinations of the mid-Pacific such as Guam, Hawai'i and Saipan to those islands such as Yap, Western Samoa, the Republic of Palau, and the Solomon Islands where tourism is very much in its embryonic stage' (Fletcher and Snee 1989: 114). In fact, in the late 1980s, Fletcher and Snee (1989) acknowledged that Guam, Hawai'i and Saipan collectively catered for 12 times the number of tourists visiting the other islands in the South Pacific. Although the existing level of tourism development in many Pacific Islands can be accounted for by a range of factors, the following are commonly cited:

- historical background and past colonial rule;
- the small size of many islands and poor communication;
- distance from the major tourism generating regions of the world (except Hawai'i', Guam and Saipan with good access to Japan);
- poor infrastructure and a low level of economic development in relation to the development of the service sector as a prerequisite for a high import content for local economies, making mass tourism development expensive and often dependent upon foreign investment and aid.

(Milne 1992a)

The issue of overlapping agencies and interests, each with their own political agenda has meant only limited regional cooperation between island states. However, the evidence in the airline sector at least is that regional cooperation is occurring through necessity in some cases: individual countries do not have the resources to single-handedly support a loss-making international airline. The colonial legacy, the emergence of indigenous cultures with an interest in tourism and the effect of transnational corporations are becoming major determinants of tourism in the region. Since 1989, there is also evidence that the dependence upon the Japanese inbound market has declined in favour of a more diversified range of sources such as the north-east Asian markets. There are also a number of important economic conditions which will encourage Pacific Islands to pursue tourism development in view of the *1994 Asian Development Bank Annual Report*, which argues that economic output and growth may drop in the late 1990s in many Pacific Island states. This means that tourism will be looked upon as an opportunity to offset such a change in national economies.

The most recent organisation which established regional cooperation in the South Pacific is the TCSP. As a regional tourism association, it is assisted by the European Development Fund of the European Union, an inter-governmental organisation based in Suva, Fiji. Its main objective is to foster regional cooperation in tourism and to assist in tourism planning, development, marketing, promotion, education, training, improving research statistics to develop a database. This has helped to raise the Pacific's profile at trade shows in Australia and Europe using its 'South Pacific village' concept promotion. But a feature article in *Islands Business Pacific* (August 1995) criticised the lack of action in relation to Visit South Pacific Year (VSPY) in 1995. Although VSPY was launched in late 1994 at world travel fairs in Europe, North America and Australia, poor performance is attributed to a lack of resources, the inability of Pacific Island tourism offices to contribute to regional promotion and a lack of action from the TCSP.

The travel trade received very limited exposure of the concept despite the planning of a calendar of events, festivals and pageants. At the same time, the resumption of nuclear testing has severely tainted the region's image and overshadowed VSPY. On a budget of $US800,000 and with a comparatively short period for planning, it was unlikely to rival the Visit Year concept actively promoted by the ASEAN countries.

Nevertheless, a ESCAP report in 1991 (see Craig-Smith and Fagence 1994) observed that the TCSP has embarked on a phase of tourism plan development, focused on the special needs of each country. By 1994, three plans had been produced for the Solomon Islands (1990), Western Samoa (1992) and Tuvalu (1992). As observed in the ESCAP research, non-TCSP tourism plans have displayed a tendency to exercise less constraint, resulting in enclave development and concentrated development related to industry pragmatism.

The region is without any doubt one of tourism potential, but the sensitivity and vulnerability of the environmental resource base of many small islands, already poses physical limits of carrying capacity. While a small number of major destinations (e.g. Guam, Fiji and Tahiti) dominate tourism in the region, for the smaller destinations the case for regional cooperation, liaison and sustainable development is now clear. For some islands, the dependence on tourism as a source of foreign exchange is developing a new dependence alongside aid. It is also evident that political instability can dramatically alter the Pacific Islands tourism image. The TCSP is an attempt to add some focus for regional organisation and cooperation, although it is now necessary for certain groups of islands and regions to establish the regional diversity of the Pacific Islands tourism product. In fact the *Pacific Islands Monthly* (September 1995) reported that the TCSP was likely to lose its EU subsidy of $US2.5 million a year in 1997, since the EU saw it as an organisation that needed to become self-funding from its country membership. This may lead to an uncertain future for regional tourism matters, although it is expected that the larger island states will continue to fund the organisation as the main focus for cooperation, development, marketing and planning. One direction which needs to be followed is the development of a stronger brand related to the cultural traits and attraction of Polynesia, Melanesia and Micronesia in the late 1990s, with regional marketing based on cooperation and a pooling of resources to avoid unnecessary duplication and competition. As Fletcher and Snee (1989: 123) acknowledged 'the development of tourism can enhance the economic development of the South Pacific Islands, but only if there is an active policy decision to develop tourism in a co-ordinated fashion . . . and thereby improve the balance of payments position of an economy', but a sound development plan based on local needs and targeted at the indigenous population appears to offer the best prospects for the 1990s.

REFERENCES

Britton, S. (1982) 'International tourism and multinational corporations in the Pacific', in M. Taylor and N. Thrift (eds) *The Geography of Multinationals*, London: Croom Helm.
Bywater, M. (1990) 'Airlines in the South Pacific', *EIU Travel and Tourism Analyst*, 1: 5–28.
Conlin, M.V. and Baum, T. (eds) (1995) *Island Tourism Management and Practice*, Chichester: John Wiley.
Craig-Smith, S. and Fagence, M. (1994) 'A critique of tourism planning in the Pacific', in C. Cooper and A. Lockwood (eds) *Progress in Tourism, Recreation and Hospitality Management, Vol. 6*, Chichester: John Wiley, pp. 92–110.
Dangroup (1991) *Western Samoa Tourism Development Plan, 1992–2001*, Apia: Government of Western Samoa and the TCSP.
Douglas, N. and Douglas, N. (eds) (1994) *Pacific Island Yearbook*, 17th edn, Suva: Fiji Times.
Fletcher, J. and Snee, H. (1989) 'Tourism in the South Pacific Islands', in C. Cooper (ed.) *Progress in Tourism, Recreation and Hospitality Management, Vol. 1*, London: Belhaven, pp. 114–24.
Hall, C.M. (1994) *Tourism in the Pacific Rim: Development, Impacts and Markets*, South Melbourne: Longman Cheshire.
Hall, C.M. and Rudkin, B. (1993) 'Ecotourism as appropriate tourism: A case study from the Solomon Islands.' Paper presented at the 13th International Congress of Anthropological and Ethnological Sciences, Symposium on Tourism as a Determinant of Culture Change, 30 July.

Hitchcock, M., King, V. and Parnwell, M. (eds) (1993) *Tourism in South East Asia*, London: Routledge.

KPMG (1993) *Investment in Micronesia*, Guam: KPMG Micronesia P.C.

Laws, E. (1995) *Tourism Destination Management*, London: Routledge.

Lockhart, D., Drakakis-Smith, D. and Schembri, J. (eds) (1993) *The Development Process in Small Island States*, London: Routledge.

Milne, S. (1990) 'The economic impact of tourism in Tonga', *Pacific Viewpoint*, 31(1): 24–43.

Marciano, C. (1996) 'Tahiti tries to rebuild image', *New Zealand Herald*, 20 February, 3: 3.

—— (1992a) 'Tourism and development in South Pacific microstates', *Annals of Tourism Research*, 19(3): 191–212.

—— (1992b) 'Tourism and development in Niue', *Annals of Tourism Research*, 19(3): 565–9.

Page, S. J. (1994) *Transport for Tourism*, London: Routledge: London.

Tourist Council of the South Pacific (TCSP) (1990) *The Tourism Sector in Western Samoa – Evaluation and Development Needs*, Suva: TCSP.

Theuns, L. (1994) 'Tourism in Western Samoa: situation, impacts and constraints', *Tourism Recreation Research*, 19(1): 49–58.

Urbanowicz, C. (1989) 'Tourism in Tonga revisited: Continued troubled times', in V. Smith (ed.) *Hosts and Guests: The Anthropology of Tourism*, 2nd edn, Philadelphia: University of Pennsylvania Press, pp. 105–18.

Wendt, N. (1992) 'Environmental problems in the South Pacific: The regional environment programme perspective', in S. Henningham and R.J. May (eds) *Resources, Development and Politics in the Pacific Islands*, Bathurst: Crawford House Press, pp. 185–94.

Wilkinson, P. (1989) 'Strategies for tourism in island microstates', *Annals of Tourism Research*, 16: 153–77.

Chapter 18

Conclusion

C. Michael Hall and Stephen J. Page

The South Pacific is unique, not because its geographical, biological, sociological and economic characteristics are found nowhere else in the world, but because the combination of these characteristics in the region is special. The region is characterised by a high degree of ecosystem and species diversity, an extraordinary level of endemicity, a high degree of economic and cultural dependence on the natural environment, vulnerability to a wide range of natural disasters, a diversity of cultures and languages, and traditional practices and customs which are central to the close and special relationship of Pacific people with their environment.

(Fuavao 1993: 22)

The chapters in this book have demonstrated that tourism is a potent force shaping the present and future structure and organisation of the economies of many Pacific Islands. One of the key themes running through all the chapters is that the image of the South Pacific as a paradise is rarely, if ever, a true portrayal of the everyday reality of the Pacific Islands. Behind the image of the Pacific tourist destinations are a number of issues which sets the economic, sociocultural, environmental and political framework within which development occurs: dependency, limited natural and financial resources, rapidly growing populations, resource depletion, and global warming are the overriding problems associated with island microstates which continue to dominate the development agenda in many of the smaller Pacific Islands.

Tourism, is but one of a limited range of development options which the governments of the region can choose. The development of tourism has in many cases not led to a greater degree of economic dependence as the reliance on foreign investment and aid continues to reinforce the dependency relationship. However, it could be argued that at least tourism dependency is a path which many destinations have chosen to pursue to shape their own development destiny, emphasising a future based on service sector activities and representing an attempt to diversify beyond the region's traditional economic dependence upon primary produce exports that is the plantation economy (Hall 1994). Nevertheless, the reality for many destinations is that the development of tourism has led to a wide-reaching impact upon local economies. The prospects for many local communities and islands is now dependent upon external interests and investments to develop a seemingly 'Western' tourism product based on large-scale integrated resort development reinforcing many of the features of the enclave development model identified by Britton (1982, 1983).

To a certain extent the responsibility for pursuing such routes to tourism development in island destinations is a function of what Crocombe (1989) calls the 'development expert'. As Crocombe (1989: 204) poignantly argues, 'A balance sheet for the post independence phase of Pacific history would probably show that a significant factor which retarded development was the so called development expert . . . those with the power so often execute projects in the way that achieves their own goals.' The problem is clearly demonstrated in the contents of some of the tourism consultants' reports for Pacific Island governments where master plans advocate mass tourism solutions rather than emphasising the concept of appropriate and sensitive development in relation to local resources and local needs (see Chapter 7). Large integrated resorts which require massive foreign investment and external control and management often eliminate local populations who are unable to participate in the closed system that enclave resort development can impose on a locality in relation to employment and revenue generating activities. This is one feature which indigenous communities are beginning to recognise and oppose, as some of the chapters emphasise (see Chapters 6 and 7). This is often a hard decision for the local population who are sold the idea on the basis of long-term economic benefits for the country. But a more critical analytical approach by indigenous people is sometimes diametrically opposed to the wishes and aims of national governments seeking tourism development as a form of economic diversification. Nevertheless, it should be acknowledged that some consultants can often become the 'piggy in the middle' between national governments and local elites who seek to drive tourism forwards and who need consultants to legitimise and endorse national and regional tourism development objectives, and local responses to tourism plans which are sometimes opposed to such routes to development. In this impossible position, impartial decision making becomes difficult, particularly when the national government are convinced that a mass tourism style of development will yield immediate benefits to offset structural problems in the local economy while fulfilling short-term political objectives. To criticise Pacific island governments for taking the soft option, however, is inappropriate given the complex nature of the economic, social and environmental problems which many Pacific Island nations face. After all, taking a determined approach to develop one's own destiny, in spite of the dependency relationship in the context of aid and inward investment is more appropriate than constantly emphasising the injustices of the colonial period.

Whether the strategy and direction which tourism takes is appropriate is open to debate, though one issue is clear: the resource basis for tourism development in many islands is strictly limited in terms of land tenure, fragile ecosystems and the delicate environmental balance which exists between humans and nature. For this reason, as many of the chapters emphasise, the specific local context is more important than generalisations on the model or type of tourism development which the Pacific Islands can support. After all, political trade-offs are increasingly based on cost-benefit analysis in which the environment is priced as a non-renewable resource which can be harnessed for tourism. While such trade-offs may not necessarily be public knowledge, it ultimately becomes the price which governments and communities have to pay for tourism development. All too often, outsiders do not give Pacific islanders the credit for their own ability to make decisions on complex matters such as this, as they have a better understanding than outsiders once the necessary implications and options are outlined.

As more Pacific Islands pursue a strategy of tourism as a path towards economic development, the impacts and repercussions of such development in the social, economic and environmental contexts of affected local communities will intensify without sensitive management and matching of development to the resource base. Although the use of the term 'carrying capacity' has invariably been used to assess the ability of the resource base to accommodate tourists and development, all too often the carrying capacity is not really understood until the threshold of acceptability has been exceeded. The implication here is that Pacific Island states do not have many options available to divert and spread the tourist capacity to alternative locations given the scale of many islands. Therefore, planning and development for small islands need to be explicit about the numbers, the seasonal spread and the spatial distribution of tourists within islands. This is to ensure that destination management is a practical exercise rather than a paper planning procedure which is not implemented due to the potential restrictions it may place upon the growth of arrivals. One thing that island destinations can be certain of is that tourism has the ability to be unpredictable: where visitor targets are set, these can easily be exceeded while in other contexts, unrealistic growth targets may never be reached due to obstacles and constraints related to transport, communications and accessibility which continue to inhibit development in some destinations. This situation was succinctly summed up by Matthews (1978: 34) when he observed that 'most ideological debate about tourism starts with the premise that the base cluster of activities which we call tourism is likely to continue in the foreseeable future. The debate is not so much concerned with tourism versus no tourism as it is with what kind of tourism'. This is increasingly the case in many of the Pacific Islands in the 1990s.

Identifying the likely changes in Pacific travel to the end of the century is a difficult task, given the diversity of the tourism destinations in the Pacific region outside of the four honeypots of Guam, Saipan, Fiji and Hawai'i. According to Edwards (1990) there are six factors which will be major determinants of the demand for tourist travel within the wider Far East and Pacific region during the

1990s. Although much of the discussion of Edwards is focused on the Far East, the factors are pertinent to econometric forecasting activities and they include:

- income growth in source areas;
- changes in the cost of travel, including exchange rate fluctuations, inflation and a downward pressure on the cost of air fares;
- the trend for holiday travel to increase at a faster rate than business travel and visiting friends and relatives;
- the emphasis among European tourists to take proportionally more beach-based holidays;
- the rise in seasonality and a decline in multi-destination trips;
- the growth of the outbound Japanese market.

A more recent analysis of European outbound travel to Asia–Pacific region by Cockerell (1994) observed that a number of other issues are also shaping travel in the 1990s including:

- the decline in the all-inclusive tour in favour of mix and match options as well as the rise of the free independent traveller (fit) and the potential of ecotourism products;
- a growing concern for quality issues;
- a greater scrutiny of the environmental dimension, particularly the quality of the environment being visited.

One additional feature which is also a major determinant of the nature and volume of tourism in the Pacific will be the relative costs of tourism activities. This will also influence the price competitiveness of destinations if airfares are excluded given the affect of certain price sensitive markets, for example the USA and the significance of destination specific costs, such as accommodation, food and tourism services.

The tourism industry in the Pacific Islands is beginning to recognise the value of the environment if King and Weaver (1993) survey of local stakeholders in Fiji holds true for other destinations where the environment was recognised as a key element in the tourism product. In addition, the political context remains a major factor shaping travel patterns since the stability of the destination affects the perception of travellers to travel there (see Chapter 6).

Some of these factors will undoubtedly shape the form and nature of tourism to the Pacific Islands. However as the chapters on specific destinations demonstrate, the Japanese tourist is no longer in the ascendancy in the Pacific islands. Many destinations still have substantial numbers of Japanese visitors to service, but the most dramatic growth has been experienced from expansion of the growing economies of Pacific rim nations, especially South Korea, Taiwan, Singapore and other ASEAN countries (Hall 1994). This has cast a new light on growth and market forecasts for islands which have previously concentrated on the Japanese as the main area of market growth (e.g. Economist Intelligence Unit 1989). Many of the destinations reviewed in this book are now aiming to expand their visitor markets by pursuing a more diverse range of tourists. But the continued impediment to such growth, as reiterated through all of the chapters in the book (with the possible exception of Hawai'i), is that of transportation and access.

The region has increasing access problems with a number of the international carriers only serving the larger destinations where the yield is profitable. The dependence upon a defined hub and spoke airline operation (see Page 1994) emanating from Auckland, Sydney, Brisbane, Pago Pago and Honolulu poses problems and potential for many smaller destinations that cannot sustain regular scheduled services provided by international carriers. In terms of problems, many nation states do not have the resources to operate a state airline due to the capital requirements and market needed to sustain a profitable range of routes. Conversely, it does offer opportunities for destinations to code share as the Royal Tongan Airlines have shown in 1995. But the distances involved in practise often mitigate against code sharing and aircraft pooling arrangements. The future development and expansion of tourism in many Pacific Island destinations will depend on their ability to accommodate jet aircraft as recent airport upgrading schemes supported by international aid suggest (see Chapter 11). But the lack of destination cooperation to date has been limited which has not facilitated a pooling of resources to promote and develop the markets for groups of destinations through a regional marketing and transportation initiatives. There needs to be a greater recognition of the benefits of cooperation as more resource efficient rather than increased competition among neighbouring destinations seeking to capture the same market.

One of the future issues which will certainly impinge on the competitiveness and image of the Pacific Islands is that of labour and human resource management (Economic and Social Commission for Asia and the Pacific 1994). Although no chapter in the book specifically dealt with this issue, a number of chapters reiterate this as a serious managerial issue for destinations seeking to develop a professional tourism business. Research using gap analysis (Gilbert and Joshi 1992), which investigates the difference between the perceived product requirements and offering by the tourism industry and tourist expectations, is becoming increasingly important to an understanding of the quality experiences which visitors are seeking. It is the staff that are the lifeblood of any tourism or service sector business when selling an experience to visitors. Human resource management issues are therefore critical in this context as well as in relation to the management and running of the tourism-related businesses. According to Baum (1993: 9), a range of common themes which affect human resource management in the global tourism industry include:

- a shrinking employment pool;
- the poor image of the tourism industry as an employer;
- the employment prospects for employees and the associated recruitment and retention problems together with the need for education;
- the training as well as skills shortages at senior management level.

The most obvious manifestation of these themes is the relationship of human resource issues, and service standards and product quality, together with a tendency for employees to develop remedial solutions to perceived problems rather than adopting a more proactive stance. In the case of the Pacific Islands, a recent report by American Express and PATA (AMEX and PATA 1994) entitled *Gearing up for Growth II: A Study of Human Resource Issues in Small to Medium-sized Enterprises in Asia-Pacific Travel and Tourism* identified a range of common themes from the survey which included organisations in Australia, the Cook Islands, Fiji, Guam, New Zealand, Papua New Guinea, the Solomon Islands, Tonga, Vanuatu and Western Samoa. The study observed that medium-sized firms faced many of the same problems as larger firms in travel and tourism (e.g. the recruitment of skilled workers), with 63 per cent of firms reporting some level of difficulty in finding managerial workers. The expansion of tourism education was deemed to be important by 62 per cent of respondents, particularly to address the shortage in skilled and semi-skilled areas. On the issue of quality, the survey found that 67 per cent of firms felt that tourism education was more related to workplace needs with the private sector interested in government subsidies for pre-service and in-service training. The issue of customer relations is seen as the most important training priority, although for many developing countries (which included the Pacific Island destinations), the role of initiative and problem-solving skills among staff were given lower ratings than in industrialised countries. Consequently, while many developing countries perceived recruitment to be a significant problem, existing legislation in some Pacific Islands prohibits external managers gaining positions and the use of expatriate staff often breeds resentment according to the report. One important recommendation here is that apprenticeship schemes which encourage domestic staff to act as understudies who accrue the necessary experience in the area would likely help overcome both the resentment and perception that there are limited career opportunities.

Nevertheless, there are other dimensions related to the development of human resources for the tourism industry, including the economic implications of the development of a flexible workforce and the potential sociocultural impacts of tourism. A flexible labour force has become one of the key characteristics of employment in the tourism and hospitality industry. Tourism employment is flexible in four ways. First, numerical flexibility, by which labour input is varied in response to changes in the level of output, for instance through the use of seasonal, part-time, casual and short-term workers. Second, functional flexibility by which employees become multi-skilled with the ability to deal with different work functions. Third, distancing, whereby subcontracting is used for various work tasks and functions. Fourth, pay flexibility, by which multi-skilled employees receive greater monetary rewards. The end result of these four factors is an employment profile which is broken down in 'core' and 'peripheral' workers (Bagguley 1990 in Urry 1990). Although research is somewhat limited, there is some evidence to suggest that in the Pacific Islands, core positions are often taken by expatriate workers while 'peripheral' positions are taken by indigenous employees (Minerbi 1992). Such a situation represents a double-edged sword for Pacific island governments and indigenous communities. On one side, there is the possibility for resentment developing between the core and peripheral workers, and the difficulties which underemployment and seasonal employment may bring. On the other, there is the opportunities created for local people, and women in particular, to obtain paid labour while at the same time being able to maintain traditional roles (Auger-Andrews 1995).

The issue of tourism employment highlights the difficult decisions many of the Pacific Islands face with tourism development. As noted above, there is recognition that tourism does not come without costs. However, for many governments and also for many of the aid donors, the question arises about what would happen if tourism development did not proceed. Therefore, the future of tourism in the South Pacific is not whether to encourage tourism development, but what sort of tourism should be encouraged.

Unfortunately, while numerous consultancies have been undertaken on tourism planning and the market and promotion of tourism in the South Pacific, relatively little consideration has been given to placing tourism within the broader development goals of the peoples of the region. Research has often been cursory and has focused on individual elements of the tourism development jigsaw puzzle rather than on the bigger picture. As several of the chapters in this book have highlighted, there is therefore a need to place tourism within an integrated context that considers all factors – economic, sociocultural, environmental and political – which affect the patterns and processes of tourism development. For example, in the case of the conservation of rainforest through tourism in Papua New Guinea, Ingram (1994: 28) argues that to simply reduce the problem of dysfunctional apparatus for conservation to flaws in the colonial system or the early withdrawal of Australia in 1975 as 'simplistic': 'postcolonial frameworks continue to interact and evolve with archaic and contemporary patterns of tenure, local institutions, investment, and regulation. In order to manage these institutional dynamics, means of identification and countering of such obstacles must be constructed.'

The development of a more appropriate intellectual and theoretical responses to the problems of tourism and development in the South Pacific is not a mere academic exercise. Theories become policies (Hall and Jenkins 1995). Both the governments of the region and aid donors are seeking such a framework. As the South Pacific Forum Finance ministers stated after their inaugural meeting in Suva in February 1995: 'We recognised that we were meeting against the background of a rapidly changing international environment, profound social and economic challenges [and] the need to promote sustainable development and the importance of positioning ourselves for the growth of the Pacific into the 21st century' (Barber 1995: 46).

There is little doubt that the Pacific Islands have, as yet, failed to participate in the economic growth of the Pacific rim. As Mak and Naya (1992: 44) stated:

'the prosperity of the Pacific Century should also include the prosperity of the Pacific islands'. Several mechanisms for greater economic, social and environmental returns to the Pacific Islands suggest themselves:

- continued diversification of the public-sector economies into appropriate tourism and service industries;
- obtaining higher returns for natural resource use and exploitation, particularly fisheries and forestry;
- greater cooperation between states in order to maximise human, natural, political and financial resources.

Tourism will clearly be a major component in the Pacific Island development equation as we head towards the next century. However, given the enormous economic, cultural and environmental problems facing the Pacific Islands, particularly with respect to population, resource depletion and climate and sea-level change, our understanding of tourism in the Pacific island context needs to be greatly improved. Clearly, progress towards the sustainable development of the Pacific will require a far better contribution from all sectors of the tourism industry, including academics, consultants and researchers, than what has hitherto been the case. It is hoped that this book will make one such contribution.

REFERENCES

AMEX and PATA (1994) *Gearing up for Growth II: A Study of Human Resources Issues in Small to Medium Sized Enterprises in Asia-Pacific Travel and Tourism*, Honolulu: AMEX-PATA.

Auger-Andrews, M.L. (1995) 'A human dimension of tourism: The impact of hotel and resort workers on the attitudes of Fijian working mothers.' Unpublished MA thesis, University of the South Pacific.

Barber, D. (1995) 'Keeping sight of that vision: The road to success for island nations in the Pacific Century', *Pacific Islands Monthly*, April: 46.

Baum, T. (1993) 'Introduction', in T. Baum (ed.) *Human Resource Issues in International Tourism*, Oxford: Butterworth-Heinemann, pp. 3–21.

Britton, S.G. (1982) 'The political economy of tourism in the Third World', *Annals of Tourism Research*, 9(3): 331–58.

—— (1983) *Tourism and Underdevelopment in Fiji*, Development Studies Centre Monograph No. 31, Canberra: Australian National University.

Cockerell, N. (1994) 'Europe to the Asia Pacific region', *Travel and Tourism Analyst*, 1: 65–82.

Crocombe, R. (1989) *The South Pacific: An Introduction*, Suva: University of South Pacific.

Economic and Social Commission for Asia and the Pacific (1994) *Review of Tourism Development in the ESCAP Region*, ESCAP Tourism Review No. 15, New York: United Nations.

Economist Intelligence Unit (1989) 'The Pacific Islands', *EIU Travel and Tourism Analyst*, 4: 70–99.

Edwards, A. (1990) *Far East and Pacific Travel in the 1990s: Forecasts and Analysis of Potential Demand*, London: Economist Intelligence Unit.

Fuavao, V.A. (1993) 'South Pacific Regional Environmental Programme: implications of Agenda 21 for the Pacific', *Pacific Economic Bulletin*, 8(2): 22–31.

Gilbert, D. and Joshi, I. (1992) 'Quality management and the tourism and hospitality industry', in C. Cooper and A. Lockwood (eds) *Progress in Tourism, Recreation and Hospitality Management, Vol. 4*, London: Belhaven, pp. 149–68.

Hall, C.M. (1994) *Tourism in the Pacific Rim: Development, Impacts and Markets*, Melbourne: Longman Australia.

Hall, C.M. and Jenkins, J. (1995) *Tourism and Public Policy*, London: Routledge.

Ingram, G.B. (1994) 'Institutional obstacles to conservation: Fergusson Island, Papua New Guinea', *Pacific Affairs*, 67, 1: 26–45.

King, B. and Weaver, S. (1993) 'The impact of the environment on the Fiji tourism industry: A study of industry attitudes', *Journal of Sustainable Tourism*, 1(2): 97–111.

Mak, J. and Naya, S. (1992) 'Economic cooperation: Asia Pacific and the Pacific islands', *Pacific Economic Bulletin*, 7(2): 39–44.

Matthews, H.G. (1978) *International Tourism: A Political and Social Analysis*, Cambridge: Schenkman.

Minerbi, L. (1992) *Impacts of Tourism Development in Pacific Islands*, San Francisco: Greenpeace Pacific Campaign.

Page, S.J. (1994) *Transport for Tourism*, London: Routledge.

Urry, J. (1990) *The Tourist Gaze: Leisure and Travel in Contemporary Societies*, London: Sage.

Author Index

Abramson, J.A. 260, 270
Acquaye, E. 98, 106
Air Vanuatu 34
Airline Business 110, 111, 127
Alleyne, G. 138, 142
AMEX and PATA 147, 152, 153, 156, 309, 311
Andeng, J. 237, 239, 241, 242, 243, 245, 246, 247, 254
Anderson, R. 258, 270
ANZ McCaughan 94, 106
Aoude, I. 192, 203
Applied Research Consultants 177, 187
Arase, D. 99, 106
Archer, E. 67, 77
Arthur, M. 151, 156
Ash, J. 272
Asia Travel Trade 136, 142
Attenborough, D. 246, 253
Auger-Andrews, M. 211, 217, 310, 311
Australian Associated Press 130, 142
Australian Bureau of Statistics 167, 168, 187
Australian Doctor 136, 142
Australian International Development Assistance Bureau (AIDAB) 66, 77, 170, 171, 172, 173, 187, 270
Ayala, H. 215, 217

Bacchieri, P. 156
Bagnis, R. 141, 142
Baines, G.B.K. 49, 62, 69, 77, 242, 248, 249, 250, 252, 253
Baker, M. 131, 145
Baker, R. 48
Bani, E. 253
Barber, D. 310, 311
Barer, M. 142
Batterham, I. 65, 66, 79
Baud-Bovy, M. 91, 101, 106

Baum, T. 273, 302, 308, 311
Beekhuis, J.V. 67, 77
Belt Collins 213, 217
Bennett, J.A. 140, 142
Bennett, M. 109, 113, 114, 127
Bergerot, J. 240, 241, 245, 246, 253
Berry, L. 149, 156, 157
Biddlecombe, C. 42, 47
Bilney, G. 11, 14
Birckhead, J. 76, 77
Bird, I. 20, 34
Bitner,M.J. 151, 156
Bjarnason, J. 43, 44, 47, 92, 101, 102, 106
Blanding, D. 34
Bolabola, C. 49, 57, 62, 211, 217
Bonnemaison, J. 250, 253
Booms, B.H. 156
Boutilier, J.A. 270
Bowman, G.A. 75, 78
BP Magazine 26, 34
Brackenbury, M. 84, 89
Brechin, S.R. 76, 80
Briand, P. 30, 34
Britton S. xx, xxii, 3, 5, 14, 49, 56, 68, 82, 83, 89, 93, 106, 110, 111, 112, 127, 172, 174, 187, 207, 212, 217, 251, 253, 273, 302, 305, 311
Brook, M. 213, 217
Brookfield, H. 12, 14, 75, 78, 93, 106
Brown, D. 23, 34
Brown, G. 156
Brown, T.J. 149, 156
Bryant, A. 111, 127
Buckley K. 27, 34
Buckley, P.J. 84, 90
Buckley, R. 67, 78
Bull, A. 43, 47
Bureau of Statistics (Fiji) 212, 214, 217
Burns, P. 86, 90, 221, 228, 230, 232, 233

Butler, R.W. 12, 14, 50, 56, 68, 253
Bywater, M. 275, 291, 302

Cain, C. 270
Cairncross, F. 125, 127
Callick, R. 66, 78
Carmen, J. 149, 156
Carpenter, R.A. 67, 78
Carper, J. 113, 114, 127
Carter, J. 30, 34
Cater, E. 75, 78, 236, 253
Chambers, M. 249, 253
Cheechi & Co. Ltd. 208, 217
Chinn, J. 136, 142
Churchill Jr, G.A. 156
Clarke, W.C. xx, xxii, 3, 14, 69, 78, 90
Cleverdon, R. 213, 217, 221, 228, 230,
    232, 233
Cliff, A. 149, 153, 157
Clift. S. 130, 142
Cockerell, N. 307, 311
Cohen, E. 19, 34, 60, 62
Cole, R. 93, 106
Colfelt, D. 140, 142
Collier, D. 109, 113, 114, 128
Commonwealth Department of Health,
    Housing, Local Government and
    Community Services 137, 142
Commonwealth Department of Tourism
    29, 34
Community Aid Abroad 66, 78
Community Resources Inc. 202, 203
Conlin, M.V. 273, 302
Connell, J. 2, 14, 41, 47, 65, 78, 82, 87, 88,
    90, 163, 175, 188, 236, 237, 251, 252,
    253
Connolly, B. 258, 270
Cook, G.C. 132, 143
Cook Islands News 225, 234
Cook Islands Tourism Authority 223, 224,
    234
Coopers and Lybrand Associates 215,
    217
Craig-Smith, S. 43, 44, 46, 47, 92, 93, 94,
    95, 97, 99, 100, 104, 105, 106, 107, 301,
    302
Crandall, L. 49, 62
Crayston, J. 112, 128
Crick, M. 82, 90, 245, 250, 251, 252, 253
Crocombe, R. 49, 63, 98, 106, 162, 164,
    172, 175, 176, 177, 178, 188, 305, 311
Crosby, A.W. 76, 78

Croves, S. 48

Dangroup 297, 298, 299, 302
Davies, B. 121, 122, 123, 124, 128
Daws, G. 19, 34
Dax, E. 136, 144
Day A.G. 19, 34, 35
De Lacy, T. 77
De Schryver, A. 136, 143
de Burlo, C. 27, 34, 49, 62, 236, 237, 239,
    240, 242, 243, 244, 245, 246, 249, 250,
    252, 253, 254, 260, 270
de Kadt, E. 51, 58, 62, 252, 254, 260, 270
Decloitre, P. 186, 188
Del Rosso, L. 120, 128
Department of Civil Aviation, Tourism and
    Culture (PNG) 270
Department of Foreign Affairs and Trade
    (Australia) 1, 2, 10, 14, 167, 169, 188
Department of Health (New Zealand) 131,
    143
Department of Trade and Industry (PNG)
    270
Diamond, J. 78
Dorrance, G.S. 2, 3, 14
Douglas, N. I. 23, 28, 33, 34, 35, 56, 60,
    62, 235, 237, 254, 270, 299, 302
Douglas, N.M. 26, 27, 28, 32, 34, 35, 53,
    56, 58, 60, 62, 235, 237, 254, 256, 260,
    263, 270, 299, 302
Drakakis-Smith, D. 48, 303
Dwyer, L. 42, 48, 49, 62

Eagles, P.F. 122, 128
Economic and Social Commission for Asia
    and the Pacific (ESCAP) 8, 14, 74, 78,
    91, 92, 97, 102, 107, 130, 143, 238, 254,
    311
Economist Intelligence Unit (EIU) 11, 14,
    93, 105, 107, 238, 245, 247, 248, 251,
    254, 255, 263, 270, 311
Edington, J.M. 68, 78
Edington, M.A. 68, 78
Edmonds, C. 140, 141, 143
Edwards, A. 306, 311
Elak, A. 99, 107
Ellig, J. 112, 114, 128
Ellis-Pegler, R.B. 130, 131, 132, 140, 143,
    145
Enloe, C. 251, 254
Erisman, H.M. 82, 90, 253
Eustis, N. 27, 35

Evening Post 143

Fagence, M. 38, 43, 44, 47, 48, 92, 93, 94, 95, 96, 97, 99, 100, 104, 105, 106, 107, 301, 302
Fairbairn, T. 37, 41, 43, 48, 93, 96, 107
Faktaufon, G. 94, 104, 107
Fallon, J. 166, 188
Farrell, B. xx, xxii, 3, 15, 30, 34, 35, 49, 56, 62, 63, 65, 78, 94, 107, 192, 196, 203, 250, 254, 261, 271
Farris, M.T. 129
Fauvao, V.A. 3, 12, 15, 74, 304, 312
Fiji Trade and Investment Board 217
Fiji Visitors Bureau 84, 90
Finney, B.R. xx, xxii, 63, 65, 78
Fisk, D.A. 72, 78
Fletcher, J. 43, 48, 51, 63, 104, 107, 270, 282, 283, 289, 297, 300, 302
Francis, J. 207, 217
Frank, A.G. 38, 48
Fuavao, V.A. 66, 67, 73, 76, 78
Fudala, P.J. 144
Furnas, J. 20, 35

Gee, C.Y. 270
Gibbings, M. J. 270
Gilbert, D. 149, 157, 308, 312
Gill, A. 146, 157
Gill, K. 114, 115, 116, 120, 128
Gillett, K. 140, 145
Gleick, J. 122, 125, 128
Go, F.M. 109, 128
Godlee, F. 135, 143
Goeldner, C. 97, 108
Gounder, R. 162, 188
Government of Fiji 217
Graburn, N.H.H. 58, 63, 260, 270
Grekin, J. 109, 111, 112, 116, 128
Gronroos, C. 149, 157
Grynberg, R. 163, 186, 188
Guadalcanal Province 139, 143
Guam Department of Commerce 63
Guam Visitors Bureau 56, 63, 276
Gunn, C. 91, 96, 102, 105, 106, 107
Gunn, J. 29, 35
Gyaneshwar, R. 137, 143

Hall, C. 220, 221, 222, 223, 228, 230, 232, 234
Hall, C.M. xx, xii, 1, 2, 9, 15, 65, 66, 67, 68, 69, 72, 75, 76, 78, 79, 81, 82, 83, 84,
85, 86, 88, 90, 93, 107, 136, 137, 138, 140, 143, 166, 167, 168, 188, 190, 203, 227, 234, 236, 237, 238, 244, 245, 246, 248, 252, 254, 262, 270, 275, 289, 291, 302, 304, 307, 310, 312
Hanton, P. 92, 95, 107
Harriott, V.J. 72, 78
Harris, L.D. 74, 79
Harris, S. 99, 107
Harrison, D. 49, 63, 161, 188
Harron, S. 262, 270
Hawai'i Department of Business and Economic Development and Tourism 193, 198, 200, 203
Hawai'i Department of Labor 199, 203
Hawai'i Ecumenical Coalition 201, 203
Hawai'i Ecumenical Coalition on Tourism 201, 203
Hawai'i Visitor Bureau 194, 195, 203
Hay, J.E. 65, 70, 73, 75, 79, 138, 140, 143
Haywood, K.M. 109, 128
Helu-Thaman, K. 49, 63, 74, 75, 79
Henderson, J. 176, 186, 188
Henry, B. 99, 107
Herbst, J. 40, 48
Hides, J. 258, 270
Hiller, H. 239, 251, 254
Hitch, T. 192, 193, 196, 203
Hitchcock, M. 275, 303
Hoadley, S. 176, 177, 188
Hoffman, E. 121, 128
Holloway, J.C. 111
Honimae, J. 133, 143
Hopley, D. 72, 79
Howarth, A. 130, 132
Hoyal, D.C. 79
Huffman, K. 63
Hughs, A.V. 186, 188
Hui Ho'Okipa o Kaua'i 201, 203

Ilaiu, M. 211, 218
Ingram, G.B. 74, 79, 310, 312
Inskeep, E. 91, 107
Interavia Air Letter 111, 128
International Bank of Reconstruction and Development 263, 265, 271
Iowa, B. 268, 271
Isaacs, R. 143
Islands Business Pacific 103, 107

Jayaraman, T.K. 237, 239, 241, 242, 243, 245, 246, 247, 254

Jenkins, C. 99, 107
Jenkins, J. 81, 90, 227, 234, 310, 312
Jennings, H. 203
Johnston, B.J. 251, 254
Johnston C. 204
Johnson, O. 246, 254
Jolly, M. 249, 250, 251, 254
Jones, D.E. 258, 271
Joshi, I. 149, 157, 308, 312
Judd, G. 20, 22, 23, 35

Kalinowski, K.M. 262, 271
Kamikamica, J. 100, 108
Karabalis, C. 166, 188
Karel, S.G. 136, 144
Keith-Reid, R. 66, 79
Kelly, M. 190, 203
Kenilorea, P. 61, 63
Kent, N. 190, 192, 194, 196, 203
Kim, K. 193, 196, 203
Kim, R. 8, 15
Kimel, S. 122, 124, 128
King, B. 97, 108, 215, 217, 307, 312
King, J.M. 110, 128
King, V. 303
Kissling, C. xx, xxii, 36, 48, 92, 94, 104,
    108, 110, 111, 127, 128, 129
Klemm, M. 84, 90
Klugman K. 27, 34
Korten, D.C. 236, 252, 254
Kotler, P. 150, 157
KPMG 279, 280, 281, 282, 284, 303
Krieger, M. 246, 254
Kroll, E. 121, 128
Kuberski, T. 142
Kudu, D. 65, 67, 76, 79
Kuhn, T. 105, 108
Kuji, T. 69, 79
Kuykendall R.S. 35, 199, 204

La Croix, S. 194, 204
Langdon, R. 30, 35
Lange, R. 136, 144
Lange, W.R. 141, 144
Laugier, S. 142
Laws, E. 295, 303
Lawson, F. 91, 101, 106
Le Fevre, T. 63, 212
Le Grand, C. 87
Lea, D.A.M. 3, 15
Lea, J. 84, 86, 90, 104, 108, 271
Leaming, M. 112, 114, 128

Lee, G. 103, 107
Lees, A. 66, 79
Le Fevre, T. 217
Levy, J.M. 40, 48
Lewis, N.D. 136, 137, 144
Lind, A. 21, 35
Lind, I. 198, 203
Lindstrom, L. 250, 254
Lockhart, D. 37, 48, 161, 188, 273, 303
Lockyer, K. 147, 157
Lombange, C. 137, 144
Lyons, M. 30, 35

Mabogunje, A. 161, 188
MacCannell, D. 150, 157, 260, 271
MacDermott, K. 245, 254
MacKenzie, M. 58, 63, 260, 271
MacNaught, T.J. 111, 125, 128, 256, 258,
    271
MacNeill, J. 252, 254
Mak, J. 9, 15, 194, 204, 310, 312
Mansperger, M.C. 49, 63
Maragos, J.E. 67, 78
Marciano 292, 303
Mathieson, A. 67, 79
Matsuoka, J. 199
Matthews, H.G. 81, 90, 306, 312
May, R. 58, 63, 260, 271
McArthur, S. 75, 76, 79
McGeough, P. 258, 271
McGraw, R. 204
McGregor, A. 235, 237, 238, 241, 243,
    244, 247, 252, 255
McIntosh, R. 97, 108
McKee, D.L. 40, 41, 45, 46, 48
McMenamin, B. 137, 144
McVey, M. 101, 108
Meheus, A. 136, 142
Mill, R. 91, 108
Millett, J. 269, 271
Mills, G.D. 134, 144
Milne, S. xx, xxii, 1, 15, 67, 70, 73, 79,
    109, 110, 111, 112, 114, 115, 116, 117,
    120, 125, 128, 129, 223, 230, 232, 233,
    234, 236, 241, 243, 244, 245, 247, 248,
    254, 256, 271, 273, 277, 295, 296, 299,
    300, 303
Minerbi, L. 65, 68, 69, 70, 72, 79, 87, 88,
    90, 130, 141, 144, 193, 198, 199, 200,
    204, 310, 312
Ministry of Foreign Affairs (New Zealand)
    164, 179, 188

Ministry of Tourism (Fiji) 215, 217
Moorehead, A. 96, 108
Morrison, A. 91
Morrison, C. 48
Mowlana, H. 109, 129
Muller, K. 246, 254
Mulley, S. 137, 144
Muqbil, I. 92, 108, 163, 188
Murdick, R.G. 147, 157
Murphy, P. 51, 63, 67, 79

Nash, D. 56, 63, 82, 90
National Evaluation Steering Committee
    137, 144
National Planning Office of Papua New
    Guinea 271
National Tourism Office of Vanuatu 87, 90
Native Land Trust Board 217
Naya, S. 9, 15, 310, 312
Nelson, H. 260, 271
New Zealand Department of Statistics 35
New Zealand Herald 130, 134, 144
New Zealand Medical Journal 135, 144
Newsweek 133, 144
Nicholls, D. 131, 144
Niukula, P. 211, 217
Nordyke, E. 198, 204
Nowosielski, L. 109, 116, 117, 125, 129
Nsanze, H. 143
Nurkse, R. 38, 48

Ohashi, Y. 204
O'Reilly and Associates 121, 129
O'Sullivan, V. 81, 84, 85, 86, 90
Office of Tourism (PNG) 271
Office of Tourism and Department of
    Labour and Industry (PNG) 271
Okotai, T. 222, 226, 234

P&O 35
Pacific Economic Bulletin 169, 170, 188
Pacific Islands Development Programme
    (PIDP) 99, 101, 104, 105, 108
Pacific Islands Monthly 238, 246, 254
Page, S.J. 94, 108, 130, 142, 244, 255, 303,
    312
Pai, G. 198, 199, 204
Pannell, J. 67, 78
Panos Institute 136, 144
Parasuraman, A. 149, 156, 157
Parnwell, M. 303
Parr, T. 35

Parry, T. 39, 48, 93, 106
Partain, B.R. 72, 79
PATA 4, 194, 241, 246, 247, 248, 255
PATA Advisory Council – Development
    Committee 131, 144
Pearce, D. xx, xxii, 45, 48, 92, 108, 111,
    129, 161, 188
Pearce, P. 146, 157
Peat, Marwick, Mitchell and Company
    266, 271
Peter, J.P. 156
Philibert, J.M. 242, 251, 255
Picturesque Travel 26, 35
Pillay, S. 143
Plange, N-K. 209, 211, 215, 217
Plowman, P. 31, 35
Pohlmann, C. 109, 114, 116, 120, 123, 129
Poon, A. 109, 113, 120, 129, 232, 234
Predmas, R.R. 235, 255
Pyle, G. 136, 144

Radburn, M. 109, 113, 114, 127
Rajotte, F. xx, xxii, 63, 210, 218
Ramsaran, R.F. 40, 48
Ranck, S. 63, 266, 268, 271
Rasmussen, C.E. 79
Reedy, M. 237, 255
Reicheld 151, 157
Reid Ross, D. 261, 271
Rendell Palmer and Tritton – Economic
    Studies Group (RPT-ESG) 228, 234
Render, B. 157
Richter, L. 14, 15, 81, 84, 90
Rimmer, P. 161, 188
Rix, A. 161, 188
Robertson, M. 10, 11, 15
Robey, B. 136, 144
Robson R. 26, 28, 30, 31, 35
Rodman, M. 237, 255
Rother, I. 193, 204
Routledge, D. 53, 63, 257, 272
Rudkin, B. 140, 143, 289, 291, 302
Ruff, T.A. 141, 144
Russell, R.S. 157
Ryan, C. 147, 149, 153, 157

Saleh, F. 149, 157
Salato, R. 211, 218
Samy, J. 56, 63, 210, 218
Sasser 151, 157
SCET-International 240, 255
Schembri, J. 48, 303

Schutz, A. 25, 35
Schwaninger, M. 262, 272
Scocozza, M. 113, 129
Scott, R. 25, 26, 32, 35, 272
Seruvatu, I. 143
Shannon, G. 136, 144
Shaw, M. 138, 144
Sheldon, P.J. 120, 129
Shineberg, D. 269, 272
Short, S. 226, 229, 230, 231, 234
Sinclair, D.P. 134, 144
Singh, K. 143
Small, J. 84, 86, 90, 271
Smith, B. 19, 35
Smith, E. 219, 234
Smith, G. 109, 129
Smith, L. 77
Snee, H. 43, 48, 51, 63, 104, 107, 270, 282, 283, 289, 297, 300, 302
Snyder, F.R. 144
Sofield, T. 49, 63, 66, 75, 79, 89, 90, 92, 108, 139, 144, 246, 250, 255, 256, 258, 268, 272
South Pacific Forum 13, 15
South Pacific Policy Review Group 186, 188
State of Hawaii Department of Business, Economic Development & Tourism 35
Statistical Digest (PNG) 272
Steele, H.T. 35
Steven, A.D.L. 79
Steves, J.S. 235, 255
Stindt, F. 20, 22, 25, 27, 30, 35
Sturton, M. 235, 237, 238, 241, 243, 244, 247, 252, 255
Sutherland, W. 205, 207, 208, 218
Swindler, W. 203

Tarte, S. 162, 188
Taylor, M.J. 110, 129
Tetreault, M. 156
Teye, V.B. 129
Thaman, R.R. 252, 255
Thakur, R. 161, 162, 188
The Economist 144
Theroux, P. 246, 255
Theuns, L. 297, 298, 299, 303
Thodey, T. 153, 157
Thomas, M.G. 145
Thomas, N. 53, 64, 64, 257, 272
Thomson, B. 24, 35
TIC/MIDS 121, 129

Tiffany, M. 138, 144
Tisdell, C. 41, 45, 46, 48
Tourism Canada 110, 111, 123, 129
Tourism Council of the South Pacific (TCSP) 67, 69, 76, 80, 91, 92, 95, 101, 102, 108, 139, 144, 210, 214, 223, 234, 261, 262, 263, 264, 265, 272, 303
Tourism Promotion Authority (PNG) 272
Townsend, K. 135, 145
Travel Weekly 112, 114, 129
Travis, A. 91, 108
Tremblay, S. 109, 113, 129
Truitt, L.J. 109, 129
Tui'maleali'ifano, M. 53, 64, 257, 272
Tuinabua, L. 103, 108
Turley, R. 133, 145
Turner, L. 272

UNCTAD 238, 255
United Nations Development Programme 170, 189
Urbanowicz, C. 295, 303
Urry, J. 309, 312

Valentine, P.S. 66, 75, 80, 262, 272
Van Trease, H. 237, 248, 249, 250, 255
van Woesik, R. 79
Vandyk, A. 111, 129
Vanuatu 238, 255
Varley, R.C.G. 46, 48, 210, 212, 218
Vlitos-Rowe, I. 120, 129
Vusóniwailala, L. 218

Wall, G. 67, 79
Wallace, E. 132, 145
Ward, R. 93, 106
Watson, K.A. xx, xxii, 63, 65, 78
Waugh, W.L., Jr. 84, 90
Weaver, S. 76, 80, 215, 217, 307, 312
Weiler, B. 70, 75, 80, 138, 143, 262, 270, 271
Wendt, A. 163, 189
Wendt, N. 189, 274, 278, 303
West, P.C. 76, 80
White, H. 162, 189
Whiteman, D.L. 269, 272
Wilcox, F. 137, 145
Wilkinson, P. 112, 116, 125, 129, 236, 237, 250, 252, 255, 273, 303
Williams, P.W. 146, 157
Wilson, B.R. 140, 145
Wilson, N. 131, 145

Woestman, L. 162, 189
Wood, R.E. 246, 250, 255
Woods, L. 99, 108
World Bank 43, 48, 82, 90, 235, 237, 238, 239, 243, 255
World Health Organization 133, 135, 145
World Tourism Organization 236, 255

Yacoumis, J. 1, 15, 42, 48, 100, 108
Yahoo 121, 129
Yahuda, M. 99, 108
Young, M. 66, 75, 80
Yukio Ohashi, Y.

Zeithaml, V.A. 157

Place Index

Africa 168
American Samoa, *see* United States
Asia 37, 135, 156, 168, 194, 214, 224, 243, 275
Australia xx, xxi, 4, 6, 7, 8, 9, 10, 11, 12, 25, 26, 29, 30, 31, 36, 44, 53, 54, 57, 68, 69, 72, 83, 84, 85, 86, 117, 118, 119, 124, 131, 132, 134, 136, 137, 142, 156, 161–189, 206, 209, 210, 213, 214, 223, 224, 243, 244, 246, 247, 256, 260, 264, 276, 280, 289ff, 301
  Australian Capital Territory
    Canberra 187
  New South Wales
    Lord Howe Island 26
    Sydney 216, 247, 258, 308
  Norfolk Island 7, 26, 168, 176
  Queensland 84, 86
    Brisbane 275, 308
    Cairns 57, 134
    Daintree 72
    Green Island 68
    Magnetic Island 86
    Rockhampton 134
    Thursday Island 26
    Townsville 134
Austria 120
  Tyrol 120

Britain, *see* United Kingdom

Canada 9, 43, 44, 53, 54, 111, 114, 194, 209, 214, 223, 224, 276
  Ontario
    Toronto 115, 116
  Quebec
    Montreal 115, 116, 119
Caribbean 73
Chile 6
  Easter Island 6

China 164
Cook Islands 3, 4, 6, 10, 29, 32, 38, 47, 52, 54, 55, 56, 102, 103, 116, 117, 119, 120, 123, 138, 165, 168, 171, 173, 174, 175, 178, 179, 180, 181, 182, 183, 184, 185, 219–234, 263, 268, 277, 309
  Aitutaki 219, 220, 228
  Rarotonga 55, 219ff, 228

Easter Island, *see* Chile
Europe 168, 194, 223, 224, 225, 264, 276

Federated States of Micronesia 6, 10, 52, 56, 65, 100, 102, 103, 171, 277, 281–282
Fiji 1, 4, 6, 8, 10, 24–26, 29, 32, 36, 37, 41, 43, 46, 47, 53, 56, 68, 69, 82, 83, 84, 85, 86, 88, 98, 99, 101, 103, 111, 116, 117, 118, 119, 120, 124, 138, 140, 165, 166, 167, 168, 169, 170, 171, 172, 173, 175, 176, 178, 196, 205–218, 243, 246, 257, 263, 268, 274, 301, 306, 309
  Bekana Island 88
  Denarau Island 69
  Treasure Island 68
  Viti Levu 55, 207
    Deuba 59
  Nadi 118, 207, 217, 221
  Suva 24–25, 103, 207
France 5, 6, 7, 8, 164, 174, 235
  French Polynesia 6, 45, 47, 52, 87, 116, 117, 134, 165, 171, 175, 176, 179, 268, 292–294
    Mururoa Atoll 87
    Papeete 117, 118, 275
    Tahiti xxi, 1, 4, 19, 30, 32, 45, 94, 117, 118, 119, 124, 138, 168, 224, 230, 274, 275, 293–293
  New Caledonia 4, 6, 28, 30–31, 37, 44, 52, 53, 84, 85, 86–87, 88, 117, 134,

167, 168, 175, 179, 243, 257, 268, 275, 286–287, 292
Noumea 25, 275, 286, 287
Wallis and Futuna 7, 165, 171

Germany 5, 7, 123, 214, 264, 280
Berlin 123
Greece 43
Guam xx, 4, 28, 31, 32, 36, 38, 44, 47, 52, 55, 56, 94, 274, 276, 277, 278–280, 300, 301, 306, 309
Tumon Bay 56

Hawai'i, *see* United States
Hong Kong 276

Indonesia 6, 135
Bali 29, 84, 246
Irian Jaya 6, 257
Sumatra 117

Japan 9, 11, 31, 52, 53, 83, 136, 156, 163, 166, 167, 190, 194, 196, 214, 243, 247, 262, 264, 275, 276, 278ff, 289, 300
Fukuoka 279
Kansai 279
Nagoya 279
Tokyo 31, 56, 216, 278

Kiribati xx, 6, 10, 32, 36, 38, 41, 52, 65, 100, 103, 115, 164, 165, 169, 170, 171, 173, 178, 179, 180, 184, 185, 277, 284–285

Malaysia 11
Marshall Islands 6, 10, 32, 38, 52, 100, 171, 277, 283–284
Mexico 9
Middle East 168, 225

Nauru 6, 10, 32, 52, 55, 57, 117, 165, 171, 276
Netherlands 6
New Caledonia, *see* France
New Hebrides, *see* Vanuatu
New Zealand xx, xxi, 4, 6, 7, 8, 10, 11, 26, 29, 31, 32, 44, 51, 53, 76, 83, 85, 115, 117, 118, 119, 131, 132, 134, 135, 136, 138, 142, 148, 151–152, 156, 161–189, 206, 209, 210, 213, 220–225, 241, 243, 244, 264, 275, 285, 286, 301, 309
Auckland 19, 138, 216, 247, 275, 308

Christchurch 152
Wellington 153, 187
Niue xx, 7, 10, 38, 51, 55, 103, 115, 117, 165, 173, 174, 176, 179, 180, 181, 182, 183, 184, 185, 277, 299–300
North America, 112, 113, 136, 168, 190, 206
Northern Marianas xx, xxi, 4, 7, 52, 275, 276, 277, 278, 280–281
Saipan 28, 44, 47, 94, 274, 278, 300, 306

Pacific Islands, *see* South Pacific; also refer to individual states and territories
Palau (Belau) 4, 7, 38, 52, 171, 277, 282–283, 300
Panama 25
Papua New Guinea xxi, 3, 4, 7, 8, 10, 26, 28, 37, 41, 50, 52, 53, 56, 57, 59, 66, 68, 84, 101, 103, 115, 133, 134, 165, 167, 168, 169, 170, 171, 173, 175, 176, 179, 183, 256–272, 309, 310
Bougainville 84, 260
Kokoda 250
Port Moresby 27, 269
Rabaul 260
Sepik River 59, 269
Phillipines 276

Samoa, *see* Western Samoa
Singapore 307
Solomon Islands xx, 3, 4, 7, 8, 10, 26, 28, 32, 41, 52, 53, 56, 57, 61, 66, 84, 88, 91, 96, 101, 102, 103, 133, 134, 139–140, 165, 167, 168, 171, 172, 173, 178, 179, 183, 184, 185, 257, 287–291, 300, 301, 309
Guadacanal 133, 139–140, 287
Honiara 133, 287
Lauvi Lagoon 139
South Korea 276, 280, 307
South Pacific 1–15, 19–145, 161–189, 273–312
Spain 6, 52

Taiwan 11, 276, 280, 307
Tahiti, *see* France
Thailand 276
Tokelau 7, 38, 165, 171, 173, 174, 176, 179, 182
Tonga 4, 7, 8, 10, 37, 38, 41, 43, 45, 46, 52, 53, 55, 56, 57, 65, 83, 87, 96, 100, 103, 111, 115, 116, 117, 118, 119, 123, 165,

167, 169, 170, 171, 173, 175, 178, 179, 180, 181, 182, 183, 184, 185, 221, 295–296, 309
Tongatupu 45, 55, 295–296
Tuvalu 7, 10, 34, 44, 52, 91, 100, 102, 103, 117, 165, 171, 178, 285, 301

United Kingdom 5, 6, 7, 38, 136, 164, 168, 214, 224, 235, 264
Scottish Highlands 120
United States of America 5, 6, 7, 9, 43, 44, 53, 54, 57, 156, 164, 209, 213, 214, 219, 223, 224, 264, 275, 276, 280
American Samoa 4, 6, 38, 52, 56, 103, 294–295
Pago Pago 275, 308
California
Los Angeles 118, 216, 225
San Francisco 194, 247
Hawai'i xx, xxi, 3, 4, 19–24, 28, 29–30, 32, 36, 37, 43, 50, 52, 53, 54, 56, 59, 69, 83, 88, 94, 115, 117, 118, 124, 138, 190–204, 300, 306, 308
Hawai'i 192, 195
Kaua'i 192, 195, 201
Lanai 195
Maui 192, 195
Molokai 192, 195
Oahu 54, 55, 199, 200

Honolulu 25, 31, 118, 198, 221, 275, 308
Laie 59
Pearl Harbour 27, 28
Waikiki 20, 54, 56

Vanuatu 3, 4, 5, 7, 8, 10, 11, 26, 27, 28, 32, 33, 37, 41, 43, 47, 52, 53, 55, 56, 69, 83, 84, 85, 86–87, 92, 101, 103, 115, 116, 117, 119, 120, 123, 133, 134, 140, 165, 167, 169, 170, 171, 173, 174, 175, 178, 179, 181, 182, 183, 184, 185, 235–255, 257, 268, 277, 309
Efate 55, 236, 244, 246
Port Vila 92, 238, 239, 240, 242, 245
Espiritu Santo 236, 240, 244
Pentecost 236, 246, 250
Tanna 236, 244, 246, 250
Vietnam 31

Wallis and Futuna, see France
Western Samoa 7, 8, 10, 37, 41, 43, 44, 47, 52, 55, 56, 57, 91, 96, 101, 102, 103, 111, 117, 118, 124, 163, 165, 169, 170, 171, 172, 173, 174, 175, 176, 178, 179, 180, 181, 182, 183, 184, 185, 296–299, 300, 301, 309
Upolu 55
Apia 57

Subject Index

aid, *see* foreign aid
AMEX and PATA 147, 152, 153, 156, 309, 311
Asia Pacific Economic Cooperation Forum (APEC) 9, 11
Association of South East Asian Nations 9
Australian International Development Assistance Bureau (AIDAB) 66, 77, 170, 171, 172, 173, 187, 270
aviation 94–95, 110–112, 194, 200–202

Closer Economic Relationship (between Australia and New Zealand) (CER) 9, 11
colonialism 5–8, 38–39, 52–54, 81–83, 96, 162, 235
and dependency 81–83
computer reservation systems (CRS), *see* travel distribution technologies
coral reefs 68–73
climate change 65–66
cruising 20, 21, 24, 25, 26–27, 31–32
cultural impact, *see* social dimensions
cultural tourism 200–203, 262

Economic and Social Commission for Asia and the Pacific (ESCAP) 8, 14, 74, 78, 91, 92, 97, 102, 107, 130, 143, 238, 254, 311
economic dimensions 36–48, 56–58, 161–189, 190–193, 198–199, 211–212, 237–239, 241–242, 247–248, 277–302
economic impact, *see* economic dimensions
ecotourism 58, 74–77, 200–203
employment 41, 42, 44, 57, 151–153, 187, 308–310
environmental dimensions 65–77, 248–249
biodiversity 73–74

of tourism 67–77
environmental impact, *see* environmental dimensions

fishing 66
foreign aid 1, 95, 161–189
Australia's to South Pacific 169–172
New Zealand's to South Pacific 176–185
foreign investment 9–11, 56–58, 81–83, 95, 161–189, 190–193

health 60, 130–142
AIDS (acquired immune deficiency syndrome) 136–137
cholera and diarrhoea 135
dengue fever 134
malaria 132–134, 139
historical dimensions 19–35, 205–210, 256, 258–260

internet, *see* travel distribution technologies

labourforce, *see* employment
logging 66–67

missionaries, effects of; *see* religion

North American Free Trade Agreement (NAFTA) 9

Pacific Regional Tourism Development Programme 102–104
Pacific Rim concept xx, xi, 8–9
political dimensions 81–89, 251
political stability 84–89

quality, *see* service quality

religion 49, 53, 54, 61

Second World War 27–28, 260
service quality 45, 146–156
social impact, *see* social dimensions
social dimensions 27–28, 49–62, 74–77,
    87–89, 230–231, 242, 249–251, 260
    authenticity 58–60
    demonstration effect 50–51
    land ownership 54, 87–89, 98–99, 201–
    203
South Pacific concept xx, xi, 1–8, 52–54,
    59–60, 93–94, 130
    myth of paradise in 19–24, 93–94
South Pacific Forum 12–13
South Pacific Policy Review Group 186,
    188
South Pacific Regional Trade and
    Economic Cooperation Agreement
    (SPARTECA) 9–11
special interest tourism 93, 138–141,
    262
sustainable development 11–13, 73–74,
    126–127, 252–253, 304–311
    and biodiversity 73–74

Tourism Council of the South Pacific
    (TCSP) 67, 69, 76, 80, 91, 92, 95, 101,
    102, 108, 139, 144, 210, 214, 223, 234,
    261, 262, 263, 264, 265, 272, 303
tourism development, also *see* sustainable
    development 11–13, 14, 54–58, 67–77,
    91–108, 130, 149–151, 161–189, 193,
    196–203, 213–215, 226–223, 245–247,
    263–269, 273, 277–302, 304–311
tourism marketing and promotion 29, 32–
    34, 86, 110–112, 115–127, 215–216,
    243, 277–302
tourism planning 32–34, 91–108, 149–151,
    240–241, 263–266, 304–311
    location and accessibility 94–95
    infrastructure issues 97–98
trade 8–11, 39–47, 161–189
travel distribution technologies 109–127

World Bank 43, 48, 82, 90, 235, 237, 238,
    239, 243, 255
World Health Organization 133, 135, 145
World Tourism Organization 236, 255